Fearless pilgrim

John Bunyan

Fearless pilgrim

The life and times of John Bunyan

Faith Cook

EVANGELICAL PRESS

EVANGELICAL PRESS
Faverdale North, Darlington, DL3 0PH, England

e-mail: sales@evangelicalpress.org

Evangelical Press USA
P. O. Box 825, Webster, New York 14580, USA

e-mail: usa.sales@evangelicalpress.org

web: http://www.evangelicalpress.org

First published 2008
Reprinted 2009

British Library Cataloguing in Publication Data available

ISBN 13 978-085234-680-8   ISBN 0-85234-680-8

All Scripture quotations, are taken from the Authorized / King James Version

Printed and bound in Great Britain by the MPG Books Group

To three other 'Johns'

to John Harris, whose love of Bunyan's 'other writings' has often stimulated my own

to John Pestell, whose encouragement and knowledge of 'Bunyan country' has been a great help

to John Thompson, a pastor to whom our family owes a great debt under God.

Contents

Illustrations

Foreword

In this new and well-written biography Faith Cook relates John Bunyan to the turbulent times through which he lived, surviving two periods of imprisonment in Bedford prison, sustained by his faith, determined, as he himself wrote, 'to live upon God that is invisible'.[1]

Faith Cook avoids the temptation of merely regarding Bunyan as one of the great figures of English literature. That he certainly is. But he is so much more — a physician of souls, much-loved pastor and powerful preacher of the gospel of grace. The authoress skilfully relates her subject to the political history of his times, in which Nonconformists won a greater measure of freedom to worship according to their understanding of the Bible during the Cromwellian period, only to be restricted again after the Restoration of the Monarchy in 1660.

Bunyan emerges from this book as a writer of plain yet remarkably imaginative prose, steeped in an amazing knowledge of the English Bible. That knowledge is not just textual: it is deeply experimental, the fruit of much meditation, as *The Pilgrim's Progress* particularly shows.

This latest book from Faith Cook's pen, or more accurately her word-processor, will surely add to her growing reputation as a biographer of such figures as Grimshaw of Haworth, Lady Jane Grey and Selina, Countess of Huntingdon. In my humble opinion it is her best yet. I heartily commend it.

David Kingdon
Former Principal of Irish Baptist College, Belfast, Northern Ireland

Preface and acknowledgements

This work is the payment of a debt — a debt to John Bunyan, one whose fierce temptations and prolonged sufferings have marked out a trail for Christians ever since the seventeenth century, that era of political turmoil and conflict into which he was born. It has been said that Satan made a serious blunder in his vicious assaults on the young tinker so soon after his conversion. For in so doing he handed to him a key of hope — a key which John Bunyan could use continually to help the tempted and despairing. Virtually all John Bunyan's fifty or more lesser-known works are autobiographical to a certain degree, for he constantly drew on his own experiences of God's delivering grace to point his readers to the way of escape from doubts and fears.

For nearly thirty years we have had a large portrait of Bunyan hanging on the wall of our home, one measuring more than twenty inches (50 cm.) in height by fifteen (38 cm.) in width, encased in a heavy gilt-coloured frame. Originating as a pencil sketch by Robert White, and first published when Bunyan was fifty-four, this portrait is cast in one of those uncanny poses in which the eyes appear to be following you wherever you stand. It has hung over my desk throughout my period of working on this biography, always reminding me to be both as accurate and as diligent in my account as I am able.

As I have been concerned to set Bunyan over against the background of the tumultuous period of history in which he lived, it has been necessary to include details of the English Civil War and the upheavals that followed during the years of the Commonwealth. His story can only be understood against the backdrop of the appalling persecution of Nonconformists like Richard Baxter and of Dissenters, represented by Bunyan himself, from the time of the Restoration of the Monarchy in 1660 and lasting until Bunyan's death in 1688.

For the purposes of this biography I have quoted almost exclusively from George Offor's 1854 edition of *The Works of John Bunyan*,[1] as most readers will find this edition more easily accessible. However, recent editions of Bunyan's works published by the Oxford University Press, with introductions and explanatory notes by Roger Sharrock and others, have been most helpful. Their quality of comment and the fact that individual books are published separately make them a handy and valuable aid. Richard L. Greaves' mammoth work, *Glimpses of Glory: John Bunyan and English Dissent*, has also been a stimulating and instructive guide.

The number of people to whom a biographer is indebted in a work of this nature is legion. Certain names spring immediately to mind, the first being our friend David Kingdon for his most helpful comments and suggestions. Three other friends have read through the manuscript: John Pestell, who has an extensive knowledge of 'Bunyan country'; John Harris, with his love of Bunyan's lesser-known writings; and Ralph Ireland, whose help in spotting mistakes has been of great assistance as always. To each of them I would like to say a warm thank you. My husband Paul reads everything I write, chapter by chapter, suggesting improvements, and to him I owe my very real thanks. Philip Green spared time from his busy farming schedule to accompany us around all the different 'Bunyan sites' in the Bedford area; the Bunyan Meeting in Bedford has kindly given permission both to photograph various artefacts and to reproduce their own quality pictures, while Clive Arnold, Curator of the Moot Hall Museum, Elstow, has kindly given me permission to use some of his pictures of old Elstow. I would also like to thank the Evangelical Library for the long-term loan of a quantity of books relating to the subject. Lastly, I have been most grateful to Evangelical Press for the care taken with this publication, and especially to Anne Williamson for all her help in editing and improving my work.

John Bunyan lived in days when it was a costly thing to be a Christian. After twelve long years of imprisonment he was still able to say:

> I have determined, the Almighty God being my help and shield, yet to suffer, if frail life might continue so long, even until the moss shall grow upon my eyebrows, rather than violate my faith and principles.

In days when active persecution is the lot of many Christians in various parts of the world and could still be so even in the West, may Bunyan's courage and example give us faith to persevere, come what may.

Faith Cook
Breaston,
August 2008

Prologue
'Coals of holy fire'

As dawn broke across London early one morning in 1685, an observant visitor to Southwark, south of the Thames, might have witnessed a surprising sight. With furtive glances to left and right, men and women were making their way swiftly and silently through the deserted streets. Some stole along Southwark Street, then down a cobbled lane known as Stoney Street. Ever fearful of watchful eyes from every window, they joined yet others who were making their cautious way up Tooley Street. Finally the stranger might have seen everyone converging on a small street known as Winchester Yard.[1] With a last quick glance around, these unobtrusive figures disappeared thankfully into the recesses of a tall building, the home of Stephen Moore.

But what had brought these people from their houses at such a time of day, and why the secrecy? Here were men and women with a single purpose: they had come to Stephen Moore's home to hear a preacher — a preacher whose words, as one among them would later write, made them feel 'as if an angel had touched their souls with a coal of holy fire from the altar'. But the days were hard. Early morning gatherings were generally safer than those at other times, for from every house 'informers' could well be watching to note down the names of any attending such an illegal 'conventicle' — as these unofficial meetings were called. Hefty fines, prison sentences and, for a third offence, even exile could be the lot of such worshippers spotted and reported to the authorities.

A silence rested on the expectant hearers as they waited, crushed into every corner of the room, some sitting up the stairway. At last the preacher himself entered from another room, a tall, strong-boned man in his middle to late fifties with shoulder-length auburn hair now streaked with grey. He paused for a moment before preaching. His commanding face gave the appearance of a man of strong character, while his largish mouth, partially hidden by a small moustache, suggested a kindly and emotional nature. But his prematurely worn features also spoke of one who had lived through days of intense suffering. With quick sparkling eyes hiding a hint of gentle humour, the preacher looked around at the sea of faces gathered about him.

Then John Bunyan gave out his text: 'The fear of the wicked, it shall come upon him: but the desire of the righteous shall be granted' (Proverbs 10:24). Yes, his hearers could well identify with such a scripture, for they lived in constant 'fear of the wicked'. Throughout England days of intense persecution threatened any whose consciences prohibited them from worshipping God in line with the dictates of the state church. In Scotland too reports were coming in daily of the sufferings, torture and death of fellow Christians on account of their faith. Known as 'the Killing Times', these were years when a faithful remnant of Scottish believers were being hounded and hunted like animals across moors and glens by the king's dragoons.

But there was one young man present at that gathering, squeezed in among the others, who felt a pang of disappointment when he heard the verse that Mr Bunyan had chosen for his sermon. Charles Doe, a Southwark comb-maker, had only recently become concerned about spiritual questions. For some time he had been struggling to live up to the standards God required, as set out in the Old Testament Scriptures — and had failed. Learning by whispered intelligence that John Bunyan, highly acclaimed as a preacher, was to be preaching not far from his home, he joined the men and women crammed into Stephen Moore's house, earnestly hoping that he might hear a sermon on a New Testament text, in order to explain how a sinner can be reconciled to an offended God.

But Charles Doe's disappointment soon evaporated: 'Mr Bunyan went on and preached so New Testament-like that he made me admire and weep for joy,' he confessed, adding, 'He was the first man that ever I heard preach to my unenlightened understanding and experience, being full of the love of God.' Tears coursed down Charles Doe's cheeks, and others wept too as they listened that day, for the preacher touched on the heart of their sufferings. Yet he also pointed ahead to the end and the fulfilment of their desires, even to the joys of heaven, when they would see the Saviour whom they had loved while on earth:

> To see Christ Jesus then, to see him as he is in glory, is a sight that is worth going from relations, and out of the body and through the jaws of death to see ... to see him preparing mansion houses for those his poor ones that are now by his enemies kicked to and fro like footballs in the world. Is this not a blessed sight?

But for the wicked, it would be far different. Though now they may gloat, a day will dawn,

> ... when death comes to steal them away from their enjoyments, lusts and delights. Then the bed shakes on which they lie, then the proud tongue doth falter, then their knees knock one against another; then their conscience stares, and roars, and tears, and arraigns them before God's judgement seat.

For the believer, however, Bunyan assured his hearers, not only can he anticipate a future glory when he sees Christ, but even today, amidst all his sufferings, he can know his consoling and sustaining presence:

> Nothing like it in all the world! His presence supplies all wants, heals all maladies, saves from all dangers, is life in death, heaven in hell, all in all. No marvel then if the presence and

communion with God is become the desire of the righteous man![2]

Such a sermon that morning made an indelible impression on those crammed into the room, and particularly on Charles Doe. After that he took every opportunity he could to listen to the preacher from Bedford, saying, 'I could weep for joy most part of his sermons.' Eventually he felt he must meet him personally. 'So by a letter I introduced myself into his acquaintance, and indeed, I have not since met a man I have liked so well.'[3]

The name of John Bunyan is well known as the author of *The Pilgrim's Progress*, that seventeenth-century spiritual classic which has been second only to the Bible in the extent of its sales. But how did Bunyan become such a preacher and writer? In the following pages we must discover the path ordained by God for this traveller to the Celestial City — a path which prepared him to be so used as a pastor to his own generation and a guide to Christ's pilgrim people still.

I

1628: that eventful year

England was in turmoil, religiously, socially and economically, in November 1628, when John Bunyan was born. Popular opinion laid the blame at the door of one man: George Villiers, 1st Duke of Buckingham. But it would be simplistic to attribute all, or even most, of the troubles that the country was experiencing to the follies and religious sympathies of this dashingly handsome, yet ill-fated nobleman.

English men and women had long memories. Some had grandparents, or even elderly parents, who were alive when the Roman Catholic queen Mary Tudor, known as Bloody Mary, was sending many of the noblest citizens of the land to a fiery and fearful death at the stake for their faith. Many could remember an event that had occurred only twenty-three years earlier, in November 1605, almost exactly fifty years after Hugh Latimer and Nicholas Ridley had 'played the man', enduring an excruciating death in 1555. On that November day Guy Fawkes and his cronies had attempted to blow up the king and his House of Commons, in order to provoke anarchy in the hope of subsequently setting another Catholic monarch on the throne. Little wonder then that the people were uneasy and not a little anxious when the Duke of Buckingham, the most prominent nobleman in the country and chief adviser to both James I and to his son Charles I, was displaying strong Roman Catholic sympathies.

Not only had Buckingham himself married a Catholic woman, Lady Katherine Manners, but in 1623, with the connivance of James I, he slipped out of the country secretly, together with the young Prince Charles, en route for Spain. The pair travelled through France in disguise,

George Villiers, 1st Duke of Buckingham

arriving at the royal court in Madrid before revealing their identity. Their object was to finalize a marriage contract for Charles, future king of England, with the Infanta Maria of Spain. In order to attain such an end, Buckingham was prepared to make huge concessions to England's Roman Catholics, and to promise that any children of the marriage would be brought up in the Roman faith. This in turn raised the spectre of other future Roman Catholic monarchs on the English throne.

Only Buckingham's brash and offensive manner lost him the marriage contract. So rude and domineering was he that the Spanish ambassador requested the English Parliament to have him executed on his return. Instead his countrymen gave him a rapturous welcome home, not because they were pleased to see him, but because the dreaded Spanish contract had failed. Intoxicated with such popularity, to which he was unaccustomed, Buckingham soon squandered it all. First, he arranged a new and highly unpopular marriage for Charles with another Catholic princess, Henrietta Maria, sister of the French king. In return he offered to help France to crush the Protestant Huguenots by promising the loan of English ships.

During 1625 and 1626 Buckingham conducted several ill-conceived and disastrous raids on Spanish targets aimed at punishing the country over the failed marriage contract. In one he planned to capture the Spanish port of Cadiz, burning the enemy fleet; in another he tried to intercept Spanish vessels carrying a cargo of silver. As a result of ill-disciplined troops, lamentable organization and insufficient supplies, each enterprise ended in defeat. England was humiliated, her troops perishing in their thousands in pitiable conditions.

When Charles I, who had inherited the throne in 1625, was forced to recall Parliament in June 1626 in order to request funds for Buckingham's exploits, a demand was made that the new king's favourite should be impeached and removed from office. But Charles, who revered and relied on Buckingham, made use of a handy expedient in order to save his friend — he simply dissolved Parliament.

Charles was now forced to raise funds by other means, and by his tactless arrogance alienated his subjects still further. If he had politely requested loans from some of his wealthier citizens there might have been no trouble. Instead he levied forced loans (which all knew would never be repaid) and threatened any who objected with either imprisonment or conscription into the army. More than this, he implemented his threats until a test case arose in which five men, known as the Five Knights, challenged the king's authority to act in such a way. When Charles coerced the courts to pronounce in his favour, the scene was set for a show-down between Charles I and his Parliament.

Until March 1628 the king and Buckingham struggled on, trying to conduct expensive foreign wars without adequate finance to back them. This only led to further defeat and suffering for the army. At last Charles I realized that he must call another Parliament to vote him the revenue he needed. And among the new members called for the first time was a young man of twenty-nine named Oliver Cromwell — elected to represent the people of Huntingdon. But Cromwell and his fellow parliamentarians had a number of grievances to settle with the king before any more money would be forthcoming. Englishmen valued their rights and privileges, and therefore these elected representatives drew up a Petition of Rights, listing matters they wished to see addressed.

Four main issues were at the heart of the 1628 Petition of Rights. First, arbitrary imprisonment without trial, as in the case of the Five Knights, must end. Arbitrary taxation, not levied through Parliament, must also cease. Thirdly, no further use must be made of martial law against non-military offences committed by soldiers and sailors. And, lastly, an end must be put to the billeting of unruly soldiers in civilian homes, where so often they had been guilty of plundering, or even murdering their hosts. If these grievances were dealt with, Parliament would agree to levy the funds which Charles requested. He had no alternative but to concede to the petition.

Parliament rose in June 1628 before any agreements had been finalized, but on 23 August, just two months later, an event occurred which put a dramatic stop to all negotiations. George Villiers, Duke of Buckingham, was assassinated. In Portsmouth at the time, Buckingham was organizing yet another naval war, continually anxious to prove his military expertise. A naval officer, John Felton, who had undoubtedly already witnessed much unnecessary death among his men, could endure no more. Swiftly and sensationally, knife in hand, he ensured that no further naval adventures would take place. Buckingham lay dead at his feet. Charles I was grief-stricken. Inhibited, lacking in confidence and uncommunicative, he had relied on his friend and favourite to an alarming extent. Now he was alone. More than this, he was angered at the national rejoicings that broke out, particularly in Parliament, in response to an event which he regarded as a personal tragedy.

Another issue was troubling Parliament deeply at this time, dominated as it was by country gentry, many of whom, like Oliver Cromwell, had strong Puritan sympathies. This was the rise of the Arminian party within the established church. With the accession of Charles I to the throne in 1625, this grouping, whose chief representative and spokesman was Bishop William Laud, was rapidly increasing in the royal favour.

Although the name 'Arminian' derived from Jacobus Arminius (1560–1609), a Dutch theologian, whose main tenet was a belief in man's free will in matters of salvation, Laud and his friends were mostly interested in ritual, dignity and order within the church. Laud's catchphrase, 'the beauty of holiness', chimed in with the religious concepts of Charles himself. But his sympathy with Roman Catholic traditions alarmed the Puritan party — a nickname given to highly principled men, mainly from within the established church, who were dissatisfied with the compromised religious settlement reached under Elizabeth I.

Bishop William Laud

William Laud was fifty-two when Charles succeeded to the throne and had been steadily progressing through the ranks of the church. With the powerful Buckingham as his friend and confidant, he held the key into the king's favours. As his position improved, his steps to control, if not to crush, Puritanism became ever more apparent. Alarmed, Parliament made an unsuccessful attempt to impeach Laud when it met in 1628, but the king's answer was to promote him yet further, appointing him as Bishop of London, a position which added enormously to his powers and influence. In the following March Charles dismissed his Parliament once again. And for the next eleven years he ruled alone, refusing to consult with any but his chosen advisers.

And in this same fraught year of 1628, far off from such scenes of royal intrigue, power-hungry nobles and ambitious churchmen, a baby was born in a poor home in a Bedfordshire village. This event, insignificant enough at the time to all but a few, was destined to arouse much interest and attention in the years to come. And even now, after nearly four hundred years, when all the incidents recounted above have been confined to the small print in our history books, the name and influence of that child live on. John Bunyan's life spanned an epoch of unprecedented change in British history. His birth in 1628 coincided with the Petition of Rights, expressing the urgent need of the people for equity and justice. His death, sixty years later, when the struggle for religious freedom was almost over, was marked by the 1688 Glorious Revolution when James II was expelled from the throne and a Protestant monarchy established.

Today Bunyan's life still stands as a symbol of endurance, a beacon of hope, for the suffering church of Jesus Christ, not only for generations long past, but also for our own times.

2

'A hint of my pedigree': John Bunyan's family

Thomas Bunyan had known Margaret Bentley all his life. Both were born in 1603 in the village of Elstow, a mile and a half from Bedford. As Elstow was then little more than a straggling line of sixty-one cottages, some clustering around the village green and the Abbey Church, the children of the village would often play together. So it may well be that Margaret was disappointed when nineteen-year-old Thomas decided to marry Anne Pinney, another local girl. He had already gained quite a reputation for his escapades, and even at the age of twenty-two still enjoyed tree-climbing. An elderly man from a neighbouring parish recorded in his diary:

> In Anno 1625 one, Bonion of Elsto, clyminge of Rookes nests in the Bery wood [Ellensbury] found 3 rookes in a nest, all white as milke and not a black feather on them.

But after only four years of married life Anne had died; no record survives of any children born to the young couple. Thomas, one who needed a woman's love and companionship, felt

Thomas and Margaret Bunyan's cottage

his loneliness acutely and within a month or two of Anne's death had asked Margaret Bentley to become his wife. An entry in the church records for 1627 reads:

Thomas Bonnionn, Junr., and Margaret Bentley were married the three and twentieth of May.

A small thatched wattle-and-daub cottage in old Harrowden, not far from the outer fringes of Elstow, would be Margaret's new home. It did not even qualify for the 'hearth tax' — a seventeenth-century tax which banded houses according to their number of living rooms or hearths. In common with twenty-five other Elstow homes, the Bunyan cottage had only one hearth.[1] Margaret herself came from one of the better homes; her mother's will listed a number of household items which she bequeathed to her children, suggesting that she was comfortably placed. Although Margaret would only receive 'the joined stoole in the chamber and my little case', her brothers and sisters were more favoured.[2]

The Bunyans of Elstow had not always been so poor. In fact at one time they had owned considerable property in the area. From early records we learn that Thomas Bunyan's ancestors had lived in that part of Bedfordshire at least from the beginning of the twelfth century. The name itself had more than thirty variant spellings, the first being 'Buignon', indicating that the family probably had French origins. In 1327 a certain William Bunion owned land which included the very spot in Harrowden where Thomas and Margaret's cottage was situated and where they brought up their family.

More than two hundred years would pass before the name 'Bonyon' crops up again in the documents of the times. In 1542, towards the end of the reign of Henry VIII, the year in which his flighty fifth wife Catherine Howard was executed, another William Bonyon is recorded as owning a significant amount of land in and around Elstow. But the village stood on monastic land, with a Benedictine nunnery established in 1078 by the niece of William the Conqueror. In 1539 the nunnery had been dissolved, in line with Henry VIII's policy to rid the country of most of its monastic houses. The abbess was pensioned off for £50 a year, each of her twenty-two nuns receiving £2. Much of William Bonyon's property reverted to the Crown.

Six years later, however, in 1548, William's son Thomas was selling off parts of the remaining property bit by bit, possibly due to a collapse in the family fortunes. In addition, he and his wife were both in constant trouble with the courts for overpricing the ale and flour which they sold. Soon there was little left of the family's original possessions. Another factor leading to the loss of land was the greed of the local gentry, who were laying claim to vast tracts of former monastic and common grazing land, which they enclosed as pasture for their own animals. The fact that the Bunyans had once been substantial landowners in the locality is reflected in the names still in common use even today such as 'Bunyan End'.

But those days were long gone by the time Thomas and Margaret married. Unusually for the times, Thomas had not followed his father's occupation, described in his will as that of a 'pettie chapman', or local trader. Instead he had struck out into business on his own as a brazier — more contemptibly known as a 'tinker'. Perhaps the family business had failed lamentably, for Thomas Bunyan's father had little to leave when he died apart from his cottage which he left to his wife, together with £5 for his

Bunyan's birthplace, marked by a stone in the far corner of the field

daughter and sixpence each for his grandchildren when they
reached the age of twenty-one.

To accommodate his business as a brazier, young Thomas built
a small forge immediately adjacent to his cottage and here he
would mend his neighbours' pots and pans, for this was no
throwaway age. To replace damaged kitchen utensils could be a
costly business, and Thomas would have many calls on his time.
Not only did he work from his own forge, but he also travelled
to the homes of the local gentry and to isolated farms in the area,
with his anvil, hammers and chisels slung on his back, doing any
repair jobs required. This fact has given rise to the notion that the
family came from gipsy stock, but there is no evidence for this.

So now in November 1628, eighteen months after their
marriage, Thomas and Margaret Bunyan were eagerly anticipating
the birth of their first baby. Their cottage, the site marked today
only by a stone in the corner of a field of wheat, stood beside a
reedy stream still known as Elstow Brook.

The placid Bedfordshire countryside, stretching away into the
distance, dotted by solitary farmsteads, may have looked peaceful
enough on that November day in 1628 when Margaret's first
child was born.[3] But far off in London a situation was developing

Stone marking Bunyan's birthplace

which would soon rip the country apart, turning neighbour against neighbour, and even father against son.

Norman font in Elstow Church in which John Bunyan was baptized

Such things were far from the minds of Thomas and Margaret as they carried their infant to Elstow Abbey Church for his christening on 30 November. Carefully they made their way alongside the brook near their home, then across the fields, gingerly navigating the marshy ground by means of stepping stones, over Cardington Brook and out on to the main Elstow Road and into the church. Here the vicar John Kellie awaited them, and after the short ceremony was over he recorded the event in the parish register:

John the sonne of Thomas Bonnionn Jun., the 30th of Novemb.

How little could he have realized that the child he had just baptized, and whom he had urged in the words of the baptismal rite to become 'Christ's faithful soldier', would not only fulfil such a calling, but would hold an honourable place in the annals of both secular and church history long after most of his own generation had been all but forgotten!

3
Childhood days

The England into which John Bunyan had been born was marked by clear social distinctions. The chances of a poor man improving his lot in life were slim, as the sight of the magnificent new Elstow Place, home of Sir Thomas Hillersdon, vividly demonstrated. Recently built out of the stones of the ruined inner cloister of the nunnery demolished in Henry VIII's time, the mansion dwarfed the nearby villagers' cottages. Each Sunday, as the Bunyan family made their way across Elstow Green and on into the dim recesses of the high-vaulted Abbey Church, they would pass the grand residence standing nearby. Week by week the vast gulf between the privileged few and the peasant majority was forcibly impressed upon them.

As we have seen, little now remained of all that the Bunyan family had once possessed. But despite the fact that John was later to describe his family as being among 'the meanest and most despised of all the families in the land', there were many who were poorer still — among them the sick, the widows and the incapacitated, not to forget the vagabonds and even the rogues. A poem John wrote as he thought back to his childhood days describes the destitution some faced as better-placed householders tried to drive such beggars from their doors:

> They within doors do him an alms deny.
> He doth repeat and aggravate his grief
> But they repulse him, give him no relief.
> He begs, they say 'Begone'; he will not hear
> But coughs, sighs and makes signs he still is there.[1]

When John was fifteen months old a second child was born to Thomas and Margaret Bunyan — a sister for John whom they named Margaret. This custom of naming an eldest girl after her mother was commonplace, and we may suppose that the two children, so near in age, were close companions throughout their childhood. Three years later, in 1633, another son, William, completed the family.

The year 1633 was highly significant in the chronology of the times. In that year Charles I made William Laud Archbishop of Canterbury — contrary to custom, for the previous archbishop, George Abbott, was still alive. During the last four years Charles I had ruled the country single-handed, without any Parliament, and throughout this time the Arminian party in the church had been making steady advances. Now, with Laud as archbishop, the pace of 'reform' towards the High Church ritual which Laud and the king favoured accelerated. First, Laud demanded uniformity in all matters of worship. Important changes were immediately set afoot: preaching was to be curtailed, and catechizing introduced in its place; weekday lectures — a method popular among the Puritans for providing the people with additional Bible-based preaching — were banned. Structural changes to the churches were ordered, with communion tables placed in a central position at the east end of the church. They were also to be railed off from the people, a move that emphasized the importance of the priesthood and recalled the Roman Catholic method of celebrating the mass.

Many objected to these changes, especially when Laud's emissaries travelled the country to see that the new religious laws were being observed. Any who refused to conform or to bow at the name of Jesus could find themselves hauled before the Court of High Commission, or the Court of the Star Chamber. These became the instruments for inflicting vicious punishment, particularly on clergy or nobility who would not submit to these latest laws. As Laud tightened his grip on religious power, brandings and mutilation, including cutting off an offender's ears, became regular practices.

All of this would have meant little enough to a boy of five, but such circumstances were to form the backdrop to John Bunyan's life and were the setting for much of the suffering endured by any who were unwilling to conform to such religious dictates. But for the present the child was much more interested in following his father into his forge to help him as he used the bellows to fan the flames of his charcoal fire, watching as the sparks flew high into the air at each skilled hammer blow on Thomas's small iron anvil.

Although Thomas Bunyan was unable to write, later signing his own will with a thumbprint, he was far-sighted and self-denying enough to decide, together with his wife Margaret, that John should have the advantage of a basic education. Perhaps they had already detected in the boy the stirrings of a remarkable intellect, for John records:

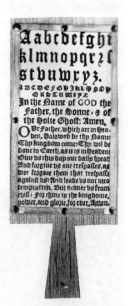

> It pleased God to put it into their hearts to put me to school to learn both to read and write; the which I also attained, according to the rate of other poor men's children.[2]

There has been some speculation about which school John attended. He may have gone out to Houghton Conquest, about three miles from his village home, where there was a free school, endowed in 1631; others think that he may have attended the Harpur School in Bedford itself. Endowed in 1556 by Sir William Harpur, this school was set up to

A horn book for learning the alphabet

teach 'grammar and good manners' to the children of the poor.[3] John would probably have learnt his alphabet with the help of a horn book, as was common in both Tudor and Stuart times.

It is possible, however, that for a small fee some provision was made for the children of the village to be educated in the precincts of Elstow Church, perhaps under the supervision of the vicar or some kindly village woman.

One of the highlights of Bunyan's childhood days was the Elstow Fair. Dating from the early twelfth century, fairs had been held annually on Elstow Green during the first week of May. These occasions, although including dances around a maypole, were not primarily designed for amusement, as many fairs are today. They were more like a busy outdoor market, with local traders shouting the virtues of their wares from behind their stalls. Before the dissolution of the nunnery in 1539 the nuns would raise funds by selling goods on the stalls.

The Moot Hall, built about one hundred years before John's birth and still a notable landmark for visitors to Elstow today, was originally designed to provide storage for the equipment and

Elstow Green and the Moot Hall today

stalls used for the fair. Then known as the Green House, it was also a makeshift court to resolve disputes arising from the fair: faulty merchandise, complaints about suspect weights and measures, and wrangles between rival salesmen. Little wonder that a village boy like John would have been intrigued to mingle with the crowds and watch all that was going on.

But young John Bunyan was not an easy child to handle. A strong character, physically tall and hardy, with distinctive reddish hair, he soon became a ringleader amongst the boys of Elstow. Undoubtedly he enjoyed rough games of a primitive type of football played on the village green. The record he leaves of his childhood days suggests that Thomas and Margaret Bunyan did little to restrain their son's erratic and wild behaviour.

> I had but few equals [he tells us in a frank admission of his unruly conduct], especially considering my years, which were tender, being few, both for cursing, swearing, lying and blaspheming the holy name of God.

He gives no hint that such language grieved his parents; indeed, he may well have first learnt it from them. Like many who blaspheme without scruple or conscience, such language became habitual to the boy:

> Yea, so settled and rooted was I in these things that they became as a second nature to me.[4]

In a vivid description of the conduct of another lawless and disobedient child which he wrote towards the end of his life, John Bunyan may well have had his own boyhood behaviour in mind:

> From a child he was very bad... Among other children ... he used to be the ringleader and master-sinner... He was so addicted to lying that his parents scarce knew when to believe he spake true; yea he would invent, tell, and stand to the lies that he invented and that with such an audacious face, that one might even read in his very countenance the symptoms of a hard and desperate heart.[5]

Little evidence remains to suggest that Thomas and Margaret Bunyan were anything other than formal in their religious views, but Sunday by Sunday, in keeping with the legal requirements of the day, they were to be found in their appointed seats in the church. What sort of sermons did the eight-year-old John and his sister Margaret hear from the vicar, John Kellie? We cannot know, but certainly John was early made aware of the spiritual realm: of heaven, hell and the coming judgement of God against sin. He later recognized the restraining hand of God in the alarming dreams that began to disturb and trouble him at this time, and has left a graphic description:

> I ... did so offend the Lord that even in my childhood he did scare and affright me with fearful dreams, and did terrify me with dreadful visions.

After each thoughtless day when blasphemies, lies and curses had poured from his mouth, John faced a nightly retribution:

> I have in my bed been greatly afflicted, while asleep, with the apprehensions of devils and wicked spirits, who still, as I then thought, laboured to draw me away with them, of which I could never be rid.[6]

The writer of an early biographical sketch, Charles Doe, who, as we have seen, knew Bunyan personally, has added details of this period which he must have heard from Bunyan himself. He tells of the 'many showers of tears' which the child shed after yet another day of uncontrolled behaviour. Doe provides a long description of John's horrific nightmares which 'made him cry out in his sleep, and alarm the house, as if someone was about to murder him; and being waked he would start and stare about him with such wildness as if some real apparition had yet remained'.[7]

Not only in the dark hours of the night was John distressed by such fears. They pursued him through his waking hours:

> Also I should, at these years, be greatly afflicted and troubled with the thoughts of the day of judgment, and that both night and day, and should tremble at the thoughts of the

fearful torments of hell fire; still fearing that it would be my lot to be found at last amongst those devils and hellish fiends who are there bound down with the chains and bonds of eternal darkness.[8]

John's capacity for heights of elation and depths of distress coupled with a powerful imagination is evident even in these early years of his life. Suddenly, as he was cheerfully playing with his friends, his mind would cloud over with dark and stormy thoughts:

These things, I say, when I was but a child but nine or ten years old, did so distress my soul that when in the midst of my many sports and childish vanities, amidst my vain companions, I was often much cast down and afflicted in my mind therewith, yet could I not let go my sins.

Troubled about his lawless behaviour, John continues:

I was also then so overcome with despair of life and heaven that I should often wish either that there had been no hell, or that I had been a devil — supposing they were only tormentors — that if it must needs be that I went thither, I might be rather a tormentor, than be tormented myself.[9]

Meanwhile, John Bunyan's education came to an abrupt end when he was about nine years old. He had mastered the rudiments of reading and writing, but now his father needed him in the forge to assist with the work, so aiding the family finances. Also it was time for him to begin his seven-year apprenticeship, which was necessary if he wished to carry on the business or to set up as a brazier on his own account. Referring to his education, John confesses regretfully, 'I did soon lose that little I learned, and that even almost utterly.' Despite such a claim, it is evident from other comments he makes that during his youth he much enjoyed reading the novels, or 'chapbooks', of the day.

George on Horseback and *Bevis of Southampton* were among young John's favourite stories. Written by Richard Johnson and republished in 1607, these tales came from a larger collection called *The Seven Champions of Christendom*, and tell of a man-eating giant done to death by the noble St George, who goes on to deal with a vicious Egyptian dragon and receives healing for his wounds from the leaves of a tree. Such tales of heroism, appealing to boys in any generation, left indelible marks on young Bunyan's imagination.

But by the time John had entered his teenage years he had managed to harden his mind against the frightening reminders of God's displeasure against his sin, and soon his terrifying dreams died out. He was able, or so it seemed, to act and speak as badly as he wished without any painful pangs of conscience:

> Wherefore, with more greediness, according to the strength of nature, I did still let loose the reins to my lusts, and delighted in all transgression against the law of God.[10]

And later he confessed sadly:

> I was one of these great sin-breeders; I infected all the youth of the town where I was born with all manner of youthful vanities.[11]

Whether the arrival of a new vicar at the Abbey Church had anything to do with such a change we cannot say. We know that in 1639, when John was eleven, a certain Christopher Hall was appointed by Archbishop Laud to the Abbey Church in Elstow. In keeping with Laud's own emphasis, he laid much stress in his ministry on the correct conduct of the services, on ritual, vestments and the importance of the priestly office.

It seemed outwardly that all John's early anxieties had now been put to rest, and he was at liberty to sin with impunity, but there is evidence that he still had some lingering traces of a tender conscience. While he felt able to curse and blaspheme freely himself, one thing disturbed his outward composure: if he ever heard or saw anyone who claimed to be religious acting in a way that contradicted those professions, he was deeply offended.

> When I was in my height of vanity, yet hearing one to swear
> that was reckoned for a religious man, it had so great a stroke
> upon my spirit, that it made my heart to ache.[12]

Although John Bunyan managed to neglect and forget God, God had not forgotten him. On two or three occasions he was remarkably preserved from imminent danger. As a non-swimmer he records an episode when the small boat he was in capsized in the River Ouse in Bedford. How he struggled ashore, or whether someone stretched out a kindly hand to help him, we do not know, but the incident remained stamped on his mind for many years. Later he would recognize God's merciful protection watching over him.

A certain impetuosity, probably inherited from his father, coupled with a reckless daring, allowed John one day to show off to a friend who was with him when he caught sight of an adder slithering across the road. Stunning the reptile with a blow from the stick in his hand, the foolish youth forced open its mouth with his stick, put his fingers down its throat and pulled out the adder's sting. 'Had not God been merciful unto me,' Bunyan comments, 'I might by my desperateness have brought myself to mine end.'[13]

An intelligent boy, John Bunyan must certainly have been aware of the alarming build-up in tensions on the national scene as the country teetered towards civil war with a fatal confrontation between Charles I and his Parliament. He may well have heard of the angry demonstrations in 1637 in the Palace Yard in London as men of influence and distinction were pilloried and mutilated for their refusal to pay the extortionate taxes being levied by the king — taxes that also angered Bedfordshire men.

As a boy who loved adventure stories, the twelve-year-old cannot fail to have been thrilled when two thousand local men marched to London on 16 March 1641. Four abreast they passed through Elstow, which lay on the high road to the capital. Displayed on their hats were the words of the petition they were carrying to the reconvened House of Commons, protesting against exploitation, evil and corrupt councillors, together with the unacceptable religious ceremonial that was burdening the people. Doubtless John would have been eager to find out the reason for such protests.

But by the following year protests had turned to the regular tramp of feet as soldiers began to muster for the forthcoming conflict. Perhaps young Bunyan, now steadily employed in his father's forge, looked with longing as the conscripts marched through Elstow, and felt his pulse quicken at the thought that one day he too might possibly become a soldier.

Another year would pass, however, before, in the late spring of 1644, a situation arose in Elstow and the surrounding district which put all such thoughts far from John's mind. One of those frightening epidemics of disease broke out in the community, sweeping young and old indiscriminately to their graves. Who would be next to develop the alarming symptoms and die? It was a question on everyone's lips. We can only imagine the distress in the small cottage by the stream in Harrowden when John's mother, Margaret Bunyan, fell ill and died at the age of forty-one. John was fifteen at the time, his sister, Margaret, only thirteen and William was eleven — all at an age when their need of a mother's love and care was at its most acute.

We know little of Margaret Bunyan's character, but, as the mother of a child like John, endowed with extraordinary natural talent, she must have been an interesting and capable woman. As the small funeral procession wound its way across the fields to Elstow churchyard on 20 June 1644, John could not have guessed that little more than a month later he would once again tread that same painful track as his young sister Margaret, his childhood companion, was also carried to her grave. The boy's desolation of spirit is not hard to imagine as both his mother and sister were taken in so short a space of time. All of the softening influences in the youth's life had vanished at a stroke.

And, as if that were not hard enough, within a month another woman was in his mother's bed. Unable to sustain his home and his business without Margaret, Thomas Bunyan had hastily remarried, without any due consideration for the feelings of his two boys, John and William. Little wonder then that John Bunyan threw himself into further youthful abandon. Now he could say:

> In these days the thoughts of religion were very grievous to me; I could neither endure it myself, nor that any other should...

Then I said unto God 'Depart from me for I desire not the knowledge of thy ways' (Job 21:14). I was now void of all good consideration, heaven and hell were both out of sight and mind; and as for saving and damning; they were least in my thoughts.[14]

Looking back on these dark days, John Bunyan could write, 'O Lord, thou knowest my life, and my ways were not hid from thee.'[15] He was right. Out of all these unpromising circumstances God was at work, forming an instrument that he would one day use to bring much glory to his name.

4

A soldier's lot

As the people of Elstow and the surrounding area struggled against the deadly ravages of disease, and John Bunyan grieved over the death of his mother and sister, a tragedy of still greater proportions was unfolding in the north of England. Just twelve days after his mother's funeral, more than four thousand young men were lying dead on a battlefield outside Long Marston, an area known as Marston Moor, seven miles west of the city of York.

On 2 July 1644 13,000 horse and 25,000 foot soldiers faced each other across a narrow divide — too narrow, as some observed. Only a rough track and a ditch lay between Parliament's united armies on Marston Hill and the armies of King Charles I on the adjacent low-lying moor. As evening fell the king's commanders relaxed, not expecting any action until the following day. The Marquess of Newcastle, commander of the king's troops, reputedly settled for a peaceful smoke in his coach while the other Royalist commander, Prince Rupert of the Rhine, the king's nephew, went off to have a meal. Quite suddenly, at 7.30 in the evening, the Parliamentarian commanders gave the order to attack. Lieutenant-General Oliver Cromwell and his cavalry charged up the left wing. 'We came down in the bravest order with the greatest resolution that ever was seen... In a moment we were past the ditch and into the Moor upon equal grounds with the enemy,' runs the report.

All through the dark hours, illumined only by moonlight, the battle raged, now swinging one way, now another. But as morning broke the Royalists were in full retreat, their casualties scattered all over the moor. The city of York, one of the king's strongholds, capitulated to the Parliamentarians and this battle proved a decisive turning point in the Civil War.

But what had happened to bring about this grievous situation, where neighbours were killing neighbours, and fathers their sons? Writers still argue about the long-term causes of the Civil War that broke out in the summer of 1642. But few would disagree with the historian Paul Johnson that the England of 1640 'seemed in ruins. It was spiritually, morally and physically bankrupt. It had lost its soul, its international credit, its domestic stability... All the ancient and familiar landmarks had gone.'[1]

However, the immediate cause of the war was the final breakdown between Charles I and his Parliament, which he had recalled in 1640 to supply funds to help him fight the Scots. Before supplying any money, Parliament had grievances of its own which it wished to see redressed. The king, unwilling to satisfy such demands or to undertake any reformation of the many ills that plagued the country, had answered Parliament's complaints by raising his standard at Nottingham on 22 August 1642, declaring war on his own people. John Bunyan was fourteen at the time and, as a youth with natural leadership ability and deep feelings, he would have followed all these events as much as he was able. Bedfordshire was one of the counties most solidly behind the Parliamentarian cause, though there were also some Royalist supporters. John and his friends must have laughed heartily when they heard that the Royalist commander Sir Lewis Dyve, from nearby Bromham Hall, had leapt into the River Ouse near his home and swum to the farther bank in order to escape Sir Samuel Luke and his Parliamentary troops.

Two years of inconclusive fighting followed, with heavy losses on both sides, but after the victory of Marston Moor in 1644 the

tide was definitely turning in Parliament's favour. The Scots had
been coaxed to enter the war on the Parliamentary side in 1643,
but the conditions of such assistance were definitely ecclesiastical.
Parliament, desperate for aid, agreed to work together with the
Scottish church towards uniformity of religion, establishing a
Presbyterian system of church order in the English churches.

Despite the undoubted help of the Scottish army under Sir
Alexander Leslie, reinforcements were still urgently needed to
make good Parliament's losses.[2] As Sir Thomas Fairfax, the
commander-in-chief, was demanding the recruitment of another
14,000 men, agents were sent throughout the country to con-
script any young men aged sixteen or over who appeared able-
bodied. Some were press-ganged; others may have volunteered.
In the autumn of 1644 Sir Samuel Luke, MP for Bedford and in
charge of the garrison at Newport Pagnell, twelve miles from
Bedford, arrived in Elstow searching for recruits.

A tall, tough-looking youth with bright eyes, a sharp intelligent
face and distinctive auburn hair attracted his attention. Not yet
sixteen, John Bunyan was too young to be conscripted, but he
may well have looked older and could therefore have been
forced into armed service. The likelihood, however, is that one as
adept at lying as Bunyan then was would have had no difficulty
in saying that he was sixteen. Besides, his home life had become
far from happy since his mother's death and his father's remar-
riage. Perhaps life in the army would provide an escape from a
difficult situation. So in October 1644 John found himself marching the twelve miles to the garrison town of Newport with a
contingent of other conscripts. Here he was to be stationed, at
least for the present. A new and highly significant phase of his life
had begun. But if John thought that the life of a soldier would
be an escape route from the bleak circumstances he faced at
home, he was sadly mistaken. Uncongenial as his home might
have been, the experiences he would meet in army life must have
made him wish he had remained unnoticed when Sir Samuel
Luke's agents came to Elstow.

Newport Pagnell is a small market town that can trace its
origins to the Iron Age; its strategic position, cradled between two
rivers, the River Ouse and its tributary the River Lovat, gave it a
natural defence against any invaders. Equally important was the

fact that the Ouse could be forded at that point. By the time the Domesday Book was compiled in 1086, Newport Pagnell was one of the more important towns in the country. Early in the Civil War, Charles I's generals had seen the importance of gaining a foothold there and using it as a garrison town from which they could launch an attack on the capital.

Consequently, Sir Lewis Dyve, the Bedfordshire man who had the indignity of performing that hasty leap into the river near Bedford, was commissioned to occupy Newport Pagnell for the king. But the Earl of Essex,[3] lord-general of the Parliamentary forces, also had his eye on the place, seeing it as a significant fortification against incursions from the north, where the Royalists were strong, and also as a useful supply route to London. In October 1643 Essex and his troops advanced towards the town, but to their amazement discovered that Sir Lewis Dyve had inexplicably evacuated, together with all his men. Later it was discovered that he had misunderstood a message from the king and thought he was being ordered to leave Newport Pagnell.

John Bunyan was stationed in Colonel Richard Cokayne's company, which consisted of 128 'centinells', or foot soldiers, together with their officers, under the overall authority of Sir Samuel Luke, Governor of the town.[4] A foot soldier's main weapon was a sword and, when supplies permitted, a musket as well. Each week Cokayne was supposed to fill in a muster roll recording the names of those men serving under him, so enabling him to claim the pay due to them for that week. John Bunyan's name first appears on the Newport Pagnell muster rolls on 30 November 1644,[5] but, as earlier records appear to be missing, he may well have been present in the town for several months already. Soon after their arrival new recruits were issued with a copy of *The Souldiers Pocket Bible*. Apart from the novels he had read, this would probably be the first real 'book' John had possessed.

Many have suggested that the Parliamentary soldiers were given copies of the Geneva Bible which they carried in their boots. But even the smallest copies, measuring four inches by two, were far too bulky for the men to take into battle. Instead *The Souldiers Pocket Bible* consisted of some twelve pages and was about the size of a modern passport. First issued in 1643, this slim

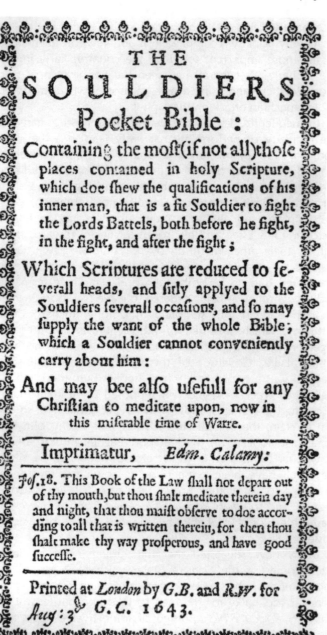

THE
SOULDIERS
Pocket Bible :

Containing the moſt (if not all) thoſe
places contained in holy Scripture,
which doe ſhew the qualifications of his
inner man, that is a fit Souldier to fight
the Lords Battels, both before he fight,
in the fight, and after the fight ;

Which Scriptures are reduced to ſe-
verall heads, and fitly applyed to the
Souldiers feverall occaſions, and ſo may
ſupply the want of the whole Bible ;
which a Souldier cannot conveniently
carry about him :

And may bee alſo uſefull for any
Chriſtian to meditate upon, now in
this miferable time of Warre.

Imprimatur,   *Edm. Calamy:*

Joſ. 18. This Book of the Law ſhall not depart out
of thy mouth, but thou ſhalt meditate therein day
and night, that thou maiſt obſerve to doe according to all that is written therein, for then thou
ſhalt make thy way proſperous, and have good
ſucceſſe.

Printed at *London* by G.B. and *R.W.* for
Aug : 3 G.C. 1643.

Title page of *The Souldiers Bible*
Reproduced by courtesy of the British Library

booklet contained a selection of 150 verses, all but four from the Old Testament and chosen mainly to encourage and instruct a soldier. A fighting man could easily slip it down his long boots or hide it in some pocket.

Collected under sixteen short headings, John would read such instructions as: 'A Souldier must not do wickedly...'; 'A souldier must be valiant for God's Cause...'; 'A Souldier must pray before he go to fight' — each with an appropriate verse of Scripture attached. In addition to this John was given a copy of *The Souldiers Catechisme*, justifying their enterprise and stating on the title page that it was 'written for the Incouragement and Instruction of all that have taken up arms in this Cause of God and his people; especially the common souldiers'. Whether John paid much attention to these things is doubtful.

Commenting on his army days, Bunyan tells us that neither judgments nor mercy 'did awaken my soul to righteousness; wherefore I sinned still, and grew more and more rebellious against God, and careless of mine own salvation'.[6]

Sir Samuel Luke, himself a staunch Presbyterian, was one who had the spiritual good of his men high on his agenda. Not only was the young Bunyan expected to attend two services each Sunday at the imposing church of St Peter and St Paul, its square tower dominating the skyline, but a service on Thursdays as well, with Bible reading and prayer each day before military duties began. In October 1644, just at the time that his new recruits from Elstow arrived, Sir Samuel records that there were at least seven 'able divines' in the town, to assist in such exercises.

The entire garrison was made up of about 800 foot soldiers although Sir Samuel had hoped to recruit 1,200. Ordinary 'centinells' were supposed to receive eight pence a day as pay from their respective home counties. But if those counties were reluctant to forward the necessary funds, or reneged on their responsibilities, the soldiers obviously suffered. Pay was hopelessly in arrears at the time that John first enrolled, giving rise to acute problems.

Unable to cover basic costs, the army quickly incurred the antagonism of the locals who were expected to accommodate the soldiers in their homes. Some nasty situations developed. A document has survived dated 14 April 1645, after Bunyan had been in the army for about six months, in which forty-one soldiers were petitioning Sir Samuel Luke urgently for money. They claimed that if they deferred paying for their accommodation any longer, 'the people may rise and cut our throats', and, as if that were not bad enough, they added that they had 'no clothes, no ammunition or supplies for their horses'.[7]

As a result the troops lost respect for their officers — leading inevitably to a breakdown of discipline. Cokayne complained to the Bedfordshire Committee, 'We are now become men of no reputation and of no command amongst our own soldiers.' Not surprisingly, scavenging and looting became commonplace. When bands of soldiers were sent out on forays against local Royalist units, prisoners were captured and brought back to the town. In many instances their clothes and personal possessions were stolen and sold. To raise money for food some men even pawned articles of their own clothing which they could scarcely spare.

Sometimes officers lent money to the men to pay for essential supplies, but accounts are extant in letters written by the governor, Sir Samuel Luke, describing the desperate situation in Newport Pagnell. 'The men have neither boots for their legs nor money to buy shoes for their horses,' he complained in an appeal to the Committee of Both Kingdoms.[8] Writing to the Earl of Essex, he added a few more colourful details: 'The wants of them are such that they are not fitting to be put on paper ... if the soldiers mutiny for want of pay I cannot help it.' He went on to describe a case of two soldiers who had to share a single pair of breeches; when one man wore the trousers the other was obliged to remain in bed all day. So cold was it that many soldiers, having no coats, refused to leave their beds at all; while at other times a shortage of townsfolk prepared to give the men accommodation could lead to three soldiers having to share one bed.[9]

Adequate weapons were equally hard to obtain, even though Sir Samuel continually sent urgent letters to London requesting further supplies of muskets, pikes, pistols, horses and boots for the men. In such circumstances many soldiers tried to abscond and return home. Only the threat of immediate death by hanging on one of the local gibbets for any found escaping prevented more men from trying such an expedient. It is not hard to imagine that John Bunyan, a youth of barely sixteen, would have been dismayed at such circumstances, but we have no record of any attempt on his part to return to Elstow. Hardy and used to tough conditions, he was not the sort to succumb to such deprivations.

While these conditions provided an ideal opportunity for many to attempt a defection from the Parliamentary army, we are not surprised to learn that in December 1644 some in the town who were still loyal to Charles I sent him a secret message informing him of the dire situation there. Scarcely more than 200 soldiers, so they reported, were still in the garrison at that time; morale was at rock bottom and even the bulwarks and outer defences were crumbling. The king could hardly wish for a better moment to mount an attack and regain the town for the Royalist cause.

In the light of such intelligence, Charles and his army advanced on Newport Pagnell. John Bunyan had not been in the garrison for more than a couple of months, with little opportunity for military training, before it appeared that he was about to have his first taste of armed combat. Sir Samuel scarcely knew what to do in the circumstances. News had arrived that '... his majesty's army both horse and foot [are] marching this way and [were] quartering last night within less than 20 miles.' If he left the garrison to seek additional troops, he feared that 'the [remaining] soldiers, for want of pay, would most of them disband... Besides my absence might encourage the enemy to come on.' All he could do was to write urgently to a nearby garrison for reinforcements: 'If you will furnish me with 50 or 60 horse to be here tomorrow betimes I doubt not but to give you good report of the enemie's quartering.'[10]

In the event only bitter weather prevented the king from taking further advantage of the plight of Newport Pagnell and of Sir Samuel Luke's men. At least the imminent threat produced one useful result: when the Committee of Both Kingdoms heard of how nearly their Newport Pagnell garrison had come under attack and could have been lost, it immediately sent £500 to relieve the situation.

Although John Bunyan had not yet tasted the bitterness of military conflict, or experienced the horror of Englishmen being called upon to kill Englishmen, he had already had to cope with a degree of deprivation and hardship which he would never forget. A soldier's lot was certainly not a happy one.

5

A babble of voices

Sir Samuel Luke, a rigid Presbyterian, was dismayed and angered at the cacophony of religious voices to which the men at the Newport Pagnell garrison were exposed. Not so the men in his charge. Most of them had come from a stratum of society that up to that time had been voiceless in terms of any political, religious or social influence. At a formative age, they now naturally and eagerly absorbed fresh ideas and convictions from the 'mechanic', or lay, preachers they could hear declaiming in various parts of the town. Before long some would become equally zealous in spreading their own newly acquired opinions. Life in the armed forces therefore brought young John Bunyan into contact with a plethora of new ideas and convictions, for many 'conventicles', or unofficial preaching services, were taking place in the area and in the town itself.

Amid the babble of voices there were a number of preachers propounding ideas that were far from biblical. At the same time in God's purposes a profound spiritual awakening was taking place in parts of the country which would shortly lead to the creation of many vibrant Independent churches. For a village boy like John, the torrent of different opinions that he met in day-to-day army life must have been an immense culture shock at first. Here he encountered men of contradictory persuasions and ideologies far removed from those he had heard in childhood as he sat under the sermons of John Kellie and Christopher Hall. Probably out of curiosity, or even boredom, he would sometimes attend these conventicles. Seed thoughts that lay dormant for many years could well have been planted in his mind at this time.

Doubtless John, who later describes himself as 'a brisk talker', also found himself at the heart of many heated debates, political as well as religious, as he lounged around the garrison. The news from home was that his stepmother Anne had just given birth to a son, controversially enough named Charles, suggesting that his father supported the Royalist cause. To name the new baby Charles was tactless at best, on Thomas Bunyan's part, since his oldest son was fighting with the Parliamentary army, and it can only have been a further grievance for John. Sceptical and profane in his use of language, the young man is not likely to have been one of Sir Samuel Luke's favourite soldiers!

While Archbishop Laud and his High Church rituals had dominated church life in the 1630s, individual opinions had been suppressed. Now, with the old bishop incarcerated in the Tower of London, every man appeared to have a different viewpoint, some wild and confused, others designed to promote true godliness and toleration for those whose conscience and under-standing of Scripture differed from that of the state church. With restrictions on publishers lifted, the market was flooded with books and pamphlets, most of them on controversial subjects. Newspapers were no longer illegal, with more than 700 different ones appearing in 1645 alone.

Then on 10 January 1645 came the execution of William Laud on Tower Hill. Elderly and frail, the seventy-two-year-old ex-archbishop was scarcely a threat any more. But many had old scores to settle, particularly William Prynne, a Presbyterian lawyer who had lost both his ears in a savage punishment in 1637 for having written a pamphlet against the godlessness of the times.

With the death of Laud the pace of change accelerated, particularly after the formation of Oliver Cromwell's New Model Army. Its generals were now appointed for ability and religious

Sir Thomas Fairfax

convictions rather than noble birth and prestige. This soon began to influence the course of the war. Sir Thomas Fairfax, a godly, just and brilliant general, was chosen by the Committee of Both Kingdoms to replace the Earl of Essex. His position as Lord-General of the New Model Army was confirmed by Parliament in April 1645. Under Fairfax the New Model Army was quickly moulded into an efficient, disciplined fighting force and, coupled with Cromwell's skilful ordering of the cavalry units, became an indispensable asset.

Other changes too were afoot in London. The Westminster Assembly of Divines, made up of 121 preachers and some laymen, had been meeting in the Jerusalem Chamber of Westminster Abbey. First convened at the request of Parliament in July 1643, the assembly's brief was to reform the life and discipline in the churches in both Scotland and England, aiming at uniformity in both countries. The members had been hard at work throughout 1644, and early in 1645 the English *Book of Common Prayer* was banned and the new *Directory for Public Worship* instituted in its place.

Of more direct relevance to Bunyan was the decision of Parliament to change the structure of pay for men serving in the army. In alarm at the number absconding and the near mutinies over arrears of pay, it was decided that in future the soldiers' pay was to come from national rather than local taxes, and by the autumn of 1645 the situation at Newport Pagnell had improved considerably.

But did John Bunyan see any action during his years in the Parliamentary army? This is a question that has often been posed, and one that has led to considerable speculation. Those, like

Bunyan, who protected the various garrisons during the Civil War were not part of the fighting units engaged for the great set-piece battles such as Marston Moor. But theirs was also a dangerous assignment as they regularly sallied forth on local missions and mounted smaller sieges. The comparative casualty figures between the garrison soldiers and those of the standing army suggest that there was little difference in terms of exposure to risk.

Bunyan's only comment on his army days has in itself puzzled many:

> When I was a soldier, I, with others, were drawn out to go to such a place to besiege it; but when I was just ready to go, one of the company desired to go in my room; to which, when I had consented, he took my place; and coming to the siege, as he stood sentinel, he was shot into the head with a musket bullet, and died.[1]

We are not told which town they were besieging when this incident occurred, but almost fifty years later an anonymous biographer, writing in 1692, made a categorical statement that this incident took place in June 1645 at the Siege of Leicester. This

same biographical sketch contains a number of in-accuracies, not least one stating that Bunyan, who, as we have seen, was still only sixteen, already had a family of his own to support at the time. In addition, the Siege of Leicester occurred in May and not June. But the greatest obstacle to this being the scene of John's escape from death is his own description, for he says he was 'drawn out to go to such a place to besiege it'. The siege referred to was therefore one being mounted by the Parliamentary forces,

Civil War Parliamentarian musketeer

whereas at the Siege of Leicester the opposite occurred. On 28 May it was the Royalists who laid siege to the town, while the Parliamentarian army struggled to defend it at considerable cost before capitulating on 31 May. When Sir Thomas Fairfax retook Leicester in June we learn that it surrendered without a single shot being fired, so Bunyan's friend could not have died on that occasion.

A leading Bunyan scholar, Richard L. Greaves, has suggested an alternative.[2] Sir Thomas Fairfax began a siege of Oxford, one of Charles I's remaining strongholds, in the middle of May 1645. To effect this siege Fairfax requisitioned 200 ladders to scale the fortifications, 2,000 spades, 600 mortar shells, in addition to 1,000 hand grenades and thirty tons of bullets. He was to be accompanied by 5,000 foot soldiers and almost as many cavalry men. Clearly this was to be a major operation. At Fairfax's request, the Committee of Both Kingdoms ordered that 400 men from the Newport Pagnell garrison should assist in the siege. Fighting was fierce and many casualties were sustained before Fairfax decided to lift the siege on 3 June.

This scenario fits the description provided by Bunyan more accurately and also corresponds with the additional information given by the anonymous biographer in 1692. He reports that the 'town was vigorously defended by the King's forces against the Parliamentarians' and that the man who replaced Bunyan 'met his fate by a carbine shot from the wall'.[3]

Another and more significant engagement soon occupied Fairfax and the New Model Army, accompanied by Cromwell and his son-in-law, Henry Ireton. For at the Battle of Naseby on 14 June 1645, the Royalist armies were shattered, leaving Charles I so weakened that the defeat marked the beginning of a final victory for Parliament. Fought twenty-five miles north-west of Newport Pagnell, the battle was close enough to Sir Samuel Luke's garrison for him to supply arms and men had they been needed.

Services of thanksgiving to God for so notable a victory were held in many parts, and Sir Samuel Luke ordered a public thanksgiving at the parish church in Newport Pagnell with a preacher of his appointment. To his dismay he discovered many empty seats on the occasion. Where were the soldiers? Apparently numbers of them had flocked to the nearby village of Lathbury to hear Captain Paul Hobson preach.

As an officer in Fairfax's army, Hobson had fought bravely at Naseby and was high in Fairfax's esteem. He was also an ardent Baptist, a man of deep spiritual experience and earnest convictions, although inclined to a degree of mysticism. His great emphasis was on the vital importance of regeneration and the work of the Holy Spirit indwelling the life of the believer. That day he chose to speak on the privileges of Christians as members of Christ's special people, the church: they enjoy 'the special love and power and sweetness of Christ to secure them from the evil that is in the world,'⁴ he told his congregation. Was John Bunyan among the men who opted for the chance to hear the soldier-preacher? It is highly likely. Possibly he heard that day a message which he would recall in years to come.

Sir Samuel was furious. Tensions were growing between the Presbyterian and Independent elements in the army. To think that an Independent preacher had grabbed the attention of his men was maddening. He ordered the immediate arrest of Hobson and a fellow preacher, another army captain, sending them back to Fairfax with a letter of protest. But Fairfax ignored Sir Samuel's protest, releasing the two.

However, Sir Samuel's days as governor of the Newport Pagnell garrison were coming to an end. A bill known as the Self-denying Ordinance had finally been passed by the House of Lords on 3 April obliging members of the aristocracy and of Parliament to resign their positions of command in the army or navy in favour of men of military experience. Only by such a sweeping measure could Parliament be sure that its commanders were single-minded in their determination to prosecute the war. Captain Charles O'Doyley was Fairfax's new appointment to be governor of Newport Pagnell. At the end of June 1645, Sir Samuel relinquished his post.

We know little of Bunyan's activities for the next year. With the king's cause rapidly disintegrating, military activity was scaled back. With the final fall of Oxford in June 1646, the First Civil War was effectively over, and the king taken into custody. Parliament ordered that the garrison at Newport Pagnell should be dismantled and its fortifications removed. This would involve heavy physical work and doubtless Bunyan was engaged in it. Some have suggested that he then returned to Elstow, but this is unlikely for Parliament ordered that:

> ... all the officers and souldiers both Horse and Foot be forthwith employed in the service of Ireland ... and it is further ordered that such common souldiers as shall refuse to go for Ireland shall be forthwith disbanded.

John Bunyan opted to go to Ireland. Perhaps the adventure appealed to him. More probably the lure of having his outstanding arrears of pay made up was a further motivation. Following many delays and setbacks a small company, intended to be an advance guard, set off in October 1646 under Captain Charles O'Hara and eventually reached Chester, where they were to await shipping to Dublin. But after some time they learnt that units from the New Model Army that were supposed to join O'Hara's men in Chester had refused to go to Ireland until their arrears of pay were settled. In the end the whole project had to be cancelled.

It may well have been while he was waiting in Chester on the Dee Estuary that John 'fell into a creek in the sea and hardly escaped drowning', as he records in his autobiography.[5] In later life he saw this incident as yet another of God's warnings to check his sinful ways. But, like the other near brushes with death, such a merciful providence appears to have had little effect upon him at the time.

With no alternative O'Hara marched his men back to Newport Pagnell once more and here Bunyan's name appears yet again on the muster rolls on 17 June 1647. Then came orders for the troops of the Parliamentary army to be finally disbanded. On 21 July 1647 John returned to civilian life in Elstow. Almost three years had elapsed since, as a youth of sixteen, he had joined the army. Ugly sights, sounds and scenes of bloodshed had been his lot; his mind had been filled with the raging controversies of the day, and now, as a young man of almost nineteen, he was coming home. Anything John Bunyan might one day become in the purposes of God was still far from evident.

6

The young brazier

To return to the dreamy village of Elstow after almost three years in an army garrison — a melting pot of ideas, opinions and speculation — needed considerable adjustment for John Bunyan and could not have been easy. In view of his father's possible Royalist sympathies and the presence of his stepmother, it is unlikely that he would wish to return to the family home. But he probably had little option. He had a further year of a seven-year apprenticeship still to serve in order to gain his Statute of Apprentices. Not till then would he be qualified to set up as a brazier in his own right.

The only record that we have of the next few years of Bunyan's life comes from the pages of *Grace Abounding to the Chief of Sinners*, an account which he wrote more than fifteen years after the events. If he had kept a diary of his early life and experiences as they occurred from day to day the result would have been far different. Diary keeping had become popular during this period. Many, like Samuel Pepys, realized that the times through which they were living were highly significant, and over 350 seventeenth-century diaries have come to light. Christians in particular were urged by their preachers, men like the Puritan John Flavel, born the same year as Bunyan, to keep a record of God's providences in their lives.

Such records would inevitably contain details of the writer's life and personal circumstances, but, as we turn the pages of *Grace Abounding to the Chief of Sinners*, we search in vain for any such observations apart from incidental references. Much that a biographer looks for is missing. We find no details of his relationships with his family or friends, his home, his business hopes and endeavours — nothing. It would therefore be unwise and also useless to try to force traditional biographical material out of *Grace Abounding*. Clearly this was not Bunyan's intention when he wrote it; his account is neither biography nor autobiography in the usual sense. Even the timescale of events which Bunyan mentions seems hopelessly tangled up and is impossible to reconcile with the known facts. 'The chronology is at best imprecise, at worst chaotic,'[1] commented Christopher Hill. If we add up all his references to the periods of time mentioned in *Grace Abounding* it comes to about seven years, which must then be squeezed into the space of five years from 1651–1656. Certain events must therefore have occurred concurrently or else overlapped.

But there are also immense gains. In *Grace Abounding to the Chief of Sinners* we have a secret window into the powerful workings of a soul in search of assurance of salvation. In a warm, dramatic, fast-moving account, Bunyan takes his readers with him from his early state of godless profanity to one of confusion, error and perplexity, and on to heights of spiritual joys. Then he allows us to crash down again with him into the depths of despair as he faces the fearsome attacks of Satan on his young faith. Yet always there is a steady, unerring progression towards his ultimate goal. This is a book with a purpose — it is didactic writing intended to put warning signs along the path of Christian experience so that others may not stumble and therefore suffer as he did. Above all, it is an extended commentary on the relationship between conscience, law and grace and the pitfalls that await those who misunderstand the connection between them.

But we must return to where we left John Bunyan as he finally received his papers decommissioning him from the Parliamentary army in July 1647. The war might be over, but there was little peace or stability in the country. The victorious New Model Army was becoming increasingly demanding and belligerent, particularly (and understandably) over its pay arrears. Authority was fast breaking down, with each man majoring on his own chosen agenda. The Levellers urgently sought a voice in government for every male; the Diggers[2] and the Ranters[3] were equally clamouring to be heard. Parliament itself was divided. Many of the Presbyterians wished to establish a rigid Presbyterian church order to replace Anglicanism. The Independents, meanwhile, represented by Oliver Cromwell, wished for a measure of religious reform and toleration.

The king, who had been in captivity since the summer of 1646, tried to take advantage of Parliament's differences. Then, in November, he made a cleverly planned escape from custody in Hampton Court Palace, absconding to the Isle of Wight. Recaptured on the island, he was held in Carisbrooke Castle. Despite this he began to negotiate with the Scots, promising them Presbyterianism for an experimental period of three years if they would raise an army on his behalf. Tempted by the king's terms, the Scottish army turned against its former Parliamentary colleagues and in April 1648 penetrated northern England. Carlisle and Berwick soon fell into Royalist hands once more.

Heartened by these victories, other defeated Royalist commanders rallied their troops and once more joined the fray with uprisings in Kent, Essex, Cornwall and Yorkshire. The Second Civil War had begun. Reacting with lightning speed, Sir Thomas Fairfax and Oliver Cromwell, together with the New Model Army, soon crushed the Royalist rebellion and once more tried to open negotiations with Charles I — a futile endeavour. The king prevaricated as before, rejecting any terms that compromised a full restoration of his royal prerogatives as he envisaged them.

Although John Bunyan would have followed the news of renewed fighting with concern, he was not recalled into active service in this further civil war, for he had never been part of the New Model Army. The country was now in a sorry state, the people frightened and troubled. Not only had thousands more died in renewed fighting, but trade was severely depressed. Continuous rain during the summer of 1648 had led to a disastrous harvest, forcing the price of wheat, barley and oats to unprecedented high levels. Many poorer families were reduced to near starvation. No one knew what would be the outcome of these things.

Then in December 1648 came the series of events which led inexorably on to the final scenes of the king's life, with his trial followed by his execution in Whitehall Palace on 30 January 1649. As Oliver Cromwell gazed one dark night at the headless body of his erstwhile king lying in its coffin, he is reputed to have described it as a 'cruel necessity', for Charles had repeatedly betrayed his own people. But many fell into a frenzy of misguided loyalty, comparing the king's death with the trial and crucifixion of Christ. John Bunyan too must have been troubled by these events, having fought for his country for almost three years. No one knew for certain what was going to happen next. Then in March came the abolition of the monarchy, together with the House of Lords. England was declared a commonwealth.

While these momentous changes were taking place on the national scene, twenty-year-old John Bunyan had been making arrangements to begin working as a brazier in his own right. Now he wished to marry and settle down. Whether he had previously met and fallen in love with a Newport Pagnell girl, we do not know. Certainly his prospective bride, an upright girl from a good home, was not from Elstow, for there is no record of their marriage in the Elstow register.

It would seem that this young woman had been left in impoverished circumstances. Her father was dead, and probably her mother too. So there may have been no one to warn her of the enormous risk she was taking in marrying someone with a reputation like John's for wild and careless living. Describing his life at this time Bunyan tells us, that

> [Christ] found me one of the black sinners of the world, he found me making a sport of oaths and also of lies; and many a soul-poisoning meal did I make out of divers lusts as drinking, dancing, playing, pleasure with the wicked ones of the world.[4]

Beyond doubt John was deeply fond of his young wife, and in all probability the tall auburn-haired ex-soldier had swept Mary off her feet. Although John does not actually tell us his bride's name, we may assume it was Mary for several reasons. The strongest is the prevailing custom of naming an eldest daughter after her mother, and we know that the Bunyans' first child was called Mary. And then there are the books. John tells us that his wife brought with her two books into her marriage — books that her father had given her. A copy of one of these books, *The Plaine Man's Path-way to Heaven* by Arthur Dent, had the name 'M Bunyan' in the front. Preserved until 1865, it was sadly destroyed in a fire at Sotheby's. A copy of the other, *The Practice of Piety* by Lewis Bayly, which might also have belonged to Bunyan's wife, has the initials M. B. in the front. This is held at the University of Alabama, and again adds credibility to the suggestion that John's wife was called Mary.[5]

Commenting on his marriage Bunyan tells us:

> My mercy was to light upon a wife whose father was counted godly. This woman and I ... came together as poor as poor might be, not having so much household stuff as a dish or spoon betwixt us both.[6]

But, poor as they were, they had at least secured a roof over their heads, a 'one hearth' cottage in Elstow High Street on the

Bunyan's cottage in Elstow, from an old print.

road to Bedford. Built of timber and plaster work with a work-shop attached, it is generally supposed that John and Mary Bunyan set up home together there early in 1649.

Before long Mary was expecting her first baby and it was vital that John tried to extend his work as a brazier in order to support her. Day after day he tramped out to farms in the area with his

Bunyan's anvil
Reproduced by kind permission of Bunyan Meeting Free Church, Bedford, England

tools strapped to his back — and a heavy burden they were, with his hammers, soldering iron and, above all, his anvil. Weighing sixty pounds, it was shaped like an enormous nail, with a flat head and a pointed end that could be hammered into the ground wherever he chose to work.

Discovered in 1905 among some scrap metal at St Neots in Huntingdon by a collector of odd or interesting items, Bunyan's own anvil has survived. Carved on one side is the name *J. BVNYAN* in John's distinctive style of signature, and on the other the old spelling of Elstow, 'H ELSTOWE', with the date '1647'.[7]

Sometimes John might be required to visit one of the stately homes in the area, and here and there we find traces of his activities. Tradition insists that he would visit such places as Houghton House on Ampthill Heights — still beautiful though now in ruins — to mend their pots and pans or undertake any other metal repair job. At Willington, five miles east of Bedford, is a strange old building known as King Henry's stables, part of John Gostwick's manorial complex where Henry VIII is known to have stayed.

King Henry's stables, Willington

Perhaps the king's horses were indeed stabled there, but there was an upper floor that may have been used to accommodate members of the royal entourage. Soon after his marriage John Bunyan was called upon to do some work for the Gostwick family and, perhaps in some idle moment, he chiselled his name on the plasterwork over the fireplace on the upper floor over the stables, adding the date '1650'. Once again bearing his own characteristic style, the signature is still to be seen today.

The year 1650 marked a change in John Bunyan's lifestyle. Shocked at her young husband's profanities and his careless attitudes, Mary frequently reprimanded him and told him anecdotes about her godly father, who would 'reprove and correct vice both in his own house and amongst his neighbours'. That was not all. She often reminded him of 'what a strict and holy life he [her father] lived in his day, both in word and deed'.[8] Surprisingly enough, it appears that John accepted his wife's reproofs meekly, and he does not seem to have resented her admonitions.

In addition to this the young couple began to read together the books that Mary's father had given her. Described as 'a sermon on repentance', Arthur Dent's book *The Plaine Man's*

Path-way to Heaven was first published in 1601 and had gone through twenty-four editions by 1637. It sold over 100,000 copies before it began to lose its popularity. The book, a chunky volume measuring about six inches by three (15 by 7.5 cm.), consists of a conversation between Theologus, a divine, and Philagathus, an 'honest man'. They meet in a meadow one pleasant May afternoon and are soon joined by Asunetus, an 'ignorant' man, and Antilegon, described as 'a caviller' — a carping, critical type. A conversation lasting over 430 pages follows, as Dent uses the interchange between these characters to set out the truths of God's Word.

With sharp rebukes against sin and fearful threatenings against those who sin wilfully, Dent also holds out the promises of the grace of God to those who repent. For John Bunyan these things came as a shock. He had spent years 'cursing and swearing and playing the madman' with little reproof. Now he learnt that these things were unacceptable to God. As he hammered away on his small anvil, the words of Arthur Dent would hammer away in his conscience:

> Let not the wicked swearers and blasphemers therefore think that they shall always 'scape scot-free because God letteth them alone for a while and deferreth their punishment; for the longer God deferreth the more terrible will be his stroakes when they come. The longer an arrow is held in the bow the stronger will be the shot when it cometh forth.[9]

Not only did John and Mary read *The Plaine Man's Path-way to Heaven*,[10] but also a book that was even more popular in the seventeenth century, *The Practice of Piety* by Lewis Bayly.[11] It was first published in about 1611, and the copy that the young couple were reading together is likely to have been the thirty-fourth English edition, published in 1643. Although Bayly himself, at one time the Bishop of Bangor, was not a very savoury character, his work is full of noble exhortations, a handbook for Christian living. Much of the guidance is directed to householders with domestic servants — certainly not to those as poor as the Bunyans — giving detailed instructions about how to prepare the heart for spiritual duty.

The first effect of Mary's concern and the books they were reading was to create in John the early awakenings of a desire to improve himself. Perhaps religion was the answer. It certainly had benefited his father-in-law. If he were to attend church regularly, not just on Sundays but twice a day together with the most devout of Elstow, that might satisfy his half-awakened conscience:

> I fell in very eagerly with the religion of the times; to wit, to go to church twice a day and that too with the foremost and there should very devoutly, both say and sing as others did, yet retaining my wicked life.[12]

As we have seen, Christopher Hall had been appointed by Archbishop Laud as vicar of Elstow in 1639. In spite of naming his newborn son 'Oliver', he clearly was Laudian in his sympathies and practice, and John Bunyan in his present ignorance fell under the spell of High Church ritual:

> Because I knew no better ... I was so overrun with a spirit of superstition, that I adored, and that with great devotion, even all things, both the high place, priest, clerk, vestment, service and what else belonging to the church.

Even worse than this, before long at the very sight of a priest,

> ... though never so sordid and debauched in his life, I should find my spirit fall under him, reverence him ... yea, I could have lain down at their feet, and have been trampled upon by them; their name, their garb, and work did so intoxicate and bewitch me.[13]

A dangerous condition in which to be, this strange fascination and delusion which gripped John Bunyan in the first movements of his soul towards God may well have been the origin of the legalism that would come near to destroying him in future days. Any exhortation from the vicar had a profound effect upon him. So it was that when the minister preached one Sunday on the evil of breaking the Sabbath day with 'labour, sports or otherwise', arrows of conviction shot through John's heart.

In 1633 Charles I had reissued *The Book of Sports*, first published under his father James I in 1618. The church calendar included many 'holy days' as well as Sundays, and the aim of this legislation was to allow the people, who normally laboured six days a week, to use leisure periods for various sports after they had attended the services. These included archery, wrestling, dancing, bowls and other games. And John Bunyan loved his sports. A strong, physically active young man, he entered enthusiastically into the rough games of football on the green and other such activities. But in 1644 *The Book of Sports* was publicly burned and such sport prohibited. So when the vicar, who appears to have bent his convictions to suit whoever was in power, dealt with this very subject John first became aware of his own sinfulness:

> Now I was, not withstanding my religion, one that took much delight in all manner of vice ... wherefore I fell in my conscience under his sermon, thinking and believing that he made that sermon on purpose to show me my evil doing, and at that time I felt what guilt was, though never before that I can remember; but then I was for the present greatly loaden therewith, and so went home when the sermon was ended, with a great burden upon my spirit.[14]

But it did not last. While Mary was cooking him a good dinner, John began to forget his worries:

> O how glad was I that this trouble was gone from me, and that the fire was put out, and that I might sin again without control! Wherefore when I had satisfied nature with my food, I shook the sermon out of my mind.[15]

It seemed that nothing had changed for the young brazier. But he would find that he could not shake off the secret workings of God's Holy Spirit as easily as he could the sermon he had just heard.

7

A 'kind of despair'

In a cheerful mood, John set off for the village green to enjoy a game of tipcat with his friends. Tipcat was a game which involved the player in first striking a small piece of wood, or 'cat', from a hole in the ground; as it rose into the air, he must strike it again. His success over his opponents was measured by the distance the 'cat' travelled. But John's game was interrupted that day. Nor was it merely the voice of conscience that arrested him: it was a supernatural intervention. Often referred to as the 'Vision on the Green', this event marks a heightened and new phase in God's dealings with this young man, and formed a significant turning point in John Bunyan's life. It is best told in his own graphic words:

> But the same day, as I was in the midst of a game at cat, and having struck it one blow from the hole, just as I was about to strike it the second time, a voice did suddenly dart from heaven into my soul, which said, Wilt thou leave thy sins and go to heaven, or have thy sins and go to hell? At this I was put to an exceeding maze; wherefore, leaving my cat upon the

Elstow Green as Bunyan would have known it

ground, I looked up to heaven, and was, as if I had, with the
eyes of my understanding, seen the Lord Jesus looking down
upon me, as being very hotly displeased with me, and as if he
did severely threaten me with some grievous punishment for
these and other my ungodly practices.[1]

Some have wondered whether Bunyan actually saw the face of
the Lord Jesus looking down upon him — and whether this was
indeed a vision. But Bunyan himself answers this in the words of
his description, for he tells us that it was 'as if I had, with the eyes
of my understanding, seen the Lord Jesus'.[2] This was not a vision
in the usual sense of the word, but a powerful and unexpected
impression upon his mind — a prototype of many of God's ways
with him. Again and again as we follow the tortuous path leading
to Bunyan's eventual conversion, this pattern of sudden and
surprising divine interventions is repeated, often occurring in the
midst of the normal activities of everyday life. Bunyan's reaction
on this occasion is typical of his response at other times:

I had no sooner thus conceived in my mind, but suddenly this conclusion was fastened on my spirit ... that I had been a great and grievous sinner, and that it was now too late for me to look after heaven; for Christ would not forgive me, nor pardon my transgressions.[3]

His understanding was correct — judged by the holiness of God, he had indeed been 'a great and grievous sinner'; but his interpretation was wrong — quite wrong. This was a pattern to be repeated many times over in Bunyan's experience during the coming months. To presume that Christ could not or would not forgive his sins was a mistake that he constantly made and one that would haunt and hinder him in his spiritual quest. His conclusion, understandably, was one of total despair:

If the case be thus, my state is surely miserable; miserable if I leave my sins, and but miserable if I follow them; I can but be damned, and if I must be so, I had as good be damned for many sins as to be damned for few.[4]

None of those playing tipcat with John Bunyan that Sunday afternoon on Elstow Green realized what was taking place before their very eyes:

Thus I stood in the midst of my play, before all that then were present; but yet I told them nothing: but I say, I having made this conclusion, I returned desperately to my sport again; and I well remember, that presently this kind of despair did so possess my soul, that I was persuaded I could never attain to other comfort than what I should get in sin; for heaven was gone already, so that on that I must not think.[5]

As John Bunyan resumed his game we can almost sense the bitterness of his despair. All the frustration of his present mood is packed into those words: 'I returned desperately to my sport again.' What more could he have done to attain the favour of God? Had he not reformed his life, attending services twice a day and venerating every object that was in any way connected with religion? How could God require yet more devotion? And, if 'heaven was already gone', then he had better blot out all thoughts of his irretrievable loss by taking his fill of sinning.

Whether John told Mary of the events on the green that afternoon we do not know. But even if he did not, she could not have failed to notice the fearful change for the worse in his behaviour. In that critical moment he had decided to try out every sin, 'that I might taste the sweetness of it', in case death should overtake him before he had found opportunity to sin to the full.

If Bunyan's language had been appalling before, now every sentence was laced with oaths and blasphemies. Describing his condition, he later admitted ruefully:

> I was one of these great sin-breeders; I infected all the youth of the town where I was born with all manner of youthful vanities. The neighbours counted me so; my practice proved me so.[6]

And again he confesses that although God showed him clearly 'both the greatness of them [i.e. his sins] and also how abomin-able they were in his sight,' he deliberately trampled underfoot such convictions: 'I was so wedded to my sins, that, thought I with myself, I will have them though I lose my soul.'[7]

But though he went on in this manner 'with great greediness of mind', he soon discovered that 'I could not be so satisfied with it as I would.'[8] Looking back, John Bunyan later commented that such a reaction in a person whose conscience has been awakened is far more common than is sometimes supposed. Abject despair is often a stratagem of Satan to destroy a soul in its first steps towards God.

But God did not permit John to experiment with sin in so frightening a manner for much longer. And the means he chose to check him in his crazy course was totally unexpected:

> As I was standing at a neighbour's shop window and there cursing and swearing, and playing the madman, after my wonted manner, there sat within the woman of the house, and heard me, who, though she was a very loose and ungodly wretch, yet pro-tested that I swore and cursed at that most fearful rate, that she

was made to tremble to hear me; and told me further, That I was the ungodliest fellow for swearing that ever she heard in all her life; and that I, by thus doing, was able to spoil all the youth in a whole town, if they came but in my company.[9]

Such a rebuke from such a person had a strange effect on Bunyan. For one who was 'a brisk talker', as John declared himself to be, we might have supposed that a torrent of self-justifications, or even a further flow of curses and swearing, might follow. Instead he reacted almost like a child before an irate headmaster:

At this reproof I was silenced and put to secret shame, and that too, as I thought, before the God of heaven; wherefore, while I stood there, and hanging down my head, I wished with all my heart that I might be a little child again, that my father might learn me to speak without this wicked way of swearing; for, thought I, I am so accustomed to it that it is in vain for me to think of a reformation, for I thought it could never be.[10]

If only Thomas Bunyan had corrected his son in early childhood, he might never have fallen into the habit of using those constant blasphemies which proved so hard to eradicate. However, against all John's own expectations, this incident, and the shame of the allegations made against him by one whose own reputation was far from savoury, brought about an amazing transformation:

How it came to pass, I know not; I did from this time forward so leave my swearing, that it was a great wonder to myself to observe it; and whereas before I knew not how to speak unless I put an oath before and another behind, to make my words have authority, now I could, without it, speak better and with more pleasantness than ever I could before.[11]

For the second time John Bunyan now attempted some measure of self-reformation, and even more so after meeting up with a local character who 'made profession of religion'. John began to read the Bible, probably for the first time. Not that he was particularly interested in the parts of Scripture which might have shown him 'the corruptions of my nature or of the want and worth of Jesus Christ to save me'. Instead it was the historical books of the Old Testament, with their stories of the exploits of faith on the part of some and the misdeeds of others, that intrigued him in much the same way as *Bevis of Southampton* had fascinated him as a child.

After factor may also have contributed to Bunyan's desire for self-improvement at this time. Mary's first baby was almost due, and John, with all the sensitivity of his nature, had honest desires to be a worthy father. Soon afterwards the baby was safely born and on 20 July 1650 the young couple carried their infant daughter along the High Street to the parish church where John himself had been baptized almost twenty-two years earlier. Here the vicar, Christopher Hall, baptized the baby and she was given the name Mary.

After some weeks, like parents the world over, John and his wife began to look for those first smiles of recognition from little Mary. But her eyes did not seem to be focusing. Then the distressing truth gradually dawned on them: their baby was blind. Was it a punishment for his sins that this helpless infant should be condemned to life in a dark world? Undoubtedly John, with all his recent past so fresh in his mind, would have made that connection. Baby Mary's helplessness and need drew out a new seriousness and measure of tenderness in her father. Throughout her life this child would hold a special place in his affections.

John Bunyan now continued his effort to improve, and this second reformation was more marked than the first. Earlier he had admitted, 'I was, notwithstanding my religion, one that took much delight in all manner of vice.' Setting the Ten Commandments of God before him, he now tried to keep them. But this worthy endeavour was accompanied by a further fatal flaw in his understanding: he regarded a mere keeping of the letter of the law as 'my way to heaven' — his passport to eternal life. And in his own estimation he managed to achieve his goal fairly satisfactorily. 'I ... did keep them pretty well sometimes, and then I should have comfort.' If he ever fell short and failed to obey one of the commandments as far as his own standards demanded, he would repent of his sin and promise God that he would do better next time. Having obtained forgiveness, as he assumed, he thought that he had 'pleased God as well as any man in England'.[12]

And his neighbours thought so too. They took him to be 'a very godly man, a new and religious man'. Most were a little baffled at the remarkable change in John from a swearing, blaspheming good-for-nothing to an apparently upright and pious citizen. They 'did marvel much to see such a great and famous alteration in my life and manners'. John Bunyan managed to keep up this conduct for a year or more: and soon became a local wonder:

> My neighbours were amazed at this my great conversion from prodigious profaneness to something like a moral life; and truly, so they well might; for this my conversion was as great as for Tom of Bedlam [a nickname for any local delinquent or drunkard] to become a sober man.[13]

Then the inevitable happened. People began to congratulate the young man for his religious life — a thing which pleased John Bunyan 'mighty well', especially as it coincided with his own opinion of himself. Later, looking back, he could see that he was nothing more than a 'poor painted hypocrite' but at the time he was well satisfied. To maintain these standards, however, was no easy task. Without the inward incentive of love to God and the help of the Holy Spirit, such ideals are irksome and displeasing to human nature. The driving motivation behind all Bunyan's endeavours now became his own reputation. 'I was proud of my godliness,' he confesses, 'and indeed, I did all I did either to be seen of, or to be well spoken of, by man.'[14]

Mary's reaction to the transformation in her young husband is unknown. But if she compared him with her father, who appears to have been a genuinely godly man, she may well have seen through John's facade of religion. The path of the legalist and religious hypocrite is hard. Having produced an elaborate code of conduct, Bunyan was obliged to try to live up to the standards he had set for himself.

In conjunction with this adherence to the letter of the law, another force was at work: Bunyan's awakening sense of right and wrong. On Elstow Green he had managed to silence his conscience by assuming that all hope of salvation had gone. Now he made a further mistake by allowing his semi-enlightened conscience to become his dictator. Coupled with the demands of the law, it became a harsh master, distorting his rational judgement. The example he gives to illustrate the effect of these twin tyrants — the bell-ringing episode — borders on the ludicrous and may well have been deliberately included in *Grace Abounding* as a warning to others of the end result of such erroneous thinking.

Certainly his account makes strange reading. John Bunyan had unusual musical gifts; one of his early endeavours after he left the army was to make himself a small metal violin — an unusual achievement — and on it he engraved his name and the name of his village as 'Helstow'.[15] We can well imagine him sitting on a small stool in the evenings playing to Mary. A further expression of his musical gift was his part in ringing the church bells.

The belfry in Elstow stands separate from the main church and here Bunyan had a regular place pulling strenuously on one of the great ropes. But now, as he joined in this activity, a new thought struck him. Was it right for a 'religious' man to engage in bell-

Metal violin with the inscription, 'John Bunyan, Helstow', with a
wooden flute said to have been made by Bunyan when he was in prison
Reproduced by kind permission of Bunyan Meeting Free Church, Bedford, England

Church and belfry, Elstow

ringing on the Sabbath? It may well be that the ringing of the bells was associated not only with the call to worship but with the sports and dancing on Elstow Green that so often followed the services.

> Now, you must know, that before this I had taken much delight in ringing, but my conscience beginning to be tender, I thought such practice was but vain, and therefore forced myself to leave it, yet my mind hankered [after it].[16]

So instead he went into the steeple house and watched as the other ringers were at work pulling on the ropes. Then the thought flashed across his mind that 'this did not become religion neither'. The more John tried to suppress his conscience, the stronger was its repressive hold. Perhaps retribution would follow and if he stood too near the bells a rope might break and one might fall on his head. If he sheltered under the main beam of the belfry he might be safe, or so he reasoned.

Then Bunyan's extraordinary imaginative powers took over — that same imagination that had led to his fearsome childhood dreams — and a fresh fear occurred to him: 'Should the bell fall with a swing, it might first hit the wall, and then rebounding upon me, might kill me for all this beam.' That possibility sent him hurrying to the door, where he decided he could watch in safety. Then a further wild imagination filled him with horror:

> How if the steeple itself should fall? And this thought, it may fall for aught I know, when I stood and looked on, did so continually shake my mind, that I durst not stand at the steeple door any longer, but was forced to flee, for fear the steeple should fall upon my head.[17]

Many biographers and commentators on this period of John Bunyan's life have suggested that this episode reveals that he was suffering from an obsessive and unstable mental condition. If it is viewed merely as a psychological phenomenon, it is possible to understand such a conclusion, but this is surely faulty reasoning. This incident demonstrates little more than John's versatile and exceptional imagination inflamed by an accusing conscience. In addition, when he wrote *Grace Abounding to the Chief of Sinners*, Bunyan had a deep pastoral concern as his primary motivation. As he wrote to the young converts to whom he addressed this book,

> If you have sinned against light, if you are tempted to blaspheme; if you are down in despair; if you think God fights against you; or if heaven is hid from your eyes, remember it was thus with your father, but out of them all the Lord delivered me...[18]

Michael Davies, in his recent work on John Bunyan, refers to 'the remorseless logic of the legalist'.[19] He points out the tortuous conflicts which a faulty understanding of the purpose of the law of God can produce on the mind, together with the tricks a sensitive conscience can play by forbidding things that are quite legitimate. It is impossible to gain a right understanding of Bunyan's plight at this time without the key of spiritual and biblical interpretation, and *Grace Abounding* is continually asking the reader whether he is prepared to view such incidents from this perspective. These were the opening rounds in that great struggle between Bunyan's present understanding of law and the grace which God provides in Christ — a conflict which would engulf John Bunyan in the years that followed.

The next thing to go was his dancing — probably morris dancing on Elstow Green. And this John found even harder to give up than the bell-ringing. But at last conscience won the day and he gave up this physical recreation:

> I was a full year before I could quite leave that, but all this while, when I thought I kept this or that commandment, or did by word or deed anything that I thought was good, I had great peace in my conscience.

Now God must indeed be pleased with him: 'Yea, to relate it in my own way, I thought that no man in England could please God better than I.'

But God was about to intervene yet again in this young man's life and to produce from such an unpromising state of mind a revolution that could only be accomplished by a powerful work of the Holy Spirit. And at the same time God was preparing someone who would be equipped in an astonishing way to help John Bunyan — a man called John Gifford.

8

What the tinker overheard

John Gifford was a man with a story even more colourful than John Bunyan's own. Imprisoned in Maidstone, Kent, he was due to be executed within a few hours for his role in the Second Civil War. As a major in the Royalist army, he had taken part in a failed uprising in April 1648 in favour of Charles I, and now must pay the ultimate penalty. Contrary to habit, Gifford decided to remain sober that night, unlike the other eleven men also condemned to be hung in the morning.

When Gifford's sister arrived at the prison gates to say her last farewells to her brother, she discovered an astonishing thing. All the guards were slumped down at their posts, heavily asleep. Without anyone to question her right of entry, she slipped into the precincts of the town jail where another surprise awaited her: she discovered that all the other captured army officers apart from her brother were inebriated. Given such circumstances, escape became a viable option and, with his sister's help, John Gifford crept past the sleeping guards and out of the town. After three days of hiding at the bottom of a damp ditch until the hunt for the lost prisoner was called off, Gifford eventually made his way to Bedford.

A violent and godless man, the ex-prisoner was not subdued by his experiences. Taking up a position as a physician in Bedford, he soon squandered all his money at the gambling tables and on his excessive drinking habits. More than this, there was one man in Bedford whom he hated and wished to murder — an admirable and upright man by the name of Anthony Harrington. Why this should be so is unknown, unless it was because Gifford found Harrington's Puritan convictions and godly way of life an unbearable irritant. Night after night he planned his means of attack. Gifford soon learnt that his quarry was in the habit of meeting regularly with a few other like-minded Christian men and women who studied the Scriptures together and shared God's dealing with their souls.

But before John Gifford could carry out his dastardly deed, God intervened. One night a particularly heavy loss at the gambling table caused him to curse God — a thing that even he had never dared to do before. Shocked at his own profanity, he hurried home and there picked up a religious book.[1] The Puritan writer Robert Bolton was not one to deal lightly with sinners and his words crashed like thunderbolts upon John Gifford's soul. His spiritual burden became intolerable, now outweighing all else. But where could he turn for help? Could God ever forgive so wicked a sinner? Then he remembered the small gathering of Christians who met together with Anthony Harrington. Perhaps they knew the answers.

Gifford's reputation had gone before him and, not surprisingly, the group did not welcome his presence and feared his motives. But Gifford would not be put off. His urgency to find the forgiveness of God was too intense for that. Each time they met, this unwanted visitor was present. And at last they realized that here was one who genuinely needed help, and before long John Gifford was a changed man by God's grace. Now all his energies were channelled into understanding God's Word and striving to please Christ.

A natural leader, Gifford soon began to urge the group, consisting of only four men and eight women, to form a church and establish regular services of worship. For twenty years they

had been meeting together from time to time, most retaining
their membership and attendance at the parish church of St Paul's.
The names of these men and women have come down to us in
the pages of the *Minute Book of the First Independent Church at
Bedford:* John Grew, a Justice of the Peace (i.e. a local magistrate), and his wife Martha; Anthony and Anne Harrington; an
elderly man by the name of John Easton, and John Gifford
himself. In addition there were a few single women, some
widowed and others unmarried, whose names were Joane
Coventon, Elizabeth Munnes, Hannah Fenne, Margaret Bosworth
and Mary Spencer, with one younger woman known only as
'sister Norton'.

So in 1650, the very year that John and Mary Bunyan's blind
baby daughter was born, this small group constituted themselves
into an Independent church and elected one of their number to
be their pastor, one who was proving an increasingly devoted
and zealous Christian — none other than John Gifford himself.
The church minute book records the solemnity that accompanied
the choice:

> After much prayer and waiting upon God and consulting
> one with another, they upon the day appointed for this solemn
> worke, being met, after prayer and seeking God as before,
> with one consent they joyntly first gave themselves to the
> Lord and one to another by the will of God. This done they
> with one mouth made choyce of brother Gifford to be their
> pastor or elder and to minister to them in the things of the
> kingdome of Christ... Wherefore brother Gifford accepted of
> the charge and gave himself up to the Lord and to his people
> to walke with them, watch over them, and dispense the mister-
> yes of the Gospell among them.[2]

John Bunyan knew little of these things, although perhaps the
story of the astonishing change in the Bedford physician, a man
called Gifford, had filtered through to Elstow, for Bedford had
only a population of less than 2,000 at the time. Nor would he
have been particularly interested in the activities of a small group
of religious people who were no longer attached to any of the
five parish churches of Bedford. Satisfied with his own zeal and

performances, he felt he had little to learn, until a day came when all was to change for John Bunyan.[3]

Much of John's time was spent away from home, sometimes working in his clients' houses and often in distant villages in search of further work. Then he would roam the streets with the well-known tinker's cry:

Have you any work for a tinker?
Have you any old bellows to mend?

Little did John Bunyan think as he said goodbye to his wife and blind baby daughter that summer morning, striding out into the bright sunshine, that the day which lay ahead would be one of the most significant in his entire life. What happened next is best told in his own words:

Upon a day, the good providence of God did cast me to Bedford, to work on my calling; and in one of the streets of that town, I came where there were three or four poor women sitting at a door in the sun, and talking about the things of God; and being now willing to hear them discourse, I drew near to hear what they said, for I was now a brisk talker also myself in the matters of religion, but now I may say, I heard, but I understood not; for they were far above, out of my reach.[4]

We can imagine this young man passing along the street and suddenly catching a few scraps of a conversation that interested him. He stops, retraces his steps a little and with quickened interest stands nearby listening to the words of a small group of women who were sitting in the sun around the doorstep of one of their homes. Lace-making was an important industry in Bedford and probably these women had brought their work outside with them and while their fingers were deftly casting the bobbins back and forth they were deep in conversation. But this was no ordinary chatter, for their talk was of spiritual concerns.

Fancying himself quite an expert at religious talk, Bunyan thought he might even have an opportunity to contribute. But what he heard disturbed him profoundly:

Their talk was about a new birth, the work of God on their
hearts, also how they were convinced of their miserable state
by nature; they talked how God had visited their souls with his
love in the Lord Jesus, and with what words and promises
they had been refreshed, comforted, and supported against
the temptations of the devil.

The new birth? No thought of such a thing had ever crossed
his mind before — he did not even know what they meant. Yet
more strangely, they spoke of the wickedness of their own hearts.
John had long since banished all such thoughts from his mind,
believing that 'no man in England could please God better than I'.
Full of an inflated sense of his own goodness, he could scarcely
credit what he was hearing:

Moreover, they reasoned of the suggestions and temptations of Satan in particular; and told to each other by which
they had been afflicted, and how they were borne up under his
assaults. They also discoursed of their own wretchedness of
heart, of their unbelief; and did contemn, slight, and abhor
their own righteousness, as filthy and insufficient to do them
any good.

The articulate John Bunyan was now silent. Whether these
women (whose names may well have been Joane Coventon,
Elizabeth Munnes, Hannah Fenne and Margaret Bosworth),
members of John Gifford's new Independent church, were aware
of the tall auburn-haired workman, his bag of tools on his back,
standing within earshot, we do not know. Possibly they were so
absorbed in conversation that they scarcely noticed him. Certainly
they can have had no idea of the effect of their words on the
bystander.

Not only was it their words that stirred Bunyan, but the way
in which they were speaking. To John religion was a gloomy
thing. Had it not taken from him all the things he most enjoyed in
life — games on the green, dancing and bell-ringing? But these
women seemed to experience a joy to which he was a total
stranger:

Methought they spake as if joy did make them speak; they spake with such pleasantness of Scripture language, and with such appearance of grace in all they said that they were to me as if they had found a new world, as if they were people that dwelt alone, and were not to be reckoned among their neighbours (Num. 23:9).

John Bunyan was shaken to the core of his being. He felt all his religious confidence slipping away, all the duties in which he had placed his hopes turning to dust:

At this I felt my own heart began to shake, as mistrusting my condition to be nought; for I saw that in all my thoughts about religion and salvation, the new birth did never enter into my mind, neither knew I the comfort of the Word and promise, nor the deceitfulness and treachery of my own wicked heart. As for secret thoughts, I took no notice of them; neither did I understand what Satan's temptations were, nor how they were to be withstood and resisted.[5]

Mesmerized, but also deeply troubled, the young brazier could hardly tear himself away, but when he did the words of these women, and their very tones, rang constantly in his ears. In a few dramatic moments God had stripped from John Bunyan all those attainments in which he had taken pride. It was as if he had everything to learn over again. Now he realized that he knew nothing spiritually and, as he confesses, 'I was convinced that I wanted [i.e. lacked] the true tokens of a truly godly man.'[6]

What could he do? To whom could he turn for help? Drawn by an irresistible desire to understand more of the joys which these women knew, Bunyan succeeding in organizing his day so that again and again he managed to be around at the very time when the women of John Gifford's church were chatting together.

Therefore I should often make it my business to be going again and again into the company of these poor people, for I could not stay away; and the more I went amongst them, the more I did question my condition.[7]

Probably the women were suspicious of him at first. Who could tell whether he was spying on them? These were hard days for any who broke from the religious mould of the established church. Disorder and confusion following the Civil War and the execution of Charles I had led to the proliferation of various radical sects, increasing suspicion of any who did not conform to the Church of England. But day after day it was the same. Whenever they took a break from their work, snatching a few minutes to talk together, this same young man always seemed to be hovering around. Soon they learnt that he was a tinker who had come into Bedford from nearby Elstow in the course of his work and that his name was John Bunyan.

Two changes began to take place in Bunyan's thinking. First came a total reassessment of himself. From being a self-congratulating religious hypocrite he now saw himself as 'a blind, ignorant, sordid and ungodly wretch'. But coupled with this, instead of despair as before, came a humility of mind and receptivity which he describes as 'a very great softness and tenderness of heart which caused me to fall under the conviction of what by Scripture they [the women] asserted'.

Before long these members of the Bedford Meeting realized that the young man who so often seemed to loiter around was no idle, prying busybody, but a man deeply troubled about his own spiritual state. Gradually, as he grew more confident, John began to ask them questions — profound, perplexing questions — for now his whole being was taken up with one intense desire. Nothing, 'neither pleasures, nor profits, nor persuasions, nor threats', could quench his all-consuming hunger to know what these humble women knew. He had to force his thoughts to concentrate on his business and his daily life, for nothing else seemed to matter except 'eternity and ... the kingdom of heaven'.

And at so sensitive a time in a man's spiritual search, we are not surprised to learn that Satan did all in his power to subvert Bunyan from his desire to know the truth. Before long members of the sect known as Ranters crossed his path. In the general confusion before Oliver Cromwell was established as Lord Protector in December 1653 this group, with their wild antinomian and pantheistic persuasions, were growing in influence. In the course of his work in some of the outlying country districts

Bunyan came across members of this sect. 'You are legal and dark,' they told him. 'Do you not know that it is possible to attain perfection and still live as you like?' John found this hard indeed.

> Oh! these temptations were suitable to my flesh, I being but a young man and my nature in its prime; but God, who had, as I hope, designed me for better things, kept me in the fear of his name and did not suffer me to accept of such cursed principles.[8]

John now shunned the godless company in which he had once delighted. A close friend named Harry was among the first to go. He was one to whom Bunyan was 'knit more than to any other', but because Harry was addicted to swearing, John managed to avoid his former friend's company until he met him unexpectedly in a narrow lane. Unable to escape him any longer, Bunyan politely enquired after his health, but when Harry replied with his customary torrent of profanities, Bunyan knew he must rebuke him.

'Why, Harry,' he asked, 'do you swear and curse thus? What will become of you if you die in this condition?' Incensed at such a reproof, all Harry could reply was: 'What would the devil do for company, if it were not for such as I?'

John Bunyan was indeed a different man. Many who read *Grace Abounding to the Chief of Sinners* puzzle over the question: when was John Bunyan actually converted? Any number of points in time have been suggested, and any number could well be sustained with biblical backing. As Bunyan himself was to struggle over this very question in the months and years ahead, it is not wise to be dogmatic, but there are several fundamental things which distinguish a Christian from an unbeliever. One of the most important is the possession of a spiritual mind,[9] and indications of this shine out in the account of Bunyan's state at this period. Who but a Christian would turn to God in dependent, self-effacing prayer in times of deep uncertainty and need, as John now did?

> Unable to judge, I should betake myself to hearty prayer in this manner: O Lord, I am a fool, and not able to know the

truth from error: Lord, leave me not to my own blindness... I lay my soul in this matter only at thy foot; let me not be deceived I humbly beseech thee.[10]

Another evidence of a spiritual mind is found in his changed attitude to the Bible. Now he read it constantly, and he records that 'The Bible was precious to me in those days.'[11] When William Grimshaw of Haworth was converted nearly one hundred years later, he declared that if God had 'drawn up his Bible into heaven and sent me down another, it could not be newer to me'. This too was John Bunyan's experience. 'I began to look into the Bible with new eyes,' he tells us and by the enlightenment of the Holy Spirit could say:

> I read as I never did before; and especially the epistles of the apostle Paul were sweet and pleasant to me [the very passages he had previously avoided]; and indeed I was then never out of the Bible, either by reading or meditation; still crying out to God that I might know the truth, and way to heaven and glory.[12]

Summing up the mercies of God to him and the changes in his attitudes after his encounter with the women from Gifford's church, Bunyan was full of gratitude to 'the infinite merciful God' who, despite his sinning, had

> ... followed me still, and won upon my heart, by giving me some understanding, not only into my miserable state, which I was very sensible of, but also that there might be hopes of mercy; also taking away that love to lust, and placing in the room thereof a love to religion.[13]

> And thus [he continues] the Lord won over my heart to some desire after the means to hear the word and to grow a stranger to my old companions, and to accompany the people of God, together with giving of me many encouragements from several promises in the Scriptures.[14]

A long dark valley might lie ahead of this young believer, with many fierce battles against the enemy of souls, with much still to unlearn as well as to learn, but such evidences of spiritual thinking surely suggest that John Bunyan's feet were now indeed planted on the rock of God's truth, even though he scarcely knew it himself.

9

The roaring lion

To throw off a past of 'cursing and swearing and playing the madman' was no light task or work of a moment for John Bunyan. A long and arduous struggle lay ahead of him in the months to come. Every scrap of his emotional and spiritual energy was engaged in the bitter conflict.

It seems as though that inner strife, with its advances and setbacks, was the only thing that mattered to Bunyan at this time. We look in vain for information about Mary's reaction to the change in her husband. Was her own religion anything more than an inherited code of practice learnt from her father in childhood? We do not know. Many other questions remain unanswered.

Was Bunyan following the drama of political events unfolding in the country between 1651 and 1653? After all, he had fought with the Parliamentary army for almost three years. Did he know that the playboy son of the executed king was crowned as Charles II by the Scots at Scone on 1 January 1651? Or had he heard of Oliver Cromwell's stunning victories over David Leslie and the Scottish armies, first at Dunbar in September 1650, and then of his 'crowning mercy' at the Battle of Worcester in September 1651?

Did he wonder what had happened to Charles after this defeat? All these questions may well perplex us and must remain without answers, for Bunyan chooses to stay silent on such issues. We may assume, however, that he would have known something of these great national events, but for the purposes of his autobiography all else was subordinated in his thinking to that one momentous issue of his life: eternal joy or everlasting perdition.

The paramount question perplexing John Bunyan shortly after his first acquaintance with the members of John Gifford's Independent meeting was 'Whether I had any faith or no?' So untaught was he that he had to confess that he scarcely knew what the word 'faith' meant — yet he realized that it was an all-important qualification for any who would enter the kingdom of heaven. Yes, he was willing to confess that he was 'an ignorant sot, and that I wanted [i.e. lacked] those blessed gifts of knowledge and understanding that other good people have.'[1] But did this mean that he had no faith?

He had not mentioned his problem to anyone and decided that perhaps the best thing to do was to put the matter to a practical test. We can imagine the troubled tinker trudging along one of the deeply rutted lanes not far from his home on his way to Bedford, his heavy anvil and other tools packed into a bag upon his back. Picking his way carefully around the rain-filled holes, John Bunyan suddenly had an idea — an idea that he would subsequently attribute directly to the work of Satan, eager to destroy his soul almost before he had begun his heavenward path.

> There was no way for me to know I had faith, but by trying to work some miracle... I must say to the puddles that were in the horse-pads, Be dry; and to the dry places, Be you the puddles.[2]

If a miracle took place, with the puddles becoming dry and the dry places turning into puddles, then he would know for certain that he had faith; if nothing happened then he was surely a castaway and had no faith.

And truly ... I was a-going to say so indeed; but just as I was about to speak, this thought came into my mind, But go under yonder hedge and pray first, that God would make you able.

God had intervened yet again to prevent John Bunyan, not yet twenty-four years of age, from extinguishing the flickering light of true faith kindled in his soul. For when he emerged from behind the hedge he decided to wait a while before trying such an experiment.

At about this time John Bunyan had a dream. Dreams had been highly significant in his life before now — as his childhood terrors could demonstrate — and dreams would play a yet more significant part in the future. But this dream was so vivid and so detailed that he tells us that he could not be sure whether it was entirely a dream. Perhaps it was a kind of vision representing the Christian life and the way to enter the kingdom of God. In it he saw those joyful, contented women of Bedford, who now appeared as if they were basking in the sunshine on some beautiful mountainside. He, meanwhile, was shivering in the cold on the far side of a great wall that separated him from them. He longed to penetrate the wall and join the favoured few. Then he tells us:

> About this wall I thought myself to go again and again, still prying as I went, to see if I could find some way or passage by which I might enter therein, but none could I find for some time. At the last I saw, as it were, a narrow gap like a little doorway in the wall, through which I attempted to pass; but the passage being very strait and narrow, I made many efforts to get in but all in vain.

But the 'dream', a representation of spiritual conversion, had a happy outcome for Bunyan. Even though he was exhausted with trying to squeeze through the narrow gap, he managed it at last by lying on one side and forcing first his shoulders and then his whole body through the entrance:

Then was I exceeding glad and went and sat down in the midst of them and so was comforted with the light and heat of their sun.[3]

Bunyan had no difficulty in interpreting this dream. The mountain was clearly a symbol of the true church of Jesus Christ, the company of believing people, while the wall was the words of Scripture which forbade anyone to enter except through Christ, the way to God. Only those who had entered in that way could enjoy the shining of God's presence. How Bunyan had longed to share in 'the sun that shone thereon', and to know 'the comfortable shining of his merciful face on them that were therein'! To enter one must be utterly in earnest, and that John Bunyan most certainly was at this time.

But despite his dream, the tinker was still beset by fears. Not only did he fear that he might not possess true faith, but now another equally daunting anxiety distressed Bunyan — a matter which has often raised doubts in the minds of those seeking to be sure of their spiritual state: 'Am I one of the elect or not?' So much did this question perplex Bunyan that at times it seemed to sap even his physical strength. He read such texts as 'It is not of him that willeth, nor of him that runneth, but of God that showeth mercy' (Romans 9:16), and commented:

Though I was in a flame to find the way to heaven and to glory, and though nothing could beat me off from this, yet this question did so offend and discourage me.

Then an even more troubling thought occurred to him: What if 'the day of grace should now be past and gone'?[4] What if God had already chosen as many as he wanted from those parts and he was too late?

In later years Bunyan would recognize that Satan, as 'a roaring lion who seeks to devour' the souls of men and women (1 Peter 5:8), was the source of these crippling temptations and fears. However, at the time he tells us:

By these things I was driven to my wits' end, not knowing what to say or how to answer these temptations. Indeed, I little thought that Satan had thus assaulted me.

Sometimes he felt like giving up the quest for assurance of eternal life altogether and collapsing beneath a burden of despair. But at a moment when his thoughts reached a nadir of gloom, some words flashed into his mind: 'Look at the generations of old and see; did ever any trust in the Lord and was confounded?'[5]

Where did those words come from? They must be somewhere in the Bible. So Bunyan started to search the Scriptures from cover to cover. It was as though all his spiritual hopes hung on that one frail thread of being able to find this single promise, and if it was not in the Bible he was lost indeed. He began to ask around, first one man well-versed in biblical knowledge, then another, but no one seemed to know. For a whole year he hunted until eventually he discovered it, not in the canon of Scripture but in the Apocrypha.[6] Did this mean the promise was invalid? Fortunately by this time he had gained enough knowledge of the Bible to see that the same promise was repeated many times over in slightly different words throughout Scripture. But his quest did have one important result. It forced Bunyan to make a detailed study of the Bible from beginning to end for answers to his perplexities.

No sooner had this young convert grasped the truth that no one who truly believed would be put to shame than his former fear raised its head again: 'Perhaps it is too late. Perhaps God has already called all those he wishes to save from these parts.' 'O, that I had turned seven years ago!' he cried out in an anguish of regret. 'To think that I should have no more wit but to trifle away my time till my soul and heaven were lost!' But once again God in his pity brought the troubled man consolation from the pages of Scripture. As he was reading the parable of the great supper (Luke 14:16-24), one sentence in particular 'broke in upon my mind': 'Compel them to come in, that my house may be filled,' and 'yet there is room'. He could now exclaim:

These words ... were sweet words to me for truly I thought that by them I saw that there was place enough in heaven for me.[7]

Gradually John Bunyan was gaining ground, inch by painful inch, towards that assurance of his part in the kingdom of Christ which he so desired. Comforted by Scripture, he would enjoy a period of calm in his mind, but Satan was not willing to lose this man without a struggle and we hardly read another few paragraphs in his account of these days before we meet with a further onslaught on his soul. As he read the New Testament he came across many references to 'calling'. His first disciples heard Christ's *call* to 'Follow me', and only those whom God *called* would inherit the kingdom of heaven.

If only he could hear a call from God, perhaps even with an audible voice! 'I cannot now express with what longings and breakings in my soul I cried to Christ to call me.' All Christians seemed lovely and privileged beyond words in his eyes, for they had received such a call.

> Gold! Could it have been gotten for gold, what could I have given for it! Had I had a whole world it had all gone ten thousand times over for this, that my soul might have been in a converted state![8]

All this time John Bunyan had borne the burden of his anxieties and spiritual fears alone. But at last, and we may probably date this event early in 1653, perhaps eighteen months after he had first met the women of John Gifford's church, he plucked up courage to tell them of his desperate plight and his longings for a certainty of his acceptance with God. They in turn told their pastor about the young tinker from Elstow and all his doubts and desires.

Kindly John Gifford invited Bunyan to his own home and spent much time trying to help him. We may well picture the scene, for the upstairs room where the two men met and even the fireplace around which they sat deep in earnest conversation can still be seen at St John's Rectory in Bedford. Gifford was in every way the right man to help John Bunyan. He had sunk to far greater depths than the twenty-four-year-old tinker and had himself experienced the astonishing forgiveness of God for his past. Nothing that the younger John could tell the older John could shock or dismay him.

St John's Church and rectory from St John's Street

It may indeed seem strange that Bunyan should be meeting John Gifford in St John's Rectory, but in fact the parish church of St John's had become the home of Gifford's small congregation. The previous rector, Theodore Crowley, had been evicted in 1653 and under Oliver Cromwell's religious settlement any viable congregation, whether Independent or from the established church, could be considered for appointment to a parish church. Congregations that applied for the use of a church were checked out by Cromwell's appointed 'triers' to judge of their orthodoxy before an appointment could go ahead. Some of Gifford's members, notably John Grew and John Easton, were members of the Bedford Council and understandably influenced the application of their own congregation for use of the vacant church and rectory of St John's.

Sometimes the two men sat opposite one another in that room, its heavy oak beams and cheerful fire leaving a permanent impression on Bunyan's mind. At other times they might pace the rectory garden together as Gifford tried patiently and wisely to disentangle John's troubled thinking and point him to the clear teachings of Scripture. On occasions Gifford invited Bunyan to listen quietly as he counselled those who came to him with spiritual problems, so that he might see that he was not alone in his perplexities. With a measure of surprise Bunyan records that Gifford 'was willing to be well persuaded of me'. Even after so short a time as a believer himself, Gifford could quickly recognize evidences of grace in the soul,

Fireplace in the room where Bunyan and Gifford used to meet
Reproduced by courtesy of Steve Nicholson, St John's Ambulance Service, Bedford

and in the case of John Bunyan he had little difficulty, even though John himself was so full of hesitancy and self-doubt.

We might have hoped that Bunyan's soul troubles were now over. But in fact the opposite was true. Many a storm would yet break over him, including an additional factor that burdened him: a frightening realization of the depths of sin latent in his own heart. As he heard others speak of their struggles against sin and their failures, he

> ... began to see something of the vanity and inward wretch-edness of my wicked heart... Nay, thought I, now I grow worse and worse; now am I farther from conversion than ever I was before. Wherefore I began to sink greatly in my soul, and began to entertain such discouragement in my heart as laid me low as hell.[9]

Many have found it incredible that this pilgrim to heaven should have had to travel so arduous a path. Perhaps, some have suggested, it was due to his complex personality, or even to a depressive nature. But it is not hard to recognize the same pattern in the dealings of God with many other men and women, and particularly those whom he has eminently used. Doubts and convictions of sin are part of the experience of all true Christians, though usually to a lesser degree.

Hugh Bourne (1772–1852), one of the founders of the Primitive Methodist Connexion, spoke of wandering in a wilderness of doubt for twenty years, fearing that 'the wrath [of God] that he saw continually hanging over his head, and which he daily expected would burst with indignation and fury upon him, [would] sink him into hell'.[10] John Cennick, a notable preacher of the eighteenth-century evangelical revival, suffered years of anguished convictions of sin before he could write, 'The fears of hell were taken away... Christ loved me and died for me.'[11] In many biographies of notable Christian men and women, we can find accounts of similar experiences.

'I was driven as with a tempest,' was Bunyan's description of these days. Sometimes he felt 'more loathsome in my own eyes than was a toad' because of his sins, and he assumed that God's view of him must be the same. Although he felt able to speak to other members of Gifford's church about his condition, no one seemed able to help him. 'They pitied me and would tell me of the promises but they had as good have told me to reach the sun with my finger,' he reports graphically. If he could not forgive himself for his past, how could he lay hold on the promises they quoted and hope that God would forgive him?

The old struggle with a conscience burdened by a misapprehension of the law of God still oppressed Bunyan at this time. So concerned was he to obey every least command that he became enslaved by legal fears: 'I durst not take a pin or a stick though not so big as a straw,' lest it was stealing. 'I saw,' he tells us, that 'I had a heart that would sin and that lay under a law that would condemn.'[12] A man who had once been 'a brisk talker' now feared even to open his mouth in case he sinned in his speech:

> My conscience now was sore and would smart at every touch... Oh how gingerly did I then go in all I did or said! I found myself in a miry bog that shook if I did but stir.[13]

However, John Gifford's pastoral help is clearly evident at this time and begins to shine through in John Bunyan's account of his life. Despite his fears, even he realized that he was now a true believer. 'Though I was a great sinner before conversion yet God never much charged the guilt of the sins of my ignorance upon me,' he admits. Gradually he was learning to look away from his own attempts to please God, for he discovered that he could never achieve 'a perfect righteousness to present me without fault before God'. The only righteousness that would avail was 'to be found in the person of Jesus Christ'.[14]

We may imagine John Bunyan joining the small congregation as he sat rather uncomfortably in the hard, tall-backed pews of St John's and listened with rapt attention to the sermons of his pastor, Gifford. One sermon in particular stirred and comforted him. The text came from the Song of Solomon, chapter 4 verse 1: 'Behold thou art fair, my love, behold thou art fair.' The theme of the message was the love of Christ for his church: a love based not on any merit in the believer, but on the constancy of the character of God; a love that remained unchanged despite the desertions, temptations and sins of the believer. Such a message

was tailor-made for Bunyan's condition and was indelibly engraved on his mind.

Above all, it was just two words that affected him most deeply
— the words, 'my love'. All the way home as he trudged back to
Elstow they rang in his mind. Could Christ really love him in spite
of all his sinning? 'Thou art my love, Thou art my love,' he
repeated to himself over and over again, and now he added
another promise from Scripture: '... and nothing shall separate
thee from my love.' Such overwhelming joy flooded his spirit as
he walked that he records:

> I could not tell how to contain until I got home; I thought I
> could have spoken of his love and of his mercy to me, even to
> the very crows that sat upon the ploughed lands before me,
> had they been capable to have understood me; wherefore I
> said in my soul with much gladness, Well, I would I had a pen
> and ink here, I would write this down before I go any farther,
> for surely I will not forget this forty years hence.[15]

How great must have been Mary's surprise when she saw
John's beaming face as he stooped to enter the doorway of their
small cottage on Elstow High Street! She was now expecting her
second child and was no doubt relieved to think that at last her
husband had found that peace he had been seeking for so long.
But Mary could not know how many more days of fierce torment
of conscience and weary self-accusation still lay ahead for John.

IO

'Satan has desired to have you'

The England of 1653 was far from peaceful. The Civil War might be over at last, but the aftermath of such a conflict, with its legacy of bereavements, anger and change, both social and political, was being felt throughout the land. Neighbours harboured deep suspicions of each other; vast tracts of countryside were scarred by battle; and poverty was widespread, with much of the cream of England's manhood dead.

The House of Lords had been abolished in February 1649, shortly after the execution of the king, when the country was declared a commonwealth. Theoretically the land was still being governed by the Rump Parliament — the remnants of the Long Parliament first elected in November 1640. In reality, however, Oliver Cromwell and the higher-ranking army officers wielded the true power. For three years Cromwell was prepared to wait while the 200 Members of the Rump Parliament struggled somewhat ineffectually to bring order out of the chaos and discontent.

Cromwell had only intended that the Rump should serve as a stopgap measure, but by April 1653 it looked dangerously like passing an act to perpetuate itself. Then Oliver's patience snapped.

Oliver Cromwell

Without even waiting to change his clothes, he rushed to the House of Commons and, after listening quietly to proceedings for a few minutes, suddenly erupted into a passion of indignant oratory. Calling for his crack troop of musketeers waiting outside, he forcibly ejected the Rump members from the House. 'You have sat too long for the good you do,' he roared, and, in a final memorable act of intolerance, grabbed the mace from the table crying, 'Who will rid me of this bauble?'

With nothing but a vacuum remaining, instead of any law-making body, a new Parliament was hastily assembled, consisting of 144 members and known in derision as the 'Barebones' Parliament.[1] This was an honest attempt, particularly by certain captains in the army, to bring in a God-fearing legislature. Influenced by the Fifth Monarchist movement, they believed that the 'rule of the saints' and Christ's millennial reign was about to be inaugurated. But this Parliament too was largely ineffectual and did not last beyond December 1653. The only alternative remaining was to declare an end to the Commonwealth,[2] and on 16 December England was proclaimed a 'protectorate', with Oliver Cromwell as Lord Protector.

If the government of England was in turmoil with internal conflicts, so too was the life of John Bunyan during 1653–1655. Summing up this entire period, he would later write:

> The Lord won over my heart to some desire ... to hear the word ... and to accompany the people of God, together with giving of me many sweet encouragements from several promises in the Scriptures. But after this the Lord did wonderfully set my sins upon my conscience, those sins especially that I had committed since the first convictions; temptations also followed me very hard...[3]

Traditional site of Bunyan's baptism, showing commemorative plaque

For the moment, however, Bunyan's 'heart was filled with comfort' as he mused on the sermon he had heard, and particularly the words, 'Thou art my love.' It is likely that this was the period when he took the step of asking John Gifford and the members of the church to consider him as an applicant for baptism by immersion — a courageous step in the mid-seventeenth century. Anyone who ventured to hold tenets of belief differing from those of the established church was regarded with suspicion. Bunyan himself does not mention the fact of his baptism, but a persistent tradition points to a small inlet in the River Ouse not far from the town bridge as the spot where he was baptized, probably at dead of night to avoid the ever-watchful eyes of those who might cause trouble. The site is marked with a plaque. Confirmation that his baptism indeed took place comes from a brief account of Bunyan's life written by his friend Charles Doe.[4]

Shortly after his baptism John joined the membership of the Bedford Meeting; his name is found in the earliest list of members as number twenty-six. But, as so often happened in Bunyan's early experiences, this season of assurance and joy soon gave way to a further period of trial and testing. But this time he received a divine warning of the temptations that lay ahead. Christ's words to Simon Peter shortly before Peter's threefold denial of his Master kept ringing in Bunyan's ears so clearly that sometimes he would turn involuntarily to see who was calling to him: 'Simon, Simon, behold Satan hath desired to have you' (Luke 22:31). Afterwards Bunyan could see that this was sent to fortify him against the coming onslaught of temptation, but he was so young in the faith that he could do little other than wonder about the strange phenomenon.

And about a month later all the battering rams of hell seemed to have been set to work to destroy John Bunyan's soul. The first temptation has a very modern ring: 'How can I know that the Bible is true? Perhaps the Scriptures are all just myth and fable.'

[Perhaps] the Turks had as good scriptures to prove their Mohomet the Saviour, as we have to prove our Jesus is... Everyone doth think his own religion the rightest, both Jews and Moors and Pagans! and how if all our faith, and Christ, and Scriptures should be but a think-so too?[5]

Then a yet more frightening thought gripped John Bunyan's mind: 'Perhaps there is no God after all, and no Christ. Perhaps the whole concept of salvation through Christ as a sacrifice for sin is one great deception.'

As such thoughts bombarded his mind, a domestic situation arose that gave Bunyan a practical proof of the truths he had embraced. It was the spring of 1654 and their second child was due soon — apprehensive days for the couple, particularly as their first child had been born blind. Then one night Mary appeared to go into premature labour. Panic-stricken, John did not know what to do. With his wife lying beside him in bed crying out in pain, John began to pray urgently. If God would intervene and cause her pains to ease, giving her quiet sleep, then he would know that he was God indeed — one who could read the secret thoughts of people's hearts. Quite suddenly he became aware that Mary had stopped crying; in fact she had fallen asleep. And shortly afterwards John too fell asleep. Only in the morning did he think of that experience and for a time was delivered from sceptical thoughts.

But, try as he might to repudiate such unwelcome reflections, another temptation followed hotfoot upon this one:

> While I was in this temptation I should often find my mind suddenly put upon it to curse and swear, or to speak some grievous thing against God, or Christ his Son, and of the Scriptures.

The temptation to blaspheme was to Bunyan one of the most disturbing, and particularly when he noticed that it was strongest when he was trying to worship, pray, or join in the Lord's Supper:

> I could attend upon none of the ordinances of God but with sore and great affliction... Yea ... uncleanness, blasphemies and despair would hold me as captive there.[6]

'Maybe I am a devil myself,' he thought morbidly, 'or at least devil-possessed. How else could I have such "horrible blasphemous thoughts" when everyone around me is praising God?'

It is not surprising that Satan should attack Bunyan at so vulnerable a point, for as a youth he had indulged in fearful blasphemies, allowing them a place in his mind. Perhaps Simon Peter too had been prone to such language before he met Christ, for when he denied the Lord, 'he began to curse and swear, saying I do not know the man' (Matthew 26:74). Nor is this tactic of Satan a rare occurrence. Many other believers can also testify to such distressing temptations. Even Charles Spurgeon, who could say:

> ... I do not remember to have even heard a blasphemy in my youth, much less to have uttered one, found rushing through my mind an almost infinite number of curses and blasphemies against the Most High God. My head became a very pandemonium; ten thousand evil spirits seemed to be holding carnival within my brain... It was the devil throwing me down and tearing me.[7]

This temptation, in its most acute phase, lasted the best part of a year for Bunyan, and yet there were moments of consolation as

well, brief rays of light in the darkness. Gradually he was beginning to lay hold of that 'way of escape' provided by God for his
tempted people:

> I remember that one day, as I was travelling into the country
> and musing on the wickedness and blasphemy of my heart ...
> that Scripture came into my mind: He hath 'made peace
> through the blood of his cross' (Col. 1:20). By which I was
> made to see, both again, and again and again that day that
> God and my soul were friends by this blood; yea I saw that the
> justice of God and my sinful soul could embrace and kiss each
> other through this blood. This was a good day to me; I hope I
> shall not forget it.[8]

Soon afterwards, as he was sitting by his fireside reading verses
from Hebrews chapter 2, the words brought such consolation and
deliverance to this beleaguered Christian that he almost fainted,
'not with grief and trouble, but with solid joy and peace'.[9] Here
he learnt of one who could 'destroy him that had the power of
death, that is, the devil; and deliver them who through fear of
death were all their lifetime subject to bondage' — even Christ
himself.

That John Bunyan should be reading and recollecting such
Scriptures is in itself an evidence that he was profiting from John
Gifford's ministry.

> At this time also I sat under the ministry of holy Mr Gif-
> ford [he recalled], whose doctrine, by God's grace, was much
> for my stability. This man made it much his business to deliver
> the people of God from all those faults and unsound rests
> that, by nature, we are prone to take.[10]

Certainly Gifford's help was invaluable to Bunyan, for yet greater
storms were soon to break on his head.

In following Bunyan's own account of his progress from self-
righteous unbelief to his conversion and initial temptations, we
have covered the first 118 paragraphs of *Grace Abounding to the
Chief of Sinners*. However, as we have noted, Bunyan does not
always attempt to set down his experiences in strict chronological

order. It seems that after paragraph 118 he may have contemplated bringing his account to a close, and so paragraphs 119-128 were intended to provide only a brief outline and summary of events that took place in the years 1654–1656.[11] It may well be that he felt reluctant to expand on the trials which almost overwhelmed him during those two years in case such an account should prove unhelpful to his readers. The fact that he changed his mind and would continue the detailed record of his early spiritual battles is one for which both his first readers and those who follow may thank God. Omitting, therefore, much of the material in paragraphs 119-130 until their rightful place in his story, we must take up his account from paragraphs 131-231,[12] where Bunyan fills in the period in more detail.

Although we are given so much detail about Bunyan's spiritual search, there is tantalizingly little information about his family life. As we have seen, John and Mary's second child was almost due. Their blind girl, Mary, was nearly four years old when her sister Elizabeth was safely born in April 1654, despite the scare a few weeks earlier. To the great relief and joy of her parents, this second child did not share the physical defects of her older sister. However, even though John had joined the Independent Meeting in Bedford, they took their baby to Elstow Abbey Church to have the birth legally registered. Whether or not Mary was in sympathy with John's new and ever-growing spiritual convictions we do not know. At no time did she join the Bedford Meeting, even though it had become the centralizing point in her husband's life. But for John himself, delivered for a short period from the tempter's fierce attacks, the safe birth of a second daughter was one further joy in his cup.

II

'Sell him, sell him!'

God did not play in convincing of me, the devil did not play in tempting of me; neither did I play when I sunk as into a bottomless pit, when the pangs of hell caught hold upon me; wherefore I may not play in my relating of them, but be plain and simple, and lay down the thing as it was.[1]

With these words John Bunyan recollected the alarming experiences through which he had passed in his long search for an assurance of his acceptance with God. The later events recorded in *Grace Abounding to the Chief of Sinners* were written ten or more years after they had happened and in his account Bunyan had one great purpose in mind: to bring spiritual consolations, warnings and explanations to young believers who were struggling to fathom God's ways with them. He spares his readers no details as he recounts the hard path he had trod, so that they might not be bewildered and distressed if they should meet similar circumstances.

Because Bunyan does not mince his words, but reveals his secret thoughts and temptations in order to help others, he has been subjected to serious misrepresentation and injustices. There were some even in his own day who were ready to heap abuse upon him for it. To write him off as mentally unstable, or even insane, was a very convenient way of avoiding the implication of his message. Following the chaos engendered by the Civil War and the rise of a multitude of sects and cranks, Michael Davies, appreciating the problem, comments, 'Bunyan could be categorized safely by any political objector as eccentric, disturbed or insane.'[2]

Some of the cruellest insults came from the pen of a man called Edward Fowler, with whom Bunyan would later find himself in conflict over important doctrinal issues. In a work entitled *Dirt Wip'd Off*,[3] Fowler's description of the tinker from Bedford is vitriolic. Bunyan, he tells us is a 'most impudent malicious schismatic ... [and among those who] tend to the subversion of all government if left unpunished'.[4]

Sadly, many of Bunyan's biographers, and those who pass comment upon him, have tended to discount the spiritual conflict he suffered during the early years of his Christian life by suggesting that much of it was self-induced. Amongst them we find men like J. A. Froude, who accuses Bunyan of 'torturing himself with illusions' and therefore 'overstraining his brain'.[5] Even so worthy a commentator as Josiah Conder, the Congregational hymn-writer, can add:

> We see no reason then to deny that the state of darkness into which Bunyan was plunged arose from that distempered action of imagination which is the ordinary effect of over-excitement.[6]

Other biographers have tried to 'rescue' him from his Calvinism, which, they say, only added to his despair.

Kinder maybe, but equally untrue is the somewhat patronizing attitude that suggests that Bunyan was suffering from a nervous breakdown, or even a mental collapse. That he experienced a measure of depression is certainly feasible, for who could endure the constant barrages of temptation without their affecting his spirit? The foremost Bunyan scholar of the twentieth century, Richard L. Greaves, gives a balanced assessment in his work

Glimpses of Glory, suggesting that Bunyan's condition was probably dysphoria, or mild depression, resulting in anxieties, doubts and restlessness of spirit. He maintains, however, that there is insufficient evidence to suggest that Bunyan was suffering from any major depressive illness.

Dr Gaius Davies goes further. He recognizes Bunyan's spiritual conflict, but as a psychiatrist studies his subject through a professional lens, seeking to explain spiritual experiences in medical terms. Bunyan was suffering, says Davies, from a 'severe obsessive-compulsive disorder',[7] and adds, '... a small proportion of obsessional patients, of whom I think Bunyan was one, are pushed to the borders of psychosis or madness.'[8] Davies does not appear to consider that the assaults on Bunyan's mind were largely satanic in origin, nor that they could come into the category of trials permitted by God, as in the case of Job in the Old Testament.

If Bunyan had indeed been suffering from an obsessive-compulsive disorder, as Dr Davies suggests, we would expect the condition to continue to manifest itself, at least at intervals, throughout his life. However, there is no record of this. Bunyan was able, moreover, to maintain a normal lifestyle throughout these difficult years of intense swings between hope and despair, continuing to support his family and follow his regular employment. Had Bunyan been living today, Dr Davies believes he might have obtained relief by means of modern medication. But this is to misunderstand the nature of the problem. Satan cannot be silenced by tranquillizers, and merely to alleviate the man's suffering would have robbed the church of the benefits which it has reaped from learning of these trials of Bunyan's early Christian life.

A further aspect in Bunyan's case, ignored by Davies, is the question of spiritual depression, as opposed to clinical depression. Even a cursory reading of the Psalms and of other biblical writers such as Job or Jeremiah, or the cry of King Hezekiah, 'O Lord I am oppressed, undertake for me' (Isaiah 38:14), brings us face to face with this condition. Christ himself could say in the Garden of Gethsemane, 'My soul is exceeding sorrowful' (Mark 14:34).

Spiritual depression is a subject with which the Puritan writers dealt extensively, though it remains a largely forgotten dimension in our own day.[9] Nor was the subject confined to seventeenth-century writings; it has been continually addressed by pastors and Christians as they have counselled perplexed and downcast believers. So we may safely categorize John Bunyan as a 'child of light walking in darkness' (Isaiah 50:10)[10] during these years, and we shall examine later some of the benefits that sprang from his trials, both for himself and for future generations.

Before that, however, we must attempt to follow him through the bewildering morass of satanic opposition which so nearly swamped his soul soon after his conversion. Delivered for a time from his former temptations to blasphemy and unbelief, Bunyan was little prepared for a further all-out assault on his young faith. But just when he felt his love for Christ 'as hot as fire' and thought that all was well with him, 'the tempter came upon me again and that with a more grievous and dreadful temptation than before'.[11] In view of his intense love for Christ it may seem strange that the onset of this period of fierce trial was the temp-tation to 'sell or part with this most blessed Christ, to exchange him for the things of this life, for anything'.[12]

'Sell him, sell him, sell him!' the devil seemed to chant over and over again in his ear until Bunyan became so distracted that he could hardly eat, pick up a tool, chop a stick, or even so much as stoop for a pin, without hearing the horrid voice whispering in his brain, 'Sell Christ for this,' or 'Sell Christ for that; sell him, sell him.' 'I will not, I will not, I will not,' Bunyan replied stoutly, 'No, not for thousands, thousands, thousands of worlds.'[13] Poor as John and Mary were, and now with two small girls to feed and nurture — one of them blind — this temptation may have originated in some enticement to reduce his spiritual commitment in return for material advantage.

Day and night it was the same. 'Sell, him, sell him,' whispered the tempter. And this went on for the best part of a year. Worn down and desperate, his mind eventually became so confused that he began to lose the power to distinguish between Satan and his own deceitful heart. At last, as he lay in bed one morning, his mind still ringing with the same old chant, 'Sell him, sell him, sell him,' and he continuing to reply, 'No! No! No!', he suddenly felt too weary to fight 'the voice' any more.

> After much striving, even until I was almost out of breath, I
> felt this thought pass through my heart, Let him go, if he will!
> and I thought also that I felt my heart freely consent thereto.
> Oh, the diligence of Satan! Oh, the desperateness of man's
> heart!
>
> Now was the battle won, and down fell I as a bird that is
> shot from the top of a tree, into great guilt and fearful despair.
> Thus getting out of my bed I went moping into the field, but
> God knows, with as heavy a heart as mortal man, I think, could
> bear.[14]

A fearful logic then gripped Bunyan's troubled mind. If he had
indeed 'sold Christ', as he presumed he had, he must have also
lost his salvation:

> Now was I as one bound, I felt myself shut up unto the
> judgment to come, nothing now for two years together would
> abide with me but damnation, and an expectation of
> damnation.[15]

And worse was to come. Reading a verse in the book of
Hebrews, he began to compare himself with Esau, 'who for one
morsel of meat sold his birthright'. Even more frightening was the
fact that when Esau regretted his folly, 'he found no place for
repentance, though he sought it carefully with tears' (Hebrews
12:16-17). What hope, then, could there be for John Bunyan?

This next period in Bunyan's life has aptly been called 'the
battle of the texts'. First one Scripture would comfort his soul, and
then all the consolation it provided would be cancelled out as he
discovered another verse, probably taken out of context, misin-
terpreted it and used it to condemn himself. Sometimes he could
even pinpoint the very time and place when God intervened to
reassure this man's tormented conscience:

> But about ten or eleven o'clock one day, as I was walking
> under a hedge, full of sorrow and guilt, God knows, and be-
> moaning myself for this hard hap [i.e. event]... suddenly this
> sentence bolted in upon me, The blood of Christ remits all
> guilt (1 John 1:7)... Now I began to conceive peace in my soul,

and methought I saw as if the tempter did leer and steal away from me, as being ashamed of what he had done... My sin, when compared to the blood of Christ, was no more to it than this little dot of stone before me is to this vast and wide field that here I see.[16]

But the comfort and relief so mercifully provided by this promise of Scripture seemed to evaporate in a few hours, as Bunyan 'sunk in my spirit under exceeding guilt again'. It appears that his oversensitive conscience was co-operating with the Evil One to condemn him. 'Maybe I have committed the unforgivable sin,'[17] was his next thought, for had he not, like Esau, also sold his birthright? And Esau was not able to find forgiveness. Little wonder that he could say:

Now was I both a burden and a terror to myself, nor did I ever so know, as now, what it was to be weary of my life, and yet afraid to die.[18]

'Perhaps,' thought Bunyan, 'I am like Peter, who denied his Master even after Christ had forewarned him. But no, I am worse than that; my case more resembles that of Judas, who actually sold Christ.' He thought of David, Solomon, Hezekiah and wicked Manasseh. They had all sinned against the light they had received. But his sin was more serious than any of theirs. They had offended under the old covenant, against the law of Moses, but he against the Saviour, against new-covenant light... And so he argued himself deeper and deeper into dejection.

It is hard to follow Bunyan into the dark valley of his doubts and despair. Sometimes it seems as though the light will never dawn for him again. Every time he attempted to pray, that same evil voice whispered in his ear, 'It is too late. You are lost,' making even prayer, as a means of grace, shut up against him.

And, as if he did not have enough to discourage him, he had the misfortune to come upon a book which seemed to confirm all his worst fears — the dreadful story of a man named Francis Spira, who had sinned irrecoverably and was pining away under the chastising hand of God. 'I am verily persuaded indeed,' said Spira to the priest who tried to counsel him, 'that God hath left

me to the power of the devil... You tell me of Christ's intercession, [but] I have denied him; you command me to believe, I say,
"I cannot, your command is impossible for me to obey." '19 Little
wonder that Bunyan found that:

> [This book] was to my troubled spirit as salt when rubbed
> into a fresh wound... Every sentence ... every groan of that
> man ... was as knives and daggers in my soul.20

Not surprisingly, Bunyan's physical health, even as a robust young
man, began to crumble under the stress of his anxieties and
temptations.

There is little relief from this appalling downward spiral for
page after page of Bunyan's account until at last we reach paragraph 173. Perhaps God allowed him to drink this cup of despair
to the very dregs so that one day he might console others. As so
often in this account, a word from the Bible seems to flash into
Bunyan's mind totally unexpectedly and bring with it either fresh
condemnation or, as on this occasion, much-needed correction
and consolation. And now it was one verse in particular that
seemed to be striving to bring him relief, even though he tried to
ignore it: 'I have blotted out, as a thick cloud, thy transgressions,
and, as a cloud, thy sins: return unto me; for I have redeemed
thee' (Isaiah 44:22). What greater assurance could this benighted
man need? Although Bunyan kept looking over his shoulder to
see whether Esau, 'who found no place for repentance', was still
on his track as well, God's promise continued to ring in his ears:
'Return unto me. Return unto me.'

As Bunyan was still hesitating, still unsure whether to classify
himself with 'Esau' or whether to believe God's promise, something so unusual happened that he scarcely knew what to make of
it. In paragraph 174 of Grace Abounding21 he describes an event
which took place as he was pacing backwards and forwards in
some workshop, probably waiting for an order to be completed.
Unsure of what to make of the event, Bunyan actually left out this
paragraph in the original version of Grace Abounding, only
adding it some years later.

As usual, his thoughts were running along the same gloomy
track, tormenting himself with his self-accusations. Quite suddenly

he heard a noise and felt a sensation which he could only compare to the sound of a wind as it 'rushed in at the window'. But,
strange to say, he was not frightened. Instead a pleasant voice
seemed to address him with a searching question: 'Did you ever
refuse to be justified by the blood of Christ?' In that moment all
his past life seemed to flash before him. He asked himself the
question: had he ever refused to be justified by the blood of
Christ? No, he had to admit, he had not. Then the voice became
more severe: 'See that ye refuse not him that speaketh' (Hebrews
12: 25).

What was this strange intervention? The Spirit of God is often
described in Scripture as the wind, and at Pentecost he came as 'a
sound from heaven as of a rushing mighty wind' (Acts 2:2). In
days of revival we read of such unusual phenomena and to
Bunyan the only explanation, and very probably the correct one,
was that in that rushing wind God had sent his messenger to him,
to bring a direct word of both comfort and reproof. Although he
could not explain what had happened, it resulted in something
that he had not known for many long months — 'a great calm in
my soul', persuading him that there might yet be hope for him.
Little wonder, then, that at first he feared to expose this personal
detail of his spiritual life to the critical gaze of those who might
read his book and discredit his account, or write him off as a mere
religious fanatic.

Although there was no immediate deliverance for Bunyan, for
Satan was not yet prepared to let his victim go, this event marks a
further turning point. 'Still my life hung in doubt before me,' he
tells us, but now he felt 'my soul desire, even to cast itself at the
foot of grace, by prayer and supplication'.[22] This was new. Only a
short time before, he had felt unable to pray at all. Satan still
slung the memory of Esau at him, knowing full well that this was
a most vulnerable point. Bunyan reeled back at this cruel thrust,
but it no longer had the same power, for now he was beginning
to dare to approach God in prayer once more and was therefore
receiving strength to believe despite his fears.

Although 'Esau' did not entirely disappear off the scene,
Bunyan gradually began to understand the passage of Scripture
that had so frightened him. Slowly he reasoned his way through
all his doubts and fears to the right interpretation:

As touching that in the twelfth of the Hebrews, about Esau's selling his birthright, though this was that which killed me, and stood like a spear against me; yet now I did consider... That his was not a hasty thought against the continual labour of his mind [as Bunyan's had been], but a thought *consented to* and put in practice likewise, and that too after some deliberation. It was a public and open act... Yea, twenty years after he was found to despise it still... (Genesis 33:9).[23]

Now at last verses from the Bible began to come as balm to Bunyan's wounded conscience. Words like 'This Scripture did most sweetly visit my soul,' and 'Oh the comfort that I had from this word!' are peppered throughout the account at this point. He even gained courage to look some of the most troubling passages in the book of Hebrews in the face. As he read about there being no more sacrifice for the sins of those who wilfully despise the Son of God,[24] he began to realize that this did not apply to him and had never done so.

But the greatest deliverance of all came in another of those special interventions by God. Still with a lingering fear 'lest all was not right', for Bunyan's conscience had become raw and damaged by the battering he had received, he tells us what happened. The passage, written in Bunyan's unique style, is deeply moving:

As I was passing in the field, and that too with some dashes on my conscience ... suddenly this sentence fell upon my soul, Thy righteousness is in heaven: and methought withal, I saw with the eyes of my soul Jesus Christ at God's right hand; there, I say, is my righteousness; so that wherever I was, or whatever I was a-doing, God could not say of me, He wants [lacks] my righteousness, for that was just before him. I also saw, moreover, that it was not my good frame of heart that made my righteousness better, nor yet my bad frame that made my righteousness worse; for my righteousness was Jesus Christ himself, the same yesterday and today for ever (Heb. 13:8).

And it is with an exclamation of joy and relief that the reader also can greet the next words of this sorely tried young Christian:

> Now did my chains fall from my legs indeed, I was loosed
> from my affliction and irons, my temptations also fled away; so
> that from that time, those dreadful scriptures of God left off
> to trouble me; now also went I home rejoicing for the grace and
> love of God.[25]

We can well imagine the smile on Mary's face as she welcomed John on his return home, and listened as he told her that
he had at last learnt Luther's great lesson, that his standing with
God did not depend on any goodness that he could achieve by a
strict adherence to the law, but on the righteousness of Jesus
Christ, who had fulfilled all the law's requirements on the sinner's
behalf.

The strength he now received as he finally grasped this vital
truth did not drain away as he faced Satan's insinuations once
more.

> Here, therefore I lived for some time, very sweetly at peace
> with God through Christ; Oh, methought, Christ! Christ!
> there was nothing but Christ that was before my eyes.[26]

And Bunyan's experience has brought relief to many sorely
tried Christians since his day. Alexander Whyte, Presbyterian
preacher of the nineteenth and early twentieth centuries, knew
this to be true. In a lecture on *Grace Abounding* he could say:

> And as many of you as are taken by the throat continually
> by God's broken law, it is for you above all men that the
> Psalms and the Romans and the Galatians and the *Grace
> Abounding* were all written.[27]

I2

'Gold in my trunk'

Long and fruitlessly John Bunyan had searched within himself for the 'gold' of a righteousness that would be pleasing to God — a treasure to offer to the one whom he had offended. And he had not been able to find it. But when he realized, as he quaintly put it, that 'my gold was in my trunk at home',[1] he had made a life-changing discovery. As we have seen, walking in the field that day he understood at last that he already possessed the righteousness of Christ, imputed to him as a free gift — it was indeed like 'gold in his trunk'. 'Now Christ was all,' he declares triumphantly, 'all my wisdom, all my righteousness, all my sanctification, and all my redemption.'[2]

Not that his many trials and temptations suddenly came to an end, but they would never again master and crush him as before. But why, we may wonder, had it taken him so long to discover this? Why had he suffered such appalling temptations — temptations that have even caused some to doubt his sanity? As if he anticipates that his readers will be asking this very question, Bunyan pauses in his narrative to suggest some answers before proceeding with his autobiography.

First, he blamed himself. He had allowed a natural trait of character, his tendency to introspection and scepticism, to dominate his thinking — like Gideon, he had asked for signs from God and had not been prepared to cast himself on the bare word of the promises. But rather than dwell on his shortcomings, Bunyan preferred to speak of the advantages that he had gleaned from his experiences. Through them the character of God in his glory and holiness had been powerfully stamped upon his consciousness. Throughout all the trials of his future pathway those lessons learnt in the darkness would never leave him. Never again would he question the being of God and his truthfulness, whatever else might happen, or whatever trials he might meet.

A second and priceless benefit that this young believer had gained from his trials was an unwavering conviction of the total reliability of the Scriptures. The threatenings against apostasy, particularly in the book of Hebrews, that had so terrified him were not to be regarded lightly. Even though they may not have applied to him, as he had once thought, they might well apply to others and therefore he warns, 'Woe be to him against whom the Scriptures bend themselves.'[3]

On the other hand, the promises of God in the Bible which he had felt so unable to claim for himself became the bedrock of his assurance in the future. In his vivid and unique style he tells us:

> I should in those days, often in my greatest agonies, flounce towards the promise, as horses do towards sound ground ... yet stick in the mire... But now a word, a word to lean my weary soul upon, that I might not sink for ever![4]

He illustrates this by quoting one particular promise on which he could now 'lean his weary soul'. The first half of John 6:37 had formerly terrified him: 'All that the Father giveth me shall come to me.' 'What', he would think, 'if my name is not among that number? How can I know if I am one of those who have been "given"?' At last he found untold solace in the second half of the verse, '... and him that cometh to me I will in no wise cast out', for that certainly included John Bunyan!

Perhaps Bunyan's richest consolation and reward was found in all that he had learnt of the grace of God:

An old view of St Cuthbert's Street, Bedford. The Bunyans' house is second from the left.

> I never saw those heights and depths in grace, and love and
> mercy, as I saw after this temptation. Great sins do draw out
> great grace; and where guilt is most terrible and fierce there
> the mercy of God in Christ ... appears most high and mighty.[5]

Now and then in those early days after his deliverance from
the tempter's clutches he was given such an indescribable dis-
closure of God's grace that he 'could hardly bear up under it, it
was so out of measure amazing'.[6] Indeed, this was yet more gold
in his trunk — a preparation both for the trials ahead and for the
life-work which God purposed for him.

With new peace in his conscience, John Bunyan, now almost
twenty-seven years of age, decided that the time had come for
him to move his young family from Elstow into Bedford itself. St
John's Church, the home of the Bedford Meeting, had become
the central point of his life. He would naturally wish his children,
with blind Mary now five years old, to come under the influence
of John Gifford's preaching. Apart from this, his work as a brazier
often involved him in visits to Stevington, some five miles north
of Bedford. Sometimes he would need to go as far as Newport
Pagnell to the west. If he moved into Bedford itself he would be
more centrally placed to fulfil such calls. The Bunyans' new home
was in St Cuthbert's Street, almost opposite the parish church. The
smallest of the five Bedford parishes, St Cuthbert's was north of
the River Ouse on the eastern boundary of the Bedford of his
day.

The cottage[7] to which the family moved had two living
rooms, one on either side of the front door, with a single room in
the gabled roof where they would sleep. At the back, overlooking
open countryside, was a small room which would later become
John Bunyan's study.

In September 1655, not long after Bunyan and his family had
settled into their new home, the Bedford church, and John in
particular, suffered a grievous loss — one that must have seemed
irreparable to Bunyan. That year, as summer turned to autumn,
the pastor, John Gifford, sickened and died. None of the other
members of the church had been able either to enter fully into
Bunyan's trials or even to help him much, with the exception of
the pastor. Although he was scarcely more than fifty years of age

and had been a believer for only five years, Gifford's ministry had been 'much for my stability', as Bunyan has previously told us. Doubtless the tinker from Bedford was amongst the few who stood around Gifford's bed as his life was drawing to an end. Perhaps he was also one of those favoured to hear the pastor's final words of passionate concern for the young church he was leaving behind. Certainly Gifford's far-seeing ideals for church life, expressed in a letter written to the church members from his deathbed, moulded Bunyan's own lifelong convictions.[8] But now Gifford had gone, and John Bunyan missed him sorely.

As we noted earlier, it would appear that paragraphs 118-130 in *Grace Abounding to the Chief of Sinners* take the form of a summary of Bunyan's life during 1654–1656, but omitting the period of his most intense confrontations with Satan when tempted first to 'sell Christ' and then to believe that, like Esau, he too had been rejected by God. It would therefore seem appropriate that we now glance back at information we may glean from that summary and fit it into the period of John Bunyan's life that we have reached, where, I believe, it belongs.[9]

With the loss of John Gifford's guidance and advice we may well suppose that this was the time when Bunyan felt most in need of a new helper — and he soon found such a friend, though only a literary one. 'I did greatly long,' he tells us, 'to see some ancient godly man's experience who had writ some hundreds of years before I was born.'[10] Perhaps someone from former generations who had gone through similar experiences to his own could be his instructor.

In days before much in the way of Christian biography was readily available, and when the cost of a printed book was virtually beyond the resources of a poor man, this must have seemed like a pipe dream. How his wish came to be fulfilled, he does not tell us apart from the simple facts:

> Well, after many such longings in my mind, the God in whose hands are all our days and ways, did cast into my hand one day a book of Martin Luther; it was his comment on the Galatians — it also was so old that it was ready to fall piece from piece if I did but turn it over.[11]

Perhaps some bookseller gave it to him, because its condition made it virtually worthless. But, old and dilapidated though it was, to John Bunyan it was a treasure trove — more gold for his trunk.

This book was everything that he had craved. All that Luther wrote rang true to Bunyan's own experience. Even the dedication in the first English edition caught his attention:

> To all afflicted Consciences which grone for salvation and wrestle under the Crosse for the Kingdome of Christ.

This was surely a book meant for him:

> When I had but a little way perused, I found my condition, in his experience, so largely and profoundly handled, as if his book had been written out of my heart.[12]

As he turned page after page, he marvelled at the relevance of Luther's words to his own case:

> When I see a man [wrote Luther] that is bruised enough already, oppressed with the law, terrified with sin, and thirsting for comfort, it is time that I should remove out of his sight the law and active righteousness, and that I should set before him by the gospel the Christian and passive righteousness, which excluding Moses with his law, offereth the promise made in Christ who came for the afflicted and for sinners.[13]

A misunderstanding of the purpose of the law given by Moses had almost crushed Luther and, in these worn pages which Bunyan now turned one by one, the great Reformer pointed to the same solution that Bunyan too had discovered when he had walked in the field that day and realized that

> ... it was not my good frame of heart that made my righteousness better, nor yet my bad frame that made my righteousness worse; for my righteousness was Jesus Christ himself, the same yesterday and today for ever [Hebrews 13:8].[14]

Luther's book also explained the source of the dreadful blasphemies that had plagued Bunyan:

> He [Luther] doth most gravely ... debate of the rise of these temptations, namely, blasphemy, desperation, and the like, showing that the law of Moses as well as the devil, death and hell hath a very great hand therein, the which, at first, was very strange to me, but considering and watching, I found it so indeed.[15]

Bunyan's conclusion regarding Luther's commentary demonstrates the influence that this one book would have on all his future thinking and the comfort it brought him in his present condition:

> I do prefer this book of Martin Luther upon the Galatians, excepting the Holy Bible, before all the books that ever I have seen, as most fit for a wounded conscience.[16]

Although it is difficult to put any firm timetable on events that Bunyan describes in his narrative, he mentions two periods of illness. The first of these we may tentatively date early in 1656. 'About the spring,' he tells us, 'I was suddenly and violently seized with much weakness in my outward man, insomuch that I thought I could not live.' He assumed his condition was the dreaded 'consumption', or tuberculosis, which so often proved terminal to both young and old. With the expectation of his impending death, John's mind turned in upon itself and, as so often happens in times of sickness, the Evil One took full advantage of his weakness in order to renew his attacks. All his sins were paraded starkly before his eyes: 'my deadness, dullness, and coldness in holy duties; my wanderings of heart ... my want of love to God, his ways and people...' Perhaps he was not a true believer after all. How could he hope for heaven in such an unworthy state?

> Now was my soul greatly pinched between these two considerations: Live I must not, Die I dare not; now I sunk and fell in my spirit...[17]

The indication that this illness occurred after he had been delivered from the dreadful condition to which he had sunk when he feared he had 'sold Christ' lies in the fact that he was now able to lay hold on the promises of God and apply them to himself:

> As I was walking up and down in the house, as a man in a most woeful state, that word of God took hold of my heart, 'Ye are justified freely by his grace, through the redemption that is in Christ Jesus' [Romans 3:24].

Deliverance came almost instantly. Other verses began flooding into the sick man's mind, and before long he could exclaim joyfully, 'Now was I got on high! I saw myself within the arms of grace and mercy.' Whereas before he had trembled at the thought of his approaching death, his fears had all evaporated:

> Now death was lovely and beautiful in my sight; for I saw we shall never live indeed till we be gone to the other world. Oh, methought, this life is but a slumber in comparison of that above.[18]

But God had further purposes for Bunyan's life and gradually his health began to show a marked improvement. Before long he was able to resume his work once more. And at about this time the piercing cries of another newborn baby rang through the house as John and Mary Bunyan welcomed the birth of their first son, a child whom they called John like his father.

Soon after Gifford's death the church began the important task of appointing a new pastor. Some of the comments which John Gifford had made shortly before he died related to such a choice for his small church — soon to be bereft of spiritual leadership. 'Spend much time before the Lord about choosing a pastor,' he urged. Then, as if he had already discerned unusual gifts in the young converted tinker, he added tellingly,

> ... for though I suppose he is before you whom the Lord hath appointed, yet it will be no disadvantage to you, I hope, if you walk a year or two as you are before election.[19]

If he had John Bunyan in mind, he knew also that John was not yet in any way ready to undertake such heavy responsibility, even though he himself had done so soon after his own conversion. In the event the church did not wait, but early in 1656 appointed another of its members as pastor, John Burton, a young and highly respected man.

Not long after this a circumstance arose which in a quite unexpected way would prove another important milestone in Bunyan's spiritual pilgrimage: the arrival of the Quakers in the area. This sect, whose teachings differed markedly from those of the Quakers of later times, had its beginnings in 1652, when twenty-eight-year-old George Fox, a wandering visionary, stood on a rocky crag in Firbank Fell, east of Kendal in Cumberland, and preached for three hours to about a thousand men and women. These were members of a sect found in many parts of the country known as the 'Seekers', his present congregation being the 'Westmorland Seekers'. Truth, he maintained, could not be stated in propositional terms, but was whispered in the heart by the Spirit of Christ, source of that inward light dwelling in every man. Fox denied that the Scriptures were the final and revealed truth of God — his own message was a direct revelation from God. His ideas gripped and excited the people.

During 1652 Fox ranged far and wide throughout the north of England propagating his views, often suffering abuse and sometimes imprisonment for interrupting services and for 'blasphemy'. The new movement gradually gained adherents, and before long the 'Valiant Sixty', as the first Quaker missionaries were later called, spread out throughout the country proclaiming their new teaching of the 'inner light'. As the movement gathered pace numbers joined it, and in 1654 Quaker representatives reached Bedfordshire. Here a prominent Bedford magistrate, John Crook, was persuaded by all that he heard, and later opened his home, a few miles south of Bedford, as a centre for Quaker meetings.

Quaker ideas soon became a talking point among the group that Bunyan had joined. As a young convert he was deeply troubled over all they were propagating, particularly the suggestion that the Bible was not the final word of God. He was also disturbed by their insistence that the Spirit of Christ dwelt in everyone, as an 'inner light', illuminating and instructing all.

Obedience to this light within was the pathway to perfection. Most crucially the Quakers denied the reality of Christ's humanity — leading to a rejection of his resurrection and ascension, together with the prospect of the physical return of Christ as judge of all.[20] Some also taught that his death did not avail for the sins of his people or satisfy divine justice. These truths were at the heart of all that had become most precious to John Bunyan — truths on which he rested for his salvation.

With ardour he now began to search the Scriptures page by page to refute such ideas. Apart from reassuring himself of the veracity of the faith, this provided him with an astonishing knowledge of the Bible. The Quakers might cast doubt on the literal physical life of Christ, but Bunyan could now declare that the Saviour's birth, death, resurrection and ascension had become so real that it was 'as if I had stood by when he was in the world, and also when he was caught up' (to heaven). This experience had a powerful impact upon him, creating 'such a change...upon my soul, it made me wonder'.[21] Describing these days and their spiritual significance Bunyan would later say:

> When the set time was come, the Lord, just before the men called Quakers came into the country, did set me down so blessedly in the truth of the doctrine of Jesus Christ that it made me marvel...[22]

Early in 1656 George Fox himself actually toured Bedfordshire and some of his followers came into Bedford during April and May of that year. Open clashes began to take place between these Quaker representatives and members of the Bedford Meeting. Bunyan, ready prepared, stood staunchly beside his new pastor, John Burton, at the Market Cross in the High Street where one encounter occurred. Another took place on 23 May when Quakers clashed with Bunyan and his pastor in front of St Paul's Church. On occasions the Quakers would attempt to disrupt public preaching services, even stripping off their clothing to create a distraction and to proclaim the natural innocence of the soul. 'Throw away the Scriptures,' yelled Anne Blackly,[23] a young Quaker woman, at one such confrontation. The proposition was unthinkable. And in a flash John Bunyan had his answer ready, an

answer born out of hard experience: 'No! for then the devil
would be too hard for me!'

This entire experience of defending the faith against error
brought an unexpected bonus to Bunyan himself, giving him what
he had lacked up till now: an unshakeable assurance of his own
salvation. Throughout the long history of the Christian church
many believers have gone through a period of perplexity, temptation and fear soon after their conversion, before being given a
full assurance of faith. William Grimshaw of Haworth (1708–
1763) is a case in point. He was two years in what he describes as
'a wilderness' after his conversion in 1742, before coming into
such an assurance in 1744.[24] In the same way John Bunyan, after
four years of uncertainty, could say: 'Now had I evidence … of
my salvation from heaven, with many golden seals thereon, all
hanging in my sight.' So significant were these 'golden seals' upon
his faith that it set John Bunyan longing for a day when

> … I might for ever be inflamed with the sight, and joy, and
> communion with him whose head was crowned with thorns,
> whose face was spit on, and body broken, and soul made an
> offering for my sins: for whereas before I lay continually trem-
> bling at the mouth of hell, now methought I was got so far
> therefrom, that I could not, when I looked back, scarce discern
> it; and oh! thought I, that I were fourscore years old now, that I
> might die quickly, that my soul might be gone to rest.[25]

Indeed, John Bunyan now had a trunk full of gold, gold that
Satan could no longer steal from him by his insidious temptations.

13

Called to preach

Coupled with John Bunyan's new and strong assurance of his salvation came an unusual sense that God had a unique purpose for his life. Bunyan himself was amazed at the strange inner conviction that he experienced, which came at the very time that he had been confronting the erroneous Quaker teachings:

> Methought I heard such a word in my heart as this — I have set thee down on purpose for I have something more than ordinary for thee to do; which made me the more marvel, saying, 'What, my Lord, such a poor wretch as I?'[1]

'Something more than ordinary for me to do' — what could these words mean? 'Have I understood them rightly?' he wondered. 'What about my weakness, my reputation for careless living in youth, my temptations, poverty, lack of education?' And yet the insistent voice in his heart kept on repeating:

'I have set thee down on purpose', and so forth, with more
fresh incomes of the Lord Jesus, and the power of the blood
of his cross upon my soul.[2]

Although puzzled, Bunyan must have guessed at the nature of
this special commission from God. For not long before his first
pastor, John Gifford, died in September 1655, some of 'the most
able for judgment and holiness of life' among the members of the
Bedford Meeting had begun to discern Bunyan's extraordinary
powers of speech and ability to express spiritual truth winsomely
and persuasively. Realizing too something of the depth of his
spiritual experiences, these people began to urge him to be willing
to 'speak a word of exhortation'[3] now and then at one of their
private gatherings for spiritual fellowship.

Bunyan shrank from the thought. To him it seemed wrong that
he should be placed in such a position, considering his recent and
often continuing battles with fears and temptations. But his friends
were insistent, and at last with much diffidence he attempted to
speak a few words to a small group of fellow members of the
meeting. The result was astonishing:

> They not only seemed to be, but did solemnly protest, as
> in the sight of the great God, they were both affected and
> comforted, and gave thanks to the Father of mercies for the
> grace bestowed upon me.[4]

Not surprisingly, the next suggestion was that John should
accompany them as they went into the surrounding villages and
that he should add a 'word of admonition' if the opportunity
arose. Again Bunyan protested his inability, but again his friends
prevailed upon him to speak, with the same result. Those who
heard told of their joy at seeing what God had done in John's
life, and urged him to continue. It is probably at this stage, shortly
after his 1656 confrontations with the Quakers, that Bunyan
himself began to sense that inward call from God and to realize
that God had indeed 'something more than ordinary' for him to
do.

Bunyan would have been well aware of the teaching of
Scripture, expounded in Puritan writings, regarding the call to the

ministry. A candidate must possess a degree of natural ability coupled with a certain stamp of authority upon him which the Spirit of God alone could give. The church to which he belonged must be able to recognize that God had specially gifted him; they should have already received encouragement and help from any contribution he had made. Lastly, the man himself must have some inner and insistent sense that this was God's purpose for his life. Bunyan's contemporary, and later his warm friend, John Owen, described the characteristics of the Spirit's call to those he was setting apart for this special work:

> He called them by furnishing them with ability and authority for their work; he commanded them to be set apart by the church, that they might be blessed and owned in their work; and he sent them forth by an impression of his authority on their minds...[5]

These things had all come together in Bunyan's experience. Not only had the church recognized his gifts, but he too had a strong inner conviction of such a call. 'I did evidently find in my mind a secret pricking forward thereto,'[6] he tells us — not out of motives of self-aggrandizement or pride, for accompanying that 'secret pricking' was always that gnawing awareness of his own inadequacy, coupled with a constant harassment by Satan's fiery darts. But despite his fears he had a passion — almost a craving — to render to God his whole strength and any gifts he possessed. I 'could not be content,' he records, 'unless I was found in the exercise of my gift, unto which I was greatly animated'.[7]

The Bedford Meeting members now numbered over ninety, a large increase on the twenty-five in membership when Bunyan had joined in 1653. Early in 1656 the church gathered with one purpose in mind: to set John Bunyan, together with several others, apart for this special calling. With prayer, fasting and appropriate solemnity, Bunyan was 'called forth, and appointed to a more ordinary [regular] and public preaching the word'.[8] Not only was he to minister to the church, but also to preach the gospel among the unconverted. Although it did not mean that he was to give up his daily employment as a brazier, he now knew that the church itself had the fullest confidence in him and had appointed him to preach as opportunities arose.

So whenever John Bunyan was able, after his long day's work mending pots and pans, he would trek out to some village, gather a congregation and begin to preach. The results were astonishing. Often he could see the tears running down the faces of his hearers as his stirring words touched their hearts and consciences. At first he could hardly believe 'that God should speak by me to the heart of any man, still counting myself unworthy'. He tried to brush aside the evidences that his preaching was effectual and souls were being awakened, but at last he 'began to conclude it might be so, that God had owned in his work such a foolish one as I'.[9]

What was John Bunyan's preaching like at this time? Helpfully, he gives us a succinct account:

> In my preaching of the Word, I took special notice of this one thing, namely, that the Lord did lead me to begin where his Word begins with sinners; that is, to condemn all flesh, and to open and allege that the curse of God by the law, doth belong to and lay hold on all men as they come into the world, because of sin.

Vehement burning words poured from the young preacher's lips as he first began his ministry. He admits that such an emphasis, without an equal emphasis on the grace and mercy of God, sprang in part from the anguish of spirit he himself had known, and still did experience in measure:

> Now this part of my work I fulfilled with great sense; for the terrors of the law, and guilt for my transgressions, lay heavy on my conscience. I preached what I felt, what I smartingly did feel, even that under which my poor soul did groan and tremble to astonishment.[10]

Bunyan's further comments suggest that he had actually started preaching before that experience later in 1656 when he was given a much deeper assurance of God's love and mercy towards him. For he adds:

I went myself in chains to preach to them in chains; and
carried that fire in my own conscience that I persuaded them
to beware of.

Sometimes, he continues:

I have gone full of guilt and terror even to the pulpit door,
and there it hath been taken off, and I have been at liberty in
my mind until I have done my work.

But no sooner had the last word of his sermon been uttered than,
'... even before I could get down the pulpit stairs, I have been as
bad as I was before.' Yet despite all this, God had supported and
carried him through, 'for neither guilt nor hell could take me off
my work'.[11]

We have noted before a remarkable similarity between the
experiences of John Bunyan and those of William Grimshaw
almost a century later. The curate of Haworth too was 'harassed
by distressing doubts and fears and fiercely assaulted by the
temptations and fiery darts of the enemy' during the period when
he first started preaching in Haworth. Commenting on this, John
Newton wrote in his biographical sketch of Grimshaw's life:

Thus many of our most eminent evangelical preachers were
led. They set out as it were in the twilight, but the dawn is a sure
presage of the advancing day. They have lived to see many
mistakes and defects in their first efforts ... but perhaps their
greatest success in awakening sinners was when their views of
the scheme of salvation were much less clear and distinct.[12]

And so it proved with John Bunyan. To his astonishment, and
doubtless to that of the Bedford Meeting, he had not been
preaching long before 'they came in to hear the word by hundreds, and that from all parts'. Many had mixed motives: we may
assume that some came merely for the novelty of hearing a tinker
preach, and others of his former associates either to mock or
wonder.

Some, however, to John's amazement and joy, showed
themselves to be 'so constant, and also in their hearts so earnestly

pressing after the knowledge of Jesus Christ' that even he had to admit that God was owning his endeavours. As he saw the tears of conviction, penitence and joy streaming down the faces of his hearers, he began to enter into the feelings of the apostle Paul and to see these men and women as a solemn seal from God on his ministry.[13]

For two years, so Bunyan tells us, the predominant note of his preaching was on the broken law of God and the fearful state of the unconverted. But gradually, as he himself gained a greater measure of peace in his own soul and Christ gave him 'many sweet discoveries of his blessed grace', his emphasis shifted. He continued to preach what he 'saw and felt', but now he 'did labour to hold forth Jesus Christ in all his offices, relations and benefits'.[14]

As Bunyan's preaching centred more fully on Christ himself and on the certainties of salvation, he began to enjoy yet more liberty in preaching. Especially was this true when he was showing that 'good works' were not a prerequisite for God's favour — a lesson that he himself had struggled to learn. His description of such occasions is vivid and moving. He tells us that:

> ... it was as if an angel of God had stood by my back to encourage me. Oh, it hath been with such power and heavenly evidence upon my own soul ... that I could not be contented with saying 'I believe and am sure;' methought I was more than sure.[15]

These very truths that he was preaching were bringing added security and confidence to his own soul.

John Bunyan's call to preach was becoming the predominant motivation for all his future life and sufferings for Christ's sake.

14

Defending the faith

If we were to call unexpectedly at John and Mary Bunyan's small cottage in St Cuthbert's Street one evening in 1656, we might well be surprised at the scene that greeted us. In all probability Mary would be sitting nursing baby John, still only a few months old, with Elizabeth, not long turned two, perhaps clamouring for her mother's attention. And there sitting at a table, making the most of the fading daylight, would be John Bunyan himself, surrounded by sheets of paper, with his blind child, Mary, standing quietly by him.

The tinker of Bedford was writing his first book — a book designed to demonstrate the errors of the Quakers' teaching and to warn the unwary. Using the words 'Ranters' and 'Quakers' almost interchangeably, for the Quaker representatives who had come to Bedford were little different in their emphases from the Ranters whom Bunyan had already met, he had scathing remarks to make about those who teach error. Time was at a premium, for some of the most prominent citizens of Bedford had already been affected. Bunyan's pen flew across his paper as all the convictions of his soul were poured into this treatise.

Bunyan's cottage, Bedford

Bunyan's defence, called *Some Gospel Truths Opened*, would run to approximately 40,000 words, mainly emphasizing the true human nature of Christ. This was a direct refutation of Quaker teaching, which minimized the importance of Christ's physical life on earth, downplaying his real birth, life, death and resurrection. By repeatedly using such expressions as the 'Son of Man' or the 'Son of the Virgin Mary, the Lord Jesus Christ...',[1] Bunyan was aiming to challenge such teaching. For Quakers, 'the Christ within, speaking, living, dying and rising', was paramount, making his actual physical life on earth of less account. As Bunyan piles on the references showing Christ to be truly man as well as truly God, his exceptional grasp of Scripture is already in evidence.

Another Quaker emphasis with which Bunyan profoundly disagreed was their stress on the 'inner light', or conscience, which they equated with the Spirit of Christ indwelling every human being. Bunyan was emphatic:

> Man, as he cometh into the world, hath not the Spirit of Christ in him; for *that* he must after receive by the preaching of the word.

To teach, as the Quakers did, that merely to follow one's conscience is all that is required is therefore serious error. Atheists also have consciences, argues Bunyan, 'yet it is their great delight to serve their lusts, this world [and] their sins'.[2] Conscience must be enlightened by the Scripture if it is to be a true guide. Bunyan's own conscience had led him up many tortuous paths before John Gifford had come to his aid. Quakerism, as Bunyan judged it, struck at the very heart of Christianity — the authority of Scripture.[3]

Diligently and methodically, Bunyan worked through all the points where he felt the Quakers were in error, always emphasizing the real manhood of the Saviour in his virgin birth, his life, death, resurrection and ascension back into the glory. He laid particular emphasis on the return of Christ to judge the world, for his readers must be prepared for that great day — a day which, in common with many other Puritans, Bunyan considered to be imminent although he would not be drawn into the dangerous business of specifying times or dates:

> I will show you that his coming will be shortly. [But] it is true, no man can tell neither the day nor the hour, yet so far as the Scriptures will give us light into the nearness of his coming, so far we may go.[4]

Again and again, as Bunyan progresses with his thesis, the preacher in him takes over from the writer. Because the time is short he is urgent and tender as he pleads with his readers. 'Art thou born again?' he asks them many times over, giving eight important tests with which they may examine themselves. And if they pass each test, he follows up, in typical Puritan style, with five advantages of true faith, assuring them that 'It will comfort thy heart against persecutions, temptations, cross providences.' Lastly, he ends with six 'admonitions' in the light of these things, with important questions and answers to consider. Then he turns the spotlight back on the Quakers with seven searching questions, demanding answers, 'Yes' or 'No', for many of them.[5]

Rather than analyse any further the details of Bunyan's first work, it is more interesting to note the sidelights which it throws on his own recent experiences — things that had so nearly brought him down in utter despair. Describing those snares which the devil had thrown across his own path, he warns against them: Satan will endeavour to keep you in love with your sins and pleasures; failing that, he will try to persuade you that your religion is nothing but 'a melancholy fit' and suggest that you pay more attention to your proper employment. If you should persist with this religion, his next strategy will be to suggest that you 'must earn heaven with [your] fingers' ends', even until you begin to congratulate yourself on your success.

All this has a familiar ring as we think of Bunyan's own pathway. He then turns on his readers, cautioning them in most stringent terms to beware of the spiritual dangers of remaining in a compromised position. Towards the end he narrows his field of attack to the Quakers themselves — with whom he had so recently contended, describing them as 'unstable souls ... deluded and beguiled at last' .[6] It may well be that Bunyan had overstated his case to some extent: certainly those Quakers whom he had met were extreme in the errors they were propagating, but, as we shall see, many of them would suffer heroically for the faith, casting themselves on Christ at the last.

Finally, John Bunyan puts down his pen. Perhaps he may read parts of it aloud to Mary, but all that now remains is for him to take his work to his pastor, John Burton, and ask if he will write a preface to it. He already knows of a London printer, John Wright, who will print his book, and an old friend from his Newport Pagnell days, Matthias Cowley, a member of the church John attended during his years in the army, who will distribute the work.

John Burton read through Bunyan's work and happily en- dorsed it, adding some comments of his own on the vital neces- sity of recognizing Christ as a real man among men, who actually took our flesh and blood. In all likelihood he put in some editorial corrections, touching up Bunyan's spelling, although the style retains its distinctive 'Bunyan' touch. But John Burton had a problem. How would readers accept the work of a man who had no university degree, who was untaught in the learning of the day and the ancient languages — a man of humble origins and employment? So in his preface Burton was at pains to underline Bunyan's credentials. Quoting 1 Corinthians 1:27, he stressed that God often chooses the foolish to confound the wise; moreover, he insisted, the writer had not been chosen 'out of an earthly, but out of a heavenly university'. In fact Bunyan possessed not one but three degrees:

> He hath, through grace taken these three heavenly degrees, to wit, union with Christ, the anointing of the Spirit, and experience of the temptations of Satan, which do more fit a man for preaching the gospel than all the university learning and degrees that can be had.[7]

Bunyan himself was acutely aware of his lack of education and experience, describing his work as 'published for the good of God's chosen ones by that unworthy servant of Christ, John Bunyan of Bedford'. But Burton's final commendation of his younger friend and church member is warm and sincere, and bears testimony to the abundant blessing already attending Bunyan's preaching even as early as 1656. Burton could testify, together with many others, 'of this man's soundness in the faith, of his godly conversation [i.e. way of life], and his ability to preach the gospel ... and that with much success in the conversion of sinners'.[8]

It can come as no surprise that at about this time John Bunyan was ill again, perhaps with influenza. Not only had he been working throughout the day, walking long miles in all weathers with his heavy pack of tools on his back, to earn enough money to support his young family; he was also taking up every possible opportunity to preach in the surrounding villages. And now, in addition, he had written a long doctrinal treatise — an exacting task since it was his first — and had seen it through the press. Very probably his illness was a relapse into his earlier condition.

As before, Satan took full advantage of his weakness.

> I find [said Bunyan] he is much for assaulting the soul
> when it begins to approach towards the grave, then is his op-
> portunity, labouring to hide from me my former experience of
> God's goodness; also setting before me the terrors of death
> and the judgment.

But he did not succumb to such insinuations for long. Soon a
verse of scripture 'did sweetly revive my spirit and help me to
hope in God' — a passage from Luke 16 referring to the angels
carrying the sick Lazarus to heaven. At that moment his darkness
was dispelled and he cried out in triumph, 'O death, where is thy
sting? O grave, where is thy victory?' As Bunyan recovered
strength, he was able to continue 'comfortable in my work for
God again'[9] — a reference which strongly suggests that this illness
came after he had begun preaching and writing.

Shortly afterwards another 'great cloud of darkness' seemed to
descend on Bunyan's spirit — a frequent after-effect of serious
illness. Gloomy and depressed, he became acutely conscious of his
spiritual deadness: 'I could not feel my soul to move or stir after
grace and life by Christ.' We can well imagine him sitting by the
fire one winter's evening, brooding on his lifeless condition, with
Mary sitting nearby, doubtless troubled that her husband should
be so downcast again. Suddenly a verse flashed into his mind: 'I
must go to Jesus.' Turning to Mary, John said, 'Wife, is there ever
such a Scripture as "I must go to Jesus?"'

Poor Mary was mystified. 'I cannot tell,' she confessed at last.

Then it came to him. 'O now I know, I know!' John exclaimed
elatedly. A passage in Hebrews 12 had sprung to mind: 'Ye are
come unto mount Sion, and unto the city of the living God, the
heavenly Jerusalem, and to an innumerable company of angels ...
and to Jesus, the mediator of the new covenant' (Hebrews
12:22-24, emphasis added). Joy flooded his soul. 'That was a
good night to me, I never had but few better,' he records. All he
longed for was an opportunity to share his ecstasy with 'a company of some of God's people'. 'Christ,' he declares 'was a
precious Christ to my soul that night.' We can imagine him, some
hours later, mounting the stairs to his loft bedroom where his

children and Mary were already asleep. But there was little sleep for John: 'I could scarce lie in my bed for joy and peace and triumph through Christ.'[10]

John Bunyan was entering on a period of great joy and usefulness in the service of the church of Jesus Christ.

I5

Repercussions

When John Bunyan published his first book, *Some Gospel Truths Opened*, in 1656, England was still in a state of uncertainty and religious turmoil. These were 'distracted and dangerous times', as he declared, times when many were 'tottering and shaking' because of the numerous sects, each clamouring to obtain a hearing for their particular ideas.

If the religious scene was chaotic, the economic and political situation was equally confusing. After Cromwell had dismissed the Barebones Parliament in December 1653, he had taken on sole rule, but was working towards the establishment of another Parliament. Convened at last in September 1655 and consisting of some 400 members as well as representatives from Ireland and Scotland, the First Protectorate Parliament also turned out to be a failure. It was unable to agree on a wide cross-section of Cromwell's proposals. Exasperated and frustrated, the Lord Protector dismissed his Parliament early in 1656 — as soon as it was legally possible to do so. Instead, he instituted the 'rule of the major-generals.' Dividing the country into twelve areas, Cromwell appointed army men to supervise and administer local government.

It is unlikely that such a system could ever have been made to work, given the deep divide that existed between the aims and ambitions of the army and those of the gentry. In addition, Cromwell may not have reckoned with the Englishman's in-grained dislike of such arbitrary rule. And soon, with the country embroiled in war with Spain, he needed more money and, like Charles I before him, knew that the only way to raise finance was to call another Parliament.

Remembering his troubles with the previous Parliament, Cromwell and the major-generals tried to ensure that only men who favoured his ideals should stand for election. Despite this more than 100 of the 400 candidates elected were unsympathetic to Cromwell's protectorate policies. By the simple expedient of banning such members from taking their seats, a largely suppor-tive Parliament assembled in September 1656. Unhappy at the mandatory exclusion of so many elected representatives, this Second Protectorate Parliament spent its first week airing its indignation.

Cromwell's overall aims in all his dealings were for 'the healing and settling' of the nation. Because these were unnatural times, following a civil war which had torn the nation apart, such dictatorial policies were probably the only way to achieve any measure of stability. His religious policies too were far-seeing and amazingly tolerant for the times. Providing that a sect was not guilty of blasphemy or of inciting political unrest, Cromwell was happy that the people should worship after the dictates of their own consciences, the only exception being Roman Catholics and High Church men, followers of William Laud. Under his rule the Jews were allowed back into the country in 1656, almost 450 years after their brutal expulsion in 1210 in the reign of Edward I.

Nor was Cromwell over-troubled about the Quakers, even though they were gaining thousands of adherents throughout the country. He had first met George Fox in March 1655, and tended to regard him as 'a character' rather than as a dangerous heretic, even though Fox had announced himself in a letter to Cromwell as one 'whom the world calles George Fox who is the son of God'.[1] But not long after Cromwell's Second Protectorate Parliament had assembled, a matter arose which pushed other complaints and

James Nayler

issues into the background: one of the Quaker leaders, James Nayler, had been found guilty of serious blasphemy.

As he travelled into Bristol on a wet October afternoon in 1656, Nayler had re-enacted the Saviour's triumphal entry into Jerusalem. Oblivious of the drenching rain, his syco-phants had spread garments on the muddy road in front of Nayler's horse crying, 'Holy, holy, holy is the Lord God of Israel.' But there were extenu-ating circumstances for such manifest blasphemy. Nayler, a charismatic figure with an undoubted preaching gift, had gained an enormous following, with many women idolizing him, extolling his virtues and attrib-uting to him a divine status. Worn out mentally and physically by his exertions in London, the Quaker preacher had fallen under the spell of a woman of dominant personality named Martha Sim-monds. It was she and other women who had set up this extra-ordinary scene. Even though George Fox had expressed his disapproval and had distanced himself from his colleague, Nayler was either too weak or too exhausted to rebuke her or to extricate himself from the hysteria surrounding him.

A furore followed. Parliament wanted Nayler to face the death penalty for blasphemy, not only for this incident, but also because letters were found on his person proclaiming him 'the only begot-ten Son of God' and suggesting that his name should be changed to Jesus Nayler. The question of retribution was debated endlessly; all London was agog with curiosity over the outcome. Cromwell, however, was open-minded enough to see that the fellow was deluded, and managed to have the death sentence waived, al-though only by a majority of fourteen votes, with eighty-two voting in favour of it. But the penalty inflicted was cruel enough: boring through Nayler's tongue, branding his forehead with 'B' (for 'blasphemer') and a public whipping in which his back was flogged with 310 lashes, followed by a lengthy imprisonment.

And it was into this background and degree of public aware-ness that John Bunyan published his first book, dealing with the errors of the Quakers. It had scarcely been out a few months before a Quaker representative wrote a scathing reply, attempting to justify their teaching and practice. Edward Burrough, the only son of a wealthy farmer from Underbarrow, near Kendal, had been disinherited and expelled from his home because of his adherence to Quaker teaching. A natural leader and a young man of high intelligence, Burrough quickly rose to prominence in the new movement. He became one of the Valiant Sixty, as the first Quaker missionaries were called, and travelled the country spreading the sect and its concepts. Many of the early Quakers had few educational advantages, so when this broadside from Bunyan was published, Burrough was the obvious one to write an answer.

Still only twenty-three, Burrough called his work *The True Faith of the Gospel of Peace.* In it he had nothing charitable to say about John Bunyan's work, describing it as 'wonderful trash and muddy stuff, unheard of before', and Bunyan himself as 'a liar, slanderer, distorter of scripture, hypocrite...' Not only did he accuse him of mixing 'many lies and slander', he poured disparag-ing and belittling censure on Bunyan's writing. 'Thy Maker will not blame thee,' he says condescendingly, 'for thou hast brought in of thy chiefest substance, though it be but clay and dirt.'[2] Closing his answer, Burrough poses twelve questions for Bunyan, in a mocking imitation of the questions with which Bunyan had ended his treatise.

Not surprisingly, before long we find John Bunyan busy writing again, this time the title being, *A Vindication of Gospel Truths Opened.* Once again he employed the services of John Wright in London to print his work and his Newport Pagnell friend, Matthias Cowley, to distribute it. Even longer than his first treatise, Bunyan's reply takes up the Quaker's arguments one by one, giving robust and scriptural answers.

Still a young Christian, Bunyan was quite able to give as good as he got, and his work is not short of insults and sideswipes against young Burrough. Warming to his theme, he begins:

There is one Edward Burrough that hath ventured to stand up against the truth ... in which book of his there is a very great number of heresies cunningly vented by him and also many things there falsely reported of me.[3]

Among other things Bunyan complained that the Quakers were little different from the Ranters and, as one who had been confused and troubled by Ranter teaching in the past, he points out that he was in a good position to know:

And really I tell thee plainly, that for the generality, the very opinions that are held at this day by the Quakers are the same that were long ago held by the Ranters. Only the Ranters had made them threadbare at an alehouse, and the Quakers have set a new gloss upon them again by an outward legal holiness.[4]

Bunyan was further stung by the comment which Burrough had made implying that he was 'one of those that do preach for hire, through covetousness, making merchandise of souls'. Considering how hard he had to work to support his family, and then to preach and write in the evenings without any financial returns, he could not refrain from an indignant rebuttal:

To defend thyself thou throwest the dirt in my face... Friend, dost thou speak this from thy own knowledge, or did another tell thee so? However, that spirit that led thee out this way is a lying spirit. For though I be poor and of no reputation in the world as to outward things; yet through grace I have learned by the example of the apostle to preach the truth; and also to work with my hands, both for my own living and those that are with me ... and to reject the wages of unrighteousness.[5]

Patiently Bunyan works through Burrough's answer, page by page, detailing with meticulous care every statement that appeared erroneous, answering it by Scripture. Here and there we have flashes of his imagery, as, for example, when he complains that with 'other lame arguments thou tumblest over, like a blind man in a thicket of bushes'.[6] Bunyan poses seven further searching questions for Burrough to answer and then puts twelve other queries into the mouths of his Quaker opponents, which he proceeds to answer one by one.

Because the Quakers were sceptical about the Second Coming of Christ, several of these questions deal with this subject. As we have seen, in common with much Puritan thought at this time, Bunyan believed that the day was imminent and that the traumatic events of the mid-seventeenth century were but a prelude to Christ's appearing in glory. Satan would be bound, and a millennial reign of a thousand years would be ushered in. He warns Burrough:

> O! how suddenly and unexpected of you will the Son of Man break down from heaven, with all his mighty angels in flaming fire and call you to judgment...[7]

Considering Bunyan's background and the fact that he had only been a true believer for about five years, this is a remarkable book. However, as John Brown points out in his *Life of John Bunyan*, had these two protagonists been able to meet face to face and discuss their differences, 'there would probably have been a better understanding and fewer hard words, for they were really not so far apart as they thought'.[8] To anyone who had the discernment to observe it, this first work held promise of Bunyan's unusual gifts and bore all the hallmarks of exceptional future usefulness.

16

Reproaches for Christ's sake

Even though Edward Burrough wrote a further reply to *A Vindication of Gospel Truths Opened*, Bunyan turned aside from controversy for the time being, and declined to continue the argument. His heart was aflame with a desire for the conversion of men and women while opportunity remained, for he was sure that soon the end would come and Christ would return to judge the earth.

Bunyan had several friends who were self-confessed Fifth Monarchists,[1] including John Childe, a fellow member of the Bedford Meeting and one with whom he had worked closely, visiting and encouraging other members.[2] At some point in his life — most probably during the 1650s — it appears that Bunyan too had a considerable measure of sympathy with the Fifth Monarchists in as far as their emphasis was biblically based.[3]

Although he continued at this time to believe that Christ's millennial reign and the 'rule of the saints' was soon to be inaugurated, there was an important difference between Bunyan's position and that of the Fifth Monarchists. In line with Christ's words that no one knows the time of his return, Bunyan refused to put any specific date on this future event. Some Fifth Monarchists, on the other hand, were ready to use force if necessary to establish Christ's kingdom on earth. The chaos of the Civil War, culminating in the execution of Charles I, had, in their view, heralded the end of all earthly monarchy — the next monarch was to be King Jesus, the Son of God from heaven. Bunyan had no sympathy with such views.

When the House of Commons, fearful of renewed civil war in the event of Cromwell's death, offered the latter the crown in February 1657, many in the Bedford area were alarmed. Had not the Civil War been fought and lives sacrificed for 'the good old cause', the expulsion of the Stuart kings and the establishment of a commonwealth? A number joined in a petition called *The Humble and Serious Testimony*, urging Cromwell to reject the proposal. Doubtless this contributed to his eventual decision to establish a second protectorate, giving him overall power with the liberty to nominate his successor, rather than accepting kingship.

Persuaded as he was that Christ would soon return, Bunyan had little time to spare for secondary issues. As a preacher he must bend every nerve to stir up his generation to seek salvation before it was too late:

> My great desire in my fulfilling my ministry was to get into the darkest places of the country, even amongst those people that were farthest off of profession ... because my spirit leaned most after awakening and converting work.[4]

Many were ready to censure John Bunyan, particularly because of the focus of his early ministry on the judgement of God against sin and the fearful results of rejecting his mercy. Much of this indignation came from those who were either incensed at his doctrine, or who challenged the right of any lay, or 'mechanic', preacher to enter a pulpit. Bunyan tells us that

> When I went first to preach the word abroad [i.e. in the area around Bedford], the doctors and priests of the country did open [their mouths] wide against me. But I was persuaded of this, not to render railing for railing but to see how many ... I could convince of their miserable state by the law.[5]

Waiting in the wings were many who wished to silence him. In March 1658 a troubling situation arose while Bunyan was preaching at Eaton Socon, a village lying north-east of Bedford, not far from St Neots. Before Bunyan had finished preaching the local constable burst in demanding John's arrest for illegal preaching. Probably stirred up by the new vicar of the parish church, the constable had no actual right in law for such action, and so, issuing Bunyan with a warrant and ordering him to appear at the next assizes, he could only release him. The troubled church in Bedford gave itself to prayer 'for counsaile what to doe with respect to the indictment against bro. Bunyan for preaching at Eaton'.[6] As nothing more is known about the case, we may assume that the matter was dropped.

Many of the villages around Bedford have their own traditions of Bunyan's visits. Stevington was certainly one that John knew well, and a Baptist church had been established there in 1655. Mention of the fellowship between this church and the Bedford Meeting is found in the Bedford record book early in 1656.[7] Cotton End, a village south of Bedford, the home of his friend George Cokayne, was another place where a small Independent meeting was established, and there was yet another in Gamlingay, to the east of Bedford.

As John Bunyan rode further afield on his various preaching missions, he met with increasing opposition. In the village of Toft, five miles west of Cambridge, another friend, Daniel Angier, born into a family with a tradition of Nonconformity, invited him to come and preach in his barn. Towards the end of the sermon a Cambridge professor of Arabic, a certain Thomas Smith, arrived unexpectedly at the entrance to the barn. 'Who is this tinker, and what right has he to be preaching?' he enquired angrily. But worse was to come. When he heard Bunyan telling his hearers that he feared most of them were unbelievers and bound for hell, he was indignant and perhaps convicted. Smith accosted Bunyan at the end of the service and demanded how he could describe a group of men and women, unknown to him personally and baptized as infants, as unbelievers? He lacked charity, Smith scolded, and was therefore unfit to preach.

Without hesitation Bunyan told Smith that in those terms Christ's ministry too was 'uncharitable', for he often described

religious people as unbelievers. Bunyan also had some provoca-
tive questions for Smith to answer: 'When were you converted,
and what signs of new life accompanied that profession?' To be
shown up by a mere tinker was more than the proud Cambridge
don could bear, and he later published an open letter to the vicar
at Toft, deriding the 'wandering preacher-tinker' and challenging
his right to preach. 'What will be the sad consequences both to
the souls and bodies and estates of you and your children in
following such strangers?' he asked.

Bunyan resolutely refrained from defending himself:

> What shall I say to those that have thus bespattered me?
> Shall I threaten them? Shall I chide them? Shall I flatter them?
> Shall I entreat them to hold their tongues? No, not I! ... It be-
> longs to my Christian profession to be vilified, slandered, re-
> proached and reviled... I rejoice in reproaches for Christ's
> sake.[8]

But help came from an unexpected quarter. Henry Denne,[9]
also a Cambridge man and a leader amongst the early General
Baptists, replied in a long letter addressed to Smith demonstrating
Bunyan's right to preach: 'You seem angry with the tinker because
he strives to mend souls as well as kettles and pans...' he wrote,
and went on to prove that if a man is sent out by his church, as
Bunyan had been, he has every right to preach the gospel.

Sometimes things went the other way, as George Offor relates
in an anecdote he has preserved.[10] In another village, also not far
from Cambridge, a Cambridge scholar noticed the crowds
gathering in the churchyard. He wondered what the attraction
could possibly be. Then he discovered that a tinker was to preach.
Intrigued, he gave a boy twopence to hold his horse, declaring
that 'he was resolved to hear the tinker prate'. Perhaps he had
read Thomas Smith's open letter. But, instead of taking offence,
the man was profoundly affected, converted and became one of
Bunyan's most constant hearers, later becoming the minister of an
Independent church himself.

Bunyan was not slow to recognize that behind the opposition
he encountered was the power of evil. If God purposed to do a
special work among the people, 'there the devil hath begun to

roar in the hearts and by the mouths of his servants'.[11] To Bunyan, therefore, the main agent of opposition was neither priest nor carping critic, but the Evil One himself. If he could not destroy Bunyan by one means, he would try another. The next stratagem he employed was to try to ruin his ministry by tempting him to pride on account of his outstanding gifts. 'I have ... been often tempted to pride and liftings up of heart,' Bunyan confesses, but the strongest antidote he had discovered to this temptation was the continual sight of his depravity of heart by nature:

> It hath been my every day's portion to be let into the evil of my own heart, and still made to see such a multitude of corruptions and infirmities therein.[12]

Words in 1 Corinthians 13 came into his mind:

> What, thought I, shall I be proud because I am a sounding brass? Is it so much to be a fiddle? ... So I concluded a little grace, a little love, a little of the true fear of God, is better than all these gifts... Therefore I came to perceive, that though gifts in themselves were good to the thing for which they are designed ... yet empty and without power to save the soul of him that hath them, if they be alone.[13]

Such thoughts caused John great 'hanging down of the head under all my gifts and attainments'. So having largely failed to destroy Bunyan's ministry through opposition or through tempting him to pride, Satan tried yet another expedient against him — slander:

> But when Satan perceived that his thus tempting and assaulting of me would not answer his design, to wit to overthrow my ministry and make it ineffectual ... then he tried another way, which was to stir up the minds of the ignorant and malicious, to load me with slanders and reproaches... It began therefore to be rumoured up and down among the people that I was a witch, a jesuit, a highwayman and the like. To all which I shall only say, God knows, that I am innocent.[14]

The accusation of witchcraft was one which the Quakers had thrown at him because he believed and taught that the ascended Christ was 'above the clouds and the heavens, now absent from his people in the world, touching his bodily presence'. Such a doctrine was inimical to the Quaker system, with their emphasis on 'a mystical Christ within'. Anne Blackly,[15] the woman who had confronted Bunyan in person on the Bedford streets urging him to 'throw away the Scriptures', had also accusingly shouted out that Bunyan 'preached up an idol and used conjuration and witchcraft'.[16]

As we have seen, throughout this period the dominant theme in Bunyan's preaching concerned the broken law of God and the approaching judgement. This too became the subject of his third book, called *A Few Sighs from Hell*, or *The Groans of a Damned Soul*. Clearly a composite work, this book was drawn from Bunyan's early sermons in line with the description later given by two of his friends, Ebenezer Chandler and John Wilson. Explaining Bunyan's method of writing up his sermons after he had preached, they were to say:

> His wit was sharp and quick, his memory tenacious, it being customary with him to commit his sermons to writing after he had preached them. His understanding was large and comprehensive, his judgment sound and deep in the fundamentals of the gospel as his writings evidence...[17]

A Few Sighs from Hell was an exposition based on the parable of the rich man and Lazarus in Luke 16. An intense, terse piece of writing, packed with warnings of the fearful end of the unbeliever, it reminds us that John himself had not long emerged from under the shackles of a condemning conscience. He still remembered his fears as he identified himself with Esau and felt the flames of hell licking around him. Such memories were imprinted indelibly on his mind, together with God's merciful intervention. As he told his readers:

> When the law curses, when the devil tempts, when hell fire flames in my conscience, my sins with the guilt of them tearing

of me, then is Christ revealed so sweetly to my poor soul through the promises.

Having been delivered from these mental torments himself, he was desperately concerned that his hearers and readers should not experience them in reality. At times he goes beyond the bounds of Scripture in his re-creation of the horrors of death and hell, but the urgency of his message is unmistakable, and was one that stirred many to seek God for mercy before it was too late. Bunyan could personify death and hell with vivid, gripping and frightening effect:

> Mark, death doth not come alone to the ungodly, no, but hell goeth with him. O miserable comforters! O miserable society. Here comes death and hell unto thee. Death goeth into thy body, and separates body and soul asunder; hell stands without, as I may say, to embrace, or rather to crush thy soul between its everlasting grinders.[18]

There is no holding back in his applications regardless of whether they were liable to cause offence:

> O thou that dost spend whole nights in carding and dancing, in rioting and wantonness; thou that countest it a brave thing to swear as fast as the bravest, to spend with the greatest spendthrift in the country; thou that lovest to sin in a corner when nobody sees thee ... thou art an enemy to the things of Christ.[19]

Time after time Bunyan's flaming eloquence breaks through his carefully reasoned argument:

> Dost thou delight in sin against plain commands? THOU ART GONE!
> Dost thou slight and scorn the counsels contained in the Scriptures and continue in so doing? THEN THOU ART GONE!
> Dost thou continually neglect to come to Christ? THEN THOU ART GONE!

As he brought this third book to a close, Bunyan decided to ask his friend John Gibbs to write an introduction. Gibbs, also a Bedford man and only a year older than Bunyan, may have been a childhood acquaintance, but he had trodden a far different path from the younger John. The son of a cooper, a tradesman who made wine casks, he had proceeded to Sydney Sussex College, Cambridge, and immediately after graduating in 1645 had been appointed as vicar of Newport Pagnell. A spiritual young man, he must have been in the pulpit on numerous occasions when Bunyan was forced to attend the services during his army days.

Now in a position to appreciate Gibbs and his courageous stand for truth, Bunyan had established a warm friendship with the Newport Pagnell vicar, and it was to him that he took his book and asked for an introductory recommendation. Gibbs was generous in his appraisal, endorsing Bunyan's emphasis whole-heartedly. Of interest are his comments on John Bunyan himself:

Concerning the author (whatsoever the censures and re-ports of many are) I have this to say, that I verily believe God hath counted him faithful and put him into the ministry [which was no easy thing for a university man to admit].

However, like John Burton before him, Gibbs had a problem and felt he must come to the defence of Bunyan, because of his background and lack of formal education:

Though his outward condition and former employment was mean and his human learning small, yet he is one that hath ac-quaintance with God, and taught by his Spirit, and hath been used in his hand to do souls good for to my knowledge there are divers [i.e. a number] who have felt the power of the word delivered by him, and I doubt not that many more may, if the Lord continue him in his work.

Gibbs goes on to give an ominous warning. Bunyan's ministry might well be short-lived. The very fact of his usefulness and success could bring down a torrent of persecution on the head of the young tinker-preacher. Quite clearly the opposition to Bunyan was increasing in its intensity. Gibbs continues:

I fear this is one reason why the archers have shot so sorely at him; for by his and others' industry in their Master's work, their slothfulness hath been reproved.

Some of John Gibbs' comments sound a little condescending: he refers yet again to Bunyan's 'meanness [i.e. his humble background] and want of human learning', reaffirming that God chooses the foolish things of this world to confound the wise. 'My meaning is, that those that are learned should not despise those that are not...' The important thing, he concludes, is faithfulness in the service of Christ.[20]

Bunyan himself was well aware of the impending storm that could engulf him. Oliver Cromwell, by his resolute lead and firm grip on the nation's affairs, had given a considerable measure of toleration to Dissenters[21] such as Baptists and Independents. If he should die unexpectedly the situation might change rapidly. And there were many ready to swoop down on the bold preacher and silence him for ever. Bunyan had been reading John Foxe's *Book of Martyrs* — a book banned for a time under Archbishop Laud, but now highly popular reading once more. Referring to Edmund Bonner, 'that blood-red persecutor' who had sent so many to a fiery death at the stake under Mary Tudor, Bunyan explains that it was loyalty to the Scriptures that had been the martyrs' great 'offence'.

And John Bunyan well knew that he could be among the first to pay a heavy price for his own staunch belief in those same Scriptures and his fearless declaration of its truths.

17

The gathering storm

On 30 August 1658 a violent storm broke over London, a storm of such magnitude that no one could remember one like it before. As crash after crash of thunder reverberated across the city and lightning split the skies in two, Oliver Cromwell, Lord Protector of England, lay dying.

1658 had been a year of personal distress for Cromwell. In February his youngest daughter's husband had died after only four months of marriage, but the grief that broke Oliver's spirit was the anguish of seeing the intense suffering of his favourite daughter, Elizabeth Claypole, affectionately known as Bettie, as she succumbed to cancer, dying on 6 August. Worn down by long vigils as he spent wakeful nights at the sick woman's bedside, Cromwell himself fell ill with a fever, thought to be an attack of malaria. Soon it became evident that, although only fifty-nine years of age, he too was dying. And at such a critical moment his prayers were for his people, the people of England:

> Lord, though I am but a miserable and wretched creature, I am in covenant with thee through grace. Thou hast made me,

though very unworthy, a mean [i.e. lowly] instrument to do thy people some good, and thee service... Pardon such as desire to trample upon the dust of a poor worm, for they are thy people too. Lord, however thou dispose of me, continue and do good for them. Pardon the folly of this short prayer, even for Jesus Christ's sake, and give us a good night, if it be thy pleasure. Amen.

On 3 September, the anniversary of two of Cromwell's greatest victories in the Civil War, this fiery and godly man was taken from the scenes of earthly strife for ever. But his loss plunged the country into a storm far greater than the one that had alarmed Londoners a few days earlier. He had not finally named his successor, and an envelope which he said contained the name of the man he had chosen could not be found. With the hereditary principle firmly embedded in the nation's psyche, Cromwell's elder son, Richard, was approached to succeed his father, though he was ill-equipped for such a charge.

While the people of England mourned or rejoiced, according to their political stance, over the passing of a great man, there was gladness for another reason in a small cottage in St Cuthbert's Street in Bedford. Mary Bunyan had given birth to her fourth baby, a second son whom they named Thomas. Their blind daughter Mary was now eight, Elizabeth was four and John two years old. But joy at the gift of this child was soon muted as it became evident that his mother was not regaining strength. Whether she fell prey to the dreaded childbirth fever, technically known as puerperal sepsis, a scourge which carried away many young mothers, we cannot know. Alternatively, in her weakened condition she may have succumbed to an infection such as smallpox or typhus fever, diseases which regularly swept through the community.

On the assumption that Mary was around nineteen or twenty when she married John in 1649, she can have been little more than twenty-eight when she died, leaving behind her young husband, scarcely turned thirty. For a man of such an emotional nature and depth of sensitivity, this loss must have been one of unimaginable pain for John Bunyan. In addition to his grief, his predicament was dire. How could he cope with four small children, one blind and another a baby of only a few weeks? And how could he support his family if he were confined to the house? Certainly his preaching would suffer. John draws a veil over his personal sorrow, but it is not hard to imagine how keenly he felt this bereavement. At such a time the closeness and compassion of fellow Christians in the church must have been an immeasurable consolation. It is likely that some of the women took it in turn to care for the bereft family and to nurture the newborn baby.

It may well have been during this period, when he was forced to limit his preaching and when his long treks mending pots and pans at far-flung farms had to be curtailed, that John Bunyan embarked on another book. *The Doctrine of Law and Grace Unfolded* would prove much longer than any he had attempted so far, and was one that marked a further milestone in his spiritual development. As Bunyan 'unfolds' the complex doctrine of the relationship between law and grace, the influence of Martin Luther's teaching in his *Commentary on the Epistle to the Galatians* is immediately evident — teaching which Bunyan had found 'most fit for a wounded conscience'.

Virtually all Bunyan's books were autobiographical to some degree.[1] He had passed through deep waters both before and after his conversion and, out of the profundity of his own experiences as he wrestled his way through the problems of a misguided and confused conscience, he had many things with which to challenge and enrich his readers. *Law and Grace Unfolded* clearly reflects the liberating help Bunyan had received from the great Reformer. As Luther says in his commentary on Galatians:

> It is necessary that men's consciences be diligently instructed, that they may understand the difference between the righteousness of the law and of grace... When you see a [Christian] man terrified and cast down with a sense and feeling of his sin, say unto him, 'Brother, thou placest the law in thy conscience... Awake, arise up, and remember thou must believe in Christ the conqueror of law and sin.'[2]

The basic thrust of Bunyan's entire book is the distinction between law and grace and the believer's relationship to both in terms of the two covenants: the covenant of works (by which he means the Ten Commandments given to the people under Moses), and the covenant of grace — God's dealings with his people in the gospel through Christ. The biblical concept of God being in coven- ant with his people was prominent in seventeenth-century Puritan thought. As we have seen, when Cromwell was dying, the comfort of knowing that he was 'in covenant' with God gave him courage to die well.

The covenant of grace, however, was unlike any covenant made between men in which two sides agree to keep certain conditions. As Bunyan explained, this was a one-sided covenant, in which God undertakes to redeem the sinner through the death and righteousness of Christ, without any prerequisites from the sinner:

> This covenant was not made with another poor Adam, that only stood upon the strength of natural abilities; but this covenant was made with the second Person, with the eternal Word of God, with him that was everyways as holy, as pure, as infinite, as powerful and as everlasting as God.[3]

Urgently he warns, not once but many times over, of the danger of remaining under the covenant of works, a condition which will eventually lead to damnation.

For Bunyan, the law, while remaining a rule of life for the believer, has lost its power to condemn him. Doubtless remember- ing the anguish of his own sufferings before he understood this, he exults in the liberating power of the covenant of grace:

> Here thou mayest hear the biggest thunder crack that the law can give and yet be undaunted. Here thou mayest say, O law! thou mayest roar against sin, but thou canst not reach me; thou mayest curse and condemn, but not my soul, for I have a righteous Jesus, a holy Jesus, a soul-saving Jesus, and he hath delivered me from thy threats, from thy curses, from thy condemnations; I am out of thy reach, out of thy bounds, I am brought into another covenant.[4]

Fearful lest his teaching should smack of antinomianism, giving rise to the concept that a Christian may therefore live as he likes because he is under a covenant of grace, Bunyan turns aside to answer such a 'hell-bred objection', pointing out that even to suggest such a thing is evidence that the one who thinks like that is not a Christian at all.

John Bunyan finds it impossible to write on this theme without constant recourse to his own traumatic experiences and the way of deliverance he had found for a distressed conscience. He deals with the two great fears that had tormented him for so long: the possibility that he had committed the unforgivable sin, and the dreadful thought that he had wilfully rejected the Saviour when he yielded in his mind to the temptation to 'sell Christ'. Whatever sin his readers may have committed, there is infinite value in the blood of Christ, the cost price of that new covenant, to cleanse the conscience of the repentant sinner. And this remains true for the one seeking to live the Christian life, as Bunyan confesses in one of the most moving passages in the whole book:

> Sometimes when my heart hath been hard, dead, slothful, blind and senseless, which indeed are sad frames for a poor Christian to be in, yet at such a time ... hath the blood of Christ, the precious blood of Christ ... so softened, livened, quickened and enlightened my soul, that truly, reader, I can say, O it makes me wonder! Again, when I have been loaden with sin, and pestered with several temptations, and in a very sad manner ... I have found that when tears would not do, prayers would not do, repentings and all other things could not reach my heart; O then! one touch, one drop, one shining of the virtue of that blood ... hath in a very blessed manner delivered me, that it makes me to marvel. O! methinks it hath come with such life, such power, with such irresistible and mar-vellous glory, that it wipes off all the slurs, silences all the out-cries, and quenches all the fiery darts and all the flames of hell fire, that are begotten by the charges of the law, Satan and doubtful remembrances of my sinful life.[5]

Not only is the believer freed from the condemnation of the law, but the devil himself can be outflanked in his attacks. In *Law and Grace Unfolded* Bunyan continues to develop a dialogue style of question and answer as he tries to come alongside the beleaguered Christian who struggles with Satan's suggestions:

Didst thou never learn for to outshoot the devil in his own
bow, and to cut off his head with his own sword, as David
served Goliath?
Quest. O how should a poor soul do this? This is rare indeed.
Answ. Why, truly thus — Doth Satan tell thee thou prayest
but faintly, and with very cold devotion? Answer him thus, and
say, I am glad you told me, for this will make me trust the more
to Christ's prayers and less to my own... And seeing thou
tellest me that I run so softly, that I shall go near to miss of
glory, this shall also be through grace to my advantage, and
cause me to press the more earnestly towards the mark for the
prize of the high calling of God in Christ Jesus.[6]

Despite the strong assurance of faith which this work demonstrates, Bunyan still felt much in need of the prayers of his readers;
bereaved and vulnerable to the assaults of those who hated his
message, he begs their intercession on his behalf:

Christian, pray for me to our God with much earnestness
[and] fervency ... because I do very much stand in need
thereof; for my work is great, my heart is vile, the devil lieth at
watch, the world would fain be saying Aha, aha, thus we would
have it... Keep myself, I cannot, trust myself, I dare not.[7]

Still deeply aware of his own inadequacy and lack of theological
training and educational advantages, Bunyan prefaces his work in
somewhat defensive terms:

Reader, if thou do find this book empty of ... scholarlike
terms, thou must understand it is because I never went to
school, to Aristotle or Plato, but was brought up at my father's house in a very mean condition, among a company of
poor countrymen.[8]

Like *A Few Sighs from Hell*, this second doctrinal book was
clearly a composite work, culled from Bunyan's more recent
preaching. If *Sighs from Hell* sums up his preaching during 1656–
1657, those first two years which he had spent 'crying out against
men's sins, and their fearful state because of them', then we may

safely say that *Law and Grace Unfolded* represents his preaching during 1658–1659, when he tells us that his emphasis changed, as he 'did much labour to hold forth Jesus Christ in all his offices, relations and benefits unto the world'. By any standard, this is an astonishing piece of work, showing a mastery of doctrine coupled with the passion of a preacher, especially considering that Bunyan himself had only known real assurance of faith for little more than three years. His publisher for this work was 'M. Wright', whose premises were at 'The Sign of the King's Head' in the Old Bailey, and who was probably a relative of John Wright, whose services Bunyan had previously used.

Although Bunyan was busy writing this important thesis, caring for his young family and earning what money he could for their support, he would also have been aware of the crucial changes taking place in the country — changes which would inevitably have serious repercussions for the small community of Christians in the Bedford church. Time and again we read of special gather-ings of the church for prayer, and in August 1659 'it was ordered that the last day of this moneth should be first spent in solemne seeking God for the nation'.[9]

And the nation was certainly in a parlous condition. Following his father's death, Richard Cromwell had somewhat reluctantly accepted the responsibilities of the Protectorate. A country-loving gentleman, he was not cut out for the rough and tumble of political life. By force of character Oliver had kept conflicting elements in the army and Parliament in check. But his son was a very different personality. Calling new elections in January 1659, Richard made an initial effort to resolve the tensions, but the army chiefs soon gained the upper hand and by April the inex-perienced Protector, known in mockery as 'Tumbledown Dick', was forced to dissolve his Parliament. Loud cries arose from all sides demanding the recall of the Rump Parliament, the name by which the remnant of the Long Parliament, first elected in 1640, had been known. Richard complied, but when the Rump, which his father had dismissed in 1653, reassembled on 7 May 1659, it voted to abolish the Protectorate. Richard resigned from office three weeks later on 24 May, plunging the country once again into uncertainty and chaos.

Even though the army had facilitated the recall of the Rump Parliament, its own aims and priorities were far different from those of the Rump. Reflecting the influence of Oliver Cromwell, the army favoured religious toleration, but many of those now restored to Parliamentary positions in the Rump wished for much tighter controls on the Dissenters, or 'sectaries', whom they viewed as potential troublemakers. Power must pass from the military to the civil government, Parliament insisted. Many in the army, on the other hand, who had fought for the abolition of monarchy and the establishment of a republic, now felt that their sacrifice had been in vain. The country was fast slipping into anarchy.

Then in October 1659 the Rump Parliament went one step too far in its attempt to reduce the power of the army. It ordered the dismissal of nine leading officers, including Major-General Charles Fleetwood, Oliver Cromwell's son-in-law, and hero of several important Civil War battles. Irate, the army marched on London and soon had the Parliament buildings at Westminster surrounded. For the second time the Rump Parliament was forcibly dismissed, and there was little it could do to prevent it. The country was now effectively without any government at all, apart from a Committee of Safety, established by the army as an interim measure. Civil war once more loomed on the horizon.

As John Bunyan surveyed the chaotic political scene and the ever-growing possibility of persecution for any who dissented from the Church of England, he was deeply concerned for his motherless family. What would happen if he should be arrested and thrown into prison? There seemed only one solution: he must remarry. Encouraged by the church, John proposed to a woman by the name of Elizabeth. Little is known of her apart from the fact that she was only young. There were several 'Elizabeth's on the membership roll of the church at this time. Perhaps she was Elizabeth Cooper, or maybe Elizabeth Burntwood — but of one thing we are certain: here was a young woman of outstanding courage and faith. To take on a man like John Bunyan and his four children was also to share his sufferings, but Elizabeth rose to the challenge. It is likely that the marriage took place towards the end of 1659, almost a year after Mary Bunyan's death.

With his family once more under the care of a loving and capable woman, John Bunyan was free to accept preaching engagements further afield. A number of north Bedfordshire towns were among those he visited towards the end of 1659. Sensing that his time might be short before his opponents succeeded in silencing him, Bunyan seized every possible opportunity to bring the message of the gospel to the people. Pertenhall and Keysoe were both places that he knew well, but the best recorded visit is the one he made to Yelden (now Yielden) on Christmas Day in 1659.

William Dell

At Yielden his friend William Dell was the rector, holding this position as well as that of Master of Gonville and Caius College in Cambridge. A fiery man with deep convictions, Dell had been a soldier-chaplain in Cromwell's New Model Army. A strong tradition exists that he came to Newport Pagnell during Bunyan's army days and was one who preached at the conventicles so despised by Sir Samuel Luke, under whom Bunyan served. Dell had a marked influence on Bunyan during the formative years of his Christian life. His passionate preaching and strong emphasis on the work of the Holy Spirit would have appealed to Bunyan. 'Without the power of the Spirit the ministry is barren [but] all Christians armed with this power walk as angels among men,'[10] he declared. His biographer sums up the dominant theme of Dell's preaching as an emphasis on 'the direct, urgent, exclusive and comprehensive bond between the individual Christian and his Creator through the medium of the Holy Spirit'.[11]

Born in 1606, Dell was more than twenty years Bunyan's senior and now, at the age of fifty-three, was nearing the end of his ministry. But he was not popular with his parishioners at

Yielden. In fact resentment had been building up against their rector for some time. Why didn't he celebrate services of Holy Communion among them? Why had he stopped singing psalms, or reading the Scriptures on Sundays? Rumour had it that he had even been cutting down trees growing in the parsonage grounds. Worst of all, they complained, some had heard him say that he 'had rather hear a plain countryman speak in the church, that came from the plough, than the best orthodox [ordained] minister in the county'.

The pulpit at Yielden parish church

Then, on Christmas Day, a day his parishioners regarded with particular veneration, who should climb the steep steps into the pulpit but a mere tinker — one called John Bunyan from Bedford? This was one insult too many for the disgruntled people of Yielden, and before long they had composed a letter written to the recently reinstated House of Lords, setting out their multiple complaints. Dated 20 June 1660, the letter censured their minister, William Dell, on numerous counts. Among them was the affront they had endured when 'upon Christmas day last one Bunyan, a tinker, was countenanced and suffered to speak in the pulpit to the congregation, and no orthodox minister did officiate in the church that day'. William Dell, whose reasons for withholding the sacraments from the people were in all likelihood due to their lack of spirituality, was unrepentant, but he knew that his days among them were numbered.

And John Bunyan too was well aware that a storm might soon break over his own head. How long he could continue preaching he did not know.

18

'One here will constant be'

Samuel Pepys, renowned diarist of the seventeenth century, was still on board the *Naseby* as he sat writing up his diary for 25 May 1660. The *Naseby*, flagship of the former Protector Oliver Cromwell and named to commemorate Parliament's important victory over the Royalists in 1645, had been hastily redecorated to remove all evidences of its past usage. For none other than Charles, son of the beheaded Stuart monarch, was on board, returning to England from Holland by popular demand of the people.

Pepys had been one of the party sent from England to escort Charles back to the country. He recorded that

> The King ... was received by Generall Monke with all imaginable love and respect at his entrance upon the land at Dover. Infinite the Croud of people and the gallantry of the Horsmen, Citizens, and Noblemen of all sortss.

As the Mayor of Dover presented the thirty-year-old son of Charles I with a Bible, the new king declared solemnly that he loved this book 'above all things in the world'. It seemed a good beginning.

Events had moved fast in the opening months of 1660. As England spiralled into chaos and the prospect of renewed civil war with the collapse of the Protectorate, General Monck, a natural Royalist, but one who had served Cromwell as commander-in-chief in Scotland, began his march south on 1 January with an army at his back. Perhaps the only one who could command any certain following, he soon discovered a widespread support for the restoration of monarchy. Wherever he went he found the people fearful and longing for nothing more than stability, even if it meant a return of the Stuarts. 'I am engaged,' declared Monck, 'to see my country freed from that intolerable slavery of government by the sword.'

Monck fulfilled his mission as he oversaw the final dissolution of the Rump Parliament and the setting up of the Convention Parliament. Assembling in April 1660, it was largely Royalist and Presbyterian in its make-up. Meanwhile Charles, who had been living in France, was asked to move to Holland so that the people would not suspect that he had Roman Catholic sympathies. Together with three close advisers, Charles drew up what has become known as the *Declaration of Breda,* named after the Netherlands town where he was living. In it he set out his terms for accepting the crown of England, but it appears that no conditions were laid down for him to fulfil before he would be welcomed as king. However, he undertook to grant a 'free and general pardon' to any old enemies as long as they would recognize him as king. The only exception would be in the case of the 'regicides', those men who had actually signed the death warrant for his father, Charles I. Above all, and most importantly for John Bunyan, together with all those Nonconformists and Dissenters who were anxiously following the swiftly developing events, he promised 'liberty for tender consciences' over matters of religion. In addition he promised to settle army pay arrears for the soldiers in the service of General Monck.

Not only did the Convention Parliament restore the status of the Church of England as the national church, it also reinstated the office of bishop which had been in abeyance since 1644. No longer must 'mechanics' or laymen like Bunyan occupy the pulpits. The *Book of Common Prayer*, replaced in 1645 by the *Directory for Public Worship*, was reintroduced; bishops and clergy who had been excluded from their former churches flocked back to take up their positions again. The new Bishop of Lincoln, Robert Sanderson, appointed in October 1660, paraded through the streets of Bedford with almost royal style.

The Bedford Meeting to which Bunyan belonged quickly felt the impact of such changes. By June 1660, scarcely a month after Charles had arrived back on English shores, the group was turned out of St John's, the parish church where it had been meeting for the last seven years. The previous rector, Theodore Crowley, dismissed from the living in 1653 because of his opposition to Puritanism, came back to claim it. A comment in the church minute book tells of the commission given to three of their men:

> ... to take care to informe themselves of a convenient place for our meeting, so soone as they can (we being now deprived of our former place) and reporte it to the Church.[1]

Nor was this their only problem. For now the church was leaderless once more, as their pastor, John Burton, had died that same month, June 1660. He had been ailing for some time, and here and there the church minutes refer to attempts made by the members to relieve him of some of the burden of pastoral care and regular preaching.

John Bunyan was well aware of the ever-increasing dangers that surrounded him as he set out on his preaching engagements. His enemies were ready to pounce, and he knew it, although no law had as yet been passed forbidding private gatherings for spiritual worship. However, Parliament was jumpy and apprehensive, for many were deeply angry over the recall of Charles. What about all the blood that had been shed to rid the country of the Stuarts? What about the religious persecution under Archbishop Laud? What of the poverty that had stalked the land after the war and all the unfair taxation that had burdened the people? Little wonder then that many in authority feared private meetings, or conventicles, as they were called, in case they should be seedbeds of revolution.

The minute book of the Bedford Meeting reflects the growing concerns of Independents at this time. Some faint-hearted and fearful members were absenting themselves from the services in case they should be courting trouble. We read that:

> Some of our brethren and sisters have neglected to come to our church meetings, and their withdrawing giveth a very ill example to others...[2]

Other members were asked to visit such people to exhort and encourage them. Meanwhile the Bedford Meeting sought a closer co-operation with other likeminded churches in order that they might all stand together in the midst of adversity. Regular days of prayer were set aside to seek God's face in these uncertain times. Bunyan's friend, William Dell, the rector of Yielden, resigned his position at Gonville and Caius College, knowing full well that it was only a matter of time before he would be cast out of Yielden as well.

When John Bunyan set out for Lower Samsell, near Harlington, some twelve miles south of Bedford, on 12 November 1660, he knew that he was under surveillance. It must have been with a heavy heart that he said an affectionate goodbye to Elizabeth and the children. Would he come home safely? He did not know. Each time he ventured out to preach he took a serious risk. Silently his 'congregation' slipped across the fields to the isolated farmstead, crossed the narrow drawbridge over the moat surrounding the farm and disappeared inside the building. As John Bunyan stabled his horse and entered, the farmer took him aside and whispered urgently in his ear, telling him of some rumours he had heard. A warrant had been issued for his arrest. Surely it would be better to disband the meeting and play safe.

Not only had the local magistrate Francis Wingate issued such a warrant, but he had also ordered that a close watch be kept on the property, 'as if we that were to meet together in that place did intend to do some fearful business, to the destruction of the country', as Bunyan later commented.[3] Possibly knowing more than Bunyan did about Wingate's unsavoury character and his determination to bully Dissenters into submission, the farmer was seriously alarmed both for the preacher and the people. But Bunyan was resolute:

> No [he replied] I will not stir, neither will I have the meeting dismissed for this. Come, be of good cheer, let us not be daunted; our cause is good, we need not be ashamed of it; to preach God's word is so good a work that we shall be well rewarded if we suffer for that.[4]

Clearly the farmer's apprehension was felt by all present. Perhaps he ought to reconsider his decision, thought Bunyan. At last he agreed to step outside and give the matter more consideration and prayer. Maybe the thought of Elizabeth and the children flashed across his mind. Elizabeth was pregnant with her first child. Nor had she much longer to wait. How she needed him at such a time! Could she possibly cope with five young children all under the age of ten if he were imprisoned? But, on the other hand, what damage it would do to the gospel cause for which he stood if he should weaken! Gradually, as he paced among the elm trees surrounding the farm, a quiet determination gripped him. Perhaps some words of Nehemiah rang in his mind: 'Should such a man as I flee?'[5] Or, as Bunyan put it:

> I walked into the close where ... this came into my mind, That I had showed myself hearty and courageous in my preaching, and had, blessed be grace, made it my business to encourage others; therefore, thought I, if I should now run and make an escape, it will be of very ill savour in the country. For what will my weak and newly converted brethren think of it, but that I was not so strong in deed as I was in word.[6]

No, he must stand firm, come what may. His example was all-important. If he should run to avoid a warrant, others might fear to stand under lesser threats. Then what would happen to the cause of truth? As he wrote later:

> Would it not be amazing should you see a man encompassed with chariots and horses and weapons for his defence, yet afraid of being sparrow-blasted or overrun by a grasshopper?[7]

If he should weaken, opponents would take the opportunity to mock the gospel, and with it the truths that he had preached — and that, he determined, must never be.

Returning to the house, Bunyan opened the meeting. We can well imagine with what earnestness he prayed for strength to endure the trials that might come. He had not been speaking for long before a rude hammering at the door alerted the worshippers to the fact that their worst fears had indeed been realized. The local constable, together with Wingate's representative, burst in demanding the immediate arrest of John Bunyan. Although instructed to accompany them without delay, John Bunyan was in no hurry. First, he insisted, he must address his distressed hearers. This suffering was in a good cause, he assured them, adding:

> We might have been apprehended as thieves and murderers ... but blessed be God it was not so, but we suffer as Christians for well doing: and we had better be the persecuted than the persecutors.[8]

Scarcely able to contain their impatience, the constable and Wingate's man kept interrupting while Bunyan tried to comfort those meeting with him. At last they moved off into the darkness of the November night, with Bunyan between them, but not to the home of Francis Wingate in Harlington. Apparently he was away for the night. It therefore fell to the constable either to guard Bunyan himself all night (because, as Bunyan commented sardonically, 'my crime was so great'), or to obtain the services of one who would stand surety for him until the morning. A friend was only too glad to help, and at least Bunyan would have the comfort of a bed to sleep in that night. Doubtless someone else hurried to Bedford to bring Elizabeth the grievous news that John was under arrest.

Faithful to his trust, Bunyan's friend conducted him to the constable's house in the morning, and from there they proceeded to Harlington, little more than a mile distant. Harlington Manor, still standing at the crossroads, and not far from the parish church, has largely been rebuilt since Bunyan's day and is now a private residence.

Bunyan continues talking while the constable is at the door

After waiting for some time, Bunyan was conducted into the 'great parlour' where Francis Wingate was seated behind a table. Also born in 1628, only a few weeks before Bunyan, Wingate eyed the young preacher carefully before questioning him. Appointed as a Justice of the Peace, with a brief to keep the peace in his area, Wingate acted as judge and jury in one. He was a convinced Royalist and his family had suffered some loss of property in the Civil War. Certainly he had no love for Puritans, least of all for John Bunyan, whom he had long regarded as a troublemaker, particularly on his preaching visits to Lower Samsell, an area which fell within Wingate's jurisdiction.

But first Wingate had to ask a few questions of the constable who had arrested Bunyan. Strongly suspecting that Bunyan and those with him at the farm were up to no good, perhaps even planning some sort of insurrection to overthrow the new and still vulnerable regime, he fired his questions like bullets. How many were there? What were they doing? What did they have with them? Perhaps these men were armed — who could tell? 'I trow,' recorded Bunyan, 'he meant whether we had armour or not.' But he was sorely disappointed. Far from uncovering some anti-government plot, the constable admitted that he had found only a few men and women gathered together to attend the preaching of God's word.

Abashed, Francis Wingate scarcely knew how to proceed. He had ordered the arrest of this man, but what accusations could he level at him? Swiftly changing course, he began questioning Bunyan about an issue where the young tinker-preacher was indeed vulnerable. 'What were you doing there,' he demanded, 'and why can you not be contented with following your proper calling? Do you not know that it is against the law for such as you to be preaching?'

Not to be beaten, Bunyan countered firmly:

> The intent of my coming thither [to Lower Samsell] and to other places was to instruct and counsel people to forsake their sins, and close in with Christ, lest they perish miserably.

And that, he maintained, he could do without any difficulty and still fulfil his normal occupation at the same time. Wingate coloured up with rage. Bunyan had touched on the very issue that maddened him. 'I will break the neck of your meetings,' he threatened angrily. 'It might be so,' was Bunyan's simple reply.

Without further ado, Wingate ordered Bunyan to arrange for men who would stand surety for him; otherwise he must go straight to prison. Although Bunyan had friends ready to support him, Wingate stipulated that they must bind themselves to prevent Bunyan from preaching. It was useless. With great courage and dignity, Bunyan released his friends from any such commitment declaring that nothing would stop him preaching:

> I should not leave speaking the Word of God [he insisted], even to counsel, comfort, exhort and teach the people among whom I came, and I thought this to be a work that had no hurt in it; but was rather worthy of commendation than blame.[9]

Infuriated at the calm boldness of the man in front of him, Wingate announced harshly that a mittimus, or legal warrant, was to be prepared immediately, committing Bunyan to the County Jail. Here he would remain until the next quarter-sessions when cases came up for trial before the circuit magistrates.

Bunyan had deliberately chosen a path of obedience to God, cost what it might in earthly terms. It was even as he would later write:

> Who would true valour see
> let him come hither.
> One here will constant be
> come wind, come weather.

19

By the light of a candle

Harlington parish church of St Mary the Virgin, built in the thirteenth century, was no more than a minute's walk from Harlington Manor. Nearby stood the vicarage, home of Dr Lindall, who had served as vicar in the village for seventeen years. He kept a close watch on all the activities in the community; if anything unusual was afoot at the Manor House, Dr Lindall was sure to hear about it. In addition, he was actually the stepfather of Francis Wingate's wife, Lettice. So for him to arrive on the scene where Bunyan was being interrogated was not surprising. He had probably been glad to hear of the arrest of that tinker who went about preaching in his and other men's parishes, and who was nothing but a worthless nuisance in his eyes.

As John Bunyan stood waiting for the mittimus, or warrant for his imprisonment, to be drawn up, Dr Lindall entered the parlour. Bunyan recognized him instantly:

> Now while my mittimus was making ... in comes an old enemy to the truth, Dr Lindale, who, when he was come in fell to taunting at me with many reviling terms.[1]

Harlington parish church

Undoubtedly Bunyan had had previous experience of this man. Perhaps he was among those whom he had in mind when he wrote:

> When I first went to preach the word abroad, the doctors and priests of the country did open wide against me. But I was persuaded of this, not to render railing for railing.[2]

Ignoring the insults, Bunyan merely replied that his business was with the magistrate, not with the vicar. When Lindall found that he could not provoke Bunyan into an argument, he began to heap further abuse on the prisoner, jeering at his predicament. What right had a tinker to be preaching, anyway?

Although Bunyan did not return 'railing for railing', even at such a moment of crisis, this censure was too much for him. Quoting from 1 Peter 4:10-11, he roundly pointed out that the apostle Peter insisted that any whom God had gifted to preach had a responsibility to do it to the glory of God.[3]

Probably it was unwise to engage in debate with the vicar, for immediately Lindall had a further double-edged jibe to level at Bunyan. 'Oh,' said he, 'I do remember that I have read of one, Alexander, a coppersmith, who did much oppose and disturb the apostles.'

The sneer was not lost on Bunyan. Clearly the reference to a coppersmith was aimed at him because he was a tinker by trade. Without a moment's hesitation he had his answer ready: 'I also have read of very many priests and pharisees that had their hands in the blood of the Lord Jesus Christ.'

The best reply that Lindall could think of was that Bunyan was the Pharisee, for, like them, 'he prayed long prayers and de-voured widows' houses'. Stung by an accusation implying that he was making money out of religion, Bunyan could not refrain from one further retort based on Lindall's own obvious wealth. At the same time he also remembered a saying in the book of Proverbs, 'Answer not a fool according to his folly' (Proverbs 26:4), and so said no more.

Doubtless Bunyan felt a measure of relief when Wingate reappeared with the warrant in his hand. Stating that the accused 'went about to several conventicles in the country to the great disparagement of the Church of England', the mittimus ordered that he must remain in prison unless he could find sureties who would stand bail for him until the next assizes, when his case would be heard by the county magistrates.

At last the end of this grievous day was approaching. But Bunyan and the constable had no sooner left the Manor House to begin the long walk to Bedford Jail before two of Bunyan's friends came hurrying up, begging the constable to wait. Deeply troubled that a man like Bunyan should be thrown into prison, these men had been taking advice, probably from a lawyer,[4] to see if anything could be done to secure the preacher's release. And now they urgently begged for an opportunity to speak to the magistrate.

Full of hope, his friends hurried in to where Francis Wingate still remained seated in order to press their case. The short November day was drawing to a close and darkness now enveloped the scene as Bunyan wearily followed them back to the house. Doubtful that any expedient could prevail, he felt that he must at least attempt to co-operate with such well-intentioned friends. But at the same time he tells us that:

> I lifted up my heart to God for light and strength to be kept, that I might not do anything that might either dishonour him or wrong my own soul or be a grief or discouragement to any that was inclining after the Lord Jesus Christ.[5]

Before long his friends were back, bright with optimism. Bunyan listened while they explained that they had been advised that all he had to do was to say 'certain words' and he could be set free. Realizing their kindly motives, Bunyan could only ask, 'What words are these?' but added that if the words were 'such that might be said with a good conscience' he would say them; otherwise he would not.

Then Bunyan noticed another door gradually opening. Someone was entering the room with a lighted candle in one hand. As the newcomer was standing in the shadows, Bunyan may not have recognized him immediately, but as the uplifted candle cast its flickering light across the man's face, he knew who it was — none other than a lawyer by the name of William Foster, one who 'had ever been a close opposer of the ways of God'.

'Who is there? John Bunyan?' cried the stranger in mock surprise. Placing his candle on a table, Foster hurried towards the prisoner, arms stretched out as though to embrace him like a long-lost friend. Bunyan records that it seemed 'as if he would have leaped on my neck and kissed me'. Such a show of unexpected affection did not fool Bunyan. 'Beware of men', he thought, recollecting the Saviour's words, and later another verse flashed through his mind: 'Their tongues are smoother than oil. But their words are drawn swords.'[6]

'Blessed be God, I am well,' answered John cautiously in response to Foster's exuberant greeting.

'What is the occasion of your being here?' asked Foster, already knowing the answer full well.

'I was at a meeting of people a little way off, intending to speak a word of exhortation to them, but the Justice, hearing thereof was pleased to send his warrant to fetch me here before him,' replied Bunyan.

'So I understand,' Foster answered. Then, clearly being privy to the 'certain words' that Bunyan must speak to secure his liberty, he continued: 'If you will promise to call people no more together, you shall have your liberty to go home, for my brother[7] is very loath to send you to prison, if you will be but ruled.'

'What do you mean by "not calling the people together"?' Bunyan enquired, explaining that his only purpose at any gathering of people was to 'exhort and counsel them to seek after the Lord Jesus Christ for the salvation of their souls'.

'Only say that you will not call people together,' Foster insisted.

Bunyan was astute enough to know that this was nothing but a trap to stop him from preaching. Realizing that the tinker was not going to be so easily hoodwinked, Foster came directly to the point. Preaching, he growled, was none of Bunyan's business. All he must do was to leave off his preaching and to follow his normal vocation.

But Bunyan was immovable. 'I can follow my calling and preach the Word,' he retorted, 'and it is my duty to do them both as long as I have opportunity.'

At this point all Foster's assumed pleasantries evaporated and, like Dr Lindall, he too became abusive, accusing Bunyan of being exactly like the 'papists'. Back and forth went the arguments, as Bunyan had an answer for everything that Foster could throw at him. At last Foster came full circle back to the 'words' Bunyan must say in order to be released. If only he would promise never to gather a congregation he would be free. 'But,' protested Bunyan, 'if people choose to come together when I speak, I cannot be held responsible for that.' Certainly he could make no such commitment.

An early picture of Harlington Manor

At last he told Foster, 'I dare say no more than I have said, for I dare not leave off that work to which God has called me.'

Outflanked by a mere tinker, Foster picked up his candle and left the room, clearly intending to advise Wingate on how he should proceed in this case. Alone in the dark, Bunyan foresaw the outcome exactly. And as he anticipated, Foster advised that the only course was to send the obstinate tinker to prison, because it was obvious that he would not see reason. As Bunyan records, 'The man that did at the first express so much love to me, told the Justice that he must send me away to prison.'

It was now too late to walk the thirteen miles from Harlington to Bedford, and a strong tradition remains that he was ushered into an attic room in the Manor House to spend the night. Alternatively, he may have returned to the home of the friend who had stood surety for him the previous night. Whichever was the case, it is not hard to imagine the thoughts that raced through his mind during the long dark hours. How could he face the coming weeks of confinement? How could he provide for his family? Somehow he must prepare his spirit for whatever eventuality might transpire. Perhaps the only way was to anticipate the very worst situation possible — even the imposition of the death sentence — so that no degree of suffering could find him unprepared. As he later wrote:

> Thus I reasoned with myself: if I provide only for a prison, then the whip comes at unawares; and so does also the pillory; again, if I provide only for these, then I am not fit for banishment; further, if I conclude that banishment is the worst, then if death come I am surprised.[8]

Whatever the thoughts that crowded Bunyan's mind that night, as morning broke, he must prepare for the long walk to Bedford Jail and an unknown future. But by this time God had given his faithful servant so marked a degree of inward peace that he could hardly stop himself from telling his scheming adversaries about it. As he later wrote, 'I carried the peace of God along with me ... and, blessed be the Lord, went away to prison with God's comfort in my poor soul.'[9]

Bunyan still had much to occupy his thoughts as he tramped along the muddy roads with the constable at his side. Through Flitwick, past Ampthill, Houghton Conquest and on through Elstow they went, places familiar to Bunyan both because of his work and from his childhood haunts. He must have wondered time and again about Elizabeth and the children. He had been away from home for two nights. Did Elizabeth know where he was? She was so young. How were these things affecting her? With her baby so nearly due, John longed to go to her. In spite of his sense of peace, he still had many fears:

> Before I came to prison I saw what was a-coming, and had especially two considerations warm upon my heart; the first was how to be able to endure should my imprisonment be long and tedious; the second was how to be able to encounter death, should that be here my portion.

Such thinking was not new to him. For almost a year he had anticipated this eventuality as he had seen the mounting opposition to his preaching. Several verses of Scripture had been of special consolation and had prepared him for the suffering that might lie ahead. One above others was 'of great use'. The apostle Paul says, 'We had the sentence of death in ourselves that we should not trust in ourselves, but in God which raiseth the dead' (2 Corinthians 1:9). Yes, Bunyan knew that he too must place all that he held dear under a 'sentence of death', for, as he expressed it:

> If ever I would suffer rightly I must first pass a sentence of death upon everything that can properly be called a thing of this life, even to reckon myself, my wife, my children, my health, my enjoyments, and all as dead to me and myself as dead to them. The second was to live upon God that is invisible.[10]

We may wonder whether John had read Miles Coverdale's 1539 translation of Martin Luther's great hymn, *Ein Feste Burg*, beginning *'Oure God is a defence and towre'*. Certainly, as we have seen, Bunyan esteemed the great Reformer's writings highly. Whether he had done so or not, the words quoted above surely echo that same courageous spirit which characterized Luther. As Thomas Carlyle would later render them:

> And though they take our life,
> goods, honour, children, wife,
> yet is their profit small:
> these things shall vanish all;
> the city of God remaineth.

And so, reaching their destination, Bunyan and the constable crossed over Bedford Bridge, walked though the streets of the town and came to a halt in front of the County Jail on the corner of present-day Silver Street.[11]

20

A prisoner of conscience

Bedford County Jail stood grim and forbidding on that bleak November morning in 1660. All that now remains of the old prison, demolished in 1802, are two of its gates that once opened onto the street.[1] Constructed of oak and heavily studded, both have bars across a central aperture or grate. Here prisoners would stand and beg for gifts of food or money from passers-by, or they might attempt to sell products they had made in the prison in order to support their families.

Calling for the jailer, the constable explained the reason for the new prisoner's arrest and handed over the warrant signed by Francis Wingate. Before many moments had passed, John Bunyan was thrust into the prison, the ominous-looking gate closing behind him with a resounding thud.

Although no pictures have survived of the former County Jail, John Howard (1726–1790), a notable eighteenth-century prison reformer who was also from Bedford, has left a description of it in his monumental work, *The State of the Prisons in England and Wales*.[2] Writing over a century after Bunyan's imprisonment, he describes the two-storeyed building and its dungeons below street

County Jail gate, Moot Hall
museum, Elstow

level. On the ground floor were two day rooms, each about eight feet square, one for men and the other for women. These were set aside for criminals: murderers, thieves, pickpockets, cheats and others guilty of various acts of felony. The rooms were small, for most inmates were only short-stay prisoners, soon being led away to be hung. Opening off the day rooms were two cells, called lodging rooms, one each for men and women, where prisoners slept at night, often in chains. Down eleven slippery steps were the dungeons, reserved for any prisoner who had proved awkward in some way. One had a small skylight, but both were dark, dank and airless — terrible places where men were often left to die.

On the upper floor was the debtors' day room, larger than the felons' quarters, and one which sometimes doubled as a chapel. Leading off from this were four lodging rooms for sleeping quarters. Nothing but straw was supplied for prisoners to lie on at night, and this had to be paid for by the prisoner.[3] If he were too poor to buy straw, mere rags might do for bedding, or alternatively, scraps of straw left over from men and women already executed. No form of heating was provided and when temperatures dropped dramatically during the winter months many prisoners would contract a serious disease and die.

To this upper floor the new prisoner was now escorted. Furnishings were scant, and Bunyan's companions were among

ON THIS SITE STOOD
THE
BEDFORD COUNTY GAOL
WHERE
JOHN BUNYAN
WAS IMPRISONED FOR
TWELVE YEARS
1660 – 1672

Stone slab marking the site of the prison

the poorest in the community, thrown into prison because of unpaid debts. Some indeed were rascals, penniless because of their own misconduct, but most were those whose lot in life had brought them and their families to the brink of starvation. Conditions for debtors could be appalling. Describing them a hundred years later, John Howard writes of men and women 'expiring on the floors in loathsome cells, sometimes in two or three inches of effluence'. We cannot imagine Bunyan's circumstances to have been much better, although it is known that his first jailer was more humane than most.

Bunyan's prison plate
*Reproduced by kind permission of
Bunyan Meeting Free Church,
Bedford, England*

Prisoners were expected to pay the jailer for their rations of food, or else they must rely on gifts brought to the jail by family members or friends. Lack of food brings out the worst in people, and when the jailer distributed the 'pennyworth of bread' or 'the two quarter loaves a week' allocated to each prisoner, the sick and friendless could easily find themselves deprived by others of their rightful share. Water too was strictly rationed, with only a couple of pints being allowed each day, not just for drinking, but for all other purposes as well. Bunyan's later comment on the state of things in the prison gives a graphic picture:

> The jail that thou seest with thine eye, and the felons that look out at the grate, they put thee in mind of the prison of hell, and of the dreadful state of those that are there.[4]

However, John Bunyan was more favoured than many prisoners, having a family who loved him. Members of the church were also anxious to help him, being deeply grieved that he should be incarcerated in this way — a portent of future suffering for Dissenters. But the first to visit him in prison brought troubling news. His wife, Elizabeth, shocked and dismayed at her husband's imprisonment, had gone into premature labour, and her progress was not encouraging. On the brighter side, Bunyan learnt that his friends were doing their utmost to secure his release. The mittimus had stated that Bunyan must remain in jail until the Quarter Sessions the following January unless some local Justice of the Peace could be found willing to arrange bail for him in the meantime.

After Bunyan had been in prison for five or six days, his friends had an idea. The Justice of the Peace at Elstow, a young man who probably remembered John from his Elstow days, might be persuaded to help. Justice Crompton agreed to come to the prison to interview Bunyan and was at first sympathetic. Yes, he might well consider arranging bail terms for him. Noting Bunyan's noble and upright bearing, he could not imagine that the prisoner would cause any trouble. But later, when he read the mittimus, which stated that John's actions had been 'greatly to the disparagement of the government of the Church of England', he was perplexed. Not since the time of Charles I had there been strictures against 'mechanics', or laymen, who wished to preach. Independent churches had flourished, and although the status of the national church had now been restored under the new king, no laws had yet been passed prohibiting conventicles or lay preaching. Had Bunyan been guilty of some other wrongdoing? Why else had he received such a severe indictment? Crompton did not know. Not long appointed as a Justice of the Peace, he became nervous and then refused to be involved in the case.

When the jailer informed Bunyan that this last hope had failed, the prisoner's reaction demonstrated the reality of his trust in God whatever the outcome:

> I was not at all daunted, but rather glad, and saw evidently that the Lord had heard me; for before I went down to the Justice I begged of God that if I might do more good by being at liberty than in prison, I might be set at liberty; but if not, his will be done.[5]

Now he must wait a further seven weeks before his case came to trial but could add:

> I did meet my God sweetly in the prison again, comforting of me and satisfying of me that it was his will and mind that I should be there.[6]

But this setback was not all. Only a day or two later came news that, after a prolonged labour lasting eight days, Elizabeth's baby had at last been born. But frail and premature, the infant's grasp on life was weak. And soon her baby died. We can only imagine the effect this incident had upon a man as sensitive as Bunyan, struggling to accustom himself to the harsh circumstances of prison life. Perhaps this was one of the lowest points of his early prison experience and it was one which he recalled with deep sorrow. Writing of these days, he penned some of the most poignant words in the whole of English literature. In them we have a glimpse into Bunyan's humanity and need, which still calls out to us across the centuries from the pages of his record:

> But notwithstanding these helps [God's comfort and grace], I found myself a man, and compassed with infirmities; the parting with my wife and poor children hath oft been to me in this place as the pulling the flesh from my bones, and that not only because I am somewhat too fond of those great

mercies, but also because I should have often brought to my mind the many hardships, miseries and wants that my poor family was like to meet with, should I be taken from them, especially my poor blind child, who lay nearer my heart than all I had besides.

The remembrance of little blind Mary, still only ten years old and much in need of her father's care, came close to breaking his spirit:

O the thoughts of the hardship I thought my blind one might go under, would break my heart to pieces. Poor child, thought I, what sorrow art thou like to have for thy portion in this world? Thou must be beaten, must beg, suffer hunger, cold, nakedness, and a thousand calamities, though I cannot now endure the wind should blow upon thee. But yet recalling myself, thought I, I must venture you all with God, though it goeth to the quick to leave you. Oh, I saw in this condition I was as a man who was pulling down his house upon the head of his wife and children; yet thought I, I must do it, I must do it.[7]

Yes, he 'must do it', for John Bunyan's conscience and desire to please his God gave him no alternative. A number of biographers, particularly men like J. A. Froude, who wrote in 1880, have criticized Bunyan severely at this point. The magistrates, they suggest, were loath to commit Bunyan to prison. All that was required of him was to attend to his vocation and to agree not to gather people together for religious purposes. Surely this was not asking too much? 'He was compelling the court to punish him, whether they wished it or not,' claims Froude, adding:

... he describes the scene as if the choice had rested with the magistrates to convict him or let him go. If he was bound to do his duty, they were equally bound to do theirs.[8]

This, however, is a double misunderstanding. First, there were as yet no new laws on the statute books prohibiting lay preaching or gatherings for worship outside the Church of England. These would certainly come, but not for another two years. Bunyan had been arrested only a few months after Charles II was recalled to the throne, promising 'liberty to tender consciences'. So the magistrates were not 'bound to do their duty' on this matter. In fact Wingate was governed by prejudice and anger rather than duty and had already declared that he would 'break the neck' of the Dissenters' meetings. In order to convict Bunyan, he had to trawl through the statute books until he came upon an old law that had been passed almost seventy years earlier under Elizabeth I. Although this law had been superseded by the laws of the Commonwealth period, it had not actually been annulled.

Called the Conventicle Act of 1593, it stated that if anyone attended any place of worship other than the parish church, together with five people apart from family members, he must be imprisoned for three months without trial. Following this he was to do public penance and promise never to repeat the offence. If he reneged on this commitment he would be exiled, and if he returned to the country again would be hung. Clearly this law, although technically still applicable, had become obsolete; without new legislation it should not have been enforced. Francis Wingate was therefore definitely going beyond the law in consigning John Bunyan to prison under this act.

A second misunderstanding on the part of those who assert that Bunyan was merely being obdurate and unreasonable lies in the relationship between his work as a brazier and his call to the ministry. For Bunyan his true vocation *was* his preaching, his daily work only a means of support for himself and his family in order to continue that vocation. The Dissenters' view of the call to the ministry was that it was essentially the call of God to a man, expressed through the collective desire of a local church. More than this, it was confirmed by an inward work of the Holy Spirit in the soul of a preacher, setting him apart for this unique calling.[9]

Once a man was chosen by the church he was not at liberty to turn his back on such a vocation, even when confronted with forbidding circumstances. As the apostle Paul expressed it, 'The gifts and calling of God are without repentance' (Romans 11:29). So, like the apostles when commanded not to teach in the name of Jesus, Bunyan could also say, 'We ought to obey God rather than men.'

In a long poem entitled *Prison Meditations* written soon after this, Bunyan declares that he was fulfilling his duty to God when he was arrested:

This was the work I was about
when hands on me were laid,
'twas this from which they plucked me out
and vilely to me said:

'You heretic, deceiver, come,
to prison you must go;
you preach abroad, and keep not home,
you are the church's foe.'[10]

The early days of a prison sentence were always the hardest. John Howard, commenting on prison life in his day, noted that deaths from jail fever were at their highest in those early months and usually struck younger men like Bunyan. Accustomed to an active life, a healthy young man suddenly found himself deprived of liberty, often with little opportunity for exercise and in overcrowded and filthy conditions. His normally healthy diet was reduced to a bare minimum. Small wonder, then, that despair set in, lowering resistance and often leading to infection and death. Describing prison conditions in Bunyan's day, G. R. Cragg writes:

Many of the prisons were fit only for beasts. Sanitation, even at the best, was extremely rudimentary, and often it did not exist at all... At the whim of a gaoler, scores of prisoners might be kept locked in their rooms for many hours — even for days — with no chance of leaving it and with conditions that can more easily be imagined than described. The discomfort because of the filth and the stench of the gaols might afflict even moderately fortunate prisoners...[11]

And Bunyan was among the more fortunate, even though he too had to bear 'the filth and the stench', listening all day long to the ugly curses of angry men and the constant rattle of chains as others were led away for execution.

Mary preparing to leave the prison for the night. (This old print reflects
a highly sanitized view of the conditions in the prison!)

Seventeenth-century jails did not impose the same restrictions
on prisoners as those of today because escape was far less likely.
In a community as small as Bedford anyone on the run could
easily be tracked down; nor could an escapee get far with poor
road conditions and no transport. It also appears that Bunyan's
family, and even friends, were fairly free to visit him, bringing
food, writing materials and warmer clothes for the winter
months. Although Bunyan was too poor to pay for anything
apart from bare essentials, his lot was therefore not as dire as that
of the friendless and destitute.

A strong tradition exists that John's young blind child Mary
used to come to the prison each day with a jug of soup for her
father. Probably Elizabeth or another adult accompanied her at
first, but the sight of his dearly-loved daughter knocking at the
prison gate with his jug of soup must have been the highlight of
her father's day. The jug itself is still on display in the Bunyan
Museum.

Following Justice Crompton's refusal to arrange bail terms for
him, John Bunyan had no alternative but to wait for the next

assizes, due to be held early in January. He sincerely hoped that the appointed judges might then be lenient and release him from prison, if only on compassionate grounds. As he thought of Elizabeth's need and of his four children, the youngest only two years old, with nothing to live on but charity, he was consoled by a verse from Scripture: 'Leave thy fatherless children, I will preserve them alive; and let thy widows trust in me' (Jeremiah 49:11).[12] Already John Bunyan was learning to pass a 'sentence of death' on all he held most dear.

Bunyan's jug
Reproduced by kind permission of Bunyan Meeting Free Church, Bedford, England

21

The trial

The magistrates filed into the Chapel of Herne one by one, taking their seats on the dais with dignity. The Bedford January Quarter Sessions were about to begin. Because the town had no assize court, this old chapel, standing near the river and adjacent to the local grammar school, served a dual purpose. Here it was that John Bunyan would face an interrogation which would determine his liberty or imprisonment.

As the tall young prisoner was led in to face his trial, he must have glanced along the imposing line of magistrates. What he saw gave him little cause for hope. Sir John Kelynge of Southill was the senior justice present and chairman of the session. Bunyan knew well that this man had old scores to settle against the Puritan party. Scarcely six months had passed since the prison gates had opened for Sir John after eighteen long years of incarceration in Windsor Castle because of his support of the Royalist cause. Among the others Bunyan would have spotted Sir Henry Chester of Tilsworth, a man with a harsh, implacable spirit, an uncle of Francis Wingate. Sir William Beecher was there; he had just received his knighthood and would certainly be most anxious

The Chapel of Herne

not to be seen to be doing religious fanatics any favours. With Thomas Snagge of Marston Manor and Sir George Blundell of Cardington Manor the panel was complete.

Another factor would have made John Bunyan pessimistic about the outcome of his trial on that January day in 1661. Serious trouble had broken out in London only a week or two earlier when Thomas Venner, popular leader of the Fifth Monarchy Movement, had led a coup against the government. During the last six years Venner had been a lay pastor of a church in Swan Alley, off Coleman Street. He and his members had been angered by the recent execution of one of the Fifth Monarchist leaders, Thomas Harrison, whose signature had appeared on the death warrant for Charles I. Venner and about fifty of his followers decided to attempt an overthrow of the new and still vulnerable government of Charles II by force of arms. Their avowed aim was to set up 'the Kingdom of Jesus', by force if necessary. For five days spasmodic fighting had broken out on the streets of London with about forty casualties. At last the army was sent out to subdue the rebellion and most of the Fifth Monarchists were killed in the subsequent fray.

While agreeing with the theological position of those who believed that Christ would soon return to set up his everlasting kingdom, Bunyan had no sympathy with men who wished to use force to bring it about. The result of this rebellion was alarming. Thousands of Quakers (who had nothing to do with the uprising) were rounded up and marched off to prison, some probably joining Bunyan in the County Jail. The government became excessively jittery, and banned all unlawful meetings, or conventicles, an action that placed Dissenters in trouble with the law. These circumstances diminished Bunyan's hopes of a fair trial, making the magistrates' attitudes to his case jaundiced at best.

Proceedings began with the indictment against Bunyan being read out to him:

> John Bunyan of the town of Bedford, labourer, being a person of such and such conditions, hath devilishly and perniciously abstained from coming to church to hear Divine service, and is a common upholder of several unlawful meetings and conventicles, to the great disturbance and distraction of the good subjects of this kingdom, contrary to the laws of our sovereign Lord the King.

If this indictment were not so serious, it would be laughable in view of the circumstances of John's arrest.

'What say you to this?' enquired Sir John Kelynge, eyeing the prisoner before him.

Without hesitation Bunyan replied that he regularly attended the church of God and was in membership with those over whom Christ was Head.

Exasperated, Kelynge clarified the point: 'Do you come to church — you know what I mean, to the parish church?'

'No,' Bunyan answered. 'I do not because I do not find it commanded in the Word of God that I should.'

Quickly out of his depth, all Kelynge could reply was: 'But we are commanded to pray.'

'Yes,' countered Bunyan, 'but not by the *Common Prayer Book*.' When asked why not (the Prayer Book had recently been made mandatory once more), Bunyan replied evenly that 'Prayers in the *Common Prayer Book* were such as were made by men, and not by the motions of the Holy Ghost within our hearts.'

Kelynge was in trouble and soon the other justices chipped in to help him out; back and forth went the arguments on the subject of written prayers. Bunyan did not dismiss them out of hand, but told the panel that for him and for those who met with him in worship, it was not their practice to write out their prayers. Unable to undermine his arguments, Kelynge made one final blunder by warning Bunyan to be careful what he said about the Prayer Book, for, he announced categorically, 'We know the *Common Prayer Book* hath been ever since the apostles' time.'

Clearly outmanoeuvred by this common 'labourer', the justices tried insults instead. 'Who is your God — Beelzebub?' demanded one, suggesting that Bunyan was possessed with the spirit of delusion and of the devil. But even this was ineffectual. Peaceably, the man in the dock ignored such remarks with a secret prayer for God to forgive them.

At last the justices began to address the matter in hand, first accusing Bunyan of speaking 'pedlar's French' and ordering him 'to leave off his canting', for he had no right to preach. Once again Bunyan quoted the reference in 1 Peter that he had used before Francis Wingate: 'As every man hath received the gift, even so minister the same one to another... If any man speak, let him speak as the oracles of God.' As if to recover his lost dignity, Justice Kelynge decided to give Bunyan a lecture on that verse of Scripture:

> Let me a little open that scripture to you: 'As every man hath received the gift' that is, as everyone hath received a trade, so let him follow it. If any man have received the gift of tinkering, as thou hast done, let him follow his tinkering. And so other men their trades; and the divine his calling.

'Nay, sir,' began Bunyan, and began to expound the true meaning of that text. Then, seeing he would never convince such prejudiced men, Bunyan ended with a breathtaking assertion in view of the issues at stake: 'If it is a sin to meet together and seek the face of God, and exhort one another to follow Christ, then I will sin still.'

Those five Justices of the Peace knew now that they had their man. 'Then you plead guilty to the indictment, do you not?' said Kelynge, a note of triumph in his voice. The indictment in question was made under article 35 of the 1593 Elizabethan Conventicle Act, which Wingate had used to imprison Bunyan. Directed against unruly sectaries or Dissenters who might stir up trouble in Elizabeth's reign, this act should not have been used against Bunyan. It said nothing about preaching without ordination by the bishops.

Bunyan realized immediately that he was trapped. 'Now, and not till now, I saw I was indicted,' he later wrote. But still he held out. The only 'confession' to which he was prepared to 'plead guilty' was that:

> ... we have many meetings together both to pray to God and to exhort one another, and have the sweet comforting presence of the Lord among us.

Of nothing else was he guilty, he insisted. But it was no use. Taking Bunyan's lack of any admission as though it were one of guilt, the justices pronounced their verdict.

'Hear your judgment,' intoned Kelynge:

> You must be had back again to prison, and there lie for three months following; and at three months' end, if you do not submit to go to church to hear Divine service, and leave your preaching, you must be banished [from] the realm. And if [he added menacingly] you be found in this realm without special licence from the king, you must stretch by the neck for it.

These were the exact terms of the 1593 act, and with that Kelynge ordered the jailer to take Bunyan back to prison.

But it was not Kelynge and his fellow justices who had the final word. Even as the jailer was tugging at his coat sleeve to take him, Bunyan called out, 'If I am out of prison today, I will preach the gospel again tomorrow by the help of God.'

Defiant, courageous and determined, Bunyan returned to prison with a heart thankful to God for his help. He declared:

> I can truly say that my heart was sweetly refreshed in the time of my examination; and also afterwards at my returning to prison.[1]

Unknown to Bunyan as he was being hustled off back to prison, in that same month of January 1661 a scene was being enacted far off in Scotland which would usher in years of intense suffering for the church of Jesus Christ. Even more severe than the trials of English Dissenters, it was suffering that would go down in the annals of history as perhaps the most widespread and brutal in the long story of the Scottish church. The new Parliament, known colloquially as the 'Drunken Parliament' because of the inebriated condition of its delegates, was in session. Illegally and fraudulently packed with representatives favourable to the government south of the border, it gleefully rescinded every act on the statute books safeguarding Reformation principles that had been passed in the last twenty years.

The Earl of Argyll, an early victim of that regime, paid for his convictions with his life. As he stood on the scaffold in May of that year, he declared:

> These times are like to be either very sinning or suffering times; let Christians make their choice ... SIN or SUFFER, and surely he that will choose the better part will choose to suffer.[2]

So too John Bunyan had chosen to suffer rather than to sin against his conscience.

Back in prison once more, Bunyan knew he had three months in which to consider his position. Only a few days earlier a fellow prisoner, John Rush, a Quaker from nearby Kempston who had also been imprisoned for his refusal to compromise his conscience, had died after almost a year in prison. 'Perhaps I too will die here', Bunyan must have thought. He had only to agree not to gather a congregation in order to preach and perhaps put in an occasional appearance at the parish church. Then all would be well: he would be restored to Elizabeth and to his young family. But if he even entertained such thoughts, he thrust them from him without delay.

> Let the rage and malice of men be never so great they can do no more, nor go no farther than God permits them [he reminded himself], but when they have done their worst, 'We know that all things work together for good to them that love God.'[3]

The prospect of banishment from the country, never again to return to his wife and children except on pain of death, was an alarming one. In days when travel beyond one's immediate community was rare, the thought of 'exile' conjured up wild and fearful mental pictures for Bunyan. Highly imaginative, he could now envisage most dreadful scenarios lying ahead for him. If he were exiled, what would he do?

> I thought about the sore and sad estate of a banished and exiled condition, how they are exposed to hunger, to cold, to perils, to nakedness, to enemies, and a thousand calamities.

And, as if all that were not bad enough, perhaps at the end he would 'die in a ditch, like a poor forlorn and desolate sheep'.[4]

But as fast as these morbid prospects invaded his mind, Bunyan manfully banished them by thoughts of the one for whose sake he suffered.

In addition to this, Satan, who had molested John Bunyan so relentlessly in the past, now came back to torment him. And what better way to attack him than to undermine his assurance? If John maintained his stand, he had been crudely told that he would 'stretch by the neck for it'. It was not death itself he feared so much as what lay after death. 'What evidence,' suggested Satan, 'have you for heaven and glory, and an inheritance among them that are sanctified?' In these dark moments of extremity, all Bunyan's confidence drained away. 'Satan laid hard at me and beat me out of heart,' he tells us. And it seemed that God himself had hidden his face from him. 'Perhaps my hopes of heaven are all misplaced after all. I am not fit to die,' thought the distressed prisoner.

This anguish of mind lasted for many weeks. And the moment of accounting drew ever closer. Again and again he cried out to his God for the comfort and grace he had known formerly, but it seemed the heavens were silent to his need. Then another thought, equally alarming, struck John Bunyan:

> [What would happen if I were taken out to die on the gallows and] I should make a scrabbling shift to clamber up the ladder, yet I should either with quaking or other symptoms of faintings, give occasion for the enemy to reproach the way of God and his people?

He imagined himself standing on the scaffold with a rope around his neck, ready to be swung into eternity, his knees knocking together with fear. What discredit that would bring on his stand! 'To die with a pale face and tottering knees for such a cause as this' would be grievous indeed.

But an end to Satan's tauntings was drawing near. Bunyan recounts it with his customary complete candour:

> Thus was I tossed for many weeks, and knew not what to do; at last this consideration fell with weight upon me, That it was for the Word and way of God that I was in this condition, wherefore I was engaged not to flinch a hair's breadth from it. I thought also that God might choose whether he would give me comfort now or at the hour of death... I was bound, but he was free; yea it was my duty to stand to his Word.[5]

With a courage and confidence that had eluded him for many weeks, Bunyan was now able to declare: 'I am for going on and venturing my eternal state with Christ, whether I have comfort here or no.' Then in words as evocative as anything he ever wrote, Bunyan records his decision:

> If God doth not come in, thought I, I will leap off the ladder even blindfold into eternity, sink or swim, come heaven or hell,

Lord Jesus, if thou wilt catch me, do; if not, I will venture for thy name.[6]

Such naked faith in God regardless of personal consequences is the stuff of which martyrs are made, and at last Bunyan's troubled mind had found a resting place.

Satan made one last desperate attempt to rob his prey of any peace of mind he might have attained. 'Doth Job serve God for naught?' he mocked, reminding Bunyan of the fearful state to which Job had been reduced. But, as so often with the devices of the Evil One, it was a suggestion too far. Bunyan immediately laid hold on the thought: 'Yes, Satan is right; I, John Bunyan, am prepared to serve God for naught, even if no heaven and no glory awaits me.' With emboldened faith he was able to declare:

Blessed be God, then, I hope I have an upright heart, for I am resolved, God giving me strength, never to deny my profession, though I have nothing at all for my pains... Now was my heart full of comfort... I would not have been without this trial for much; I am comforted every time I think of it, and hope I shall bless God for ever for the teaching I have had by it.[7]

So with renewed confidence — even with joy — John Bunyan awaited his forthcoming appearance at the next assize. But just before it was due, on 3 April 1661, he had an unexpected visitor.

22

Seeking a royal pardon

'Neighbour Bunyan, how do you do?' greeted the visitor in a cordial voice. Bunyan had been called from his upstairs prison room to meet a certain Paul Cobb, who had been sent from the Justices of the Peace to interview him.

Cautiously Bunyan replied, 'I thank you, Sir, very well, blessed be the Lord.' Could the magistrates have sent their clerk to tell him that his sentence was to be waived and he would soon be a free man, or had they a more sinister intent? Not many moments passed before Bunyan realized that Paul Cobb's mission was to make a final attempt to persuade him to relinquish his firm stand and submit to their demand that he discontinue his preaching. With the spring assizes fast approaching, these justices knew that they would soon be in the position of having to banish the tinker-preacher from the country, according to the sentence they had imposed if he would not yield. They could well have been uneasy about the terms on which this man had been condemned, knowing full well that he had been arrested and imprisoned when he had not been acting illegally.

After his genial greeting, Paul Cobb's initial tactic was to threaten the prisoner. 'I come to tell you that it is desired you would submit to the laws of the land, or else at the next sessions it will go worse with you, even to be sent away out of the nation,' Cobb warned. Perhaps his three months in prison had weakened Bunyan's resolve. 'I am sent,' he continued 'to tell you that they [the justices] do intend to prosecute the law against you if you submit not.' Certainly, after the uprising of the Fifth Monarchists led by Thomas Venner only three months earlier, an interim law had been passed banning conventicles, but this law had not been in force when Bunyan was first arrested.

Patiently Bunyan explained this to Paul Cobb: 'Sir, I conceive that that law by which I am in prison at this time doth not reach or condemn either me or the meetings which I do frequent.' The meetings condemned by the Elizabethan law under which he was arrested were those of men who gathered together to perpetuate some evil design, Bunyan continued, but the ones which he attended were only to exhort and encourage men and women in the way of God.

Cobb's reply to this was that obviously everyone would say that his particular gathering was innocent. Then, coming immediately to the point, he referred to the recent Fifth Monarchist revolution, adding in a cynical tone: 'You see the late insurrection at London, under what glorious pretences they went; and yet indeed, they intended no less than the ruin of the kingdom and commonwealth.'

Bunyan's reply indicates that he totally repudiated Venner's action. 'That practice of theirs I do abhor,' he maintained, adding that, as a Christian man, he considered it important to submit loyally to his king and government. Back and forth went the arguments. Because some people meet in secret to practise evil, it does not follow that all who attend private meetings have wicked intentions, Bunyan asserted. Perhaps a homely illustration would make Cobb understand his point:

> Set the case that, at such a wood corner, there did usually come forth thieves to do mischief; must there therefore a law be made that everyone that cometh out there shall be killed? May not come out true men as well as thieves out from thence?[1]

Seeing that confrontation of this sort was not helping his cause, Cobb changed his ploy, thinking that a different approach might win Bunyan over. He would try softer tactics.

'Goodman Bunyan,' he said in gentler tones, 'methinks you need not stand so strictly upon this one thing... Cannot you submit and notwithstanding do as much good as you can in a neighbourly way without having such meetings?' It sounded plausible enough. 'Why do you insist on preaching?' Cobb wanted to know. After all, Bunyan was free to attend and to hear preaching.

Bunyan was ready with his answer. Clearly familiar with the writings of Wycliffe, he told Cobb firmly that, according to that fourteenth-century Reformer, anyone who failed to obey God for fear of men 'shall in the day of judgment be counted a traitor to Christ'. This comment sparked off further argument on the nature of the final judgement and on Bunyan's right to preach in the first place, but, like Kelynge before him, Cobb soon found that he was out of his depth in attempting to debate with this tinker. At last he tried the emotional argument: 'You have not long before the next assizes.' Surely it would be better to submit to the demands of the law, for, 'You may do much good if you continue still in the land; but alas, what benefit will it be to your friends or what good can you do to them if you should be sent away beyond the seas into Spain or Constantinople, or some other remote part of the world? Pray be ruled.'

The very mention of such far-off places must have sent a shudder down Bunyan's spine. But still he remained firm. 'I hope God will help me to bear what they shall lay upon me,' he said courageously, but added, 'I know no evil I have done in this matter to be so used; I speak in the presence of God.'

If this man would not be 'ruled', Cobb had no more to say, except to demand obedience to the king and his government. And to this Bunyan replied that in all areas where the king had lawful authority he would obey, but, like the apostles, he dared not yield in matters of conscience. Paul Cobb had also failed in his task to persuade Bunyan to relinquish his preaching, and so relapsed into silence.

As the clerk of the justices rose to go, Bunyan thanked him for his 'civil and meek discoursing with me', and expressed his wish that they might one day meet again in heaven.

As John Bunyan awaited the spring assizes, the political scene in London was changing yet again. The Convention Parliament,

which had voted for the return of Charles II, was dissolved and a
new Parliament, known as the Cavalier Parliament, elected.
Whereas the previous Parliament had been largely conciliatory
towards Dissenters, the Cavalier Parliament was far different in
character. Composed of men of Royalist persuasion, it has been
described as 'more Royalist than the king himself', and many of
the members had old scores to settle against the Presbyterian and
Puritan parties. They represented families that had suffered
grievous loss in the Civil War, with the confiscation of property
and estate. Now they were bent on revenge.

The king, who had discovered the folly of religious persecution
in observing the fate of his father and of Archbishop Laud, was
anxious to be as accommodating as possible in the new religious
settlement for his country; not so the High Church men who
came to power in the Cavalier Parliament. On 15 April 1661 the
Savoy Conference, consisting of twelve bishops and twelve
Presbyterian divines, met at the Savoy Palace in London to thrash
out future religious policy. Among the former group was Gilbert
Sheldon, Bishop of London, a man who could show little mercy,
and among the latter Richard Baxter, hopeful to the last that a
degree of religious toleration could be achieved.

But it was not to be. Bishop Sheldon and his High Church
supporters were determined to push through an agenda which
would restore ritual and ceremonies that were High Church, or
even Catholic, in character. They showed little regard to the
sensitivities of the Presbyterians, and even less to those of other
Dissenters. The *Book of Common Prayer* was to be revised, and
in July 1661 a Bill of Uniformity was drafted which, when it
became law, would require the 'unfeigned assent and consent' of
the people to all its contents. Many of these struck at the very
heart of evangelical and biblical truth.[2] From now on the Church
of England was set on a path of intolerance which would bring
untold suffering to Dissenters for the next twenty-five years.

Whether news of these developments had filtered through to
Bunyan in the Bedford County Jail we do not know. He would
have been well aware, however, that the coronation of Charles II
was to take place on 23 April. He then learnt that, contrary to his
expectations, the spring assizes, which would have determined his
fate, were not to take place after all. At any coronation it had

become customary to declare a general pardon for many of those currently serving prison sentences, in order to demonstrate the new king's goodwill towards his subjects. As the prison gates swung open for a considerable number of Bunyan's fellow prisoners, he discovered to his dismay that the name of a certain tinker-preacher was conspicuously absent from every list compiled by the local magistrates of those to be released. John Brown, one of Bunyan's earliest biographers, comments: 'Barabbas was preferred to the Master, no wonder then that felons were preferred to the disciple.'[3]

The only answer that Bunyan could obtain to his repeated enquiry as to why his name was not included was that he had already been convicted and therefore did not qualify for the general pardon — a thing which he believed to be manifestly untrue, for, as he stoutly maintained, he had never pleaded guilty to any indictment against him. One possibility still remained, however. For one calendar year from the date of the coronation it was possible for those not included in the king's pardon to 'sue out a pardon', or to apply directly to the king for clemency.

As he pondered the available options, the only expedient John could propose was that Elizabeth herself should travel to London and present an appeal to the House of Lords on his behalf. Elizabeth was prepared to try, though it must have been a frightening undertaking for a young seventeenth-century woman. Her courage in being ready for such an enterprise speaks highly of the sterling character of John Bunyan's second wife. The sixty miles or more between Bedford and Westminster would have taken at least four days on foot, and it is doubtful whether Elizabeth could afford to travel any other way. The roads were poor, footpads[4] and highwaymen lay in wait for the unwary, and crowded inns along the way afforded little comfort at night.

John had heard of a certain Lord 'Barkwood'[5] — whose name was actually William Russell, fifth Earl of Bedford — who was known to be sympathetic to Dissenters and other Nonconformists. So it was to this man that he instructed his wife to make her appeal. And in the early summer of 1661 Elizabeth began her journey, carrying with her John's written petition which explained his circumstances and his request for justice and freedom.

Whether she went alone, or was accompanied by someone from the Bedford Meeting to offer protection, we are not told.

Arriving at her destination, this intrepid young woman ventured into the august precincts of the House of Lords, enquiring for the Earl of Bedford. He received her petition sympathetically enough, but said he would need to present it to other members of the House of Lords for a joint decision on the case. This probably spelt the end of Elizabeth's hopes, for the answer came back that their lordships had no power to release her husband: Elizabeth must wait for the midsummer Bedford assizes, and present her petition before the circuit judges on that occasion. It is not hard to imagine the crushing disappointment Bunyan's wife must have experienced as she prepared to turn homeward, realizing that her endeavours had been little less than fruitless. All she had gained was a warrant from the peers to back up John's petition at the next assizes. Whether that would carry much weight, she had no means of knowing.

In all probability Elizabeth had one further task to undertake on John's behalf while in London — a visit to his publisher, Francis Smith, with another manuscript, this time written within the confines of his prison. *Profitable Meditations* is a long poem covering thirty-one pages in its original form, with 186 verses. Bunyan urgently needed to raise money to support his family and this may well have been in his mind as he wrote this metrical 'Conference between Christ and the Sinner'. Divided into nine sections, it addresses both believers and unbelievers but, as ever, Bunyan's primary aim was to urge his readers to seek salvation while the opportunity remained. Yet his own doubts and struggles also find expression, particularly in a section called 'A Discourse between Christ and the tempted soul':

Soul: My loving Lord, my sin it is so strong
and mighty, and foils me though I strive
against it; and I fear 'twill do me wrong.
Oh! I beseech thee let my soul revive.

Christ: I love thee dearly, groaning heart, I come
with grace and faith and love to lift thee out

> of sin and death and hell; and to my home
> I'll have thee. This by grace I'll bring about.[6]

Prison life had indeed been hard for John Bunyan, but in spite of every setback, he was still able to declare: 'I never knew what it was for God to stand by me at all turns ... as I have found him since I came hither.'[7]

And, as he would later declare, 'In times of affliction we commonly meet with the sweetest experiences of the love of God.'

23

'He dares not leave preaching'

Nothing more now remained for John and Elizabeth Bunyan but to wait for the midsummer assizes, due to be held in August. Elizabeth's hopes must have risen when she learnt that Sir Matthew Hale was to be the senior judge — a man with a reputation for fairness and mercy. Only two years earlier Sir Matthew had used his influence to release the Quaker leader George Fox from prison. Perhaps he could be persuaded to release her husband too. Born in 1609, Hale had practised at the bar since 1637, and had held a prominent position in Oliver Cromwell's protectorate government.

Described by the Puritan writer and preacher Richard Baxter 'as sharing a regenerating, illuminating, quickening spirit,' he was in Baxter's opinion, 'most precisely just, insomuch as I believe he would have lost all that he had in the world rather than do an unjust act'. Hale was clearly a good, godly and fair-minded man. But he was also a little nervous. Even though Charles II had recently honoured him with a knighthood, Hale had formerly participated in Cromwell's parliaments and was anxious not to do anything further to damage his reputation with the king.

The other judge at the assizes was to be Judge Thomas Twisden. Born in 1602, he was fifty-nine at this time and had gained a reputation for severity, bordering on cruelty, in his judgements. But Elizabeth probably did not know this. To assist the judges, one or two of the local justices were also present, most noticeably in this case, Sir Henry Chester of Tilsworth, uncle of Francis Wingate, and one of the original panel of magistrates who had imprisoned Bunyan earlier that year.

The grounds of John Bunyan's appeal written on the petition that Elizabeth would present were twofold: firstly, he had been arrested before any new laws against conventicles had been passed, his conviction resting on an old law resurrected for the purpose; and secondly, he had not pleaded guilty to any indictment; the panel of magistrates had only twisted his words and claimed that he had confessed himself guilty. Probably neither John nor Elizabeth realized that any refusal to plead either 'Guilty' or 'Not Guilty' would be considered as an admission of guilt.

As the judges alighted from their coach at the door of the Chapel of Herne, where the assizes were held, Elizabeth was waiting. As the poor countrywoman gazed at these dignitaries in

Sir Matthew Hale

their scarlet robes decorated with ermine, the sight must have been intimidating. Approaching the younger man, whom she knew to be Sir Matthew, Elizabeth presented John's petition. Hale received it 'very mildly', glanced briefly at it and said kindly to the apprehensive young woman, 'I will do the best good I can for you and your husband, but,' he added, 'I fear it may be none.'

Slightly heartened by Hale's considerate tone, Elizabeth determined to try again the following day, fearful that Hale might forget her case in the mass of affairs to which he must attend. With an audacity born of her need, Elizabeth decided on a risky strategy. As the coach carrying the distinguished visitors rumbled down the High Street, Elizabeth stood by the road, with a second copy of John's petition in her hand. As the coach passed she threw the petition in through the open window. Stooping to grab the offensive piece of paper, Judge Twisden, who had clearly been informed of the nature of the case, shouted angrily at Elizabeth that her husband was a convicted man and could not be released unless he would promise not to preach any more.

This was indeed a setback. 'If only,' thought Elizabeth, 'I could speak to Sir Matthew himself, and plead John's cause, I would stand some chance of a hearing.' So on the third day of the assizes, with yet another copy of the petition, this resolute girl pressed through the crowds at the Chapel of Herne and flung herself before Judge Hale as he sat on the bench. Once again Sir Matthew listened sympathetically to Elizabeth's plea, but seeing what was happening, Sir Henry Chester hurried to the bench and spoke to Hale, describing Bunyan as 'a hot-spirited fellow', and assured him that the tinker was indeed lawfully convicted. As one of Sir Matthew's tasks was to check up on the decisions of the local magistrates, it was vital to Chester that nothing amiss should be discovered in their dealings with Bunyan.

Crushed with disappointment, Elizabeth fell back into the crowd as Sir Matthew waived her case aside. All her endeavours had been to no avail. But the High Sheriff, Edmund Wylde, had witnessed the young woman's brave attempt; drawing her aside, he had a further suggestion. If she could speak to Sir Matthew when he was 'off duty', relaxing with the other magistrates and perhaps enjoying a drink together at the nearby Swan Inn, she might stand a better chance. Motivated by her own desperate situation and her husband's need, Elizabeth summoned up all her courage and, when the hearings were concluded, made her way to the Swan Inn. Pushing her way through the noisy gathering, her heart hammering with apprehension, face flushed and anxious, Elizabeth flung herself once more before Judge Hale.

'My lord, I make bold to come once again to your lordship, to know what may be done with my husband,' she faltered.

The old Swan Inn, Bedford

Astonished and slightly exasperated, Hale replied, 'Woman, I told thee before, I could do thee no good; because they have taken that for a conviction which thy husband spoke at the sessions; and unless something can be done to undo that, I can do thee no good.'

'My lord,' answered Elizabeth, knowing this was her last chance, 'he is kept unlawfully in prison; they clapped him up before there was any proclamation against the meetings; the indictment also is false. Besides, they never asked him whether he was guilty or no; neither did he confess the indictment.'

'My lord, he was lawfully convicted,' shouted some other magistrates standing nearby.

'It is false,' repeated Elizabeth. 'When they said to him, "Do you confess the indictment?" he said only this, that he had been at several meetings, both where there was preaching the Word and prayer, and that they had God's presence among them.'

At this point Judge Twisden joined in, already angry at Elizabeth's persistence. 'What!' he exclaimed. 'Your husband is a breaker of the peace and is convicted by the law.'

Indignation had taken over from fear and Elizabeth's boldness was astonishing as she stood her ground, insisting that the conviction was false. The situation became quite nasty as Justice Chester kept shouting, 'It is recorded. It is recorded,' as if the mere fact that it was recorded made it correct. 'He is a pestilent fellow,' added he, 'there is not such a fellow in the country again' — an unintentional witness to the effect of John Bunyan's preaching.

'What?' intervened Judge Twisden again. 'Will your husband leave preaching? If he will do so, then send for him.'

Elizabeth Bunyan's next comment showed the tenacity and strength of her Christian conviction: 'My lord, he dares not leave preaching as long as he can speak.'

Unable to persuade the judges that John had been falsely convicted, Elizabeth had only her own desperate circumstances left as a plea to move Sir Matthew to compassion. Turning from the angry magistrates, she directed her words solely to him: 'All my husband wants is to follow his calling, that his family might be maintained,' she said, adding with a degree of pathos which obviously touched Sir Matthew, 'My lord, I have four small children that cannot help themselves, of which one is blind, and have nothing to live upon but the charity of good people.'

Four small children — how could so young a woman, probably little more than nineteen or twenty, have such a family? Hale wondered.

'My lord, I am but mother-in-law [i.e. stepmother] to them, having not been married to him yet two full years. Indeed, I was with child when my husband was first apprehended; but being young and unaccustomed to such things, I being [di]smayed at the news, fell into labour, and so continued for eight days, and then was delivered, but my child died.'

'Alas, poor woman,' said Hale with genuine sympathy. But seeing that his fellow judge was being swayed in favour of this persistent woman, Twisden intervened. 'She makes poverty her cloak,' he said with a sneer. 'Her husband is better maintained by running up and down a-preaching than by following his calling.'

'What is his calling?' enquired Hale.

'A tinker, my lord, a tinker,' cried a chorus of voices.

Elizabeth was quick on the rebound. 'Yes, and because he is a tinker and a poor man, therefore he is despised and cannot have justice.'

Elizabeth pleads with the judges

Clearly Hale was now taking Elizabeth seriously, but still felt there was little he could do in the circumstances. He now spoke 'very mildly' to her: 'I tell thee, woman, seeing it is so, that they have taken what thy husband spake for a conviction, thou must either apply thyself to the king, or sue out his pardon or get a writ of error.'

This last alternative upset Justice Chester all the more. A 'writ of error' would obviously reflect badly on the court decision which he had helped to make. 'My lord,' he said vehemently, 'he will preach and do what he lists [i.e. likes].'

'He preaches nothing but the Word of God,' retorted Elizabeth promptly.

'He, preach the Word of God!' snarled Judge Twisden, lunging towards Elizabeth as though he would dearly like to strike her across the face. 'He runneth up and down and doth harm.'

'No, my lord,' interrupted Elizabeth, 'it is not so; God hath owned him and done much good by him.'

'God!' responded Twisden angrily. 'His doctrine is the doctrine of the devil.'

With all the verve of a woman who knew she had right on her side, Elizabeth responded, directing her words straight to Judge Twisden: 'My lord, when the righteous Judge shall appear, it will be known that his doctrine is not the doctrine of the devil.'

Understanding full well that Elizabeth was implying that he was an *unrighteous* judge, Twisden could only comment to Hale, 'My Lord, 'do not mind her, but send her away.'

Caught in the crossfire of this exchange, Hale was in a difficult position. He could not be seen to dissent publicly from his fellow judge. All he could do was to apologize to Elizabeth and repeat his former advice, but he emphasized once again that her best and cheapest option was to get a writ of error. At this point Justice Chester appeared even angrier, and although Elizabeth begged again and again that John should be sent for out of prison to plead his own case, she could soon see that nothing more could be done.

Bursting into tears, Elizabeth pushed her way out of the crowded Swan Inn. But, as she afterwards explained to John when she told him all that had transpired, these were not tears of self-pity, nor even of grief at the failure of her endeavours, but 'to think of the sad account such poor creatures will have to give at the coming of the Lord, when they shall there answer for all things whatsoever they have done in the body whether it be good or whether it be bad'.

Clearly Elizabeth Bunyan was a worthy wife of such a man as John Bunyan.

24

Living on the invisible God

I have suffered as much misery as soe dismall a place can be
capable to inflict and soe am likely to perish without your Ma-
jestie's further compassion and mercy towards me.

The words quoted above were written by John Bubb, a fellow
inmate in Bedford County Jail with John Bunyan. Bubb had been
convicted for murder after being involved in a drunken brawl in
which he had stabbed a man who had later died of his wound.
But Bubb had influential friends, and none more so than Francis
Wingate, who had been responsible for Bunyan's original imprisonment. Wingate even raised money on Bubb's behalf to
finance his appeal before the king. Bubb was granted his eventual
acquittal.[1] Not so John Bunyan.

Sir Matthew Hale had suggested that Bunyan should try again
to apply to the king for a pardon, but this was an expensive
course of action costing £30, a sum that neither Bunyan nor his
friends could afford in days when a poor man's income was often
little more than £10 a year. Alternatively, Hale recommended that
he could try to obtain 'a writ of error', but once again Bunyan

would have needed to engage a lawyer who could fight his corner, and as a tinker he did not move in such circles. The situation looked bleak.

However, during the period following the assizes, and for most of the following year, when he was theoretically able to seek out a royal pardon, Bunyan's jailer felt justified in giving his prisoner a considerable amount of liberty. It would appear that this first jailer was more humane than most. He had also discovered in John Bunyan a very different sort of prisoner from those he usually handled. For, like Joseph in Egypt, the Lord was with him and 'gave him favour in the sight of the keeper of the prison'. Each night, however, except on rare occasions, Bunyan had to be back within the confines of the County Jail.

Consequently we find Bunyan's name occasionally appearing in the church records of the Bedford Meeting at this time. But the days were difficult and we read:

> Our meetings having bene for some time neglected through the increase of trouble, the 28th of the 6th moneth 1661, the Church through mercy againe met.

A few sentences further on we read that 'our brother Bunyan' was commissioned to visit two church members. And in the following month the record continues:

> At a meeting of the Church at Bedford the 26th of the 7th moneth ... We desire brother Bunyan and John Fenne to go again to Sister Pecock.[2]

'Sister Pecock' had evidently been absenting herself from services of worship through fear of the consequences, and who better than John Bunyan to go and encourage, or even admonish her?

As fearless as ever, Bunyan seized every occasion possible to preach, knowing that his opportunities would undoubtedly be cut short at any moment. And the burden of his message was:

> ... to be steadfast in the faith of Jesus Christ, and to take heed that they touch not [i.e. avoid] the [Book of] Common Prayer but to mind the Word of God.[3]

In October of that year, John Bunyan took an even greater risk: he decided on a trip to London to visit friends and colleagues. Perhaps he also hoped to see his publishers to check up on the progress of his manuscripts.

The government was still jittery and suspected that secret plots were being hatched at every unofficial gathering. So when Bunyan travelled again to London in the spring of 1662, it was one risk too many. Someone recognized the tall, auburn-haired young man and reported Bunyan's activities to his enemies. The anger unleashed against his jailer for allowing the prisoner so much liberty was virulent and extreme. Not only did he almost lose his job, but he too was threatened with an indictment and warned that punitive measures would be taken against him if anything of the kind should ever happen again. As for Bunyan himself, 'They charged me also that I went thither to plot and raise divisions, and make insurrection, which, God knows, was a slander.'[4] Now Bunyan was treated with a heavy hand, and his prison conditions were more stringent than ever before, 'so that I must not look out of the door'.

Records of meetings of the church became less and less frequent and after 1663 they ceased altogether for a number of years. Clearly the Independent Church at Bedford no longer dared to meet openly. Now they could only carry on gathering secretly, varying the location each time in order to avoid the vengeance of the law. The iron hand of persecution was gradually tightening on Dissenters, as the Cavalier Parliament began to pass repressive legislation against them. In November 1661 the Corporation Act was introduced, preventing any who would not take communion in a parish church from being elected to positions of influence on municipal corporations. This effectively silenced all voices of protest at a local level.

Following the midsummer assizes, the next session when the cases of Bedford prisoners were to be heard was due in November 1661. Once more Bunyan made strenuous efforts to gain a hearing before the judiciary of the day. He fully expected that on this occasion his indictment would come up for review, but the assizes came and went, and his name was yet again omitted from any list presented to the magistrates. Nothing remained but for him to face the cold winter months in Bedford Jail for a second year.

Determined to gain a hearing at the spring assizes to be held in March 1662, John Bunyan took the desperate measure of begging his jailer to add his name to the list of felons whose cases were to come up, even though he did not fall into that category of prisoner. In addition, he managed to gain the goodwill of the High Sheriff, probably the same Edmund Wylde who had been the only one to speak an encouraging word to Elizabeth when she was rebuffed in her appeal on John's behalf. 'Yes', said the sheriff, he would make certain that Bunyan's name appeared in the 'calendar', or list of cases to be judged. Even the judge himself assured Bunyan that this time he would receive a hearing. But when the names of those to appear in court were called out, once again Bunyan's was missing.

How had this come about? Bunyan soon found that it had been engineered by one whom he had thought to be well-disposed towards him — Paul Cobb, clerk of the justices. Despite calling him 'Goodman Bunyan' and other conciliatory names, in reality Cobb proved himself to be 'one of my greatest opposers', and Bunyan discovered that Cobb had personally scrubbed his name off the list. Instead of an unbiased statement of the indictment against Bunyan, he had written, 'John Bunyan was committed to prison being lawfully convicted for upholding of unlawful meetings and conventicles.' Nor was that all. Cobb threatened Bunyan's jailer that if by any chance Bunyan managed to receive a hearing and was released, he, Paul Cobb, would force the jailer to pay the fee[5] due on the release of a prisoner, instead of Bunyan himself. In addition he would file a complaint against the jailer at the next quarter sessions. These threats were enough to intimidate the most considerate of prison keepers and to harden the prisoner's conditions.

All Bunyan's hopes of release in the near future faded. He thought of his young family in all their need, of Elizabeth, of the believers whom he loved and had served, of his young converts in the faith for whom he could now do little. Certainly he was called upon to 'pass a sentence of death' upon all that he had held dear, and instead 'to live upon God that is invisible'.[6] Like Moses, who also 'endured as seeing him who is invisible', so too

John Bunyan found great 'reward' through his sufferings. 'I never had in all my life so great an inlet into the word of God as now,' he declared, adding:

> Those Scriptures that I saw nothing in before are made in this place and state to shine upon me. Jesus Christ also was never more real and apparent than now; here I have seen him and felt him indeed.[7]

But it was far from easy. Satan took every opportunity to taunt the imprisoned man; sometimes fears troubled him and those wild imaginations that he had known in his youth returned to harass and distress him. But at such times he found the tender grace of God to be his support and comfort:

> Yea, when I have started, even as it were at nothing else but my shadow, yet God as being very tender of me, hath not suffered me to be molested, but would with one scripture and another strengthen me against all.[8]

Sometimes his comforts were so overwhelming that he confesses that 'Were it lawful, I could pray for greater trouble, for the greater comfort's sake.'[9] Turning his thoughts into verse, John Bunyan wrote:

> For though men keep my outward man
> within their locks and bars,
> yet by the faith of Christ I can
> mount higher than the stars.
>
> Their fetters cannot spirits tame,
> nor tie up God from me;
> my faith and hope they cannot lame,
> above them I shall be.
>
> God sometimes visits prisons more
> than lordly palaces,
> he often knocketh at our door,
> when he their houses miss.[10]

Bunyan could have echoed the words of Samuel Rutherford, a Scottish pastor exiled during William Laud's period as archbishop, who also testified to an unusual presence of God during times of suffering. Under house arrest in Aberdeen between 1636 and 1638, far from his Anwoth home, Rutherford had written:

> My prison is my palace, my sorrow is with child of joy, my losses are rich losses, my pain easy pain, my heavy days are holy happy days. I may tell a new tale of Christ to my friends.[11]

Meanwhile the situation for Nonconformists — a term originally applied to members of the Church of England who, while agreeing with the general position of the church, opted out of some of the rubric of its ceremonial — and Dissenters, such as the Baptists and Independents, was looking increasingly gloomy. On 19 April 1662 the Bill of Uniformity passed into law. The terms of the act were harsh and were largely drawn up by Sir John Kelynge himself, the one who had presided at Bunyan's trial, and was described as a 'violent cavalier'. G. R. Cragg lists some of the requirements of the act:

> Prior to St Bartholomew's Day 1662 everyone who had held any ecclesiastical office was to read morning and evening prayer, and then 'openly and publicly before the congregation there assembled declare his unfeigned assent and consent ... to all and everything contained and prescribed in and by the Book of Common Prayer'. The Solemn League and Covenant [sworn in 1643 between England and Scotland] was to be explicitly renounced... Only those who had received episcopal ordination might henceforth officiate in the Church of England... Schoolmasters and even private tutors came within the terms of the Act...[12]

Black Bartholomew's Day, as it came to be known to posterity, fell on Sunday, 24 August 1662. Bunyan would have known that many of his associates suffered severely, having their ministries cut short by the terms of the act. His friend William Dell of Yielden, for whom Bunyan had preached, was only one of many to be seriously affected. And these were good, capable and godly men. 'I do not believe,' wrote Richard Baxter, ejected from his ministry at Kidderminster, 'that ever England had as able and faithful ministry since it was a nation as it had this day.'[13] And as Oliver Heywood, Nonconformist leader in Lancashire and Yorkshire, commented, 'The Act of Uniformity struck all Nonconformists dead on St Bartholomew's Day.'[14]

On that day the sufferings which Bunyan had been enduring for almost two years became the lot of many. 'I have eleven arguments for conformity,' said one man, looking at his wife and ten children, 'but Christ has said, "Whoso loveth wife or children more than me is not worthy of me."'[15] Nearly two thousand ministers and schoolmasters chose that same course, losing their homes, ministries and incomes rather than compromise their consciences by conforming to the terms of the act. Harried, imprisoned and often homeless, their sufferings form a sorry episode in the history of the Church of England and have scarred for ever the memory of the Restoration period.

Burning with indignation against such compulsory use of the *Book of Common Prayer* and the suffering it had brought to those who refused to use all or part of it, John Bunyan took up his pen once more and began to write a treatise on the character of real prayer. Men might silence the voice of the preacher by incarcerating him in a cold prison, but they had not reckoned on the power of his pen. The question of the true nature of prayer had been discussed at length during Bunyan's trial before Kelynge and his justices in January 1661, and he had been mulling over it ever since. With an ironic twist he writes:

> Look into the jails of England and into the alehouses of the same; I trow [i.e. believe] you will find those who plead for the spirit of prayer in the jail, and them that look after only the form of men's inventions in the alehouse. It is evident also, by the silencing of God's dear ministers, though never so powerfully enabled by the Spirit of prayer [that] they in conscience cannot admit of [i.e. agree to] that form of Common Prayer.[16]

And before long Bunyan would produce a remarkable book on this same subject, bearing the title, *A Discourse Touching Prayer*. The work of one who had been taught by God in the hard school of suffering, Bunyan's first prison treatise is a spiritual gem, and had it proved to be the only fruit of his trying circumstances the gain for his readers, both then and now, would have been incalculable.

25

A prisoner of hope
(1662–64)

A stained-glass window in the Bunyan Meeting Free Church inserted in 1978 depicts a well-dressed man with a seraphic smile on his face, hair neatly combed, sitting by a window, quill in hand and blank paper before him. With a sturdy table on which to write, the sun streaming in through the window onto the coloured floor tiles, this window presents an idealistic but thoroughly erroneous picture of John Bunyan's prison conditions. How he managed to write at all amidst those overcrowded, filthy, rat-infested surroundings, with the groans of prisoners resounding in his ears and the ever-present clank of chains reminding him of the death sentence imposed on many inmates, is astonishing.

Yet write he did, perhaps with his paper resting on his knee, his quills and ink faithfully brought to the prison by Elizabeth, or even by his blind child Mary, now twelve years of age.

Few letters have survived from John Bunyan's pen, but one, which takes the form of a poem of seventy stanzas, throws much light on his state of mind at this time. Called *Prison Meditations*

directed to the heart of suffering saints and reigning sinners, this
long poem was written in answer to a letter John had received:

> I take it kindly at thy hand
> thou didst unto me write;
> my feet upon Mount Zion stand,
> in that take thou delight.
>
> I am indeed in prison now
> in body, but my mind
> is free to study Christ, and how
> unto me he is kind.

It must be said that John Bunyan's poetry does not equal his
prose, and yet much of it makes compelling reading. His style was
in keeping with the popular ballads of his day, which were probably sung with enthusiasm in the local taverns.[1] It also bears a
resemblance to the metrical psalms of Thomas Sternhold and John
Hopkins which he would have sung as a youth in Elstow parish
church.

From other verses in this poem we learn that the threat of
banishment, or even of execution, was often in John's mind
during his early imprisonment. The terms of the Act of Uniformity
were harsh and certainly provided for the death sentence for
anyone who continued to flout its regulations and worship God
in accordance with Scripture and his or her own conscience. In
1664 twelve ordinary Christians, ten men and two women, were
caught at a meeting in Aylesbury and ordered to conform within
three months. Refusing to do so, they had the death sentence
passed on them, their homes ransacked and their goods confiscated. Only the intervention of William Kiffin, a leader among the
Particular Baptists, who pleaded their cause with the king himself,
prevented the death sentence from being carried out.[2]

It is not surprising, therefore, that Bunyan should write in his
Prison Meditations:

> The prison very sweet to me
> hath been since I came here,

and so would hanging also be,
if God would there appear.

When they do talk of banishment,
of death or such like things;
then to me God sends heart content
that like a fountain springs.

Such words give the lie to those who suggest that Bunyan was a severe depressive. Certainly, he suffered periods of depression, but it is hard to imagine anyone who would not do so in his circumstances.

In this poem, written after Black Bartholomew's Day, Bunyan grieved over those men whose courage and spiritual convictions had collapsed as they faced the cost of suffering for their principles:

Here we can see how men all play
their parts, as on a stage,
how good men suffer for God's way
and bad men at them rage.

Here we can see who holds the ground
which they in Scripture find,
here we see also who turns round
like weathercocks with wind.

Even Bunyan cannot have failed to be moved when he heard that his former antagonist, Edward Burrough, the Quaker who had replied to his early work, *Some Gospel Truths Opened*, had died in prison. Lying on filthy straw near an open sewer, his body wracked with fever, and surrounded by blaspheming inmates, Burrough had nevertheless died well, counting it a privilege to suffer for Christ's sake. He was still only thirty years of age.

Gradually, as the weeks lengthened into months, Bunyan began to realize that any hopes of his own release were far distant and, like Burrough, he was able to set the privilege of suffering for Christ over against the joys of home, family and freedom. He had little doubt about which was the more precious:

Though they say then that we are fools
because we here do lie,
I answer, gaols are Christ his schools,
in them we learn to die.

Then let us count those things the best
that best will prove at last;
and count such men the only blest
that do such things hold fast.

This perspective on his sufferings did not cancel out Bunyan's
anxieties, and most of all those concerning the needs of his family.
He had confessed that he felt like 'a man pulling down his house
upon the head of his wife and children'. And yet he could see no
alternative. But at least he could do his best to provide for them.
Being a practical man, Bunyan quickly mastered the skill of fitting
metal tags on the ends of the long laces used to secure boots and
shoes.

Every spare moment found the prisoner busy either writing,
reading or twisting and fastening these tags. One who spent some
time in prison with Bunyan, John Wilson, originally a member of
the Bedford Meeting, but later the pastor of an Independent
church in Hitchin, records that Bunyan made 'many hundred
gross' of such tags for sale. Possibly he stood at the prison gate
himself trying to attract the attention of passers-by, or his child
Mary may have sold them in the marketplace, her blindness and
need touching the sympathy and purses of those bustling around.
Added to this, Bunyan wrote a number of shorter poems and
articles, probably for sale to support Elizabeth and the children,
for, according to her own words, the family had 'nothing to live
upon but the charity of good people'.

For his reading material, his fellow prisoner John Wilson tells
us that Bunyan had only two books with him in prison: first, his
Bible and, secondly, John Foxe's *Book of Martyrs*. This latter was
not the slimmed-down version still in print today, but a massive
three-volume set, each volume containing more than 1,000 pages
of double-columned text. In it Foxe traces the sorrows and
sufferings of the Christian church from earliest times. First published in English in 1563, it went through four editions before

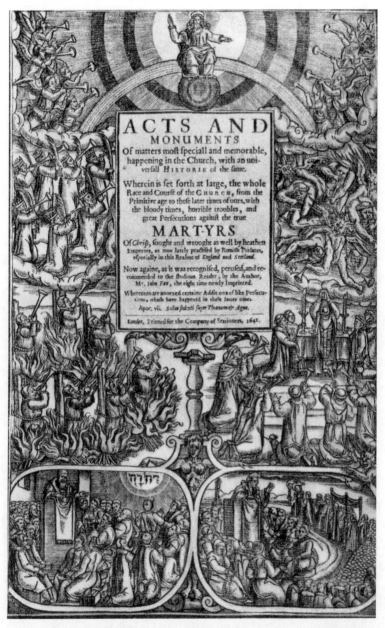

Title page of the edition of Foxe's *Book of Martyrs* used by Bunyan

Foxe's death in 1587, concluding with some martyrdoms of Elizabeth I's reign. In 1571 a copy was placed in every cathedral in the country, the book doing more than any other to shape the thinking of the Protestant church.

Bunyan's own copies of these volumes, more properly called *The Acts and Monuments of the Church,* are still extant. We can well believe that he spent many hours poring over the close print, reading of the fearsome cruelty with which the enemies of Christ tried to crush the faith of believing men and women. As he read he found fresh courage to endure his own sufferings. In each copy he wrote his name, adding the date '1662' in volume 3.

JOHN·BVNYAN·1662.

Opportunities for private prayer in the dirty, degrading and crowded prison must have been non-existent. And yet in spirit John Bunyan soared above his sordid surroundings as he communed with God, receiving new strength for his circumstances. Here he gained sights of that heavenly city, destiny of the people of God, where suffering would be gone for ever.

> This gaol to us is as a hill
> from whence we plainly see
> beyond this world and take our fill
> of things that lasting be.[3]

As we have seen, the Act of Uniformity, compelling preachers to use the *Book of Common Prayer* and to declare their assent to all its wording, was the crisis that forced many both in England and Scotland out of their churches; it was one about which John Bunyan felt deeply. Apart from the poem, *Profitable Meditations,* the first book which he wrote in jail was *A Discourse Touching Prayer,*[4] expounding his understanding of true prayer. Based on the verse, 'I will pray with the spirit, and I will pray with the understanding also' (1 Corinthians 14:15), this began with a short but powerful statement. Bunyan's opening definition of prayer is perhaps one of the simplest but most profound in the whole of religious literature:

> Prayer is a sincere, sensible [i.e. acutely felt], affectionate pouring out of the heart or soul to God, through Christ, in the strength and assistance of the Holy Spirit for such things as God hath promised, or according to the Word, for the good of the church, with submission, in faith, to the will of God.[5]

In his first chapter Bunyan proceeds to take different words and clauses of that definition, enlarging and expounding them with all the sensitivity of a true pastor. Only a man who had communed often with God in secret could write as he does. In a second chapter he turns to his main text and explains what it means to 'pray with the Spirit' — something that is essential if prayer is to be in accordance with his earlier exhortations. But even those who most earnestly seek the help of the Spirit in prayer may still find it hard to continue in such a frame:

> O the starting-holes that the heart has in time of prayer! None knows how many by-ways the heart has, and back-lanes, to slip away from the presence of God. How much pride also if enabled with expressions! How much hypocrisy if before others![6]

Clearly Bunyan wrote out of personal experience of the difficulties of this spiritual exercise.

A third chapter explains what is meant by 'praying with the understanding', and a fourth deals with 'queries and objections'. Here Bunyan's pastoral heart shines out ever more clearly. To the one who longs to pray, but who finds he 'can scarce say anything at all', Bunyan replies:

> Ah, sweet soul! It is not your words that God so much regards ... his eye is on your brokenness of heart, and that it is that calls forth his compassion.

A final chapter deals in typical Puritan style with 'uses and application', and throughout this work Bunyan takes several sideswipes at those who insist that the only way to pray is by means of the written prayers in the *Book of Common Prayer.* This is followed by twelve short admonitions which a believer would do well to heed in order to keep his praying warm and effectual.

As he laid down his pen, Bunyan no doubt wondered who would publish a prisoner's work. Even if his publisher Francis Smith was willing to take it, how would he get the manuscript to him? At present Bunyan was kept under the strictest supervision, and not allowed to step outside his prison for any cause whatsoever. It appears that he must have handed the treatise either to Elizabeth or to some member of the church, for this most moving and valuable work was printed privately.

Still the weary prison days stretched out before Bunyan. He may have heard various items of news concerning events taking place outside his prison walls and learnt with dismay that Bishop Gilbert Sheldon had now become Archbishop of Canterbury. In future days this harsh High Churchman would be the architect of many of the sorrows of the persecuted Dissenters.

But Bunyan would be encouraged with news from the Independent Church of which he was a part. They were continuing to meet as they were able, although always in different homes and locations. The church minutes for October 1663 state:

> The church (not withstanding their sore persecutions now come upon them) having spent many dayes in prayer with fasting, to seek the right way of the Lord in this matter, did joyntly make choice of brother Samuell Fenne (now lately delivered out of prison) and John Whiteman for their pastors and elders to minister the word and ordinances of Jesus Christ to them.[7]

To know that those young believers to whom he himself had preached, many of them his own children in the faith, were receiving pastoral care and were remaining faithful despite the difficulties and persecutions which were now their lot, would have brought much consolation to the prisoner incarcerated in the County Jail. Despite this, Bunyan longed to help them further, and so resorted to the only means he knew in his present condition — the written word.

Calling his new treatise *Christian Behaviour*, Bunyan began to lay down spiritual guidelines for them to follow. Above all, he was anxious that these men and women should express in the quality of their lives and behaviour the reality of their Christian profession. The days were hard, and some had already quailed before the challenge and reneged on the faith. Others had backslidden and no longer attended the public worship of the church for fear of reprisals. 'Take heed,' he urges such people, 'thy soul, heaven and eternity lies at stake.'

The work is divided up into many categories of relationships, giving guidance as to the standards expected: to the husband, the wife; to parents with their children and children with their parents; to servants and masters, and to neighbours. Lastly, he details the dangers of such temptations as pride and adultery, the latter a sin which he considers a 'pervasive sin — a very taking sin' because it is 'natural above all sins to mankind'.[8]

There is, however, a special pathos in this work. Although George Offor, in his edition of Bunyan's writings, dates it in 1674, an edition is extant in the British Library bearing the date '1663', which makes it one of Bunyan's earliest prison writings. Discovered in 1864 among the books belonging to a farmer in Kent, this edition carries in its title the evocative words, *By John Bunyan — a prisoner of hope.* The treatise closes with the words: 'Farewell, From my place of confinement in Bedford this 17th of the 4th month, 1663'.

It is also evident that Bunyan expected his death to be imminent — at any moment the jailer could unlock the gate and summon him forth to the scaffold. This is borne out by his concluding words. Fearing that he might never have another chance to urge his converts to the standard of godliness expected of believers, he wrote:

> Thus have I in few words written to you before I die, a word to provoke you to faith and holiness, because I desire that you may have the life laid up for all them that believe in the Lord Jesus and love one another when I am deceased... Wherefore I, not knowing the shortness of my life ... have

taken this opportunity to present these few lines unto you for your edification.[9]

Nothing remains to mark the spot where this 'prisoner of hope' suffered, prayed and wrote apart from a plaque in the pavement indicating where the old prison once stood, on the corner of Silver Street and High Street. But these written memorials still have power to move the heart more effectively than any other monument.

26

The city of gold

The sweet sound of someone playing a flute could be heard coming from the upper prison day room in Bedford County Jail. Who could be creating such music in the midst of the squalor and degradation of a prison? None other than John Bunyan, prisoner of the Crown, a man who would rather obey his God and his understanding of the Scriptures than buy his freedom at the expense of his conscience. But when the jailer came up to investigate the source of the music, he was puzzled to find nothing more than his prisoner occupied as usual, perhaps making metal tags, or else absorbed in some stirring account of bygone days recorded by John Foxe in the *Book of Martyrs*.

From his youth Bunyan had enjoyed music. He had abandoned his early practice of bell ringing in the Elstow parish church when his conscience was awakened and he feared he might be doing wrong, but the love of music remained strong. As we have seen, before he left Elstow in 1655 he had made himself a small violin, carefully crafted from metal and inscribed with his name. Whether he had been able to bring his violin into the prison with him, we do not know. But one day the prisoner had an idea. If he

Bunyan's flute (see also picture on page 76)
Reproduced by kind permission of Bunyan Meeting Free Church, Bedford, England

removed one leg from his stool, hollowed it out and notched it in the correct places, he could make an acceptable flute. Then if he heard the jailer approaching, he had only to slip the leg quickly back into place.[1]

And Bunyan also loved to sing. Little besides metrical psalms, chants and paraphrases of Scripture was sung in the churches of his day — the use of other religious verse in song was still taboo.[2] As already noted, many of Bunyan's poems followed the style of the popular ballads and could easily be put to music. Some were hymns in all but name. In that same year of 1664, a contemporary, Benjamin Keach, was put in the stocks in Winslow, Buckinghamshire, for publishing a work called *A Child's Instructor,* a question-and-answer instruction primer which included some hymns. Although all copies of it were torched, Keach was undeterred, and later republished his book. Like Bunyan he faced constant suffering for his views as a Dissenter.

The situation for the persecuted Dissenters was becoming steadily more oppressive. Whereas the pastors and teachers had suffered under the terms of the 1662 Act of Uniformity, now it was the turn of the people. In May 1664 the first Conventicle Act was passed. This legislation ordered that no more than five people in addition to the immediate members of a family should gather together for any form of religious activity. The rank and file of Baptists, Independents, Presbyterians, Quakers, and any other grouping outside the established church, now became the target of this new Conventicle Act.

From the point of view of the government of the day such an act was to some extent understandable. Having enjoyed extraordinary religious freedom under Cromwell and under the protectorate parliaments, many were seething with discontent against the restrictions imposed by the new regime, especially those still loyal to 'the good old cause'— the Commonwealth. Such people felt that everything for which they had fought, and for which their sons had died, had been lost. In York twenty-six men were executed in late 1663, sixteen of them hung, drawn and quartered, for allegedly being involved in the Farnley Wood Plot, which aimed at overthrowing the government. In addition the Fifth Monarchist rebellion in 1661 had done a great deal of damage to the Dissenting cause. One Presbyterian, Thomas Horrockes, preached a sermon in 1664 in which he threatened that the Cavalier Parliament would 'lye in the dust' before the year ended, and George Cokayne, a personal friend of Bunyan's from Cotton End near Elstow, dared to suggest that Charles II deserved to be beheaded as his father had been. To the government, therefore, security was all-important and the Conventicle Act was seen as a way of stamping out not only religious dissent, but any secret gathering that might be plotting an uprising of some kind.

The new Conventicle Act was harsh in its terms. For anyone discovered at a service of worship, however innocent it might be, a fine of £5, or three months imprisonment, was immediately imposed. For a second offence the penalty was doubled. A third offence called for a fine of £100, or seven years banishment. Private homes could be suddenly surrounded and searched to count the number of people gathered together. This new law, introduced by the Cavalier Parliament under legislation known as the Clarendon Code,[3] brought a fearsome degree of suffering upon the people. On occasions a small group of friends gathered together at a funeral could face the same penalties if more than five were present.

Often men and women were too poor to pay such exorbitant fines; then the consequences could be still worse. Armed with a warrant to seize whatever goods they could find in lieu of payment, constables would ransack the homes of the poor, sometimes even in the middle of the night. Kitchen implements, bedding, tools vital for trade and even food for sick children were all taken at will, often condemning the victim to abject poverty. Rarely would sufferers put up any resistance — indeed there was little they could do in their own defence. Even a time-server like Samuel Pepys the diarist felt a stab of compassion for the injustices inflicted on Dissenters. A note in his diary for 7 August 1664 recorded that he had seen 'several poor creatures carried by, by constables for being at a conventicle,' and added, '... they go like

lambs without any resistance. I would to God they would conform or be more wise and not be catched.'

A number of congregations devised their own means of
escape. As magistrates could only administer justice within the
borders of their respective counties, Dissenters might worship in
meeting houses which bordered several counties. If a look-out
man warned of the approach of magistrates from one county, the
congregation could quickly disappear into another to be beyond
their reach.[4] Even so, the prisons were now packed to overflowing with men and women who had been discovered worshipping
in some hidden corner.

Although it was little compensation to John Bunyan that his
fellow Christians were also suffering, he now had an unexpected
bonus of sweet companionship within those prison walls. Sometimes a whole congregation caught worshipping was marched
straight to prison.[5] A certain John Donne, ejected from his church
in Pertenhall in 1662, had gathered his congregation together in
nearby Keysoe Woods in the middle of the night. Surely none
would molest them there. But he was wrong. All of those present
— sixty or more people — were hustled off to Bedford County
Jail. So too were Samuel Fenne, co-pastor of the Bedford Independent Church, and his brother John, a seller of haberdashery in
Bedford, together with many others from their church. At times
that upstairs day room was packed to capacity with Dissenters.

If he must be severed from his congregation, John Bunyan
now discovered that a congregation had come to join him. We
can only imagine the depth of joy and fellowship those suffering
Christians experienced as they worshipped their God together in
such circumstances, well knowing that no cruel constable could
burst in and molest them further. One who was imprisoned
among them has left an early record of those memorable days:

> In the midst of the hurry which so many newcomers oc-
> casioned I have heard Mr Bunyan both preach and pray with
> that mighty Spirit of faith and plerophory [i.e. fulness] of di-
> vine assistance that has made me stand and wonder.[6]

A number of John Bunyan's most memorable printed sermons
started out as messages addressed to his fellow prisoners. One

remarkable example is found in a work entitled *The Holy City or The New Jerusalem*. The preacher himself describes the origin of this piece:

> Upon a certain first-day, I being together with my brethren in our prison chamber, they expected that, according to our custom, something should be spoken out of the Word for our mutual edification; but at that time I felt myself, it being my turn to speak, so empty, spiritless and barren, that I thought I should not have been able to speak among them so much as five words of truth with life and evidence; but as it fell out providentially I cast mine eye upon the eleventh verse of the one and twentieth chapter of this prophecy [Revelation] upon which, when I had considered a while, methought I perceived something of that jasper in whose light you will find this holy city is said to ... descend; wherefore having got in my eye some dim glimmerings thereof ... I with a few groans did carry my meditations to the Lord Jesus for a blessing which he did forthwith grant according to his grace; and helping me to set before my brethren we did all eat and were well refreshed.[7]

Rising to preach amid the squalid surroundings of the jail, John Bunyan directed the gaze of his hearers beyond those strong walls that held them captive, beyond 'the lumber and cumber of this world', to the beauties of the New Jerusalem — a city of gold, the true church of Jesus Christ. He saw a threefold picture of the church.

First there was the church as she was in her early days — the period described in the Acts of the Apostles, together with the first couple of centuries of her life.

Secondly, he envisaged the church in the days of her apostasy and captivity. By this Bunyan meant a period stretching from the third century onwards until his own day. This period he describes as 'the days of antichrist'. During it the church had been constantly under the domination of her enemies. Towards the end of this second period, Bunyan placed a phase in the life of the church which he described as 'altar work' — a period when the great doctrines of Scripture were recovered through the work of the Reformers such as Luther and Calvin. This 'altar work' was followed by 'temple work' — a description of Bunyan's own time, marking the end of this second period. 'Temple work' was characterized by the emergence of a pure church, 'a select company of visible believers, walking in the faith and holiness of the gospel', separate from 'carnal gospellers'.[8] In other words, this period marked the growth of Independent churches like Bunyan's own. However, this entire second phase, as he visualized it, was fast drawing to a close.

Soon Antichrist would be overthrown and a third epoch in the life of the church, or 'city work', would be ushered in.[9] Many who delved into dating such events thought that the year 1666, bearing that unusual threefold 'six', the number of the beast,[10] would witness the final overthrow of Antichrist[11] and the advent of Christ's millennial reign. To what extent Bunyan was affected by this thinking we do not know, but the dating of this treatise in 1665 may well be significant.[12]

In *The Holy City*, Bunyan is mainly taken up with 'city work', this third era, in which he foresees 'the gospel church returning out of antichristian captivity' — into a millennium of prosperity which will end in a final consummation of glory when Christ returns to judge the nations. As we have seen, Bunyan had once anticipated an imminent return of Christ when he would reign together 'with his saints'.[13] But now, as he writes *The Holy City*, he appears to have modified this view.

As Bunyan pictures the start of this millennium of favour and blessedness, with 'that great city, the holy Jerusalem descending out of heaven from God', he is captivated by the glory and beauty of the true church of Jesus Christ during this coming period of her prosperity. Many would then be converted and brought in, for Satan, 'that great red dragon', would be 'delivered up into the hand of Christ who hath shut him up and sealed him down for a thousand years'.[14] Not that the church would be without her enemies. Just as there were snipers and opponents when the walls of the first Jerusalem were being rebuilt under the leadership of Nehemiah, so too, as the walls of this New Jerusalem are being erected, she will still have her enemies. But these walls, described in Revelation 21, are built on sturdy foundations and are therefore a strong defence against the enemy.

Spiritual life and zeal in the hearts of God's people will run high in those days, for, as Bunyan explains:

> Satan [being] thus tied up, we shall, together with this mercy, receive such a plentiful pouring forth of the Holy Ghost, that though there will remain in us still reminders of our corruptions, yet, by the plentiful indwelling of the Holy Ghost, and the joy and peace and heavenly sweetness thereof, these things shall lie like lean, withered, blasted things.[15]

In this graphic sermon, which Bunyan later expanded into a lengthy treatise, he began to reveal his genius for allegory. Now and then flashes of it had already entered his writings, but with such a theme as the coming glory of the church, his imagination had full rein. For each part of this golden city, the true church of Christ, Bunyan allocates a meaning. The twelve gates symbolize both the ready access his people may have to spiritual communion with God and also the diverse peoples that will enter the city during this millennium of increase and joy. Bunyan shares the hope that the Jewish people will then be converted in large numbers through the preaching of the gospel, so he tells us that these twelve gates signify 'the happy return and restoration of those poor distressed creatures the twelve tribes of the Jews that are scattered abroad'.[16]

Imprisoned as he was within a gloomy jail where the brightness of full daylight rarely penetrated, one of the most desirable features of the heavenly city for Bunyan was its light. The apostle John described it as 'like unto a stone most precious, even like a jasper stone, clear as crystal' (Revelation 21:11). For a prisoner like Bunyan, the very thought of a day when all darkness will be dispelled for ever, and with it 'the spiders and dragons and owls and foul spirits of antichrist', brought him joy. In a rare reference to his own circumstances, he writes wistfully, 'You know how especially pleasant [this light] is to such men that have for several years been held in the chains of affliction.'[17]

Not only is the New Jerusalem a place of light, but its streets are made of pure gold, like 'transparent glass'. And why, asks

Bunyan rhetorically, should the streets be of gold? Among his other reasons he assures his hearers that gold symbolizes:

> ... how invincible and unconquerable a spirit the people of God are possessed with. Gold is a metal so invincible and unconquerable that no fire can consume it; it may burn it indeed and melt it, but the gold remains, and holds its ground ... the more it is burned and melted, the more it recovers its colour and the more it shakes off its dross and dishonour. Just thus it is with the people of God...[18]

We can almost sense the consolation these words must have brought to his first hearers, incarcerated within the dingy walls of Bedford Jail, their earthly prospects all but ruined. And for Bunyan himself, these grand hopes of the Christian gospel gave him the strength to endure his sufferings with the long separation from his family.

Progressing in his exposition of Revelation 21, Bunyan reaches verse 22, and here there is a marked change. For we read that the holy city has no temple, for 'the Lord God Almighty and the Lamb are the temple of it'. Bunyan is quick to recognize that the glory of the church which he has been describing is now 'swallowed up' with a yet brighter radiance. The millennium of blessing for the church on earth has been exchanged for those more glorious joys of heaven itself.

Whether or not we concur with Bunyan's apocalyptic views, there is no doubt that he seeks to support every statement he makes with scriptural references: the only textbook in his hand is the Bible itself. To the passage in Revelation 21 he adds quotations from the Old Testament, particularly the prophecies of Daniel and Ezekiel. And, in this context, he also quotes Haggai 2:7-9, where the Lord of glory suddenly comes to his temple: 'I will shake all nations, and the desire of all nations shall come; and I will fill this house with glory, saith the LORD of hosts.' The initial fulfilment of these words, as Bunyan readily acknowledges, lies in the first coming of Christ, but he suggests that they carry a double interpretation: 'So shall the New Jerusalem temple-worship be swallowed up by the glory of the appearing of Christ the second time.'[19]

John Bunyan is almost lost for words as he describes this eternal state:

> Then will be a golden world... It will be then always summer, always sunshine, always pleasant, green, beautiful, fruitful and beautiful to the sons of God ... the mountains shall drop down new wine, and the hills shall flow with milk... O blessedness![20]

27

'A drop of honey from the carcase of a lion'

When Samuel Pepys saw a comet in the night sky on 24 December 1664, he made a special note of it in his diary. It seemed to him 'larger and duller than any other star'. Who could tell whether this unusual sight could presage some strange event, possibly even a national disaster? That very week a man died of the plague in Drury Lane, in the St Giles area of London. Called the Black Death because of the colour of the swellings that accompanied the dreaded disease, the plague had already made several sweeping scourges through London earlier in the century. During the fourteenth century it had wiped out a million and a half from a population of four million in England. So the appearance of the comet filled many with foreboding, and nervous people were quick to link any unusual signs and portents with some fresh outbreak of the alarming disease.

Only the previous year Holland had been ravaged by plague. Charles II had forbidden any further trade between the two countries, but everyone knew that this was not just for fear of infection being transmitted. Fresh hostilities had recently broken out between the Dutch and the English over the possession of colonies in the New World. Londoners, however, were more concerned about the encroaching threat of plague than about any Dutch war and watched apprehensively to see if their fears would be confirmed. By early spring the death rate was rising, although the authorities ignored it at first. Still the numbers of the dead and dying mounted as the infection gradually spread ever further across London. By June a general panic set in. Charles II and his courtiers retreated to the safety of Hampton Court Palace, Parliament moved to Oxford and the mad rush to flee the city began. Every road out of London was clogged with horses, carts, wagons and coaches as all who were able to do so tried desperately to escape the ever-encroaching menace.

The summer months of 1665 were exceptionally hot, and by mid-July the death toll had soared to more than 1,000 a week. In August it had reached over 6,000 dead in a single week and by September had peaked at 7,265. Daniel Defoe, in his account of these frightening days, reports that 40,000 dogs and 200,000 cats were killed, as it was feared that these domestic animals might be carrying the disease. In fact this was the worst possible action to take, for the real culprits were the fleas carried by the black rats. In the absence of their natural predators, these rats multiplied and the plague spread.

Terrified by the rapid increase and the virulence of the disease, the Lord Mayor ordered that all victims and their families should be locked into their homes together. The house was to be marked with a red cross and sealed up for forty days until either all were dead, or the disease had been conquered. Guards posted outside the houses refused to respond to the desperate cries from within, and families were known to break down the walls of their homes in order to escape. Nurses and those appointed to care for the sick were forced to carry coloured sticks so that the public could give them a wide berth. And each evening the death carts trundled down the roads with the doleful cry: 'Bring out your dead.' Eventually the plague would kill one in five of all Londoners.

Among the first to flee the city were the clerics who had flooded in to take up the vacant pulpits following the Great Ejection of St Bartholomew's Day, 1662. But there were faithful pastors, banned from their pulpits, who now saw their opportunity and duty to return to their pulpits in order to minister to the sick and the dying. Richard Baxter, ejected from his own pulpit in Kidderminster, has left this description:

> Divers [i.e. several] nonconformists, pitying the dying and distressed people that had none to call the impenitent to repentance, nor to help them to prepare for another world, nor to comfort them in their terrors when about ten thousand died in a week, resolved that no obedience to the laws of any mortal men whosoever could justify them for neglecting of men's souls and bodies in such extremities...[1]

Records of the devastation caused by the Black Death in previous epidemics sent a chill of fear throughout the land. During the fourteenth-century outbreak whole villages had been wiped out in a matter of days. Rumours of the fearful death rate in London would have reached John Bunyan in prison. Doubtless some of his friends in the city had already died. Perhaps the plague would soon spread beyond the capital, eventually sweeping through the country. Many who observed these things were convinced that this outbreak of the plague was evidence of the righteous anger of God on the nation because of the cruel measures inflicted on many innocent Dissenters.

The County Jail in Bedford would be particularly vulnerable to the infection due to its filth and overcrowding. But, rather than brood on the very real possibility of the contagion reaping its grim harvest in the prison and among his own family and friends, John Bunyan busied himself with further writing.[2] It may even have been the possibility of imminent death that caused him to begin an account of his own early life and conversion, especially for the sake of his converts, and perhaps also for his children and Elizabeth.

However, as we have already seen, *Grace Abounding to the Chief of Sinners* was not intended primarily as autobiography. Bunyan carefully explains in his preface that he was addressing his words to his own spiritual children, those converted through his preaching, in order to point out a way of deliverance from the temptations and the pain of spiritual anguish which he had suffered. Even though Justice Kelynge might wish to silence the tinker-preacher by recourse to an old Elizabethan Act of Parliament, clapping him up in jail, Bunyan was still able to maintain the close bond with his 'dear children' and to minister to them with his pen.

In parts Bunyan's preface to *Grace Abounding* reads more like a New Testament epistle. 'I thank my God upon every remembrance of you,' he writes. All letters need an address and, understandably enough, Bunyan gives his own as the 'Lion's Den', commenting that he can 'rejoice even while I stick between the teeth of lions in the wilderness' — an eloquent commentary on his prison conditions. He now hoped that younger Christians might be able to benefit by his experiences, so avoiding the pitfalls that had ensnared him:

> If you have sinned against light; if you are tempted to blaspheme; if you are down in despair; if you think God fights against you; or if heaven is hid from your eyes, remember it was thus with your father, but out of them all the Lord delivered me.[3]

In addition Bunyan wanted them to recollect God's early dealings with their souls:

> Remember, I say, the word that first laid hold upon you, remember your terrors of conscience, and fear of death and hell; remember also your tears and prayers to God; yea, how you sighed under every hedge for mercy.

Such recollections can prove a powerful antidote to spiritual depression.

Because of his earnest desire to encourage these younger believers, he points out that he is deliberately writing in a down-to-earth, straightforward style. There must be no possibility of any misunderstanding. He is determined therefore to 'be plain and simple and lay the thing down as it was'.[4]

Bunyan realized that only those with spiritual insight would be able to understand him. He did not wish to publish anything which his antagonists might take hold of and use against him, further aggravating his sufferings. So in his introduction he indulges in the use of a riddle borrowed from Samson when he wished to outwit the Philistines:

> I have sent you here enclosed a drop of that honey that I
> have taken out of the carcase of a lion (Judges 14:5-9). I have
> eaten thereof myself and am much refreshed thereby.

He then explains his 'riddle'. Temptations, he tells his readers, are
like the lion Samson slew, but when they are overcome they
become like honey, strengthening and sustaining the believer to
face any subsequent trial. We can almost hear Bunyan chuckling
to himself, as he comments, 'The Philistines [i.e. his jailer and
those men who had imprisoned him] understand me not.'

In *Grace Abounding* Bunyan strays for the first time from the
style of a sermon or theological treatise into one of gripping
narrative. The reader immediately senses a new freedom of
expression and a graphic style of writing that were largely absent
from his previous books. Here we have the immediacy of the
storyteller who takes the reader from one paragraph to the next
with breathless intensity, inviting him to read on by intriguing
introductions. 'But the same day as I was in the midst of a
game...'; 'At this I felt my own heart begin to shake...'; 'By these
things I was driven to my wit's end...'; 'I remember that one day
as I was travelling ...' and 'Thus I went on for many weeks...' are
but a few examples.

There is a poetry in Bunyan's prose, a cadence and rhythm in
his sentences, which makes them memorable. Describing the
women of Bedford whose conversation he overheard, he writes,
'They spake as if joy did make them speak.' When at last he
discovered that Christ was his righteousness, he exclaims:

> Now did my chains fall from my legs indeed, I was loosed
> from my afflictions and irons... O methought, Christ! Christ!
> there was nothing but Christ that was before my eyes.

Quaint images startle the reader: 'I did shook the sermon out
of my mind'; 'This sentence lay like an ill-post upon my back';
and 'These words were to my soul like fetters of brass to my legs',
to quote just a few.

It would appear that Bunyan wrote the bulk of *Grace Abounding* during 1665 and had it ready for the printer either late in that
year or early in 1666. But who would print it? Described as

'condensed, severe, and naked in style beneath the pent fire of Bunyan's feelings and pressure of conscience',[5] it was not the sort of book that might immediately attract a publisher. Francis Smith, the Baptist publisher who tended to live dangerously near the edge of the law, often printing work which the government considered 'seditious', had printed Bunyan's last six or more titles. Smith, however, was now enduring one of his many spells in prison, and in any case, as Bunyan well knew, Smith's warehouse was in constant danger of raids. The ever-vigilant officials of the Stationers' Company who oversaw the licensing laws frequently targeted his premises. Perhaps someone had recommended to Bunyan a young publisher named George Larkin, and it was to him that the prisoner entrusted the first edition of this remarkable book.

Until 1883, a period of almost two hundred years, it was thought that no copies of this first edition had survived. Then a single copy came to light. A probable reason for the disappearance of all other copies of the first edition was the devastating Great Fire of London of 1666. According to a contemporary account, vast quantities of books stored in London warehouses were destroyed. As the writer vividly records:

> None received so grand losses and damages by that devouring conflagration as the Company of Stationers, most of whose ... storehouses and shops, together with all their books, bound and unbound ... were not only consumed in a moment, but their ashes and scorched leaves were scattered in sundry places about 16 miles from the City.[6]

This sole copy, bought by the British Museum and now safely housed in the British Library, immediately revealed an interesting fact. Bunyan had left out from this first edition published in 1666 a number of fascinating pieces of information which he had later inserted into subsequent editions.

Absent from this edition are a number of personal anecdotes from Bunyan's youth, including his risky extraction of an adder's sting and his falling into the Ouse with its near-fatal consequences. The narrative of the strange fears regarding his bell-ringing at Elstow parish church, recorded in paragraphs 33-35, is also

GRACE

Abounding to the chief of Sinners :

O R,

A Brief and Faithful

RELATION

Of the Exceeding Mercy of God in Christ, to his poor Servant

JOHN BUNYAN.

Wherein is particularly shewed, The manner of his Conversion, his sight and trouble for Sin, his Dreadful Temptations , also how he despaired of Gods mercy, and how the Lord at length thorow Christ did deliver him from all the guilt and terrour that lay upon him.

Whereunto is added,

A brief Relation of his Call to the Work of the Ministry, of his Temptations therein, as also what he hath met with in Prison.

All which was written by his own hand there, and now published for the support of the weak and tempted People of God.

Come and hear, all ye that fear God ; and I will declare what he hath done for my soul, Psal. 66.16.

LONDON:

Printed by *George Larkin.*   1666.

Title page of the first edition of *Grace Abounding*
Reproduced by courtesy of the British Library

missing from his initial account; so too was the record of the help he discovered in Martin Luther's *Commentary on the Epistle to the Galatians*, recounted in paragraphs 129-130. No mention is made of his army days. The reason for this is obvious. Bunyan was a prisoner of the Crown, and if it were widely known that he had fought in the Parliamentary army against Charles I, this could have seriously undermined his hopes of any release. Only in later years would it be safe to reveal facts about his army career, and even then Bunyan does not disclose on which side he fought. Some early writers have argued that he might have fought on the Royalist side, but had he done so, he would undoubtedly have included some record of his endeavours. To show that he had fought *for* the king's father might well have enhanced the prisoner's chances of liberty.

Although *Grace Abounding* was republished the following year, no copy of this 1667 edition has survived. In all likelihood its content was largely similar to the previous edition, for Bunyan's circumstances were unaltered. A third edition, printed by Bunyan's original publisher, Francis Smith, now back in business, was published in 1672, and this included much of the material mentioned above. Not until then did Bunyan at last feel confident enough to recount also the strange experience which had partially led to his deliverance from the crippling attacks of Satan, as recorded in paragraph 174, when he heard that unexpected voice asking if he had ever refused to be justified by the blood of Christ.[7]

Various other alterations and additions to *Grace Abounding* followed in further editions, particularly in a fourth edition, thought to have been published in 1677. A final version, consisting of 339 numbered paragraphs, was published shortly before his death. This is the version that we know today.

Omitted from any version published during Bunyan's lifetime are the records of his trial and imprisonment. These appear to have been written in four or five short instalments, possibly pastoral letters, each ending with a 'Farewell' salutation to his readers. Judging by the detail included, he must have written them shortly after the events which they record. However, it would have been highly prejudicial to the prisoner's cause to publish such facts, sabotaging any possible hope of release. A careful account of Bunyan's hearing before Francis Wingate, following his arrest, is the first of these, followed by one of his trial before Kelynge, one of Paul Cobbs' visit and, lastly, of Elizabeth Bunyan's heroic attempt to gain John's freedom. It was not until 1765, some seventy-five years after Bunyan's death, that this manuscript was first published and combined with future editions of *Grace Abounding.*

How little could those men, Francis Wingate, Kelynge, Foster, and Judge Twisden, whose merciless inhumanity had imprisoned John Bunyan, have foreseen that in so doing they were unintentionally benefiting future generations of men and women through the writings of this poor tinker! *Grace Abounding* has been numbered amongst the outstanding spiritual autobiographies of all time, and compared with such classics as Augustine of Hippo's *Confessions.*

Many even today are glad to add their names to the long list of those who can identify with John Bunyan both in his temptations and ultimate triumphs. *Grace Abounding to the Chief of Sinners* has lifted countless men and women from despair to hope. Fourteen-year-old Andrew Fuller, who would go on to become the influential Baptist pastor of Kettering in the late eighteenth and early nineteenth centuries, was among them. Weighed down by an accusing conscience and torn with doubts, he could record: 'Sometimes I was very much affected ... in reading such books as Bunyan's *Grace Abounding to the Chief of Sinners.*'[8]

28

A masterpiece in the making

When Thomas Farynor, Charles II's baker, forgot to shut down his oven fire one night in September 1666, he could not know that his carelessness would ignite the greatest conflagration that London had ever known. Sparks from his fire fell on an adjacent pile of kindling wood, and by the time Farynor had been in bed for three hours his shop and house were ablaze. A high wind carried the sparks from the burning shop in Pudding Lane to the Star Inn in nearby Fish Street Hill. Hay provided to feed the animals of travellers staying the night at the inn soon caught fire … and so the fire spread.

In a city of buildings largely half-timbered and covered with pitch, many with thatched roofs, the risk of fire was high. For five dreadful days the inferno consumed everything in its path. By order of the king many homes were purposely blown up by gunpowder to check the course of the blaze. The panic and tragedy that followed were recorded by Samuel Pepys in his diary:

> So I [went] down to the waterside ... and there saw a lamentable fire ... Everybody endeavouring to remove their goods, and flinging [them] into the river or bringing them into lighters [flat bottomed barges] that lay off; poor people staying in their houses as long as till the very fire touched them, and then running into boats, or clambering from one pair of stairs by the waterside to another.

Richard Baxter adds:

> The loss in houses and goods is scarcely to be valued. And among the rest, the loss of books was an exceeding great detriment to the interest of piety and learning.[1]

As we have noted, the Great Fire probably destroyed most copies of the first edition of John Bunyan's *Grace Abounding to the Chief of Sinners.*

Before the fire was finally brought under control, one and a half square miles of the city had been reduced to cinders. Eighty-seven of London's old churches had succumbed to the flames and more than 13,000 homes had been destroyed. The Monument now marks the spot where Thomas Farynor's house once stood.

To many it seemed that the Great Fire, following so soon after the Great Plague, was God's answer to another cruel measure instigated by the Cavalier Parliament in order to crush any dissent from the national church. As one contemporary writer put it:

> The late dreadful fire, kindled by our God-provoking sins and abominations ... hath within three days turned nearly eighty-eight parishes and parish churches into heaps of ashes and rubbish to the just horror and amazement of all spectators.[2]

Harshly Anglican in its stance, Parliament had been angered at the apparent audacity of Nonconformist ministers and Dissenters who had defied the Conventicle Act and had gathered the people together for worship during the Great Plague. Archbishop Gilbert Sheldon, an implacable opponent of Nonconformity and Dissent, was convinced that the ejected ministers were 'holding unlawful assemblies under colour or pretence of exercise of religion'. In fact, so he maintained, they were taking advantage of national disasters in order to destabilize the government even more. So, from the safety of Oxford, these politicians did not hesitate to burden the oppressed Dissenters yet further.

Although the king himself was unhappy about the laws being passed against a substantial number of his subjects — particularly as they also discriminated against Roman Catholics — Parliament was unrepentant. The Five Mile Act, passed in October 1665, was intended to put a firm stop to ejected pastors preaching in their own pulpits again. By this act no pastor or teacher was allowed to live within five miles of the town or the place where he had formerly ministered unless he was prepared to swear a stringent oath of loyalty to king and church. A crippling £40 fine was to be imposed on any who were discovered in breach of the act. So, in addition to their expulsion from their pulpits, many ministers consequently faced the added dilemma of homelessness as well.

In several instances the result of this new legislation was counterproductive, particularly in the wake of the two national disasters. People were even more prepared to listen attentively to the preachers who, despite the Five Mile Act, were still preaching to devastated and homeless Londoners. A number of meeting places were hastily built where churches had been destroyed by the Great Fire to accommodate the anxious congregations.

Although the Great Fire had finally eradicated the last pockets of plague infection in London, this was by no means true of the rest of the country. Stories of the heroism of the villagers of Eyam, in the Peak District of Derbyshire, are well known. The disease had entered the village through a parcel of cloth sent from London. Instead of fleeing their homes, and so spreading the contagion to all the surrounding areas, the villagers agreed to a self-imposed quarantine, thus containing the disease. But out of a population of 350 all but ninety had perished by September 1666. One woman lost her husband and six children within the space of a few days; their graves are still to be seen today. In July 1666 the plague also broke out in Newport Pagnell, the garrison town just twelve miles from Bedford where Bunyan had served during the Civil War. Before the year was out 600 deaths had been recorded in the town, the vast majority from the plague. John Bunyan's friend and first bookseller, Matthias Cowley, was among the victims.

Clearly, extra precautions needed to be taken in nearby Bedford, which probably explains why John Bunyan was released from prison for a few short months at this time. The grime and rat infestation of the prison made it a vulnerable target, and prison staff may well have been depleted as a result of either sickness or fear. Plague did indeed find some forty victims from an area of the town not far from the jail, influencing the prison authorities to grant Bunyan a temporary release. Charles Doe's brief account of his friend's life in *The Struggler* records this information for us.[3] It is also corroborated by an anonymous biographer, and by the fact that Bunyan's name is missing from a list of prisoners in the County Jail in 1666.

To have her husband home at last must have been a deep joy for Elizabeth. Her courage and faithfulness over the years, mothering John's family and supporting John himself, make this woman's name shine out in the annals of Christian heroism. John's blind elder daughter, Mary, now sixteen, was far from well; his second daughter, also named Elizabeth, was twelve and the boys, John and Thomas, were ten and eight. Before long John's second wife had the added happiness of knowing that she was expecting her own child, a compensation for the baby she had lost when John was first arrested.

But John Bunyan's freedom did not last long. And we can well imagine that the prison floor seemed harder and the straw filthier when he found himself back in his old surroundings. Charles Doe informs us that he had been rearrested while he was once more engaged in his well-loved work of preaching to the people. John must have found this second imprisonment hard indeed. During his first six years in prison he had written and published at least nine treatises, sermons or poems. Now he temporarily fell silent, publishing nothing between the years 1666 and 1672, although, as we shall see, he was still engaged in writing. It is also likely that his blind daughter Mary, whom he had described as 'nearer my heart than all I had besides', died at about this time. The very thought of added suffering for this girl 'would break my heart in pieces', he had once declared. Perhaps more than ever before, with Elizabeth expecting another child, John found that he must 'pass a sentence of death' on all he held most dear. Yet, as he had written earlier, such afflictions made him 'look to God through Christ to help me and carry me through this world'.

These events might well have caused him to recall a sermon he had once preached on 1 Corinthians 9:24: 'So run that ye may obtain.' Very probably this sermon, which he had entitled *The Heavenly Footman*, was actually preached before he was first imprisoned in 1660. His friends, Ebenezer Chandler and John Wilson, writing about Bunyan in later years, recalled the preacher's habit of writing up his sermons, or at least of writing extensive notes of them, shortly after he had preached them. These notes would later become the raw material of his printed works.

So, faced with his present grievous circumstances, John Bunyan might well have realized the relevance of this message to his sufferings and to his own need for endurance. 'THEY THAT WILL HAVE HEAVEN MUST RUN FOR IT', he wrote in capitals on his paper as he began to urge upon all who hoped to reach heaven at last the vital importance of active perseverance in the Christian race. Perhaps he preached the sermon again to his fellow prisoners, for some might have been tempted to succumb to despair under their trials. But his real target was those whom he addressed in his introductory 'epistle' as 'all the slothful and careless people'. Bunyan knew well that many outside the prison walls who had once professed faith were now complying with the values of the times and neglecting spiritual issues. More than this, he was aware of a widespread antinomianism in the churches which had been incipient from the days of the Civil War and was now prevalent among many who made high-sounding religious claims. Because of God's abundant grace, they were saying, he did not require holiness on the part of those who professed faith — in fact the greater their sins, the more God's grace would shine out. Bunyan felt the necessity of warning such people of their imminent spiritual danger.

The Heavenly Footman, subtitled *A Description of the Man that Gets to Heaven*, is perhaps one of the most convicting and searching books that Bunyan ever wrote. He allows no one to remain complacent. 'All or everyone that runneth doth not obtain the prize,' he cautions, and adds, '... there be many that do run, yea, and run far too, who yet miss of the crown at the end of the race.' He then gives seven reasons why it is incumbent upon all who claim Christian faith to strive to obtain that crown. 'They that will have heaven must run for it,' he reiterates over and over again. Opportunities do not last for ever:

> ... perchance the gates of heaven may be shut shortly. Sometimes sinners have not heaven-gates open to them so long as they suppose.[4]

In answering the question of one who enquires anxiously, 'But how should a poor soul ... run?' Bunyan provides nine directions on how to run the Christian race. Nothing, he tells the enquirer, must be allowed to hinder him:

> What, will you go, saith the devil, without your sins, pleasures and profits? ... Soul, take this counsel and say, 'Satan, sin, lust, pleasure, profit, friends, companions and everything else, let me alone, stand off, come not nigh me, for I am running for heaven, for my soul, for God, for Christ, from hell and everlasting damnation: if I win, I win all, and if I lose, I lose all; let me alone, for I will not hear.' SO RUN.[5]

These nine directions are followed by nine motives to spur on those that would win the prize. Yet Bunyan is a compassionate pastor and knows that the believer often grows weary in the Christian life. Despite this, he must continue to run, but Christ will come to the aid of his exhausted people:

> When thou hast run thyself down weary, then the Lord Jesus will take thee up and carry thee. Is not this enough to make any poor soul begin his race?[6]

Finally, in typical Puritan style, Bunyan adds nine 'uses' that must follow from his teaching, concluding that a man must run for his life, not falling into the trap of looking back, as Lot's wife had done. This small book contains some of the strongest imperatives in all Puritan writings urging Christians to press the harder after heaven. Always Bunyan holds out the real and fearful possibility that if anyone turns back and gives up the race he may lose his own soul in the end.

Although Bunyan's teaching may seem at first glance to run contrary to the Reformed doctrine of the final perseverance of believers, it does in fact echo the biblical tension that a believer's assurance of acceptance with God must go hand in hand with persistence and spiritual diligence. Even the apostle Paul, in the passage from which Bunyan was preaching, said, 'I therefore so run ... lest ... when I have preached to others, I myself should be a castaway.' The passages in Hebrews that had once so frightened Bunyan are now seen as signposts warning all who profess the faith of the dangers awaiting them if they fail to persevere — a biblical emphasis.

Evidences that this message was almost certainly first preached before Bunyan was imprisoned in 1660 can be found in the sermon itself. For example, he refers to the length of time that he had been a true believer as only short.[7] In addition there are constant references to issues that were alive and crucial to Bunyan in the late 1650s. He warns twice against the fate of Francis Spira, a man who had sinned against light and mercy, and whose case had brought Bunyan himself to the brink of despair. He even cautions against the danger of emulating Esau, whose record had also so nearly caused him to stumble.[8] He urges his hearers not to be waylaid in their race to heaven by the teaching of sects such as 'the Quakers, the Ranters, and the Freewillers', all of whom had figured prominently in his mind in the mid to late 1650s. He describes himself as an 'Anabaptist', a term he would have avoided in a later work. A final evidence that this was an early sermon to which he was now returning comes from the fact that the only two books of his to which he refers were both written in the late 1650s: *A Few Sighs from Hell* (published in 1658) and *The Doctrine of Law and Grace Unfolded* (1659).

However, the date when Bunyan was writing up this powerful sermon is highly significant for another reason — a reason which he himself explains:

And thus it was: I writing of the Way
and race of saints in this our gospel day
fell suddenly into an allegory

about their journey and the Way to Glory;
in more than twenty things, which I set down;
this done, I twenty more had in my crown,
and they again began to multiply
Like sparks that from the coals do fly...[9]

It was while he was urging men and women to run for heaven regardless of hindrances that Bunyan first conceived the idea for his great allegory, *The Pilgrim's Progress*. The exact words from *The Heavenly Footman* which grabbed his imagination and sent new ideas tumbling through his brain might well have been these:

Because the way is long (I speak metaphorically), and there is many a dirty step, many a high hill, much work to do, a wicked heart, world and devil to overcome; I say, there are many steps to be taken by those that intend to be saved... Thou must run a long and tedious journey through the vast howling wilderness, before thou come to the land of promise.[10]

And so, laying aside his present manuscript for the time being and reaching for a fresh wad of paper, Bunyan began to scribble down the new ideas that were flooding his mind. Addressing them as if they were living people, he writes:

Nay then, thought I, if that you breed so fast
I'll put you by yourselves, lest you at last
should prove *ad infinitum* and eat out
the book that I already am about.[11]

It has traditionally, even romantically, been thought that John Bunyan's masterpiece, *The Pilgrim's Progress*, was written almost ten years later in a small prison cell on Bedford Bridge known as the Town Clink, a prison demolished in 1795 because of storm damage.[12] Attractive as this idea may seem, it is highly improbable. The place and date of the composition of this great book have been the subject of considerable scholastic scrutiny coupled with the discovery of various documents.[13] The burden of evidence makes it virtually certain that the Bedford County Jail was the birthplace of the great allegory.

An old print of Bedford Bridge shows the Town Clink, which has traditionally (though probably incorrectly) been identified as the place where *The Pilgrim's Progress* was written.

Taking Bunyan's own testimony that the seed thoughts for *The Pilgrim's Progress* sprang from a book he was already writing on the 'race of saints in this our gospel day', we may safely assume that this book was indeed *The Heavenly Footman*.[14] He must therefore have started to write his great allegory in about 1667–68.[15] When the ideas first came to him, John Bunyan had no thought of turning them into a book; it was merely as a diversion from his present depressing circumstances that he wrote:

> When at the first I took my pen in hand
> thus for to write, I did not understand
> that I at all should make a little book
> in such a mode. Nay, I had undertook
> to make another, which, when almost done,
> before I was aware, I this begun...
>
> Nor did I undertake
> thereby to please my neighbour; no, not I;
> I did it mine ownself to gratifie.
> Neither did I but vacant seasons spend

in this my scribble; nor did I intend
but to divert myself in doing this,
from worser thoughts, which make me do amiss.

The *Heavenly Footman* and *The Pilgrim's Progress* must
therefore be regarded as complementing each other, both urging
his readers to persevere in the race for heaven. Words in *The
Heavenly Footman* remind us again and again of ideas developed
more fully in *The Pilgrim's Progress*.

Beware of by-paths [Bunyan warns his readers in *The
Heavenly Footman*] take heed thou do not turn into those
lanes which lead out of the way. There are crooked paths,
paths in which men go astray, paths that lead to death and
damnation, but take heed of all those. [16]

We are immediately reminded of the way Christian and Hopeful
wandered into By-Path Meadow and soon found themselves the
helpless captives of Giant Despair.

Again in his introductory lines to *The Pilgrim's Progress*
Bunyan repeats the grand themes which had occupied his mind
when writing *The Heavenly Footman:*

This book it chalketh out before thine eyes
the man that seeks the everlasting prize...
It also shows how he runs and runs
till he unto the gate of glory comes.

The overall object he has in view in *The Pilgrim's Progress* is to
press home the vital importance of perseverance if one would
obtain 'the everlasting prize'. This too is the urgent exhortation in
The Heavenly Footman: 'The prize is heaven and if you will have
it, you must run for it,' Bunyan declares, adding in the final words
of the book:

Be sure that thou begin by times [early]; get into the way;
run apace and hold out to the end; and the Lord give thee a
prosperous journey.

Although *The Pilgrim's Progress* takes the crown of all Bunyan's writings, this small introductory book, *The Heavenly Footman*, has had a profound effect on many Christians both in the past and in our own day, and to read it cannot fail to spur the believer onwards in his race to heaven.

29

From a den in the wilderness

'As I walked through the wilderness of this world, I lighted on a certain place where was a den.' These are among the best-known words in all literature. With them John Bunyan introduces his readers to what he modestly calls 'my scribble' in his versified 'Apology' for *The Pilgrim's Progress*.[1] Setting the tone for his entire book, he immediately unites two opposite concepts. The first is that of the 'den'. In his autobiography, *Grace Abounding*, Bunyan had described his prison as a 'Lion's Den', and now, in case his readers need reminding, his new book also has its genesis in such a den — the harsh circumstances of a seventeenth-century prison, where Dissenters like Bunyan languished, many spending the best years of their adult lives there.

Married to this earthy and material concept of a 'den', a small and confined space, abode of vicious and frightening creatures, Bunyan adds, as his second image, the words 'the wilderness of this world', conveying the sense of a wide and trackless place. This alerts us to the fact that *The Pilgrim's Progress* is not only born out of the grim realism of the prison, but is also an allegory. The author is creating a backdrop for a right understanding of all that follows. Some modern writers have tried to discover the source of Bunyan's 'wilderness' imagery, suggesting that it may have come from earlier literature. But such a search is needless, for it clearly springs directly from the Scriptures, in which Bunyan had steeped himself for many years. The words themselves echo the narrative of Genesis 28 where Jacob, escaping from his brother Esau, 'lighted upon a certain place, and tarried there all night ... and lay down in that place to sleep. And he dreamed...'[2] In addition God describes himself as the one who led his people 'through that great and terrible wilderness, wherein were fiery serpents, and scorpions, and drought...' (Deuteronomy 8:15).[3]

So with these twin concepts, the den and the wilderness, Bunyan notifies us that his book is both allegorical and literal. Some indeed have seen it as a mere replay of the events of his own life, which he had recently recorded in *Grace Abounding.* However, as Richard Greaves points out, only about thirty per cent of the material in *The Pilgrim's Progress* actually reflects Bunyan's own personal experiences; the remaining seventy per cent represents the character of the Christian life in this world, with its ultimate and glorious destiny in the Celestial City.

'And in that place I laid me down to sleep: And as I slept, I dreamed a dream.' John Bunyan had ever been a dreamer. Dreadful dreams had marred his childhood. He had recorded that:

> I have in my bed been greatly afflicted, while asleep, with the apprehensions of devils and wicked spirits, who still, as I then thought, laboured to draw me away with them, of which I could never be rid...

And when he woke he would stare about him, unable to grasp for the moment that it was only a dream. Later on, when he was urgently seeking salvation, he dreamt of the believers in the Bedford Meeting basking in the sunlight on a grassy mountainside. Happily in this dream he had eventually been able to squeeze through a narrow gap and sit down among them.

The narrative of a dream was therefore a natural medium for Bunyan to begin to express the thoughts that were crowding into his mind. 'Providence, grace and genius,' were the basic ingredients that uniquely equipped John Bunyan to write *The Pilgrim's*

Progress, according to one writer. Long years in a prison cell, cut off from all the family activities which would normally have absorbed his time, had given Bunyan the opportunity to meditate deeply on the great issues of life, death, heaven and hell. Most of all, he had pondered that all-important question of perseverance in the Christian race, one that had engrossed his attention as he wrote *The Heavenly Footman.*

Why God chose the poor tinker from Bedford jail to accomplish what many talented theologians, educated in the universities, could never hope to achieve, is one of the mysteries of his providence. At the very time that Bunyan began to write his allegory, another whose name has been linked with his, John Milton, among the greatest English poets, was preparing his classic *Paradise Lost* for the press. As Lord Macaulay was to write in a review essay of Robert Southey's work on Bunyan's life:

> We are not afraid to say that though there were many clever men in England during the latter half of the seventeenth century, there were only two minds which possessed the imaginative faculty in a very eminent degree. One of those minds produced the *Paradise Lost,* and the other *The Pilgrim's Progress.*[4]

The analogy in *The Pilgrim's Progress* of a journey leading away from the familiar surroundings of home to a destination still not fully disclosed also springs directly from biblical narrative. Abraham is called to leave the comforts of Ur of the Chaldees to look for 'a city which hath foundations, whose builder and maker is God'.[5] Christians are described in the New Testament as 'strangers and pilgrims' on earth.[6] Bunyan's readers would therefore have no difficulty in identifying with his lonely hero as he flees the City of Destruction, his face set towards 'yonder shining light'.

Again, lying just beneath the surface of the allegory is the realism of the suffering which Dissenters and Nonconformists of various descriptions had endured and which they still faced. Bunyan may well have heard of Ezekiel Rogers' epic journey in 1638 as he and the entire population of the village of Rowley in East Yorkshire piled all their goods into wagons and, leaving their homes, set out for the New World, where they could worship God without compromising their consciences. But much more recently the Five Mile Act had turned many preachers into 'itinerants' as they wandered homeless from place to place, preaching wherever they could snatch an opportunity without endangering the lives of their hearers. Oliver Heywood, to quote just one example, would traverse thousands of miles in Yorkshire and Lancashire before his death in 1702.

Benjamin Keach, another of Bunyan's contemporaries whose sufferings at the hands of an aggressive government were real and acute, wrote a book in a similar vein to *The Pilgrim's Progress,* published in 1673. Calling it *War with the Devil,* Keach depicts a young man whom he calls Youth being instructed by Truth, but also facing conflict with the powers of evil. Keach too is deeply concerned about the need for perseverance and adds a dialogue at the close of the book in which an old man named Apostate has reneged on his desires to journey to Canaan and is returning to 'Egypt' — the place of bondage. Apostate disparages Youth's hope:

> What grounds have you, my friend, for to believe
> If you forsake all things, you shall receive
> This land you speak of, for your own possession?

But Youth remains steadfast and Apostate's end is one of horror, as he cries out:

> I must confess, I know not what to say:
> If there's a God, then cursed be the day
> That ever I was born.[7]

Whether Bunyan had read *War with the Devil* or not, we cannot know, but if so, then its popularity, for it ran into many editions, may have encouraged him in his own allegory. The universal appeal of *The Pilgrim's Progress,* however, lies in the fact that anyone, whether a Christian or not, can readily identify with the opening concept of distress with which Bunyan begins his allegory. To read of a man bowed low beneath a terrible burden and crying out, 'What shall I do?' touches on a frame of mind immediately compatible with the human condition. And, like the skilled preacher that he was, Bunyan takes up the initial empathy we may feel and soon reveals that the man, whose name is Christian, is distraught because of the burden of his sins; the book he is reading is none other than the Bible, warning him that his home town, the City of Destruction, is about to be burnt up in the fires of God's judgement. 'I looked,' wrote Bunyan, 'and saw him open the Book and read therein; and as he read he wept and trembled.'

Using mainly words of a single syllable, Bunyan builds up a dramatic picture of the fearful fate that awaits all who remain in such a doomed place, and it is with a measure of relief that we learn of Evangelist's arrival on the scene, pointing the way to 'yonder wicket gate'. This introduction to *The Pilgrim's Progress* is graphic and unforgettable: a burdened man running across the fields, with his fingers in his ears to shut out the cries of those who would detain him and crying out, 'Life! Life! Eternal Life!'

Most of Bunyan's first readers would immediately relate this unfolding story to his autobiography, *Grace Abounding to the Chief of Sinners.* His own anguish under the burden of his sins is clearly in John Bunyan's mind as he sits in his 'den' penning these memorable words. The Slough of Despond, which Bedford people will readily point out to visitors as they view the marshy land near John's childhood home of Elstow, also has its equivalent sense not only in Bunyan's own experience but in the Scripture itself.[8]

To explain further the presence of this fearful marshy ground on the pilgrim's way, Bunyan cannot avoid the temptation of intruding himself into the scene of his 'dream'. He has a crucial question to ask. Why, he wants to know, are poor sinners not spared the torment of falling into such a 'slough'? Why has the ground never been made sound? Help, who has rescued the struggling man, answers:

> This miry Slough is such a place as cannot be mended: It is the descent whither the scum and filth that attends Conviction of Sin doth continually run, and therefore it is called the Slough of Despond.

Nor can we be surprised when we discover that the next crisis facing the aspiring Pilgrim before he reaches the Wicket Gate is the temptation to think that a careful observation of the demands of the law of God will be an adequate means of obtaining God's favour and his salvation. The subsequent failure of such an attempt had all but crushed John Bunyan's own spirit. Bowed low beneath the burden on his back, Pilgrim now meets up with Worldly Wiseman, who, plausibly enough, directs him to the home of Legality by way of Mount Sinai where, he assures him, his burden will quickly be removed. But, following Worldly Wiseman's directions, the troubled man soon finds his burden heavier still and is overcome by fear:

> There came flashes of fire out of the Hill that made Christian afraid that he should be burned: here therefore he sweat and did quake for fear. [9]

This is a vivid pictorial representation of the teaching Bunyan had set out almost ten years earlier in *The Doctrine of Law and Grace Unfolded*.

The influence of Martin Luther at a crucial time in Bunyan's life and the liberating effect he had known in reading Luther's *Commentary on the Epistle to the Galatians*[10] is clearly evident in this part of his dream. Bunyan is anxious that his readers should not strive to rid themselves of the burden of sin by following a merely legal code as he had done. It is only through the work of Christ, as he had urged in *Law and Grace Unfolded*, that the believer can withstand 'the biggest thunder crack that the law can give and yet remain undaunted', and can say,

> O law! thou mayest roar against sin, but thou canst not reach me; thou mayest curse and condemn, but not my soul... I am out of thy reach, out of thy bounds. [11]

As he trembles under the overhanging mountainside of Sinai, Christian is rescued by Evangelist, severely admonished and set back on the right path towards the Wicket Gate. Before long he is knocking importunately at the gate, and Goodwill, a represent-ation of Christ himself, as Bunyan later makes clear, pulls the bedraggled seeker to the safety within. A wicket gate, as the *Oxford English Dictionary* points out, is a narrow door, often set within a larger one, and corresponds here to the 'strait gate' of the Lord's teaching.[12]

This door at Elstow parish church is traditionally thought to have provided the inspiration for the image of the Wicket Gate

Again tradition indicates a small door in the parish church in Elstow as a possible origin for Bunyan's imagery. Whether this was so or not, we cannot be certain, as he does not tell us himself, but certainly this Wicket Gate symbolizes far more in *The Pilgrim's Progress* than a mere gate. As Goodwill, the keeper of the gate, is a representation of Christ, so the gate itself captures the same image, for Christ declares himself to be both the door and the way to heaven.[13]

John Bunyan undoubtedly uses entry through the Wicket Gate as a symbol of spiritual conversion. It is to the gate that Evangelist directs the troubled man, and once through the gate Goodwill assures the pilgrim that 'An open door is set before thee and no man can shut it.' The gate stands at the head of the way, and as Christian journeys he meets a number of phoney travellers who have not entered by the gate, but had jumped over a wall or chosen some other entry. None of these are seen to be genuine pilgrims.

The fact that the Wicket Gate represents conversion in *The Pilgrim's Progress* has raised problems for some. Why, they ask, does Evangelist point Christian to the Wicket Gate, and not to the Cross? Why does Christian not lose his burden immediately, but instead carries it beyond the House of the Interpreter until he reaches the Place of Deliverance — the Cross? Why is there this 'separation' between the gate and the cross? Even though Bunyan adds a marginal note to the effect that only the death and blood of Christ can relieve any of the guilt and burden of sin, C. H. Spurgeon is unhappy about this ordering of events. Although his admiration for Bunyan was second to none,[14] Spurgeon says in a sermon on 'Christ Crucified', preached one Sunday evening in 1858:

> John Bunyan puts the getting rid of the burden too far from the commencement of the pilgrimage. If he meant to show what usually happens, he was right; but if he meant to show what ought to have happened, he was wrong.[15]

Over the centuries theologians have argued about the order of salvation (or *ordo salutis*). No general agreement exists about the exact sequence of the various acts of grace by which the Holy Spirit leads a man or woman from a state of unbelief to the assurance of salvation. Some view it from the divine perspective — seeking to understand the mind of God as he planned a way of salvation for fallen man. Others view it from the standpoint of human experience, and trace the order of God's working in terms of the conscious awareness of it felt by those who seek salvation.

Certainly, John Bunyan is picking up on his own experience and expressing it in the life of his pilgrim. His conversion, probably in 1653, shortly after meeting the women from the Bedford Meeting, and recorded as early as paragraph 45 in *Grace Abounding*, occurred when he was still in almost total ignorance of biblical truth. He carried a burdened conscience for many long months after this and not until paragraph 115 could he record a day when he was walking along a country path and, suddenly:

> ... the scripture came into my mind, 'He hath made peace through the blood of his cross'. By which I was made to see again and again that day that God and my soul were friends by this blood.

Even so, Bunyan's sense of relief at this point is short-lived.[16]

Perhaps it is true to say that in our own day biblical conversion has been presented too simplistically, and such expressions as 'coming to the cross' or 'coming to Christ,' or even 'making a decision', are used to cover an experience both profound and infinitely varied. William Grimshaw, commenting on the wide variety of conversion experiences in Haworth in 1744, could say, 'Nay, there are not two in 500 of God's children that are born again or brought to Christ every way alike.'[17] Even the disciples of Christ, undoubtedly regenerate men, struggled with the concept of the cross. Peter, who had just confessed, 'You are the Christ, the Son of the living God,' could soon afterwards upbraid the Saviour when he spoke of his forthcoming death.[18]

However, before giving Christian further directions, Goodwill questions him about his journey so far, about the two men, Obstinate and Pliable, who had accompanied him for part of the way, about Worldly Wiseman's mischievous advice and about the family he had left behind in the City of Destruction. Then in his dream Bunyan sees Goodwill pointing out the way ahead, and directing the traveller towards the House of the Interpreter. But, above all, Christian is anxious about the grievous burden that he still carries.

> As to thy burden [responds Goodwill], be content to bear it, until thou comest to the Place of Deliverance [the Cross]; for there it will fall from thy back by itself.

With quickened interest the reader turns the pages of *The Pilgrim's Progress* to discover how the pilgrim loses his burden; and we may well imagine that, absorbed in his dream-story, Bunyan also found his own prison circumstances easier to bear, for he tells us in his versified 'Apology':

> Thus I set pen to paper with delight,
> And quickly had my thoughts in black and white.

30

Beyond the Wicket Gate

Unexpected crises and important political changes were taking place far from the scenes of degradation and hopelessness within the Bedford jail. Even though Bunyan was still busy chronicling the progress of his pilgrim, he would have been well aware of these things. The Great Plague, followed so soon by the Great Fire, had troubled and unsettled the people. Many felt certain that the face of God was turned in anger towards the land, the prime cause undoubtedly being the persecution of godly men and women. Then the unthinkable happened. To a people as proud as the English it seemed the ultimate insult when in June 1667 the Dutch, with whom they had been at war, actually sailed up the River Medway as far as Chatham, capturing and burning English ships. The *Royal Charles,*[1] the very ship that had brought Charles II back to England in 1660, flagship of the navy, was towed away as a trophy of war, together with three other ships. All were badly damaged by fire.

The navy had been unprepared for such an attack and was seriously short of ammunition. Furious at this national humiliation, the people looked round for someone to blame. They began to recollect, with a degree of nostalgia, the days of the Protectorate when Oliver Cromwell had accomplished his stunning victories. The royal court, with its frivolity and licentious behaviour, became a prime target for the nation's discontent. Writing long years after, Rudyard Kipling recaptured the mood:

Mere powder, guns and bullets,
we scarce can get at all;
Their price was spent in merriment
and revel at Whitehall,
while we in tattered doublets
from ship to ship must row,
beseeching friends for odds and ends —
and this the Dutchmen know!
No King will heed our warnings,
no Court will pay our claims —
our King and Court for their disport
do sell the very Thames![2]

With the Treasury owing the navy at least one million pounds, and a king more interested in his mistresses than in the affairs of state, it is not surprising that some head had to roll for this national disgrace. Unpopular in any case, the Lord Chancellor, Edward Hyde, Earl of Clarendon, became the scapegoat. Not only was he intolerably conceited, particularly after the marriage of his daughter Anne to James, brother of the king and heir to the throne, but Hyde had also been one of the main influences behind the laws against the Dissenters. The Cavalier Parliament, supported by Archbishop Gilbert Sheldon, had passed these laws, known collectively as the Clarendon Code. When a popular demand was made for Edward Hyde to be impeached he fled to France, where he remained until his death in 1674.

In place of one man with overall power under the king, five Privy Councillors took over the effective government of the country, becoming known as the Cabal, an acronym made up of the initial letters of their names.[3] While this brought no dramatic changes in John Bunyan's circumstances, it was widely thought that the persecution against Dissenters would ease, particularly as the Earl of Shaftesbury, Lord Ashley Cooper, was a member of the

Cabal. The earl, who became Chancellor of the Exchequer, had strongly opposed Clarendon's religious policies and his support for toleration was well known. In addition the Conventicle Act which had come into effect in 1664, forbidding more than five to be present at any act of worship, was due to expire in 1669. Many were hopeful that the harsh conditions imposed by this act would not be renewed, and that the worst days of suffering for Dissenters and Nonconformists were a thing of the past.

In Scotland too the sufferings of the Covenanters had eased. The violent persecution endured by John Blackader and his family only the previous year is just one example of the sorrows experienced by many others. At two o'clock one morning in 1666, a party of dragoons had raided Blackader's home in search of the preacher. His furniture was smashed up, curtains were ripped down and his precious books consigned to the fire. His ten-year-old son ran half a mile, clad only in his nightshirt, after one dragoon offered to add him to the fire. Even the family's poultry lay dead about the yard before the dragoons had finished. But, with power now vested in the Cabal, of which the one-time Presbyterian Earl of Lauderdale was also a member, a degree of toleration prevailed.

Adding to this new spirit of hopefulness came the safe birth of Elizabeth's child, Sarah — conceived during John's short release in 1666. The recent death of his blind daughter Mary had been a deep grief to John, making the birth of another daughter a source of much-needed comfort. At last, after seven years of caring for her stepchildren, Elizabeth had a child of her own to nurture and love. And for John himself, the possibility that he might soon be released from prison to preach freely and to support his young family once more was a further consolation.

Meanwhile the ideas for Christian's pilgrimage to the Celestial City were still pouring into Bunyan's mind. Before his pilgrim could lose his burden at the Place of Deliverance, Goodwill had directed him to the House of the Interpreter, where he would learn valuable lessons to help him on his journey. The comparison at this point between Bunyan's pilgrim and Bunyan himself, as he had once sat in John Gifford's upstairs room at St John's Rectory, is unmistakable. Here his first pastor had answered the tinker's many perplexing questions, and here too Bunyan had been taught important lessons about the Christian life. So now, in a similar way, his pilgrim is instructed by the Interpreter — a representation of the Holy Spirit.

Because many faithless clerics now filled seventeenth-century pulpits, one of the Interpreter's first objectives — and one which Bunyan wished to impress on any who might one day read his book — was the importance of distinguishing between a true pastor and a false one. Bunyan's words describing the sort of guide whom Christian must heed are among the best known in *The Pilgrim's Progress*. They almost certainly depict John Gifford himself as Bunyan remembered him — a man to whom he owed so much:

> Christian saw a picture of a very grave person hang up against the wall... It had eyes lifted up to heaven, the best of books in his hand, the law of truth was written upon his lips, the world was behind his back; it stood as if it pleaded with men, and a crown of gold did hang over its head.[4]

Such was the man Christian must follow. Here too in the House of the Interpreter the pilgrim learnt the vital importance of perseverance, of striving ceaselessly to attain that crown of gold at the end of the journey. This had been the subject of *The Heavenly Footman*, and is the dominant theme of the entire book John was now writing. But constant effort is needed in order to persevere. To impress this upon the hopeful pilgrim, the Interpreter shows him a palace with its gate heavily guarded by armed men. Anyone who would enter there must be prepared to face a bitter fight: few had the courage. At last Christian saw one valiant volunteer, 'a man of a very stout countenance', coming forward to make the attempt. 'Set down my name, Sir,' said he to the one sitting by the gate ready to enrol volunteers. Donning his armour, this brave man began 'cutting and hacking most fiercely'. At last, though 'he had received and given many wounds', he broke through and pressed forward into the palace, there receiving a hearty welcome. With this graphic word picture, Bunyan was emphasizing the vital importance of biblical perseverance, however difficult — a lesson he and his fellow Dissenters were learning at great personal cost.

The Interpreter gave the new pilgrim many other valuable instructions before he set out on his journey once more. Several of these can be traced back to particular incidents which Bunyan himself had learnt through his own personal circumstances. But suddenly we are jolted back to Bunyan's dream: 'Now I saw in my dream...' — at last the Cross. It was standing by the wayside on a small elevation, and not far away the pilgrim saw what appeared to be a large hole, or a sepulchre.

As Christian approached the Cross he felt the cords binding the burden to his back snapping one by one. Unexpectedly his burden 'began to tumble and continued to do so, till it came to the mouth of the sepulchre, where it fell in, and I saw it no more'.

Interestingly, in view of Spurgeon's comments regarding the relationship between the Wicket Gate and the Cross, there is no mention here of Christian casting himself down in repentance and faith before the Cross, or of his begging forgiveness for his sin

According to tradition, Bunyan may have had this site, near Stevington in Bedfordshire, in mind in his description of the 'sepulchre'

before his burden rolls away. It would seem that in the case of Bunyan's pilgrim, as in his own, this present experience represents not conversion itself, but an assurance of his acceptance by God and a seal of the forgiveness of his sins. Christian's reaction to these things is one of unutterable joy as he weeps with sheer relief and happiness. Then three Shining Ones appear, giving him confirmations, or pledges, of this new-found assurance. One declares, 'Thy sins be forgiven thee'; a second strips off his rags, clothing him with 'a change of raiment' (i.e. clothing), or a 'broidered coat', as he later describes it;[5] while the third sets a distinguishing mark on his forehead and gives him a sealed roll, or scroll, which he must read often and carefully guard, for, like a passport, it would be a guarantee of his welcome in the Celestial City.

Giving 'three leaps for joy,' Christian proceeds on his way, singing:

Thus far did I come laden with my sin;
nor could aught ease the grief that I was in
till I came hither; What a place is this! ...
Blest Cross! blest Sepulchre! Blest rather be
The man that there was put to shame for me!

31

Palace Beautiful: an Independent church

I have determined, the Almighty God being my help and shield, yet to suffer if frail life might continue so long, even until the moss shall grow upon mine eyebrows, rather than ... violate my faith and principles. [1]

John Bunyan's words are little less than heroic considering all that he had already endured. Even though the best years of his vigour and manhood were slipping away while he remained incarcerated in Bedford jail, he would not compromise or deny the principles for which he suffered. And one of those principles, strongly held, was the right of the gathered church of believing men and women to worship in accordance with their understanding of the Word of God. To represent such a church in his allegory, Bunyan chose the image of a stately palace.

When Christian arrives at Palace Beautiful he is weary and dispirited. Not only has he undergone a long and hard climb up Hill Difficulty, but he has had the misfortune of losing the scroll that was given to him at the Cross — the Place of Deliverance. It had slipped down unnoticed under his seat while he was asleep in a wayside arbour on the way up the hill. After retracing his steps and at last recovering his scroll, Christian hastens forward again, still chastising himself for his indolence, especially as night is now falling. By this word picture Bunyan is showing that it is possible for a true believer to lose, at least temporarily, a sense of assurance regarding his salvation, especially in times of physical exhaustion and spiritual difficulty. This incident springs evidently and directly from his own experiences as he struggled with doubts and satanic taunts before he joined the Bedford Meeting — his own Palace Beautiful.

As he hurries along, Christian meets Mistrust and Timorous, who are rushing terror-stricken in the opposite direction. Two fierce lions, so they tell him, are lurking by the roadside ahead, waiting to devour any would-be pilgrims. They dare not venture any further for fear that they will be torn in pieces. Thrown into a dilemma, Christian decides that he has no alternative but to go on, even to face death if need be. Encouraged, however, by the sight of 'a very stately palace before him', where he might obtain a night's lodging, he presses forward. His fear of the lions is relieved to some extent by the reassuring words of Watchful, the porter at the palace lodge, who tells him that the vicious-looking creatures are actually chained. 'Keep in the midst of the path, and no hurt shall come unto thee,' the porter advises. Nervously Christian threads his way between the lions and arrives at last at the gate of the Palace Beautiful.

As Christian views the magnificent house, Watchful informs him that it was 'built by the Lord of the Hill, for the relief and security of pilgrims'. Traditionally it has been thought that Houghton House, above the town of Ampthill, south of Bedford, was the origin of the palace of Bunyan's dreams. It stood in all its one-time splendour at the top of an incline, which was probably steeper in Bunyan's day than it is now, and it is likely that as a youth he may even have done some work there as a brazier.[2]

Under this image Bunyan is summing up his own doctrine of the church as a gathered community of 'visible saints', or true believers. Although remaining in the world, they are not part of it. The true church, in Bunyan's understanding, provides a sanctuary and a place of refreshment where members will be encouraged,

Houghton House as it appeared in its prime
(showing the north and west fronts)

instructed and armed to face the battles that lie ahead.[3] The lions
chained by the wayside are probably intended to symbolize those
twin threats, the national church and the state, that in Bunyan's
day 'roared' at any seeking to enter the palace, as he had discovered to his cost.

Bunyan himself had found such fellowship with other believers, as well as much-needed help from a faithful pastor, at a time
of extreme need. So now his tired pilgrim seeks entry to the
Palace Beautiful. However, admission is not granted automatically. Watchful tells Christian that only if his conversation pleases
Discretion, one of the girls who live in the palace, will he be
admitted. By this Bunyan is emphasizing those qualifications for
church membership which he himself had learned from John
Gifford. Admission to the Bedford Meeting did not depend on
outward credentials, such as baptism by whatever mode, but on
evidences of spiritual life. As Gifford had written in his pastoral
letter just before he died:

> Now concerning your admission of members ... this much I
> thinke expedient ... that after you are satisfyed in the worke of
> grace in the party you are to joyne with, the saide party do
> solemnly declare (before some of the church at least) that

The ruins of Houghton House (showing the south front)

union with Christ is the foundation of all saintes' communion, and not any ordinances of Christ, or any judgement or opinion about externalls.[4]

In a later treatise[5] Bunyan would set forth his own views on the standards required for those wishing to be accepted into membership of an Independent church. They must have a credible testimony of God's dealing with them, he insists, and will show their sincerity by a life of holiness, devoid of outward or obvious blame. New members should not be received without 'a discovery of their faith and holiness and their declaration of willingness to subject themselves to the laws and government of Christ and his church'.[6] Bunyan does not discount the importance of baptism for any who profess faith in Christ, but will not reject an obvious 'saint', or refuse him admittance to the Lord's Table just because he has not been baptized as a believer. As we shall see, this stance was to lead him into deep trouble, especially with the Particular Baptists of his day.

After Watchful, the porter, who represents a pastor figure in the allegory, calls for Discretion, she plies Christian with questions before admitting him to the palace. Where had he come from? How did he begin his journey? Whom had he met so far?' Satisfied with his answers, she invites him in, and soon the questioning begins again, as Piety, Prudence and Charity (whose names indicate the characteristics expected of church members) all have much that they wish to know about the newcomer.

In answer to a question by Piety on his pilgrimage up till that point, Christian speaks of his experience at the Cross:

> I went but a little further and I saw One, as I thought in my mind, hang bleeding upon the tree, and the very sight of him made my burden fall off my back, (for I groaned under a very heavy burden), but then it fell down from off me. It was a strange thing to me, for I never saw such a thing before.[7]

Prudence questions him about his attitudes to his sinful way of life in the City of Destruction and about his present way of confronting those sins that still trouble him. She asks how he deals with 'annoyances', or sins to which he falls prey which he had thought were already vanquished. The answer Bunyan puts into the mouth of his pilgrim is memorable:

> When I think what I saw at the Cross, that will do it; and when I look upon my 'broidered coat, that will do it; also when I look into the Roll that I carry in my bosom, that will do it; and when my thoughts wax warm about whither I am going, that will do it.[8]

Lastly, Charity takes it in turn to question Christian, and her great concern is for the wife, children and neighbours whom the pilgrim has left behind in the City of Destruction. Did he warn them adequately? Did he pray for them, plead with them? The standards required of would-be church members was high indeed, and such a procedure of close questioning, typical of Dissenting practice, was followed in the Bedford Meeting whenever anyone applied for membership. We read in the church minute book for 1656, three years after Bunyan himself had joined:

> Upon the desire of brother Smith of Kempston to joyne with us, our brother Crow and brother Robert Wallis were appointed to commune with him, and if they were satisfyed, to desire him to come to give in his experience the next meeting.[9]

Some were refused, others required to wait a while before being accepted but, as we discover the name of a certain 'Brother Smith' listed among the church members shortly after this, we may assume that there was a satisfactory conclusion in his case. The importance of being able to give a credible account of God's dealings with the soul before a welcome into the membership was extended to an applicant was clearly paramount among the Independent churches.

Following these prolonged conversations, Bunyan again jolts his readers back to the dream structure of his narrative, for he wishes to introduce the subject of the Lord's Supper, with all its significance and sweetness for the believer. We read, 'Now I saw in my dream that thus they sat talking together until Supper was ready.' Christian's answers had clearly proved acceptable, and he was welcome to join in this most solemn celebration of the church. Shortly after joining the Bedford Meeting, Bunyan himself had been welcomed at the Lord's Table. At first he had struggled against fierce temptations on these occasions, as if the Evil One would try to destroy the benefits of the sacrament for this young Christian. But later, he tells us, he found much blessing as he 'discerned the Lord's body as broken for my sins'. Perhaps his prison experiences made it yet more precious, for two of Bunyan's friends, Ebenezer Chandler and John Wilson, could later record:

> At his administration of the Lord's Supper it was observable that tears came from his eyes in abundance for the sense of the sufferings of Christ.[10]

John Kelman, in his two-volume work on *The Pilgrim's Progress* called *The Road,* maintains that the description here of this communal meal in Palace Beautiful 'ranks ... as one of the most perfect of Bunyan's writings,' adding:

> ... for delicacy of touch, for unconscious art and exquisite simplicity, for fullness of religious meaning and wealth of spiritual imagination, it would be difficult to find its equal.[11]

As those around the table enjoyed the meal together with 'wine that was well refined', they spoke much of 'the Lord of the Hill', and of his sacrifice for sin. He 'is such a lover of poor pilgrims', they declared, 'that the like is not to found from the east to the west'.

Far into the night they talked, until at last Christian is taken to 'a large upper chamber whose window opened towards the sun rising', where he was to sleep. Little wonder that he could exclaim:

> Where am I now! Is this the love and care
> of Jesus for the men that pilgims are,
> thus to provide! That I should be forgiven,
> and dwell already the next door to heaven![12]

John Bunyan had a high view of church life and Christian fellowship. 'Like the flowers in a garden that stand and grow where the gardener hath planted them,'[13] so Christians standing together bring honour to Christ in the context of church fellowship, each adding to the beauty and sweetness of the garden. In another work Bunyan was to describe the joy of true believers gathering together as:

> ... the place where the Son of God loveth to walk... No place, no community, no fellowship, is adorned ... with these beauties as is a church rightly knit together to their head and lovingly serving one another. [14]

But Bunyan cannot forbear also to give a warning to all who consider themselves to be members of a church that they must 'take heed of being ... painted flowers which retain no smell, and of being painted trees whereon is no fruit'.[15]

More privileges follow for Bunyan's pilgrim in Palace Beautiful, each designed to prepare and strengthen him for the journey ahead. In the study he learns of the heroic achievements of those who have trodden the pilgrim path before him, and in the armoury he is shown the armour detailed in Ephesians 6, with which pilgrims of old had fought and won their battles: sword, helmet, shield, breastplate and shoes that will not wear out. And before he allows his pilgrim to set out on his travels once more, John Bunyan adds one final touch — a lesson he himself had learned through the rigour of his prison experience — to keep his eyes fixed on the ultimate goal of his journey, the Holy City. Christian is conducted to the roof of the palace, where he can look into the far distance. From there he is able to see:

> ... a most pleasant country, beautified with woods, vineyards, fruits of all sorts, flowers also with springs and fountains, very delectable to behold.

The country, he learnt, was called Emmanuel's Land.

Equipped with a fine suit of armour from the armoury in case he should meet 'with assaults in the way', Christian leaves Palace Beautiful at last, accompanied by the women until he reaches the bottom of the hill. He is encouraged by Watchful, the porter, who tells him that another pilgrim, named Faithful, has recently passed that way before him. And through all this elaborate imagery Bunyan is demonstrating the joys and benefits of belonging to the true church of Jesus Christ.

32

The pilgrim path

Many have noticed the similarities between John Bunyan's autobiography, *Grace Abounding to the Chief of Sinners*, and *The Pilgrim's Progress*. George Cheever, writing in 1872, commented, 'As you read *Grace Abounding* you are ready to say at every step "Here is the future author of *Pilgrim's Progress*."'[1] However, as we have noted, Bunyan's allegory extends beyond the personal experiences of his own conversion covered in his autobiography. Long hours spent meditating on the nature of the Christian life had given the prisoner in Bedford jail an abundance of other material for 'this my scribble'.

'This my scribble' should more correctly be rendered 'this my inspiration', for perhaps one of the best definitions of 'inspiration' to be found anywhere in literature, as C. S. Lewis points out,[2] follows these words in 'The Author's Apology for his Book':

Neither did I but vacant seasons spend
In this my scribble; nor did I intend
but to divert myself in doing this...
For having now my method by the end,

still as | pull'd, it came; and so | penn'd
it down; until at last it came to be
the length and breadth, the bigness that you see.

'Still as I pull'd, *it came*; and so I penn'd it down,' sums up the basic ingredient for such a work of imaginative genius. As fast as new ideas crowded into his mind, so he wrote them down.

Other factors, in addition to Bunyan's powers of creative thought and his own Christian experience, contribute to the make-up of *The Pilgrim's Progress*. As a youth, John had enjoyed the 'chap books', or adventure fictions, of his day. *George on Horseback* and *Bevis of Southampton*, tales by Richard Johnson, extracted from his larger collection, *The Seven Champions of Christendom*, were early favourites. These were tales of man-eating giants and dragons, together with noble warriors who risked their lives to conquer vicious ogres. Johnson describes in lurid detail 'A tyrrible battaille betwixt St. Anthonie and the Giant Blanderon and afterwards his strange entertainment in the Giant's Castell'.[3] Commenting on Bunyan's own use of such imagery, C. S. Lewis, whose own ability to write of giants, witches and lions in his *Narnia Tales* needs no introduction, writes:

> Bunyan's high theme [the spiritual life] had to be brought down and incarnated on the level of an adventure story of the most unsophisticated type — a quest story, with lions, goblins, giants, dungeons and enchantments.[4]

We are not surprised, therefore, to meet with a monster of horrific proportions as Bunyan's pilgrim ventures into the Valley of Humiliation. Yet even here there is little fictional material in this incident. All the terror that Bunyan himself had endured in his worst moments of satanic onslaught is packed into his description of the 'foul fiend' named Apollyon who comes out to meet Christian. Straddling across his way, the fiend demands to know why this pilgrim has left his kingdom, and where he thinks he is going.

Hideous to behold: he was clothed with scales like a fish ... he had wings like a dragon, feet like a bear, and out of his belly came fire and smoke.

Christian's words as he declares his new allegiance to the King of princes resonate with courage:

O thou destroying *Apollyon,* to speak the truth, I like his service, his wages, his servants, his government, his company and country better than thine; and therefore leave off to persuade me further, I am his servant and will follow him.[5]

After the ensuing fight between Christian and Apollyon, Bunyan describes the pilgrim's night-time trek through the Valley of the Shadow of Death, a circumstance which relates easily to his own early circumstances. Groping his way through the dark and dreadful valley, with its deep ditch on one hand and its bottomless quagmire on the other, the pilgrim hears doleful voices and groans echoing all around and sees flames and smoke billowing about him. As he wrote, Bunyan must have constantly recalled his own dire state of mind when he could scarcely distinguish any longer between the barbs of satanic assault and his own sane and rational thoughts.[6] Little wonder that he could add, 'The way to heaven lies by the Gates of Hell.'

But there is relief for Christian as he hears another pilgrim somewhere ahead of him who is quoting Scripture. Morning breaks before he manages to catch up with this man, but before he does so he sees by the light of day the mangled remains of other pilgrims who had been murdered as they had passed that way before him, their bones now scattered about. Two giants, Pagan and Pope, were responsible for this carnage, and Christian's path lies near their cave. Only Pope is sitting in the mouth of his cave,[7] but he has now become a decrepit and impotent creature who can do nothing other than threaten the passing pilgrim. This reflects the fact that at the time when Bunyan was writing Roman Catholicism had become abhorrent in the country. Following the cruelties of Mary Tudor and the reaction to the Catholic stance of earlier Stuart kings, it now posed little threat.

At last Christian manages to draw level with Faithful, the pilgrim whom Watchful the porter had seen. This man also came from the City of Destruction and had set out on pilgrimage as a result of all the commotion in the town following Christian's own departure. Because the lions near Palace Beautiful were asleep as he passed, Faithful had continued on his journey and so, according to Christian, had missed out on the many benefits of that palace.

Since Bunyan names this pilgrim Faithful, he clearly represents any faithful traveller to the Celestial City, but undeniably there is a unique bond between Christian and Faithful. Some have wondered whether Bunyan had a special friend in mind as he wrote. If so, who was he? In the narrative both pilgrims came from the same city and they had known each other previously. Perhaps it was Martin Luther, suggest some; others think it may have been Bunyan's first pastor, John Gifford, but probably Dr Barry Horner is nearest the mark when he identifies Bunyan's early friend William Dell as the prototype for Faithful.[8]

William Dell, once a chaplain in the New Model Army, had befriended Bunyan when the younger man had just started preaching. Although rector of Yielden, as well as Master of Gonville and Caius in Cambridge, he was glad to welcome the young tinker to his pulpit on Christmas Day in 1659. As we noted, the Yielden parishioners were angered and insulted by this and wrote a letter of complaint to the House of Lords. William Dell was ejected from his pulpit by the 1662 Act of Uniformity and compelled into homelessness by the Five Mile Act of 1665. Because Dell was a churchman and had therefore not joined an Independent church — typified by the Palace Beautiful — Bunyan pictures him as going on ahead without calling there. In 1669, the very time that Bunyan was writing *The Pilgrim's Progress*, news may well have just reached the prisoner in Bedford jail that his old friend had died at the age of sixty-three. Perhaps Bunyan wished to add his own tribute to William Dell, this faithful, suffering servant of Jesus Christ.

Another aspect of Bunyan's genius as he develops his allegory lies in his choice of names for his various characters. These are people we may all know well, and with Bunyan we either smile gently at the caricature, or else take to heart the warning of the dangers that such individuals pose. Some of these personify those whom Bunyan knew before his conversion: Legality and his son Civility, and of course Mr Worldly Wiseman, all dubious types who mislead pilgrims. Obstinate and Pliable epitomize many who show initial interest in the Christian faith and then draw back. Talkative, the son of Say-well, is full of religious conversation but has little or no understanding of inward heart-religion. Ignorance is 'a brisk lad' whose intractable insistence on his own 'good thoughts', and indeed his own righteous life, sets him beyond any influence for good. Characters with names such as Formalist, Hypocrisy, By-Ends, Lady Feigning, Mr Temporary, Turn-Away, and many others, all conjure up vivid mental pictures of time-serving and false professors of religion.

An evocative and memorable use of names follows when Christian and Faithful reach Vanity Fair. Here in the town of Vanity we have Bunyan's most all-embracing description of a world system as it stands in opposition to God — a description matching that of the apostle in 1 John 2:16: 'All that is in the world, the lust of the flesh, and the lust of the eyes, and the pride of life, is not of the Father, but is of the world.' Bunyan's day was not far different from our own, as we see a portrayal of undisguised wickedness placarded across our hoardings, newspapers and television screens. Christian and Faithful know there will be suffering ahead as they enter the town of Vanity, where a year-long fair is set up devoted to the acquisition of all things legitimate and illegitimate, and where nothing but 'jugglings, cheats, games, plays, fools, apes, knaves and rogues of every kind' is to be seen. Undoubtedly, Bunyan had his own Elstow Fair in mind, where a special court had to be set up in the Moot Hall on fair days to adjudicate against such rogues.

Bunyan does not recommend any form of liaison with the world in order to win it. Rather, the pilgrims gain attention and a hearing by their very distinctiveness, both of dress and speech. Distinguished too by their genuine lack of interest in the goods on sale, they declare, 'We buy the truth,' when asked what merchandise they fancy. Such a stand evokes the rage of the men of Vanity Fair. Charged, like the apostle Paul at Ephesus, with being 'Enemies and Disturbers of their trade', the two pilgrims are put into an iron cage and abused, their feet held fast in the stocks.

The end is predictable as they are brought to trial and Bunyan employs every weapon of irony in his arsenal as he describes the proceedings. The two men stand no chance of justice as witnesses bearing such names as Envy, Superstition and Pickthank are called in and the judge is named Lord Hate-Good. It is no surprise when, despite Faithful's courageous testimony, the jurors, made up of men like Mr Blindman, Mr Malice, Mr Heady, Mr Hate-light, Mr Live-loose, Mr Cruelty, and others, bring in a guilty verdict. Bunyan knew these men well: they might well have been named Sir John Kelynge, Judge Twisden, Henry Chester, George Blundell, William Foster and Francis Wingate.

> Then said *Mr No-good*, 'Away with such a fellow from the earth.' 'Ay,' said *Mr Malice*, 'for I hate the very looks of him.' Then said *Mr Love-lust*, 'I never could endure him.' 'Nor I,' said *Mr Live-loose*, 'for he would always be condemning my way.' 'Hang him, hang him,' said *Mr Heady* ... then said *Mr Implacable*, 'Might I have all the world given me, I could not be reconciled to him, let us forthwith bring him in Guilty of Death.' And so they did.[9]

Faithful's cruel martyrdom combines all the worst forms of physical torture inflicted on an innocent man, as he was buffeted, lanced with knives, stoned, pricked with swords and then 'burnt to ashes at the stake'. Bunyan had read well his Foxe's *Book of Martyrs*; perhaps he had also heard of the recent martyrdom of the young Scottish Covenanter, Hugh Mackail. A year or two earlier this attractive and godly man, only twenty-six years of age, had his leg smashed to pulp in order to force him to betray his fellow Covenanters before he was eventually hung at the Grassmarket in Edinburgh. Crying out, 'Farewell, the world and all delights... Welcome, sweet Lord Jesus, Mediator of the new covenant,' Hugh Mackail had joined that innumerable throng who 'loved not their lives to the death'.

However, Bunyan's ethic of trial and affliction for the Christian is a positive one. He only devotes one short paragraph to the details of Faithful's cruel death before he brings himself into his own story once more to tell us of God's answer to his people's sufferings:

Door at the present Bunyan Meeting depicting scenes from *Pilgrim's Progress.* (The top left-hand panel shows the chariot waiting to take Faithful to the Celestial City)

Reproduced by kind permission of Bunyan Meeting Free Church, Bedford, England

Now I saw that there stood behind the multitude a chariot and a couple of horses waiting for *Faithful*, who was taken up into it and straightway was carried up through the clouds with sound of trumpet, the nearest way to the Celestial Gate.

One who had himself endured as much as John Bunyan was well qualified to point out to his readers the benefits that suffering can bring to the Christian:

Righteousness thriveth best in affliction, the more afflicted, the more holy... The prison is the furnace, thy graces are the silver and gold ... so the Christian that hath and that loveth righteousness, and that suffereth for its sake, is by his sufferings refined and made more righteous.[10]

But this is not the end, for Bunyan is also anxious to emphasize that, by casting Christians into prison or even killing them, their enemies cannot crush the church of Jesus Christ. For from the ashes of the fire that consumed Faithful's martyred body another pilgrim rises up. As Bunyan tells us, Hopeful, seeing the bold stand of Christian and Faithful, begins his pilgrimage as Christian's new companion: 'Thus one died, to make testimony to the truth and another arises out of his ashes.'

Sing, Faithful, sing, and let thy name survive
For though they killed thee, thou art yet alive![11]

33

The suffering church

A surprising entry can be found in the Bedford Meeting church record book for 30 October 1668.[1] It reads:

> Many of the friends [of this church] having in these troub-
> lous times withdrawne themselves from close walking with the
> church ... some also being guilty of gross miscarriages ... the
> congregation having kept certaine dayes with fasting and
> prayer bewailed their fall ... [and] did agree that brother John
> Fenne and brother Bunyan should speake with brother
> Robert Nelson and admonish him for his withdrawing from the
> church and other miscarriages.[2]

For almost five years, covering from early 1664 until this date, no entries had been made in the church records and the book itself was probably hidden in some secure place away from prying eyes. Clearly the persecution of Dissenters must have eased enough by late 1668 to make it safe both to hold and record details of a church meeting. But most surprising of all is the inclusion of John Bunyan's name with that of his fellow prisoner

John Fenne to oversee some matter of discipline in connection with a church member.

After eight years in prison, and at the age of forty, John Bunyan must have wondered at times whether he would end his days within those stern walls, incarcerated by the state for conscience' sake. At one point, as he wrote the allegory which he would call *The Pilgrim's Progress,* he imagined Christian and Hopeful, poor captives of Giant Despair. We may well surmise that as Bunyan pictured their circumstances his story became almost autobiographical, particularly when Christian plumbed the depths as he contemplated the giant's suggestion that he should take his own life.

> Brother, said *Christian* [to his fellow prisoner], what shall we do? The life that we now live is miserable! For my part I know not whether 'tis best to live thus, or to die out of hand ... the grave is more easy for me than this dungeon.

Only Hopeful's words, warning of the sin of suicide and exhorting him to patience and hope, raise the pilgrim's thoughts above such despondency. Then, after finding new strength through prayer, Christian suddenly remembers that he carries in his pocket a key called Promise which can open any lock in Doubting Castle. With this he and Hopeful escape from the grasp of Giant Despair.

Later, putting the same truths into a sermon, Bunyan was to exhort any of his hearers who are tempted to despair to look again to the promises of God:

> This is not the time to despair: as long as mine eyes can find a promise in the Bible, as long as there is the least mention of grace, as long as there is a moment left me of breath or life in this world, so long will I wait or look for mercy, so long will I fight against unbelief and despair.[3]

How then, we may wonder, did John Bunyan gain a modicum of liberty during late 1668? The answer lies in the political situation which had developed. Events such as the Great Plague and the Fire of London, together with the ignominy of the Dutch incursion up the Medway and the burning of English ships, had bred a widespread discontent with the Cavalier Parliament and with its repression of Dissenters. Added to this, people feared that a continuing war against the Dutch, many of whom held a theological position similar to that of the Puritans and Dissenters, could easily inflame the situation. The king himself favoured toleration, but mainly because it would include improved circumstances for Roman Catholics.

Talk of a declaration of religious toleration was widespread. Even Samuel Pepys, the diarist, writing on 20 January 1668, could comment, 'There is a great presumption that there will be a Toleration granted.' Such circumstances, therefore, combined to ease the heavy hand of the law against Dissenters. With the new Cabal ministry in charge and the approach of the time when the 1664 Conventicle Act was due to expire, John Bunyan had clearly been allowed a measure of freedom by his jailer. In all likelihood he was only released from prison during the daytime and expected to be back within the jail by nightfall.

Once again engaged in service for the church outside the prison walls, he had less time and opportunity to write. His family was at a demanding age; Elizabeth, his eldest child following the death of Mary, was fourteen years of age, the boys, John and Thomas, twelve and ten respectively, and Sarah still a baby of little more than eighteen months.

This temporary release is thought to be the explanation for the strange break in the narrative of Bunyan's allegory, *The Pilgrim's Progress.* After their escape from Giant Despair and Doubting Castle, the pilgrims arrive at last at the Delectable Mountains, seen in the distance by Christian from the roof of Palace Beautiful. Here, as in the palace, they are taught valuable lessons by some shepherds, who represent pastors of the churches — their names being Knowledge, Experience, Watchful and Sincere. Then, as the pilgrims prepare to leave the delights of the shepherds' company and resume their journey, Bunyan unexpectedly and dramatically writes, 'So I awoke from my dream.' His readers are left in suspense, wondering if the pilgrims will ever gain the Celestial City.

How gladly must John have taken up once again his role as a family man with church responsibilities! His name appears twice more in those same minutes of 30 October 1668, and on both occasions he was commissioned to undertake some matter of discipline with regard to those whose courage and convictions had failed them when suffering was the likely outcome of any bold stand. 'Brother Coventon' was another whom Bunyan was asked to visit. This may well have been Edward Coventon, one of the earliest church members and also a deacon, a fact which would make it a particularly difficult assignment for Bunyan. Nor was the result a hopeful one, for we read in a later entry in the minutes that the church found Coventon guilty of 'utter neglect' and that they were forced to 'judge [him] unworthy of that honourable imployment and divest [him] of all authority and trust of that nature'.[4] On a happier note, there were also new applicants waiting to be admitted to the membership of the church.

Heartened by an easing of their circumstances, Dissenters began meeting openly again. New meeting houses were built, and pastors who had been banished by the Five Mile Act were emboldened to appear in their former pulpits. Some Nonconformists, such as Richard Baxter and Thomas Manton, hoped that their views might yet be accommodated within the established church. But at times these persecuted Dissenters went too far, disrupting church services and reclaiming pulpits now occupied by clergy who had conformed in order to retain their ministry.

All this increased activity on the part of the Dissenters provoked a negative reaction. Parliament became alarmed and yet more anxious to suppress conventicles, fearing that the latter were hotbeds of revolution. Archbishop Gilbert Sheldon called for a census to discover how many conventicles were taking place in any given area and also the numbers of those attending.[5] In Bedford William Foster, the lawyer who had been present at Bunyan's first interrogation by the magistrates, was active. Described by Bunyan as 'a close opposer of the ways of God', he was still searching out and arresting any 'conventiclers' whom he could find. Anthony Harrington, one of the original founder members of the church, now elderly and infirm, had to flee his home in order to avoid being cast into prison — a circumstance which would probably have led to the old man's death. Bunyan wrote him a pastoral letter in the name of the church, one straight from the heart of his own experience:

We are comforted in remembrance of thee, brother, while we consider that notwithstanding thy naturall infirmity, yet thou prizest good conscience above thine owne injoyments... You, brother Harrington, have lived to see the slippery and unstable nature that is in earthly things; wherefore we beseech you to expect no more there-from than the word of God hath promised... God is wise and doth all things for the best for them that love him... When we are desolate then we trust in God and make prayers and supplications to him night and day.[6]

Then on 11 April 1670 came an offensive against Dissenters more vicious than anything they had known in recent years: the Second Conventicle Act was passed by Parliament. Described by the poet Andrew Marvell as a piece of 'arbitrary malice', it struck the Dissenting churches with added ferocity because their new-found strength made them less willing to comply with its terms. Its reprisals against those discovered worshipping in any place other than a parish church were vicious. For a first offence a fine of five shillings was to be levied, and this would be doubled for any further offence. A preacher was to pay £20 on the first occasion that he was caught, and £40 for a second time. If he could not pay, the congregation would be charged instead, while the owner of the premises where a conventicle was taking place would face a similar fine.

Just one month later, on 15 May 1670, the Bedford Meeting felt the full impact of the heavy hand of the law, put into effect with almost unbelievable brutality. Doors were broken down, homes ransacked and personal belongings 'distrained', or seized in lieu of money, if the person attending a conventicle was unable to pay the fine demanded. A good-for-nothing by the name of Feckman, a spendthrift who had sunk to desperate poverty, welcomed the new act, seeing in it a lucrative means of 'recovering an estate and raising himself a fabrick out of the ruines of those whose kindnesses had refreshed him'. This man gladly entered the service of the Bedford lawyer William Foster, to earn himself a handsome income by raiding the meeting places and homes of the Dissenters. An early document describes the 'more than usual diligence' of this man:

[He acted with] extraordinary rage and violence, so that by his fierceness and cruelty he appeared more of a resemblant of Satan than an officer of the court.

Breaking into the home of John Fenne, who had been a fellow prisoner of Bunyan, on Sunday, 15 May, Feckman discovered a service of worship in progress. He and an accomplice drove all the worshippers present off to Foster's house, where the amount of the fine to be levied against each individual was announced. Nehemiah Coxe, who was preaching at the time, together with John Fenne, was sent straight to prison, joining John Bunyan, who had already been placed back under close guard. Edward Coventon's wife was present at the meeting (we may assume that her husband was not, in view of the discipline already imposed on this ex-deacon). She was ordered to pay five shillings, a sum Coventon could not or would not pay. Because of this a handsome brass kettle was seized in its place. But the neighbours, ordinary Bedford citizens, were so angry that no one could be found who was willing to carry it away.

The fifteen-page account of the sufferings of the Bedford church, now held in the British Library, is called *A true and impartial account of some illegal and arbitrary proceedings by certain Justices of the Peace and others against several innocent and peaceable nonconformists in and around the town of Bedford 1670*. Its record, a valuable insight into the sufferings of Christian men and women under the terms of the Second Conventicle Act, contains many instances of heartless cruelty. We read of Thomas Arthur, a pipe-maker, who locked his doors against Foster and his cronies. His fine was £11, claimed Foster but, being an astute businessman, Arthur demanded to see the warrant on which the amount was recorded. It was for £6. Foster hastily told Arthur that the extra £5 had been added as a penalty for locking his door. We read that:

[When the pipe-maker] perceived that Mr Foster would distreyn all his goods, he said, 'Sir, what shall my children do? Shall they starve?' Mr Foster replied that as long as he was a rebel, his children should starve...

Foster then promptly ordered that all Arthur's household goods should be carried away, not leaving him with as much as a stick of wood with which to light his kiln in order to set the pipes which were ready to be fired.

Despite the fact that fines were to be doubled if these people were caught worshipping again at an illegal conventicle, the Bedford Meeting church members did not hesitate to gather the next Sunday. This time Edward Isaac, a blacksmith, was fined forty shillings (£2) for himself and his wife — a prohibitive sum for a working man at the time — and, as if that were not enough, he was also robbed of 'locks, shovels and the very anvil upon which he forgeth his work'.

A weaver called Thomas Thorowgood, from the nearby village of Cotton End, dared to allow his home to be used for a meeting. Betrayed by the chatter of a little child, the premises were raided by Foster and his men. Thorowgood, who could not pay the £20 fine, was dispossessed of all he had, right down to the loom with which he earned his living.

The 'impartial account' of these events contains story after story of the injustices perpetuated against innocent people — so manifestly excessive that in many cases the other citizens of Bedford threatened violence against collaborators such as Feckman. Sometimes as many as a hundred people gathered in silent support of their fellow citizens. These were honourable Bedford tradesmen — a grocer, a cutler, a heelmaker, a shoemaker, a baker, a constable, etc. All were members of the Independent church and all were heavily fined, with some being stripped of everything they possessed and having goods confiscated, the value of which often amounted to far more than the original fine.

In the case of one well-to-do widow, a Mrs Mary Tilney, her home was emptied; tables, chairs, cupboards, mattresses, blankets were all seized, even down to the sheets on her bed. Her neighbours wept openly at this manifest robbery — a thing which grieved the kindly woman more than her own losses — '... and so the officers left her, having finished this dayes work', we read. The account concludes that 'poor and industrious families are utterly ruined, some made wholly incapable to provide for their future subsistence'. We are not surprised, therefore, to read that when Feckman died unexpectedly no coach-owner would agree to bear his coffin from the house to the grave.

The success of the move to crush any nonconformity to the established church was enormously strengthened by the work of 'informers', their function now legalized by the Act of Parliament and made hugely profitable by offering such people a fixed share in the fines imposed. Informers were everywhere; men, or even women, who had often been brought to penury by their own feckless lifestyle now hoped to regain some position in society by betraying neighbours and one-time friends. An informer might be lurking in some part of a wood waiting to spy on a secret congregation. Some even professed conviction of sin in order to gain an entry into a gathering of Dissenters. They had been known to visit the bereaved and dying to extract information, or to bribe children to follow a 'suspect' to see where a group of worshippers was meeting. In a later book John Bunyan describes an informer as 'a man of a very wicked life' who would 'watch of nights, climb trees, and range the woods of days if possible to find out the meeters'.[7] One never knew whom to trust.

It is not hard to imagine the distress which John Bunyan must have experienced, now that he was a helpless prisoner again and unable to share in or relieve the sufferings of his fellow church members. Whether Elizabeth and the family were involved in such fines or deprivations we are not told; possibly not, as there is no certain record of her actually being a member of the Bedford Meeting, unless she is listed under her maiden name. But for Christians, as Bunyan pointed out in a later sermon:

> [Suffering] comes not by chance, or by the will of man, but by the will and appointment of God ... and as God has appointed WHO shall suffer, so he has appointed WHEN they shall suffer for his truth in the world ... and as God has appointed who and when, so he has appointed WHERE this or the other good man shall suffer...[8]

It was such truths as these that had sustained Bunyan under years of harsh imprisonment and family deprivation and could alone uphold his fellow believers in their present circumstances.

For John himself there remained nothing else but to take up his pen again and continue his dream from where he had left off:

> And I slept and dreamed again, and saw the same two pilgrims going down the mountains along the highway towards the City...

And in these final, well-loved chapters of *The Pilgrim's Progress* men and women the world over have reaped untold benefit from the sufferings of one member of the Independent church at Bedford.

34

A strange conclusion

As John Bunyan sat once more in his sordid prison cell, with little natural light penetrating the gloom, his thoughts were far away. In his mind's eye he could see two men standing in a land of extraordinary beauty:

> Here they heard continually the singing of birds and saw everyday the flowers appear in the earth... In this country the sun shineth night and day, wherefore this was beyond the Valley of the Shadow of Death and also out of reach of Giant Despair, neither could they from this place so much as see Doubting Castle. Here they were within sight of the city they were going to.[1]

Christian and Hopeful had arrived in Beulah Land — a country that in Bunyan's mind lay in immediate sight of the Celestial City. After leaving the shepherds on the Delectable Mountains, the pilgrims had encountered such characters as Atheist and Ignorance and had fallen prey to the wiles of the Flatterer. Having crossed the Enchanted Ground safely — that place where many pilgrims fall asleep and are lost — they are now in the Land of Beulah, spoken of by the prophet Isaiah,[2] a place of light and joy, a place of vineyards, gardens and birdsong.[3]

Only the River of Death — that deep and bridgeless river — remained to be crossed before the travellers reached the Celestial City, their ultimate destination. Bunyan was under no illusions about the nature of death. In the margin of his story he wrote, 'Death is not welcome to Nature, though by it we pass from this world into glory.' He had experienced the anguish of bereavement early in life when both his mother and sister died within a single month. In addition his first wife and his well-loved blind daughter Mary had been taken from him in death. So in Bunyan's allegory Christian finds the waters dark and menacing when he enters that last river. He fears he will be lost. Crying out, 'I sink in deep waters, the billows go over my head,' he sees all his sins of a lifetime rising up against him to condemn him. Satan can often launch his most bitter assaults at a dying believer, and in *The Pilgrim's Progress* Bunyan describes Christian's 'Horror of Mind and Heart-fears that he should die in that river and never obtain Entrance in at the Gate'. Hopeful, true to his name, finds the passage easier, and struggles to keep Christian's head above the waters. 'Brother, I see the Gate and Men standing by to receive us,' he calls out to encourage his struggling companion.

At last Christian cries in a loud voice, 'Oh, I see him again! And he tells me, "When thou passest through the Waters I will be with thee..."' Finally he feels solid ground under his feet once more. 'Then they both took courage and the enemy was after that as still as a stone, until they were gone over.' Together the two pilgrims reach the farther bank, and Bunyan's description of the glories of heaven awaiting them on the farther shore is among the finest in all literature:

> Now I saw in my dream that these two men went in at the Gate, and lo, as they entered, they were transfigured: and they had raiment put on that shone like Gold... Then I heard in my dream that all the bells in the City rang again for joy... Now just as the gates were opened to let in the men, I looked in after them; and behold the City shone like the sun, the streets also were paved with gold...[4]

Little wonder, then, that John Bunyan, sitting in his unwelcome prison, was carried away by his own account and could add sadly, '… and after that they shut up the gates: which when I had seen, I wished myself among them.' We can almost imagine him looking around his gloomy 'den', with the glory still shining in his eyes, and wishing that he too could have been there.

And so the narrative ends — but not quite. *The Pilgrim's Progress* was never intended to be a mere story, full of entertainment value for his readers. Like all Bunyan's best works, it was evangelistic before anything else. Although he had been prevented from preaching to the crowds who once thronged to hear him, this book is effectively a sermon from start to finish. Again and again he warns his readers of the dangers of entering the pilgrim path in any other way but by the Wicket Gate. The message of the book is the same as that of the smaller work which inspired it, *The Heavenly Footman:* 'He who would have heaven must run for it,' a truth he had reiterated many times over. A number of characters in *The Pilgrim's Progress* appear to begin well, but fall at various hurdles along the way. Their fate is to be taken as a warning to all would-be pilgrims that the way to heaven is both narrow and hard. Constant perseverance is required in order to be fully assured of attaining heaven at last.

Bunyan's strange concluding paragraph to *The Pilgrim's Progress* should be read in that light and then comes as no surprise. In his dream he sees Ignorance, that 'brisk lad' with whom Christian and Hopeful had held long and fruitless conversations, approaching the river. Although they had tried to persuade him again and again that his own righteousness could never be good enough for God, he would not listen. Instead he insisted that his heart was sufficiently good and pure to merit heaven. Ignorance then crosses the river easily with the help of a ferryman named Vain Hope, but when he reaches the gate of the Celestial City he is unable to produce a certificate to prove himself one of the King's true subjects. Bound hand and foot, Ignorance is taken to a door in the side of the hill and thrust in. Bunyan ends his book with these sombre words: 'Then I saw that there was a Way to Hell even from the Gates of Heaven as well as from the City of Destruction.'

Certainly, from a literary perspective, such an ending 'spoils' Bunyan's book, but, as we noted, his purpose is primarily evangelistic. Many commentators on *The Pilgrim's Progress* are uneasy about its conclusion, including C. S. Lewis. In *The Last Battle*, the final volume of his *Narnia Tales*, C. S. Lewis includes among those accepted by Aslan into 'the real Narnia' a young man who was sincere enough in what he believed, but had been ensnared in a false religion all his life.[5] Lewis therefore finds Bunyan's teaching hard to accept: 'The dark doctrine has never been more horrifyingly stated than in the words that conclude Part 1' (of *The Pilgrim's Progress*), he complains. However, even Lewis admits that the book 'would be immeasurably weakened as a work of art if the flames of hell were not always flickering on the horizon'.[6]

Why, then, does Bunyan single out Ignorance for such a dreadful end? He had entered the pilgrim path through 'a crooked lane' rather than the Wicket Gate, but many other so-called pilgrims had also deviated from the right path in different ways. The answer perhaps lies in the fact that Ignorance persistently denied a doctrine that Bunyan held to be of supreme importance: the doctrine of the righteousness of Christ credited to the believer as a free gift. Martin Luther's *Commentary on Galatians* had emphasized this teaching, bringing enormous release to Bunyan at the beginning of his spiritual life. It had been 'gold in my trunk' to discover that:

> ... it was not my good frame of heart that made my righteousness better, nor yet my bad frame that made my righteousness worse; for my righteousness was Jesus Christ himself, the same yesterday and today, and for ever.[7]

But Ignorance denies this doctrine. As the pilgrims pass over the Enchanted Ground they meet up with him for a second time and speak with the young man at length, but all in vain. At last Christian exclaims in desperation:

> Thou neither seest thy original nor actual infirmities, but hast such an opinion of thyself ... as ... plainly renders thee to be one that never did see a necessity of Christ's personal righteousness to justify thee before God... Be awakened then, see

thine own wretchedness and fly to the Lord Jesus: and by his righteousness ... thou shalt be delivered from condemnation.[8]

All this takes on a greater significance when we realize that at about the same time as he was concluding *The Pilgrim's Progress*, Bunyan was locked in fierce literary combat with a certain Edward Fowler, vicar of Northill in Bedfordshire. Fowler was a typical 'Vicar of Bray'[9] who, as Bunyan scathingly commented, could adapt himself 'for every fashion, mode and way of religion'. He had once favoured Presbyterianism, but had balked at the suffering he might have endured in 1662 and had conformed with the terms of the Act of Uniformity. He was a man who would, as Bunyan remarks, 'hop from Presbyterianism to a prelactical mode [i.e. to accepting the government of the church by prelates, or bishops], and if time and chance should serve you, backwards and forwards again...'[10] Bunyan, who had suffered so acutely for the truth, despised such a 'weathercock'. To him Fowler was one of those whom he represented in *The Pilgrim's Progress* as Lord Turnabout, or even Mr Facing-both-ways.

Bunyan was roused to take issue with Fowler personally when he read the latter's book, *The Design of Christianity*, a work licensed for publication in June 1671. In it Fowler sets out his concept of the purpose and intent of God in salvation. It is quite probable that Bunyan actually knew Fowler, but this did not prevent him from pouring scorn both on the vicar and his views in a manner common at the time.

Obtaining a copy of *The Design of Christianity* in January 1672, Bunyan wrote solidly for six weeks, producing a 46,000 word answer. This he called *A Defence of the Doctrine of Justification by Faith*. Few are at their best in controversy and Bunyan's answer is prolix and somewhat repetitive, and certainly not very polite. Mustering all his verbal artillery, he did everything in his power to shoot down the arguments of Edward Fowler. His indignation was twofold — not only was Fowler a representative of those turncoat churchmen who had been partially responsible for all the sufferings of the Dissenters, but his popular book was robbing poor sinners of the knowledge of the way of forgiveness of sin.

Among the basic tenets of Fowler's argument is that the work of Christ was primarily intended to restore man to that original purity he had once known in the Garden of Eden — to renew the natural goodness of the human heart. He asserts that, though man is sinful, he has the power to control 'his brutish passions and affections'.[11] In his claims for this basic goodness in human nature, he is making use of the same arguments as those used by Ignorance in conversation with Christian and Hopeful. 'I will never believe that my heart is thus bad,' declared Ignorance when Christian described man's natural sinfulness, quoting Romans 3:10-12: 'There is none righteous ... there is none that doeth good.'

Like Fowler, Ignorance had denied the doctrine of Christ's gift of righteousness imputed to the believer:

> What! [declares Ignorance] would you have us trust to what Christ in his own person has done without us? This conceit would loosen the reins of our lust... For what matter how we live if we may be justified by Christ's personal righteousness?

In exasperation Christian replies, 'Ignorance is thy name and as thy name is, so art thou.'

The heart of Bunyan's contention with Fowler lies in his defence of this vital doctrine of Christ's imputed righteousness, making the believer acceptable to God. As with Ignorance, so now with Fowler, Bunyan does not trouble to hide his indignation over his denial of the truth. Such an unworthy representative of the church was part of a 'whole gang of rabbling ... counterfeit clergy' and, like the others, he was misleading the people. Bunyan sarcastically accuses Fowler of being 'a glorious latitudinarian that can, as to religion, turn and twist like an eel on the angle'.[12]

Not surprisingly, Fowler struck back. If Bunyan had expressed himself in discourteous language, his vocabulary appears mild in comparison with Fowler's invective. The title itself is almost sufficient evidence: *Dirt Wip'd Off — A manifest discovery of the gross ignorance and most unchristian and wicked spirit of one John Bunyan, lay-preacher in Bedford which he hath showed in a vile pamphlet by him against The Design of Christianity.*

Throughout his seventy-eight-page reply Fowler sprinkles un-called-for insults against the imprisoned preacher. He finds it hard 'to defile his fingers with so dirty a creature'. Bunyan's book, Fowler maintains, 'is full of brutish barkings'; it contains 'scurrilous and vile language and horrible revilings'. As we may expect, the doctrine that most offended this proud churchman was the one insisted upon by Bunyan — that only by Christ's imputed right-eousness can a sinner be accepted before God. 'How sottish is this Ranter,' exclaims Fowler, deprecating Bunyan's belief that all the sinner needs is 'to trust to and venture the eternal concerns of his soul upon the righteousness that is nowhere to be found but in the person of his [God's] Son'. 'That is all,' comments Fowler, 'and as much as anyone can expect from him.'[13]

John Bunyan did not reply. He had learnt long ago not to 'answer a fool according to his folly'. But, as he was putting the finishing touches to his allegory, *The Pilgrim's Progress*, and not yet certain whether or not he would attempt to publish it, he may well have decided to add those final sentences, consigning Ignorance, a religious, though misguided and unteachable man, to hell, and we cannot but think that he may well have had Edward Fowler in mind. Perhaps the conclusion to *The Pilgrim's Progress* was not so strange after all.

35

Freedom at last

After John Bunyan's brief taste of semi-freedom in 1668 and 1669, opening as it did the vision of opportunities to serve his church once more, his fresh imprisonment in April 1670 must have been hard to bear. On what grounds, he asked himself time and time again, was he enduring these long years of confinement? Was he right or just misguided? Such questions pulsed through his mind continually, and we may well imagine that as he tossed back and forth through the long night hours on his hard straw 'bed' they became particularly acute and problematic. As Bunyan confessed,

> [It was] continually dogging of me to weigh and pause and pause again the grounds and foundation of those principles for which I have thus suffered.[1]

If John himself felt the need of reassurance that he was not suffering needlessly, nor depriving his growing family of his presence and of a regular income without good cause, others too might certainly wonder about it. Primarily, he reminded himself, it was because he was unwilling to attend the parish church, taking communion with those devoid of true faith; added to this was his unshakeable conviction of his call to preach. Another matter was also weighing on his mind. In a church meeting held on 24 October 1671 in Haynes (not far from Bedford), the proposal to appoint John Bunyan to the pastoral office of the church was raised for consideration — a fact that suggests that there was a general expectation that he might well be permanently released in the near future. With such a proposition under discussion by the church members, it was important for Bunyan to give time and thought to those beliefs and principles which had governed his own actions and which would underpin any future ministry he might undertake.

In the enforced isolation and idleness of a prison cell, he had time for much reflection and, as he turned over in his mind each facet of truth for which he was suffering, Bunyan decided to jot them down. And, as with so much that he wrote, his material seemed to expand as he worked and before long he had yet another treatise on hand ready for his publisher, Francis Smith. The first part was entitled simply: *A Confession of my Faith.* Reading much like an expanded church statement of faith, each numbered paragraph of Bunyan's *Confession* begins with the words, 'I believe ...' Succinct and scripturally satisfying, the first twenty-one articles cover, among other topics, the nature of the Godhead, the fall of man, the deity of Christ, redemption through his blood, heaven, hell and the return of Christ in judgement. Bunyan then elaborates in more detail on the great doctrines of salvation: justification, election, calling, faith and repentance.[2] Of repentance Bunyan declares:

> Godly repentance doth not only affect the soul with the loathsome nature of sin that is past but filleth the heart with godly hatred of sins that may yet come.

Bunyan frequently appended a preface, or introductory letter, to the many items which he wrote. But on this occasion he decided to address his letter to one unnamed individual in particular — one who had voiced doubts over the necessity of the suffering Bunyan was enduring. Perhaps this was a fellow prisoner who was questioning his own position as well as Bunyan's, for he concludes his letter with the words, 'Yours in bonds for the gospel'.

Meanwhile developments were taking place on the national scene which would profoundly affect Bunyan's future. Charles II hid a cunning and devious nature under a playboy exterior; for, although he appeared outwardly little interested in anything apart from women, sport and spaniels, he was in fact plotting a Stuart despotism far more radical than anything practised by his father, Charles I. Much English blood had already been shed during the Civil War to rid the country of such autocratic rule. Now Charles II planned to restore it by subtle intrigue and a betrayal of the trust of his people.

First, he schemed to dispense with Parliament. He would do this by freeing himself of dependence on the finance which these elected representatives voted for the royal exchequers.

Ruling alone and not accountable to any, he next planned to bring his country back to the Roman Catholic fold — by force if necessary. All this would be impossible without the aid of the French king, Louis XIV. Charles had natural links with France, being half French by birth himself. So, together with his sister, Henrietta Anne, who was an ardent Catholic and also sister-in-law to Louis, he laid his plans to remodel the English church after the French pattern, subservient to Rome in all but the papacy.

Already a covert Catholic himself, the king negotiated a secret treaty with Louis XIV which was signed in Dover in May 1670 and is therefore known as the Treaty of Dover. Included in this treaty were certain clauses, hammered out by Arlington and Clifford, two members of the Cabal ministry with Catholic sympathies, but kept hidden from the other three members. These clandestine agreements specified that Louis XIV would give Charles substantial financial aid to free him from dependence on Parliament. In addition, Louis would provide 6,000 troops to help Charles force through the conversion of the English church back to Catholicism. Charles, for his part, would repay Louis, first by announcing his personal conversion to Roman Catholicism and, secondly, by aiding Louis in his attempt to overrun the Dutch republic.

The following year a sham Treaty of Dover was presented to Parliament, largely the same as the one negotiated in 1670 but omitting any reference to the re-establishment of Catholicism. By it England annulled her earlier settlement with the Dutch, declaring war against them once more. As a direct result of the treaty a third expensive Anglo-Dutch war began, but Charles decided to delay the public declaration of his own conversion to Catholicism until a more propitious moment.

In the meantime the king must prepare the ground for the English church to embrace Catholicism once more. To do this Charles would need to extend religious toleration to English Catholics, who now faced the same penal laws as the Dissenters and Nonconformists. The only course open lay in granting a general religious indulgence to all outside the established church. In that way he hoped that his real motive, which was to reinstate Catholicism, might pass undetected. Because Parliament would never have agreed to any such indulgence, it was in the king's interest to keep it in abeyance, at least for the present, and act unilaterally.

So, calling on his royal prerogative, the king announced a Declaration of Religious Indulgence on 15 March 1672:

> We do ... declare our will and pleasure to be that the execution of all penal laws in matters ecclesiastical, against whatever sort of nonconformists or recusants, be immediately suspended; and all judges, sheriffs, justices of the peace ... and other officers whatsoever, whether ecclesiastical or civil, are to take notice of it and pay due obedience thereunto.

Up and down the country prison doors swung open, as hundreds left their foul and dingy cells as free men and women. But there were conditions as well. To prevent religious anarchy, the king stipulated that, upon application, he was willing to grant licences for as many places of worship as might be required for Dissenting gatherings and also to give licences to certain named preachers who would be permitted to officiate at services of worship.

John Bunyan was quick with his list of such places and preachers, for who could tell when the situation might change yet again? Doubtless Bunyan's request list for licences had been compiled while he was still in jail, in conjunction with some of his fellow prisoners. No less than thirty different meeting sites in the immediate Bedford area were specified as requiring licences for Dissenting worship. Some of these were church buildings, others private homes and some only barns. A barn which a certain Josias Ruffhead hoped to purchase in Mill Street, Bedford, was on the list; so too was Widow Read's home in Stevington; in addition there were buildings in Cotton End, Keysoe, Ampthill, Haynes, Kempston, Cardington, Edworth, and other nearby places. Clearly Bunyan and his friends had long-term plans for the future of the gospel in the Bedford area.

These small groups of Dissenters, linked by belief and suffering, were already establishing a pattern of biblical church unity, and their existence provided a base for Bunyan's future ministry. Regardless of any persecution that might lie ahead, a circuit of Independent churches was being established which was now strongly entrenched and could no longer be permanently trampled upon or extinguished by fierce penal laws. Together with these applications for meeting venues were the names of twenty-six men who wished to receive licences to preside at services of worship; among them were John Bunyan, the Fenne brothers, Nehemiah Coxe from the Bedford Meeting, and John Gibbs, Bunyan's friend from Newport Pagnell who had also suffered imprisonment.

Three months before this date, anticipating that the king would soon announce such a declaration, the church in Bedford made a significant decision — one that would affect John Bunyan for the rest of his life. As we have seen, in October 1671 the proposal to appoint him to be pastor of the church had been discussed at a church gathering. Since then the church members had given themselves to 'much seeking God by prayer and sober conference'. And on 21 December 1671, at a full church meeting held no doubt in some secret location in Bedford, those gathered made their solemn and significant resolution: John Bunyan was officially appointed to undertake the pastoral oversight. The church record book reads:

> The congregation did at this meeting with joint consent (signified by solemne lifting up of their hands) call forth and appoint our brother John Bunyan to the pastorall office or eldership. And he accepting thereof gave himself up to serve

Christ and his church in that charge, and received of the eld-
ers the right hand of fellowship.[3]

Buffeted over many years by the storms of persecution,
Bunyan had stood unbowed and firm. When he was first imprisoned, as a zealous young man recently turned thirty-two, he had
displayed outstanding gifts of preaching and leadership. Tall,
vigorous and auburn-haired, with clear fresh features, he was
youthful, eager and dedicated in the service of God. Now at
forty-four years of age, matured by suffering and experience, John
Bunyan was a much older-looking man, but in every way even
more equipped to lead a church which had itself been tried in the
storm. Eleven books, some highly significant, had been the fruit of
the prison years.

Although he was already allowed a measure of freedom, in
view of the king's Declaration of Indulgence, John's release was
not to be granted automatically. He must still apply to have his
name included in the lists of those eligible for discharge on the
grounds that his sole 'misdemeanour' had been to worship or
preach at a conventicle. Many prisoners might otherwise attempt
to escape from jail under false pretences. Nor were the magistrates forward in granting the ill-treated preacher his freedom.

Persecution of Dissenters had never been equally intense in all
parts of the country. Many constables had shown marked reluc-
tance to harry and repress their inoffensive neighbours for their
religious beliefs. In London and the south-west, however, grievous
accounts exist of heartless inhumanity meted out to men and
women caught worshipping in secret. The presence of a man like
the lawyer William Foster in Bedford, together with the clerk of
the justices, Paul Cobb, ensured that a preacher as influential as
John Bunyan would not be readily released.

The Quakers too had suffered more than most in the long
repression since 1662. Only after personal pressure on the king by
members of the sect did they manage to ensure that they were
included in the general pardon. And, similarly, for John Bunyan
there was no automatic discharge until he succeeded in having his
name added to a list of 471 Quakers who were currently serving
prison sentences. At last the Bedfordshire County Sheriff, a certain
Thomas Bromsall, confirmed that Bunyan's release was legitimate,

and that attending conventicles had indeed been his only offence. Even then, not until 13 September 1672 was his pardon officially ratified by the king's Great Seal.

Despite having enjoyed some freedom before May 1672, it was probably not until then that John was finally able to pack up his few belongings for good: his Bible, his hefty volumes of Foxe's *Book of Martyrs* and other personal items. Perhaps tucked under one arm he carried a sheaf of papers containing 'this my scribble' — a story of a lonely man who had set out on pilgrimage to the Celestial City and of all the trials he had encountered before reaching his goal. What to do with the manuscript, he hardly knew. But for the time being he had enough matters of concern on his mind to delay any decision on the matter.

John Bunyan in 1673

A portrait is extant dated 1673 — the year after John Bunyan emerged from prison — showing a very different-looking man from the more popular pencil sketch by Robert White. The face looks pale and a little strained — a contrast with the surviving description of him as a man with a fresh-looking, reddish complexion. Maybe this was the result of long years of living in semi-darkened surroundings. But the eyes are intense and piercing — eyes that had looked on the filth and degradation of a seventeenth-century jail, yet eyes that had looked into the Celestial City and seen its glories.

36

A painful controversy

The joy of John Bunyan's homecoming was not without its shadows. In many respects he was a stranger to his own children, for Elizabeth had brought up his family single-handedly for almost twelve years. When John was first thrust into prison on that November day in 1660, his older son, also called John, was only four. Now he was a young man of sixteen, probably as tall as his father. Thomas, who had been just two years old, was now fourteen. Possibly Thomas resented the deprivations suffered by the family, and had allowed his father's imprisonment to rankle and embitter his spirit. Certainly he had missed his father's strong hand of discipline on his life and may already have been a difficult young person to handle. Not many years after this we discover Thomas Bunyan involved in petty crime, much to the shame and embarrassment of his godly father and stepmother. Blind Mary had died, and John's second daughter Elizabeth was now a young woman of eighteen; his young daughter, Sarah, child of his second marriage, was an energetic five-year-old.

Nor were things straightforward on the business front. His son John had been training as a metal worker, doubtless with the hope of one day taking over his father's braziery business. But the business itself was in ruins; as one contemporary records, '… his temporal affairs were gone to wreck, and he had as to them to begin again as he had newly come into the world.' All his former customers had found other tradesmen to undertake their work, and if the ex-prisoner wished to start up again he would need to establish new contacts — no easy thing when he had a prison record to account for.

But in spite of his problems, Bunyan rejoiced to be out of the dank and fetid prison at last. Turning his back on the jail that May day in 1672, he would have walked along Mill Street before reaching his home in St Cuthbert's Street where Elizabeth and the family awaited him. As he passed by, however, his eyes would have turned naturally to an old orchard that lay a little below street level to his right. Nearby stood an equally old barn. The land on which the orchard grew was reputed to have once been part of the former moat that had surrounded Bedford Castle, and was immediately adjacent on one side to the home of John Easton, an influential founder member of the Bedford Meeting. On the other side stood a dovecote, property of another church member, Josias Ruffhead.

But the real object of Bunyan's interest was the barn itself. It could easily be turned into a meeting place for the church, at least as a temporary measure. Without doubt Josias Ruffhead thought so. A shoemaker by trade, Josias had also known his share of sufferings as a Christian, but now he had offered to buy the property with the church's needs in mind. Since being turned out of St John's in June 1660, the church had known no settled home. Often they would gather in small groups in secret, and they would always be moving from place to place for fear of informers. At present the orchard and barn both belonged to Justice Crompton, the very one who had refused to arrange bail for Bunyan when he was first imprisoned in 1660. But with the sum of £50 offered for the barn, Crompton was tempted to agree to the sale.

As we have seen, Bunyan had had the foresight to add that barn to the list of properties included in his application for licences as 'a place for the use of such as doe not conforme to the Church of England who are of the perswasion commonly called

Congregationall'. The indenture for the barn was then conveyed from 'Josias Ruffhead to John Bunyan of the Towne of Bedford, Brasier', and it is not hard to imagine the flurry of activity as church members speedily began to strip down the old building, perhaps apply a coat or two of whitewash and furnish it with benches, ready for the day when their new pastor should preach the opening services.

A fresh opportunity of service had begun for Christ's suffering servant, John Bunyan. The licence to use the barn took effect from 9 May, the same date that John Bunyan's licence to preach also became valid. Undoubtedly opening services were soon held in the new church. It might well have been a cause of passing regret that Sir John Kelynge, chief instrument in the imprisonment of the young tinker-preacher twelve years earlier, had died the previous year, and did not witness that unexpected turn of events.

The fact that Bunyan should describe the church as 'Congregational' rather than 'Baptist' in his application for a licence is significant. Apparently since 1657, a period of at least sixteen years, there had been some degree of friction between those Baptist churches that urged the importance of believers' baptism as the 'initiating ordinance' both for membership of a church and for the privilege of taking part in the Lord's Supper, and those churches that held the 'open communion' position adopted by the Bedford Meeting, which extended these privileges to all who gave evidence of being true believers. Over the years a number of members had left the church because of this issue. Pressure had even been put upon Bunyan himself to abandon his convictions. As he was about to assume the pastorate, Bunyan was anxious both to clarify his position on the role of baptism in the life of the church and to heal any breaches which might exist between his church and those holding a differing position.

As we have seen, not long before he left prison Bunyan had spent time writing what he had called *A Confession of my Faith and a Reason of my Practice in Worship*. Following his *Confession*, the remaining two-thirds of his book handle in some depth these far more problematic and divisive issues of worship.

First he dealt with a straightforward matter: 'Those with whom I dare not hold communion.' As we noted earlier, one of

the main reasons for his long prison sentence was his refusal to
attend a parish church, which would also entail taking the sacrament with those whom he knew well to be unregenerate. With
such he dared not hold communion, especially with any whom he
regarded as 'openly profane'.

Then, more controversially, and at greater length, Bunyan
turned to the opposite subject: 'Those with whom I dare [hold
communion]'. Apart from the Scriptures, two men had influenced
Bunyan's early thinking. One was his own first pastor, John
Gifford, who had laid down bold parameters for the fledgling
church just before his death in 1655. He had urged them to avoid
the sin of breaking the fellowship and union which they enjoyed
over 'externals', which included the vexed question of baptism by
immersion.

The other was Henry Jessey, pastor of a Separatist church in
London to whom the Bedford church had turned for advice in the
past. Although a firm advocate of believers' baptism, Jessey had
also contended that repentance and faith, together with godliness
of life, were more important as qualifications for church membership than the mode of baptism. He set out his position in a book
published in 1650 and called *A Storehouse of Provision in Server-
all Cases of Conscience.*

> Differences [over baptism, he wrote], should not hinder
> the receiving of each other or their sweet communion in the
> Lord together.

Much harm had been done in the churches, he continued, because
of misunderstandings over the function of baptism:

> Water baptism hath not only rent [Christ's] seamless coat,
> but divided his body which Christ hath purchased with his own
> blood ... thereby pulling in pieces what the Spirit hath joined
> together.[1]

Bunyan advocated a similar position. The ordinances of
baptism and the Lord's Supper were appointed as 'servants to
teach and instruct us in the most weighty matters of the kingdom
of God,' he wrote, and he declared his 'reverent esteem' of them

and their 'excellent use to the church ... being to us representations of the death and resurrection of Christ'. However, he
refused to 'ascribe to them more than they were ordained to have
in their first and primitive institution'.[2] In any case, most of the
early members of the Bedford Meeting and their children had
already been baptized as infants.

In a long and elaborate dissertation, Bunyan insisted that
baptism was not an 'initiating ordinance' into the church of Jesus
Christ. It was largely for the benefit of the individual concerned,
giving him a seal of assurance that he was accepted by God. Its
purpose, as Bunyan saw it, was that the new believer's 'own faith
... might be strengthened in the death and resurrection of Christ'.[3]
Bunyan himself had been baptized in 1653 and certainly did not
discount or dismiss the significance of the ordinance, but to shut
someone out from the benefits of church membership and the
comfort of partaking at the Lord's Table for lack of this ordinance
was surely wrong in his view. His reasoning is lucid:

> Strange! Take two Christians equal in all points but this,
> nay, let one go beyond the other far for grace and holiness,
> yet this circumstance of water shall drown and sweep away all
> his excellencies, not counting him worthy of that reception that
> with hand and heart shall be given to a novice in religion be-
> cause he consents to water.[4]

But if baptism is relegated to a secondary position and is mainly
for the benefit of the individual believer, as Bunyan insisted, on
what grounds should an applicant be received into membership?
His answer is clear. 'Their faith, experience and conversation' (i.e.
manner of life) must be examined in the light of the standards set
out in the Word of God, and if the evidence is 'found good', then,
says Bunyan, 'the church should receive them into fellowship'.[5]

Bunyan sincerely thought that such a statement of his convictions would dispel any misunderstandings between the position
held by 'open communion Baptists' like his own church, and that
of the Particular Baptist churches. Closing his treatise, he addressed
those who had been in contention with each other, urging them
to resolve their differences. 'Brethren,' he begs, 'CLOSE, CLOSE; be
one as the Father in Christ is one.'

If Bunyan imagined that he had healed the wounds by his plain speaking, he was sadly mistaken. Not many months later came the answer from the London Baptists in a book called *Some serious reflections on that part of Mr Bunyan's Confession of Faith touching church communion with unbaptized believers.* Written by a Thomas Paul, who is thought to have been a member of Devonshire Square Baptist church, it was harsh and insensitive. Thomas Paul's pastor was the influential Baptist leader William Kiffin, a wealthy merchant and also a Member of Parliament. It would appear that Kiffin himself wrote the introductory letter to the treatise, and although Bunyan was dismayed at the tone he adopted, this was much kinder than that of the bulk of the book. Bunyan could write in reply:

> What Mr Kiffin hath done in the matter I forgive, and love him never the worse, but must stand by my principles because they are peaceable, godly [and] profitable.[6]

Much of the tenor of the book was vitriolic and unjust. Parts of Thomas Paul's attack on Bunyan's position can be reconstructed from Bunyan's lengthy reply: *Differences in Judgment about Water Baptism, no bar to Communion.* Thomas had described Bunyan as 'a man devilish, proud, insolent, presumptuous and the like'. He had gone even further, pouring scorn on Bunyan because of his lowly origins. This stung Bunyan to the quick, and he replied angrily

> You closely disdain my person because of my low descent among men, stigmatising me for a person of THAT rank, that need not be heeded or attended to.

As we have seen, Bunyan was well able to defend himself and even to add his own measure of acerbic comment. Much of Bunyan's reply is a repeat of the arguments in his first treatise and it scarcely makes uplifting reading. Few people are at their best in contention. It was published in the autumn of 1673 but, unlike most of his other work, was soon forgotten and not republished in his lifetime. Answering the accusation that he was favouring the position of those who believed in infant baptism, Bunyan replies stoutly, 'We indulge them not,' but adds, '... being commanded to bear the infirmities of each other, [we] suffer it ... till God shall otherwise persuade them.' He then throws Christ's own challenge at Thomas Paul: 'If you be without infirmity, do you first throw a stone at them.'[7]

Bunyan had tried to persuade his friend John Owen to write a foreword for him, and although Owen had at first agreed, he later withdrew after Thomas Paul and his friends had put pressure upon him not to do so. Making light of his disappointment, Bunyan wrote:

> Perhaps it was more to the glory of God that truth should go naked into the world, than as seconded by so mighty an armour-bearer as he.[8]

In order to sort out their differences on this vital subject, the Particular Baptists in London, doubtless including Thomas Paul himself, tried to persuade Bunyan to meet them for a public debate when he was next in London. However, Bunyan left the city without replying, but set out his reasons for declining the invitation in his written reply.

First, and most obviously, he feared a fresh round of insults because of his lack of formal education. With a twist of irony he says:

> The reason why I came not amongst you was partly because I consulted mine own weakness, and counted not myself, being a dull headed man, able to engage so many of the chief of you.

But more seriously, he feared that, as had happened with his written work, 'both myself and my words would be misrepresented'. They could well 'alter and screw arguments out of their place and make my sentences stand in their own words, not mine'.

Further verbal missiles were flung at Bunyan, including a long and unpleasant diatribe called *Truth Outweighing Error* from Paul Denne, a General Baptist. This was especially hard for Bunyan because Paul Denne's father, Henry, had proved a helpful and kindly friend to Bunyan in his early days as a preacher, and had come to his defence on occasions.[9]

Clearly this whole controversy was a painful one. To dispute with those, like Edward Fowler, who rejected important elements of the faith was one thing, but to clash with true believers was indeed hurtful. Another Particular Baptist, Henry D'Anvers, joined the fray and Thomas Paul made a further attack on Bunyan's position. This is evident from Bunyan's final short reply, *Peaceable Principles and True*, published in 1674. Although no copy of Paul's work has survived, its general theme can be gathered from Bunyan's answer, with one gem in particular gleaned from these unhappy exchanges. In reply to Paul's question, 'How long have you been a Baptist?' with the added cut, 'It is an ill bird that betrays his own nest.' Bunyan answers:

> And since you would know by what name I would be distinguished from others; I tell you, I would be and hope I am A CHRISTIAN; and choose, if God should count me worthy, to be called a Christian, a Believer or other such name that is approved by the Holy Ghost.[10]

In 1681, some years after these heated exchanges, William Kiffin himself wrote a much more measured response called *A Sober Discourse of Right to Church Communion*. Like Bunyan, Kiffin, a kindly and godly man, hoped to heal the breaches between true believers, and he does not mention Bunyan by name, although his position on the importance of baptism as the gateway to church membership and the Lord's Supper is unaltered. Bunyan, doubtless weary of controversy, did not reply and was by this time engaged in more profitable writing.[11]

At this difficult time, when even fellow believers were casting ignominy on his character and standing, John and his wife Elizabeth were cheered by the birth of another child, their last, Joseph. One final twist in the controversy over baptism lies in the fact that baby Joseph was taken to the parish church of St Cuthbert's to be baptized on 16 November 1672 — a source of embarrassment to many who have valued Bunyan's courageous stand on important church issues.

Some have made the unlikely suggestion that Joseph was in fact Bunyan's grandson, born to his own elder son, John. This is improbable because the youth was only sixteen at the time. Since Bunyan himself disagreed with the baptism of infants, others have surmised that this may have been Elizabeth's stated wish, one to which her husband felt he must yield. It is not known for certain whether Elizabeth was actually a member of the Bedford Meeting; she may possibly have retained her affiliation to the national church. Joseph's baptism must therefore remain an anomaly hard to explain.[12]

With fresh opportunities now opening up before him, John Bunyan was glad to put the controversies of these recent months behind him and give all his energies in service to his God and to his Bedford congregation while he had the opportunity.

37

The Bedford pastor

Although the Dissenters celebrated their new-found liberties in 1672, no right-minded person supposed that days of persecution were gone for ever. Their freedom could only be tenuous at best, and if a fickle king or antagonistic Parliament were to reverse the present policies, further days of harassment could well lie ahead. Many churchmen expressed serious disquiet over the turn of events in favour of Dissenters. For instance, Bishop William Fuller of the Lincoln diocese, which included the area around Bedford, could write, regarding the king's Declaration of Indulgence:

> Wee now feel the sad effects of the Declaration. Bold Presbyterians and Anabaptists with the Quakers are exceedingly increased: Insomuch as if there is not a sodain stop put to their daring growth: I dread to write the Consequences.[1]

More than this, the bishop had heard on the ecclesiastical grapevine that some Dissenting preachers — and Bunyan would certainly have been among the number — were actually travelling around from place to place, strengthening smaller fellowships and preaching in locations other than their immediate licensed building.

Nor were clerics alone in their dismay. When the elected representatives of government, the Cavalier Parliament, which was at present in abeyance, heard what the king had done, there was great consternation. Many suspected the king's secret agenda, and the fear of Roman Catholicism was rife. If the king could favour one select grouping of the population, why not another? Who could tell where this would end? This was surely the downward path leading back to the autocracy exercised by his father Charles I, or so they thought. Parliament's moment of protest came sooner than they might have expected.

The Third Dutch War, which had been declared in March 1672, was not going well for England and France. Young William of Orange was called upon to organize his nation's defence. Dykes were opened, land flooded and Holland's indomitable navy sent out to face the combined ships of England and France. And when Spain and Austria rallied to the Dutch cry for assistance, the war was all but over. In desperation Charles was forced to recall Parliament to ask for more finance to fight this expensive war. Parliament was willing enough to oblige, but at a price — the repeal of the Declaration of Indulgence. Parliament was not entirely unwilling to help Dissenters, but a growing fear of Catholicism was now looming on the horizon and they wished to ensure that conditions were not eased for Catholic adherents. A humiliated king was forced to break open the royal seal on his Declaration of Indulgence with his own hands.

When Parliament was recalled in March 1673, it promptly repealed the Declaration of Indulgence and passed instead a bill for 'the Ease of Protestant Dissenters'. But this foundered after being thrown out by the House of Lords, where a preponderance of bishops held sway. All liberties granted to Dissenters were withdrawn once more and the Test Act was introduced. Under this legislation no one could hold any sort of civil or military office without conforming to the established church, thus dashing any hopes of normality for Dissenters. Soon the Cabal ministry itself collapsed, as Sir Thomas Osborne, Earl of Danby, came to power. A rabid opponent of any deviation from the Church of England, whether Dissenting or Catholic, Sir Thomas was intent on introducing yet harsher measures to deal with those who wished to worship outside the orbit of the establishment, in an attempt to crush the spirit of Nonconformity totally.

But this proved impossible. A year or more of freedom had led to an explosion of Dissenting causes: new buildings had been licensed, their preachers issued with the king's own permission to officiate. No preacher seemed quite sure, however, whether the repeal of the Declaration of Indulgence also meant that his licence to preach had been cancelled. In the absence of any overruling directive to the contrary, most were determined to continue their ministries. And the government knew that unless such licences could be officially annulled, there was little they could do to curb the influence of such men as John Bunyan and his fellow preachers. Nevertheless, the church in Bedford was deeply concerned about the situation, with the minute book recording days of prayer and humiliation to seek God's favour and intervention.

Meanwhile, regardless of the darkening situation and while opportunities remained, John Bunyan gave himself steadfastly and unremittingly to his work as a preacher and pastor. Church gatherings were held in many nearby places — Gamlingay, Edworth, Cotton End and Haynes, to name a few. But a study of the church minute book, some of it written up in John's own untidy handwriting, indicates that discipline in the church had suffered during the long period of repression. Again and again we read of members being rebuked, disciplined, or even excommunicated, for various misdemeanours. Most commonly it was for non-attendance at services, but disobedience to parents and debt are also mentioned as offences. Among the more serious cases for discipline was that of John Rush, excommunicated in April 1673 on the following grounds:

> ... being drunke after a very beastly and filthy manner, that is above the ordinary rate of drunkenness for he could not be carried home from the Swan to his house without the help of no less than three persons ... he was so dead.[2]

Alarmed at the situation which had developed, John Bunyan began to preach a series of sermons on *The Barren Fig-tree*, or *The Doom and Downfall of the Fruitless Professor*. These sermons were based on Christ's parable about the owner of a vineyard who had planted a fig tree which was proving barren (Luke 13:6-9). For three years the owner had come searching for fruit, and had eventually instructed his vineyard keeper to cut the tree down. The keeper pleads that the tree should be nurtured for one more year — that it should be given one more chance, and then if it still proved fruitless, it would be felled. A subject such as this was apposite to the situation which confronted the new pastor, and with a pastor's heart he pleads, warns, threatens and encourages his hearers as he expounds this parable.

As was his custom, Bunyan gathered these sermons together and wrote them up, sending the finished manuscript to a publisher in the autumn of 1673.[3] Modern commentators on Bunyan frequently suggest that he had a 'sub-text' in many of his writings, a second and hidden message that he was trying to express in coded language. Certainly, he was living and writing in the context of a fraught political and religious situation, one under which he had suffered acutely; he may well have intended some of his remarks to have a wider implication, or more subtle nuance, than the obvious message on the surface. But to suggest, as some do, that Bunyan had a double-edged political agenda hidden in his writings is to fail to understand him. The Bedford pastor was gospel-orientated through and through, and the main thrust of all his spoken and written work was directed to the hearts of his immediate readers or hearers, warning, exhorting and building them up in the truths of that gospel.

The Barren Fig-Tree was addressing the same acute problem as *The Heavenly Footman* and *The Pilgrim's Progress* — the presence of religious hypocrites within the church. Never one to mince his words, Bunyan goes to the heart of the problem:

> Many make religion their cloak, and Christ their stalking-horse, and by that means cover themselves and hide their wickedness from men: but God seeth their hearts.[4]

God is the owner of the vineyard and Christ the vineyard-keeper who pleads for another year's chance for the fruitless tree, but, as Bunyan points out again and again, the all-important mark of the true believer is 'fruitfulness', or holiness of life. Absence of such evidence, or 'fruit', is 'a dreadful sign that thou art to come to a dreadful end'. Time after time, the preacher addresses his hearers as 'barren fig-trees'. With tender yet penetrating persistence he asks:

> Barren soul, how many showers of grace, how many dews from heaven, how many times have the silver streams of the city of God run gliding by thy roots, to cause thee to bring forth fruit!

With a delightful human touch Bunyan pictures a woman — perhaps he had his own Elizabeth in mind — who plants a small tree in her garden:

> The woman comes into her garden towards the spring ... and sets to gathering out weeds, and nettles and stones and takes a besom and sweeps the walks...

But if, after all her effort, the tree is fruitless, she will say, 'It is dead, it is dead at root: if I had let it stand it would have cumbered the ground.'[5]

Towards the end of his sermon, Bunyan is at his most fearsome as he describes the state of the man or woman who, like Esau, 'can find no place for repentance'. The possibility that the day of grace may be past for an individual even before this life is over is one with which Bunyan himself had wrestled, almost to the point of distraction. Next Bunyan lists signs which might suggest a person to be in such a condition.

Then comes one of the most terrifying passages in all of Bunyan's writings as he describes the approaching end of the 'barren fig-tree':

> And now he begins to shake the fig-tree with his threatenings: Fetch out the axe! Now the axe is death; death therefore is called for. Death, come smite me this fig-tree. And withal the Lord shakes the sinner and whirls him upon a sick-bed, saying 'Take him, death, he hath abused my patience and forbearance, not remembering that it should have led him to

repentance, and to the fruits thereof. Death, fetch away this fig-tree to the fire, fetch this barren professor to hell!'[6]

But the passage has a surprising twist. Just as we imagine that the end of the unfruitful person is about to unfold, the God of pity hears the man's desperate pleas for a further opportunity to mend his ways. Bunyan pictures this man as he 'is come down from his bed and ventures into the yard or shop, and there sees how all things are gone to sixes and sevens', and 'he begins to have second thoughts...' And so, as in the case of so many 'death-bed repentances', he soon returns to his old habits once more.

On a similar theme, Bunyan preached a further series of stringent exhortations based on the words of Christ: 'Strait is the gate, and narrow is the way, which leadeth unto life, and few there be that find it' (Matthew 7:14). The depth of the preacher's concern for those who think their spiritual state is secure but who are deluded by a false confidence is evident throughout. In conclusion he urges his hearers to examine their own hearts, for he fears that many of them may fall into this category:

> Dost thou love thine own soul? Then pray to Jesus Christ for an awakened heart, for a heart so awakened with the things of another world that thou mayest be allured to Jesus Christ... Beg again for more awakenings about sin, hell, grace and about the righteousness of Christ. Cry also for a spirit of discerning...[7]

Later Bunyan would publish his work under the title, *The Strait Gate*.

To preach such sermons as these was bound to arouse fresh opposition. For twelve years his antagonists had tried and failed to silence the voice of the preacher. But now, deceived by Satan himself, his opponents knew an even more potent method to bring John Bunyan's reputation to ruins — scandal. Nor has he been the only honourable servant of Jesus Christ to find his character defamed by a whispering campaign. The pages of Christian biography are sprinkled with examples of men and women who have suffered in this way.

In 1674, therefore, John Bunyan faced one of the supreme trials of his life — one that led him to defend himself hotly and indignantly in print.

First, the rumours were spread about that he 'was a witch, a Jesuit, a highwayman and the like'. So ridiculous were such accusations that Bunyan could dismiss them with little more than a metaphorical wave of the hand and the comment, 'God knows that I am innocent',[8] adding that he would pray that his accusers might be brought to repentance.

But when the rumour-mongers suggested that he 'had my misses, my whores, my bastards, yea two wives at once', Bunyan was incensed, but also recognized that Christ had forewarned his followers that men would say 'all manner of evil against you falsely for my sake'. Accusations came to a head early in 1674, when Bunyan had been pastor for little more than two years.

One charge concerned a young woman named Agnes Beaumont. On 31 October 1672 the name 'Agniss Behement' was entered on the church register — the first entry in John's own handwriting. Agnes, an articulate and intelligent young woman, was a twenty-two-year-old farmer's daughter from Edworth, not far from Biggleswade. She has left a detailed account of the events which occurred on a bitterly cold February day in 1674 — events which sparked off a malicious character assassination of John Bunyan.

Agnes kept house for her widowed father, John Beaumont, a man who had shown passing spiritual concern, but had then become a virulent opponent of Bunyan and the Bedford Meeting. For Agnes the great desire of her life was to be at the meetings and to hear Bunyan preach, a thing her father was now reluctant to permit. Then came a day when the Lord's Supper was to be celebrated at Gamlingay and for a whole week beforehand Agnes had been praying that God would soften her father's heart so that he would allow her to attend.

At last the young woman gained the coveted permission but, as her brother and his wife were also going, and using the only available horse, Agnes would need a lift to Gamlingay, seven miles away. She asked John Wilson, a fellow church member who was later to become her pastor, to call at the farm to take her riding pillion on his horse. Such an arrangement was not considered at all

Agnes Beaumont's cottage at Edworth

improper; indeed, it was a regular practice in those days. Great was the girl's disappointment as she waited patiently by the farm gate for Wilson to come and eventually realized that her plans had gone wrong and that he was not coming. But she brushed away her tears when she heard another horse and rider approaching the farm — and who should it be but John Bunyan himself, on his own way to the meeting?

Too shy to ask for a lift, Agnes appealed to her brother to ask Bunyan on her behalf. Knowing the antagonism of the girl's father, Bunyan refused, despite the earnest pleas. Also he was well aware that his enemies were only waiting for some supposed indiscretion on his part. Only after seeing Agnes's distress and hearing her repeated entreaties, along with a promise she made that she would accept the consequences, whatever they might be, did Bunyan at last agree to take her. But they were spotted — first by Agnes's father, who threatened to pull her off the horse if he could catch them, and then by the local Church of England curate, Anthony Lane. He caught sight of them as they rode along, and looked at them 'as if he would have stared his eyes out'. John Bunyan had given his enemies the very opportunity for which they had been waiting. Afterwards, as Agnes reported, Lane 'did scandalise us after a base manner, and did raise a very wicked report of us'.

The consequences for Agnes were serious. Not only did her father lock her out of the house for the following two nights, but when he died unexpectedly three days later of a heart attack, she was accused of poisoning him. The case was brought to trial; had she been found guilty, she would undoubtedly have faced the death penalty. But who had helped Agnes plan the supposed murder? Who had supplied the poison? The gossips had a ready answer. Why, surely, it must have been John Bunyan, they whispered. Agnes's story, told in her own artless style and with breathless intensity, has been printed many times, perhaps presented most grippingly by the artist Lewis Lupton in 1963, under the title *Behind Mr Bunyan*, complete with his own dramatic line drawings depicting events as they unfolded.

But if the situation was serious for Agnes, who was eventually pronounced innocent, it was yet more so for Bunyan. Adding eleven indignant paragraphs to be included in the next edition of *Grace Abounding*, he struggled to clear his name:

> My foes have missed their mark in this their shooting at me. I am not the man. I wish that they themselves be guiltless. If all the fornicators and adulterers in England were hanged by the neck till they be dead, JOHN BUNYAN, the object of their envy, would be still alive and well. I know not whether there be such a thing as a woman breathing under the copes of the whole heaven, but by their apparel, their children, or by common fame, except my wife.[9]

John Bunyan realized that his real enemy was none other than the Evil One himself, and the plan behind these 'reproaches and slanders to make me vile among my countrymen' was in order that 'if possible my preaching might be made of none effect'. Well might he write as a true soldier of Jesus Christ:

I bind these lies and slanders to me as an ornament; it belongs to my Christian profession to be vilified, slandered, reproached and reviled...[therefore] I rejoice in reproaches for Christ's sake.[10]

Without doubt these unseemly accusations against Bunyan succeeded to some small degree in making him 'vile among my own countrymen'. Otherwise he would not have felt that he must defend himself as robustly as he did; but there is no evidence that this incident caused any permanent damage to his reputation. In the wisdom of God, Bunyan declared, he had always been 'shy of women from my ... conversion until now'. So circumspect had he been in all such relationships that he had constantly avoided being alone with women members of his church — maintaining a standard of integrity higher than was the general practice. Few therefore could take such libellous charges against the new pastor seriously.

It was just as Christ had warned his first disciples: 'The servant is not greater than his lord. If they have persecuted me, they will also persecute you' (John 15:20).

38

Tenuous liberty

John Bunyan was on the run. On 3 February 1675 the bishops and those members of the government most virulently opposed to any toleration of dissent from the Church of England had at last compelled the king to issue a proclamation declaring that the licences granted to Dissenting preachers were now retracted, and so were invalid. Anyone caught officiating at a religious service other than in accordance with the state church liturgy would henceforth be liable for a fine of £20 for a first offence and £40 for any subsequent offence — a charge well above a labouring man's wage for a year. If the preacher were unable to pay, his household goods could be commandeered up to the worth of his fine, although, judging by the inequity of fines in 1670, possessions taken in this way could far exceed the value of the fine. However, one mitigating clause in the legislation stipulated that nothing could be sequestered unless the 'offender' himself was present.

William Foster, the Bedford lawyer whom Bunyan had once described as 'that close opposer of the ways of God', now occupied the position of Commissary of the Archdeacon's Court.

Unrepentant over his vicious treatment of church members in 1670, he was still as zealous as ever to destroy the Independent church, and in particular to silence John Bunyan. The cancellation of the preaching licences gave Foster just the opportunity he was wanting. Only four weeks later this arch-enemy organized a warrant for Bunyan's arrest, signed on 4 March 1675[1] by thirteen justices of the peace on the grounds that he had been preaching at a conventicle during the previous month. Addressed to 'the Constables of Bedford', it complained that:

> One John Bunnyon of your said Towne, Tynker, hath divers times within one month last past in contempt of his Majties good lawes preached or teached at a Conventicle Meeting or Assembly under colour or pretence of exercise of religion in other manner than according to the Liturgie or practise of the Church of England...

To protect Elizabeth and the children, and also his church, Bunyan had no option other than to go into hiding. It must have been a wrench to leave his family once more. Joseph, his youngest son, was little more than two at the time and Sarah barely eight. As magistrates had jurisdiction only over their own counties, it was vital for John to leave Bedfordshire. But where could he go? Several possible locations have been suggested, but in the absence of definite evidence much of this must be guesswork. The most likely answer is that he did not stay long in any one place, to avoid causing trouble for his hosts. He may well have spent time with John Gibbs, his friend in Newport Pagnell, in Buckinghamshire, or with John Wilson, until recently a member of the church in Bedford but now the pastor of an Independent church in Hitchin, Hertfordshire.

William Foster had also discovered a further expedient to make certain of trapping his prey. More than a year earlier Bunyan had received an order to attend his local parish church of St Cuthbert's and take the sacrament there. Predictably he had refused. As a result he had been excommunicated — the usual measure in the circumstances. Forty days were then allowed for the excommunicated person to appear before the Archdeacon's Court; if he failed to comply he would be liable for arrest and

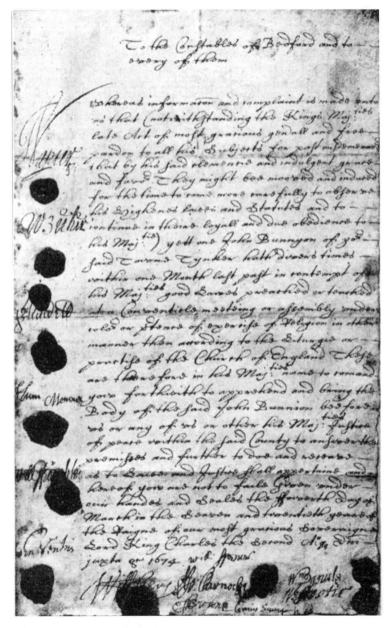

The warrant for John Bunyan's arrest

imprisonment. Generally this remained no more than a threat, with such action rarely being carried out. However, Foster decided that in Bunyan's case it would be different. Gloating over this piece of information, which he himself had written into the records at the time, Foster notified the Bishop of Lincoln in writing that John Bunyan had not only been excommunicated, but had also neglected to appear before the Archdeacon's Court. Bunyan could now be arrested on either the warrant for preaching at a conventicle or on this charge. Little wonder that he went into hiding.

No mention of their pastor occurs in the church minute book during 1675 and 1676,[2] and evidence that he was indeed an exile from his own home comes from a short catechism which he compiled and published in 1675. Deeply concerned that he could no longer preach and teach those new Christians who had recently joined the Bedford church — young people like Agnes Beaumont — Bunyan wrote a simple series of questions and answers, designed to help them personally and also to instruct them in answers to give to any who enquired concerning their faith. In the short preface to this catechism Bunyan describes his special bond with the church in Bedford, but then adds that at the time of writing he had been 'driven from you in presence, not affection'. He ends with the words: 'Yours to serve you by my ministry when I can to your edification and consolation.'[3]

A number of locations in the counties around Bedford have strong associations with John Bunyan. Some of these links may well have been created at this time of extremity. Many Independent and Baptist meeting places had secret escape routes so that if the local constables were seen approaching, the preacher could 'disappear' before they arrived. One 'pulpit' which Bunyan is reputed to have used could also double up as a high-backed pew, thus hiding the preacher from sight if necessary. This pulpit can still be seen today, stored in the vestry at Breachwood Green Baptist Church, near Hitchin.

Some cottages could provide a concealed cupboard or even an unused chimney into which a hunted preacher could squeeze until the danger was past. An old chimney stack in Coleman Green, near Wheathampstead, is all that remains of a cottage where Bunyan is reputed to have stayed when preaching nearby. It now bears an inscription to that effect, while the public house on the green opposite, taking advantage of the association, is called the John Bunyan.

Perhaps the most evocative of all the places associated with Bunyan's name is Wainwood Dell, not far from Hitchin. The five Foster brothers lived at Hunsden House, near the village of Preston, and welcomed the preacher whenever he was in the area. Anyone who ventures into the woods beyond the house can still discover among the trees what appears to be a large circular hollow shaped like a natural 'amphitheatre' that is now over-grown and wild. To this spot, so tradition tells us, John Bunyan's congregation would creep at dead of night and listen with rapt attention to their preacher as he sought to raise their eyes above the struggles and sufferings of this life to see the glory in store for the people of God. We can almost hear him speaking:

> Now we know but in part ... then shall we have perfect and everlasting visions of God, and his blessed Son Jesus Christ, a good thought of whom doth sometimes so fill us while in this world, that it causeth joy unspeakable and full of glory... Then will our conscience have that peace and joy that neither tongue nor pen of men or angels can express...[4]

In all likelihood much of John Bunyan's time was actually spent in the relative safety of London, for it would be harder to track him down in the city. Understandably, he had books he wished to see through the press, and also the security afforded in the home of a friend would give him the coveted opportunity to write. Men like George Cokayne, from Cotton End near Bedford, who was pastor of an Independent church in St Giles, Cripple-gate,[5] may well have offered him shelter. We know for certain from the Bedford Meeting record book that the church had regular contact with a number of the London Congregational churches. Pastors or members of these churches would have willingly given Bunyan refuge at this time.

Another purpose John Bunyan had in visiting London was to seek advice from his friends as to whether to allow his 'scribble' — that story he had written of a pilgrim travelling to the Celestial City — to be printed or not. To many good men such a novel form of writing came as something of a shock. Not all were happy about it. As Bunyan tells us in his versified 'Apology':

> Well, when I thus had put my ends together,
> I show'd them others, that I might see whether
> they would condemn them, or them justify:
> and some said, Let them live; some, let them die.
> Some said, John, print it; others said, Not so.
> Some said, It might do good, others said, No.
> Now was I in a strait, and did not see
> which was the best thing to be done by me.

Torn by all the conflicting opinions, John made up his own mind:

> At last I thought, Since ye are thus divided,
> I print it will; and so the case decided.

There are other possible reasons why Bunyan delayed publishing this particular book, the main one probably being the national and political situation. Censorship was strict and the government's Surveyor of the Press, Robert L'Estrange, was determined to stamp out all Dissenting literature. Francis Smith, Bunyan's most regular publisher, was constantly in and out of prison, his warehouse frequently raided and his stock confiscated. Not long out of prison himself, Bunyan was anxious not to print anything that might prejudice his freedom or invite censorship. Several scenes from the narrative of *The Pilgrim's Progress*, particularly the description of the trial of Christian and Faithful at Vanity Fair under Lord Hategood, might well be interpreted as a commentary on the government's iniquitous handling of Dissenters.

In addition, since leaving prison in 1672, Bunyan had been under considerable pressure of work. First, he had all the concerns of the church and preaching ministry on his shoulders. Then, as we have seen, he was involved in a painful controversy with men whom he knew to be fellow believers over the issue of the place of believer's baptism in admittance to church membership and the Lord's Table. Edward Fowler invited further discord by his poisonous reply to Bunyan's work entitled *A Defence of the Doctrine of Justification by Faith*. Then he had his family concerns. He was probably seeking to train his eldest son John to take over the family business, and Thomas's behaviour may also have been causing concern. And, as if all this was not enough, he had to deal with the smear on his character over the incident involving Agnes Beaumont. A final reason for the delay in publication of *The Pilgrim's Progress* was obviously Bunyan's unsettled existence during 1675 and 1676, with his constant travel from place to place.

The books that John Bunyan did write and publish during his two years of exile were innocuous enough. As we have seen, his catechism was among them; another was *Light for them that Sit in Darkness*, actually licensed by L'Estrange in June 1675. The burden of this book was a theme close to Bunyan's heart, and one denied by men like Edward Fowler: the certainty of the believer's secure standing before God by having the righteousness of another — that is, Christ — imputed to him. *The Strait Gate*, which addressed the same problem as *The Barren Fig-tree*, with its warning to those whose religious professions were little more than hypocritical, was also published in 1676.

A further book, published that year, which once again was an expanded sermon, bore the simple title *Saved by Grace* and was an exposition of Ephesians 2:5, a simple but profound treatment of the amazing grace of God towards sinners. Full of pastoral concern, Bunyan deals with subjects such as the fear of death experienced by many Christians. Sometimes the sins of many years ago come back to haunt the dying believer, and Satan mocks him by pointing to his inadequacies:

> True, sick-bed temptations are oftimes the most violent, because then the devil plays his last game with us,[but] he is never to assault us more; besides, perhaps God suffereth it thus to be, that the entering into heaven may be sweeter.

Charles Doe, who was later to become a friend with enormous admiration for Bunyan, once declared that *Saved by Grace* was 'the best book that was ever writ or I read except the Bible', although he was quick to add, '... and then I remembered I had received a great deal of comfort from all his books.'[6] Doe's estimate of this one book may well have been based on passages such as:

Thou Son of the Blessed, what grace was manifest in thy condescension! Grace brought thee down from heaven; grace stripped thee of thy glory, grace made thee poor and despicable, grace made thee bear such burdens of sin, such burdens of sorrow... O Son of God! Grace was in all thy tears... Grace came out where the whip smote thee, where the thorns pricked thee, where the nails and spear pierced thee. O blessed Son of God! Here is grace indeed! Unsearchable riches of grace. Grace to make angels wonder, grace to make sinners happy, grace to astonish devils.[7]

At last, as 1676 drew to a close, Bunyan made the critical decision to return to Bedford. Elizabeth needed him; the children were being deprived of their father; the church had no pastor. But what would happen if he were arrested and imprisoned again? Perhaps John felt it was a risk he must take. And the joy of his homecoming was indeed soon muted. Having defaulted on the order to appear before the Archdeacon's Court within the fixed forty-day period following excommunication, and with his enemy William Foster as the archdeacon's commissary ready to ensure that Bunyan was brought to account, the outcome was predictable. A loud rap on the door and a sharp demand for 'John Bunyan' was all too soon followed by the familiar walk 'home' to prison once more.

39

A publishing venture

John Bunyan was back behind bars. His family and church must have felt unimaginable dismay as the well-loved preacher's liberty was forfeited once more after only four years of relative freedom. Tradition has always maintained that during this second imprisonment John was put into the Town Clink, situated on the picturesque old bridge that once spanned the River Ouse. The present-day bridge now bears a plaque alerting visitors to the fact that the town's renowned former resident was once locked in the old Clink.

Some have questioned, however, whether this was indeed Bunyan's prison, suggesting that in all probability he would have been sent back to the County Jail. But John Brown, his most important early biographer, vigorously asserts that the Clink on the bridge was indeed the scene of Bunyan's second imprisonment. Brown, himself the pastor of the Bedford Meeting from 1864 to 1903, rests his contention on a strong unbroken tradition. The prison had suffered severe flood damage in 1671, but was extensively repaired in 1675 and therefore in use again by 1676 when Bunyan was jailed.

An old print of the Town Clink on Bedford Bridge

Brown's arguments in favour of the Clink over against the County Jail are hard to refute, for he appeals to the personal testimony of William Bull, Congregational minister at Newport Pagnell and friend of John Newton. Born in 1737, some fifty years after Bunyan's death, Bull had previously lived in Bedford and had been a member of the church at a time when Bunyan's own great-granddaughter was also a member. Bull's pastor, Samuel Sanderson, had been co-pastor of the church at the same time as Ebenezer Chandler, Bunyan's direct successor in the pastorate. Each time that Bull crossed the bridge, he would pause to remember Bunyan — the heroic prisoner who had suffered there.

Another possible pointer to the Town Clink on the bridge being Bunyan's prison was the incidental discovery of a ring marked 'JB' buried in the rubble when the prison was finally demolished in 1765.

This strong local tradition has been set over against a document which has subsequently come to light suggesting that the 'writ of excommunication' under which Bunyan was jailed constituted him 'the King's prisoner' and, as such, the arresting sheriff would have consigned him to the County Jail once more.[1] It seems, however, that John Brown has the stronger case and that within the walls of that dank and dismal Clink, with the waters of the Ouse lapping beneath, John Bunyan was imprisoned once more, at least for a time.

Snatched from his valued work of preaching and watching over the spiritual lives of his church members, the imprisoned pastor would naturally have turned his mind to his writing. Doubtless he had brought with him that manuscript written during his earlier imprisonment which he had called *The Pilgrim's Progress*. While some could see little good in his work and advised him against publishing it, others were encouraging him to go ahead. The only way to discover who was right, Bunyan had decided, was to test out the market:

> For, thought I, Some, I see, would have it done,
> though others in that Channel do not run:
> to prove then who advised for the best,
> thus I thought fit to put it to the test.

Also feeling the need of some vindication for writing in so unusual and unorthodox a way, Bunyan began a lengthy 'Apology' in verse, attempting to explain his method and purpose, and to justify his use of allegory. Some of the long, lonely days in his prison cell were probably spent in writing this poem. In it he compared himself with the fisherman who uses various baits to catch the unwary fish:

> Behold how he engageth all his Wits;
> also his Snares, Lines, Angles, Hooks and Nets...

Even then, some fish will not swallow the bait, yet it is not wrong to try every possible means. But Bunyan is strongest when he turns to biblical reasoning:

> My dark and cloudy words they do but hold
> the Truth, as Cabinets inclose the Gold.
> The Prophets used much by Metaphors
> to set forth Truth. Yea, whoso considers
> Christ, his Apostles too, shall plainly see,
> that Truths to this day in such Mantles be.

Despite all he said, many might still disapprove, so Bunyan goes on the attack instead, giving three reasons why he has chosen to write in allegory. His third and strongest reason again derives from biblical example:

> I find that holy Writ in many places
> hath semblance with this method, where the cases,
> do call for one thing, to set forth another;
> use it I may then, and yet nothing smother,
> truth's golden Beams.

Turning from a justification of his method, Bunyan sets out his real objective in writing the book, addressing not his critics, but his potential readers:

> This book it chalketh out before thine eyes
> the man that seeks the everlasting Prize;

it shows you whence he comes, whither he goes,
what he leaves undone; also what he does:
it also shows you how he runs and runs
till he unto the Gate of Glory comes.

If his work is read with an open mind and a desire on the part of the reader to profit, then, certainly:

This book will make a Traveller of thee,
if by its Counsel thou wilt ruled be...
O then come hither,
and lay my Book, thy Head and Heart together.

In addition to putting the finishing touches to *The Pilgrim's Progress*, it is thought that John worked on the fourth edition of his autobiography, *Grace Abounding to the Chief of Sinners*. Originally published in 1666, with a third edition in 1672, this record of Bunyan's fraught and arduous search after true faith in Christ and assurance of that faith had attracted a wide readership. But now Bunyan wished to add to the record. He wanted to vindicate his character from the evil slurs heaped upon him after he had taken Agnes Beaumont to a meeting behind him on his horse. And this he did, in eleven indignant paragraphs.[2]

Some of his time was also spent in writing up a series of sermons that were probably preached shortly before his imprisonment. Based on John 6:37, the series had an evocative title, *Come and Welcome to Jesus Christ*, and the verse itself was one that had brought Bunyan great encouragement in the early days of his spiritual search. As he writes, we detect a new urgency and tenderness in his address to those who seek Christ:

Coming sinner [he pleads], the Jesus to whom thou art coming is lowly in heart, he despiseth not any ... he will bow his ear to thy stammering prayers; he will pick out the meaning of thy inexpressible groans; he will respect thy weakest offering... Now, is this not a blessed Christ, coming sinner?[3]

Although Bunyan filled as much time a possible with his writing, it must have been difficult to keep a sense of despair at bay in the circumstances. Days turned to weeks, and weeks to months, and still there seemed no prospect of his release. Perhaps he was going to die in that damp, desolate place. When a man had been excommunicated from the established church, as Bunyan had, the law of *habeas corpus* — that legal process which required a judge to investigate the legitimacy of a man's imprisonment — no longer applied. A prison sentence under such conditions could easily last until death, and for Bunyan this seemed a distinct possibility, for he was now almost fifty years of age. Would there be no redress for the honoured pastor of the Bedford Independent church, no new law to which he could appeal? An anonymous friend, who wrote a brief biographical sketch of Bunyan's life, has recorded a gloomy outlook on Bunyan's prospects.[4] He expressed the fear that Bunyan might well die in that prison because of the appalling conditions he was enduring.

But God had not forgotten the sufferings of his faithful servant, and was able to use the most unexpected means to deliver John Bunyan. And who more unexpected than the Bishop of Lincoln, Thomas Barlow? As Bedford came within the bounds of his diocese, this meant that William Foster, Bunyan's relentless antagonist responsible for his imprisonment, was now directly answerable to the bishop. Barlow has sometimes been identified as the prototype of the Vicar of Bray — that cleric who changed his politics and religious sympathies in accordance with whichever king was on the throne. He certainly would not have been a natural friend of Dissenters.[5]

Though poor and forgotten by those in authority, John Bunyan had influential friends, and none more so than Dr John Owen. A prominent Puritan theologian, and pastor of Leadenhall Street Congregational Church in London, Owen was one who actually had the ear of the king himself. And he grieved for the treatment meted out to John Bunyan. When a mutual friend, probably George Cokayne, spoke to him on Bunyan's behalf, Owen decided to act. His opinion carried some weight with the Bishop of Lincoln, for Thomas Barlow had been Owen's tutor during his student days at Oxford, and was therefore well disposed towards him.

From John Asty's *Memoirs of the Life of John Owen*, published in 1721, we learn that Owen wrote to Thomas Barlow, describing the Bedford pastor's plight, and with the letter he enclosed a 'cautionary bond' for Barlow to endorse. This was a legal document signed by two sureties — men who were willing to vouch that the prisoner in question would 'conform within half a year', and who were also prepared to vouch that he would abide by the terms of the bond. The prisoner could then be released by the bishop of his diocese — in Bunyan's case, Thomas Barlow. Probably procured on Bunyan's behalf by his friend Cokayne, the bond was dated 21 June 1677 and had been signed by Thomas Kelsey and Robert Blaney, who were in all likelihood members of Cokayne's congregation.[6]

Although legally all was in order, Barlow hesitated, true to character. He needed time to consider the matter, he told the bearer. A fortnight later he was still hesitating, fearing to act on his own account lest he should offend men like William Foster. Meanwhile he continued to protest his respect for John Owen, saying he would be happy to co-operate if at all possible. At last Barlow suggested that Owen should approach the Chancellor, Lord Finch, first; if he agreed, then Barlow would be happy to oblige and endorse the bond. This alternative shifted any possible blame away from Barlow, but it would also involve the prisoner in a hefty fee. Whether Owen paid the fee on Bunyan's behalf, we do not know, but after the Chancellor had approved Bunyan's release, Barlow at last consented to add his own signature, and the prison doors swung open for John Bunyan once more.[7]

Thomas Barlow was known to have possessed several of Bunyan's latest books, and the anonymous writer of the *Continuation of Mr Bunyan's Life* suggests that the bishop had also been impressed by Bunyan's patience under his afflictions and 'was moved to pity his hard and unreasonable sufferings'.[8] However 'moved' the bishop may have been, and despite his declared desire to 'strain a point to serve' his former student John Owen, he actually did the minimum to bring about Bunyan's release.

What this cautionary bond entailed in Bunyan's circumstances, however, is not entirely clear. Certainly an initial reading suggests that a prisoner freed in this way was agreeing to conform to the Church of England within six months. This, as Bunyan's friends well knew, was out of the question. After remaining resolute through all the fearful trials he had borne since his first imprisonment seventeen years earlier, it was inconceivable that Bunyan would now crumple and agree to conform in order to gain his freedom. Had he not declared that he would endure 'even until the moss shall grow on my eyebrows rather than thus violate my faith and principles'? Perhaps their recourse to this scheme was merely a desperate stratagem employed by these men to free the preacher in view of his harsh circumstances. They may well have hoped that once he was released, no action would be taken to force Bunyan to comply with the conditions of the bond, or perhaps these requirements had become just a formality. As no more is known of the matter, it is likely that this was indeed the case.

A free man once more, John Bunyan's priority in the summer of 1677 was to find a publisher for *The Pilgrim's Progress*. Fears of a fresh wave of persecution against Dissenters were abroad, and Bunyan knew he must act without delay. Dr John Owen had used a certain Nathaniel Ponder to publish his own writing, and it may well be that he recommended him to Bunyan. Ponder, the son of an Independent pastor who had founded a church at Rothwell in Northamptonshire, had already risked much to publish the work of Independent preachers, and was prepared to take on Bunyan's new and intriguing work. In December 1677, the book was submitted to the Stationers' Hall for a licence; this was granted the following February, and before long the first copies of this unusual book were coming off the press at The Peacock in the Poultrey, in Cornhill, London.

So popular did the first edition of *The Pilgrim's Progress* prove to be that it sold out within months, and still the public was clamouring for more. Just one highly valued copy of this first edition remains today; it is kept in a padded box in the British Library, with viewing only allowed under close supervision. This slim volume, containing 233 pages and sold for one shilling and six pence, is in beautiful condition, after having been discovered virtually unused in some nobleman's library.

Astonished by the success of his publishing venture, Bunyan immediately began to work on a new and improved second edition. A number of important passages were inserted, some among the better-known portions of the entire book. The first addition follows immediately after the introductory paragraph in which Bunyan depicts a burdened man clothed in rags, weeping and trembling as he reads the book he holds:

> In this plight therefore he went home, and refrained himself as long as he could, that his wife and children might not perceive his distress; but he could not be silent long...

Bunyan then adds a passage telling of the efforts on the part of the distressed man's wife, relations and neighbours to dissuade him from his 'folly'. The author only returns to the original story when Christian meets with Evangelist, who points him to the Wicket Gate.

A further passage added to this second edition is longer and includes the entire episode of Christian's encounter with Mr Worldly Wiseman. This vivid extract contains the disingenuous advice which Worldly Wiseman gave to Christian, sending him to the village of Morality to get rid of his burden. It continues with the terrified pilgrim cowering under Mount Sinai, fearing that the rocks will fall on his head, until Evangelist meets him again, reproves him and directs him back to the Wicket Gate. Another passage added to the second edition during that same year, 1678, was introduced into the scene at the Palace Beautiful, where Charity is questioning Christian about why he has left his wife and children behind.

A number of other small changes are also to be found in this second edition, including a paragraph in which Bunyan parodies the residents of a town called Fair-Speech. With his experience of such characters as Edward Fowler in mind, he clearly has a point to make as he introduces characters bearing such memorable names as Lord Turnabout, Mr Smooth-man, Mr Anything, not to omit the parson, Mr Two-Tongues.

Hard days still lay ahead for Dissenters, and John Bunyan knew that at any moment he might find himself trapped into a situation in which he could be thrown back into prison. But for the moment this deeply tried Christian must have experienced much joy as he noted in amazement the overwhelming popularity of *The Pilgrim's Progress*.

40

A time of fear

When the body of Sir Edmund Berry Godfrey, a well-reputed London magistrate, was discovered lying in a ditch on Primrose Hill, Marylebone, in October 1678, with a sword protruding from his heart, all London fell into a fearsome panic. And not without cause. For this dastardly murder appeared to add credibility to the frightening words and publications of a certain Titus Oates. The son of a Baptist who had formerly been one of Cromwell's chaplains, Oates was nothing but a ne'er-do-well and a villain. His apparent conversion to Roman Catholicism in 1677, the year of Bunyan's release from prison, might have been of little significance had he remained in the English Jesuit colleges to which he had attached himself, first in Spain and then in Holland.

Soon, however, his Catholic patrons discovered that Oates was a fraud and expelled him. Perhaps by way of vengeance, he reverted to Protestantism and conceived the idea of spreading the rumour in England of a fearful 'Popish Plot'. Detailing it in a massive portfolio of 'evidence', Oates alleged that the English Jesuits planned to set fire to the City of London, to murder Charles II and place his brother James, a Roman Catholic, on the throne instead. Every Protestant who would not convert to Rome would then be murdered without mercy. In the light of his assertion that he himself had been privy to the secret planning of this operation, Oates' words certainly seemed feasible. The Gunpowder Plot of 1605, with its attempt to blow up king and Parliament, had not been forgotten; nor had the recent Great Fire of London. Oates appeared before the Privy Council in September 1678, and his dossier of allegations and supposed evidence was submitted to Sir Edmund Godfrey for investigation. When Sir Edmund disappeared and was later discovered brutally murdered, fear reached new proportions.

Certainly, the people of London must have thought the plot was already being carried out, with Sir Edmund as its first victim. Society women carried daggers with them, and men hid whips in their garments for self-protection. Fear was etched on every face. When they bolted their doors at night no one knew whether they would wake up again in the morning. Looking back on the situation, Bunyan wrote:

> Our days indeed have been days of trouble, especially since the discovery of the Popish Plot, for then we began to fear cutting of throats, of being burned in our beds, and of seeing our children dashed in pieces before our faces.[1]

As a result, Catholics were expelled from the capital, and some were rounded up and executed. To cast even the slightest doubt on the assertions made by Oates could bring the accusation of being a secret Catholic.

These were days when informers earned a lucrative reward for their treachery, and neither Dissenter nor Catholic knew whom to trust. Titus Oates himself grew rich, with apartments in Whitehall and an annual allowance of £1,200; his allegations of foul play grew ever more brazen as he accused one after another of some felony. Suspects were arrested and thrown into prison, with a number of them being proclaimed guilty and executed. The king himself was among the few who did not believe Oates and his fabrications, probably because he knew enough already of ineffectual Catholic plans for the conversion of England.

Bunyan's concern with the problem of fear ran far deeper than questions of physical safety and whether some cut-throat might be running wild in the community. He had known days when he had lain 'trembling under the mighty hand of God, continually torn and rent by the thunderings of his justice'; he could recall the crippling effects of fears concerning his spiritual state. A verse which had brought him relief was John 6:37, where Christ says, 'Him that cometh to me I will in no wise cast out.' That verse had been 'a word, a word to lean a weary soul upon that I might not sink for ever!'[2] During the autumn of 1678, when many people were afraid of what each new day might bring, Bunyan took his manuscript of sermons based on this verse to Benjamin Harris, a printer with radical political views.

Like Francis Smith, his earlier printer, whom he had already used at least twenty times, Harris was in constant trouble with the law for printing politically sensitive material. But this new series of sermons, probably written up while Bunyan was in prison, was of a different ilk. Called *Come and Welcome to Jesus Christ*, it strikes a new note in Bunyan's publications — a pastoral tenderness and compassion for the plight of the troubled sinner who scarcely knows how to resolve his spiritual fears. Using the form of a dialogue between the sinner and the words of his text, Bunyan wrote one of his most striking passages:

> But I am a great sinner, sayest thou.
> 'I will in no wise cast out,' says Christ.
> But I am an old sinner, sayest thou.
> 'I will in no wise cast out,' says Christ.
> But I am a hard-hearted sinner, sayest thou.
> 'I will in no wise cast out,' says Christ.
> But I am a backsliding sinner, sayest thou.
> 'I will in no wise cast out,' says Christ.
> But I have served Satan all my days, sayest thou.
> 'I will in no wise cast out,' says Christ.
> But I have sinned against light, sayest thou.
> 'I will in no wise cast out,' says Christ.
> But I have no good thing to bring with me, sayest thou.
> 'I will in no wise cast out,' says Christ.

> Thus I might go on to the end of things, and show you that
> still this promise was provided to answer all objections.[3]

Such words, with their deep understanding drawn from his own experience, made this book, following so soon after the second edition of *The Pilgrim's Progress*, one of the best-loved of all Bunyan's publications. It went through six reprints during his lifetime and many more afterwards.

As a true pastor, Bunyan was also anxious to use this time of national anxiety to bring relief and consolation to his hearers, many of whom looked for assassins around every corner. Returning to Nathaniel Ponder, Bunyan submitted a further series of sermons, expanded into book form, which he called *A Treatise on the Fear of God*. Basing his work on the words in Revelation 14:7, 'Fear God, and give glory to him, for the hour of his judgment is come,' Bunyan addressed the problem of fear, maintaining that only a true fear of God can drive out craven fear. Roman Catholicism itself was based on fear, he asserted.

> [These misguided fears had] racked and tortured Papists
> for hundreds of years together ... with their penances, going
> barefoot on pilgrimage, wearing of sackcloth, saying so many
> pater-nosters, making so many confessions to priests...

But Bunyan is not harsh:

> This fear would vanish [he tells his readers], could they be
> brought to believe that Christ was delivered up for our of-
> fences and raised for our justification.[4]

A right fear of God is the antidote to every other fear. It was the answer to their present distresses:

> Remember what a world of privileges do belong to them
> that fear the Lord ... namely that such shall not be hurt, shall
> want no good thing, shall be guarded by angels, and shall have
> a special licence, though in never so dreadful a plight, to trust
> in the name of the Lord, and stay upon their God.[5]

Meanwhile the idea of a 'Popish Plot' was gaining even more credibility. Among those whom Titus Oates accused of being involved was a certain Edward Coleman, a Roman Catholic and a secretary to James, the heir apparent to the throne. Charged with hatching plans to murder Charles II and make James king in his place, Coleman had his property searched. Hidden behind his chimney there was discovered a box of secret papers containing his correspondence with prominent Roman Catholics in Italy and France. The contents were incriminating. Coleman had written:

> We have a mighty work upon our hands, no less than the conversion of three kingdoms and by that the subduing of a pestilent heresy, which has domineered over a great part of this northern world a long time. There was never such hope of success since the death of Queen Mary as now in our days...[6]

Such revelations caused public fears to be whipped to a yet higher pitch, and on 3 December 1678 Coleman was hung, drawn and quartered — that fearful punishment reserved for traitors. Although with hindsight historians have discredited the entire Popish Plot as a fabrication, we may well wonder, in view of Coleman's correspondence, whether it actually contained some degree of credibility. Certainly men like John Owen and John Bunyan believed it to be true. We know from the secret Treaty of Dover of 1670 that plans had been devised to convert England to Catholicism, using force if necessary. Perhaps Titus Oates was indeed privy to some elements of covert scheming.

Although deeply troubled about the situation, both for himself and for members of his church, John Bunyan used every spare moment he had for his preaching and writing. His publisher, Nathaniel Ponder, who now acquired the nickname 'Bunyan Ponder', was busy producing a third edition of *The Pilgrim's Progress*. Little more than a year had elapsed since the first had been published, and still the public were clamouring for more. Substantially the same as his second edition, this third one, published in 1679, contained only one change of any significance: the introduction of a character called By-Ends. Coming from the town of Fair Speech, By-Ends meets Christian and Hopeful not long after Faithful's martyrdom at Vanity Fair. Soon he introduces the pilgrims to his unworthy companions, Mr Hold-the World, Mr Money-Love and Mr Save-All. By-Ends wishes to join Christian and Hopeful on pilgrimage, but Christian remarks sagely:

> If you would go with us, you must go against wind and tide...
> You must also own religion in his rags as well as when in his
> silver slippers; and stand by him too when bound in irons as
> well as when he walketh the streets with applause.[7]

Not surprisingly, By-Ends is not willing to accept such conditions — ones that Bunyan himself had learnt through hard experience.

Much of Bunyan's time during 1679, however, was taken up with a far different project. As a follow-up to *The Pilgrim's Progress*, he had planned to write the story of a life journey that led in the opposite direction from the Celestial City. It was the story of one who travelled through this world on a downward path leading to hell. The idea had been simmering in his mind for some time; as he finished *The Pilgrim's Progress* he had warned any careless or hardened readers:

> But if thou cast all away as vain,
> I know not, but 'twill make me dream again.

The result was a book with the grim title, *The Life and Death of Mr Badman.*

Unlike *The Pilgrim's Progress*, Bunyan chose to write this follow-up to it in a style similar to the one used by Arthur Dent in *The Plaine Man's Path-way to Heaven*, one of the two books belonging to his first wife, Mary.[8] In it Dent had recounted an imaginary conversation between four characters, but for Mr Badman's life Bunyan decided to restrict the dialogue to just two — Mr Wiseman and Mr Attentive. As they meet up one morning, these men begin to discuss the wickedness of the days in which they live. Wiseman is especially burdened because of the recent death of a neighbour of his — a thoroughly corrupt individual called Mr Badman.

In creating the misdemeanours of this fictitious character, Bunyan packs into his story many of his own observations of the vices to which unregenerate men can stoop. Much of his material may well have been gleaned from his twelve years in Bedford Jail, as he came into contact with villains guilty of gross acts of wickedness. However, in view of the state of the nation, it may well be that Bunyan was also looking beyond the wicked life of one individual and its consequences and that he had a message for a nation that had deliberately turned away from the high ideals of Puritan godliness and was condoning a licentious lifestyle practised both by the court of Charles II and by the ordinary citizen.

Told through the words of Wiseman, Badman's steady down-hill drift into evil is set before the reader. Even his childhood held all the seeds of his dishonest lifestyle. 'From a child he was very bad,' declares Wiseman. 'His very beginning was ominous.' It would seem that Bunyan's own unruly childhood behaviour may well have been in his mind as he wrote. Attentive interrupts the narrative at intervals both to ask further questions and to point out the lessons to be learned from Badman's conduct.

We learn how Badman robs his parents and by pretending to be religious he tricks a wealthy but godly girl into marrying him. He defrauds his customers in business, files for bankruptcy, cheats his creditors out of their due and resists all his wife's pleas and prayers. One of the most dastardly aspects of Badman's behaviour was his opposition to his wife's faith, which led to his refusal to allow her to worship with other believers. We hear echoes of Agnes Beaumont's account of her father's callous behaviour in the description of Badman's treatment of his wife. He is even prepared to act as an informer, proposing to betray his wife's Christian friends to the magistrates, 'to make them pay dearly' for their convictions. Only the thought of losing custom for his business prevents him from doing so.

Attentive chips in at this point with a lurid anecdote of the fearful fate of another informer, whose dog bit his master's leg. As the bite turned gangrenous, we learn that the informer's 'flesh rotted from off him before he went out of this world'.[9] Clearly this was a cautionary tale which Bunyan intended would-be informers to note well.

Occasionally Bunyan lightens the distasteful narrative with moving descriptions. When Badman's first wife dies, we read:

Die! She died bravely; full of comfort of the faith of her
interest in Christ, and by him of the world to come... She be-
haved herself like some who were making of them ready to go
meet their bridegroom. Now, said she, I am going to rest from
my sorrows, my sighs, my tears... Then shall I have my heart's
desire; there I shall worship without temptation or other im-
pediment; there I shall see the face of my Jesus, whom I have
loved...[10]

Badman's second wife is a woman more wicked than he, a fact
which Bunyan sees as a just recompense for his treatment of his
first, godly wife.

Here and there, through either Attentive or Wiseman, Bunyan
weaves into his account local stories and folklore relating to
various acts of wickedness. Some anecdotes have names attached
to them. An unsavoury character named Dorothy Mately of
Ashover in Derbyshire was swallowed up in a large hole nine feet
deep which suddenly opened up in the ground; she died when a
great rock fell in on her head. Some of the stories are coarse, even
crude; some are credulous, demonstrating that John Bunyan was
also a child of his time.

Into his ghastly account of Badman's downward spiral, Bunyan
skilfully weaves an element of mystery. 'Wait until you hear how
he died,' Wiseman keeps telling Attentive. Again and again we are
warned to expect a shocking account of the deathbed of such a
wicked man. Bunyan maintains an element of suspense right until
the end. 'Pray, how was he in his death? Was death strong upon
him?' enquires Attentive. Instead of dying in terror, as we might
expect, we learn from Wiseman's answer that he died 'as quietly
as a lamb'. For this unexpected twist in his conclusion, Bunyan
had in mind Psalm 73:4, where the psalmist complains of the
wicked that 'There are no bands in their death: but their strength
is firm.' A peaceful deathbed, Bunyan points out, does not mean
that someone is accepted by God at the last. 'By their childlike,
lamblike death they think that all is well,' but that may be far
from the case.

A deathbed such as that of Badman forms a stark contrast to
Christian's experience in *The Pilgrim's Progress*. As we have seen,
Bunyan's pilgrim struggled in the waters of that last river. 'Ah, my

friend,' Christian cried out to his companion, Hopeful, 'the sorrows of death have compassed me about.' Troubled by 'heart-fears that he should die in that River', his passage was far from easy, for this was Satan's last attempt to destroy him. The unbeliever, on the other hand, may often die peacefully, like Badman, without such assaults.

Bunyan's follow-up book to *The Pilgrim's Progress, The Life and Death of Mr Badman,* was printed by Nathaniel Ponder in 1680, but in view of its subject, we are not surprised that it did not enjoy the same reception as its predecessor — a fact that may have set John Bunyan thinking about the possibility of some other sequel to his highly popular book.

Meanwhile, for a period of three years the country had remained in a state of terror amounting to national hysteria over the Popish Plot. Numerous prominent Catholics found their names on Oates' list of suspects. Many were released after trial, but at least thirty-five faced death at the hands of the public executioner. In March 1679 Charles II had attempted to allay the nation's fears by dissolving his Parliament and holding a further election. As a result the Cavalier, or Court Party, which had held power since the Restoration, was outvoted. Instead a large majority of the Country Party, which came to be known as the 'Whigs', was returned. Bedford alone spent £6,000 on ensuring that their Whig candidate, Lord William Russell, was elected.

To curb the progress of the supposed Popish Plot, this new majority in Parliament made a determined effort to exclude James, the Catholic heir, from the throne. And in May 1679, Ashley Cooper, Lord President of the Council and 1st Earl of Shaftesbury, introduced a bill known as the Exclusion Bill, ruling out James from the succession. Flushed with triumph, the Whig party continued to inflame the nation's fear of a plot to their own advantage. Cries of 'No Popery' rang out across the streets of London, while effigies of the pope were burnt each November to mark the anniversary of the accession of Elizabeth I. Furious at the continued attempts of Shaftesbury and his party to force through the Exclusion Bill, cutting out his brother from the succession, Charles dissolved his Parliament on two separate occasions, but each time a substantial Whig majority was returned once more.

As time passed and the terrible things predicted by Oates failed to materialize, the Whigs began to lose their power and credibility. At last in 1681 the party was forced to concede failure when the Exclusion Bill was defeated for the third time in the House of Lords. Many of the Whigs, and Shaftesbury among them, had favoured the Duke of Monmouth, a nominal Protestant and the king's illegitimate son, as heir apparent in place of James, the king's brother. In anger, Charles suddenly dissolved his Parliament for the third time. Having secured the assurance of French support and finance from Louis XIV, he decided to rule without the aid of politicians.

Gradually the deceptions foisted on the country by Titus Oates were becoming clearer. After the execution on 1 July 1681 of Oliver Plunkett, Archbishop of Armagh, the tide of opinion began to turn against Oates. One after another of his victims was cleared of wrongdoing. Finally, on 31 August 1681, Oates was banished from his lavish apartments at Whitehall. Arrested for sedition, he was fined the enormous sum for those days of £100,000 and thrown into prison, to await further punishment.

41

'Come wind, come weather'

The Dissenters were in serious trouble once more. The panic over the threat of a violent death as a result of the alleged Popish Plot hatched by the Jesuit hierarchy had temporarily eased their burden. Now things were changing again. In promoting the Whig party, the Earl of Shaftesbury had deliberately set out to woo the votes of the middle classes of England, the tradesmen and towns-people. Most of all, he had sought to attract the Nonconformists and Dissenters, whose sufferings at the hand of the Cavalier Party had been so intense. Many had fallen for the bait and had given the Whigs their wholehearted support, thinking this would bring days of persecution to an end. But, by linking their cause to the vicissitudes of a political party, they were in fact preparing the way for an intensification of their own sufferings should the Whigs ever fall from power.

And fall they did for, as we saw, Charles II dismissed his Whig-dominated parliament early in 1681. This change ushered in a period of persecution for Dissenters more brutal than anything that most of them had previously experienced. Formerly the king had pressed for religious toleration for all, hoping to ease the burden on Roman Catholics. In reality, he cared little about Protestant Dissenters. His support base lay with the High Church nobility, and if these men wished to hound Dissenters and Nonconformists out of their homes and jobs, it was of no concern to him. In his eyes their recent support for the Whig Party had sealed their fate.

Despite the fact that the allegations made by Titus Oates had been largely discredited, many Dissenters still accepted his assertions, believing them to be at least partially true. John Bunyan and his friend Dr John Owen were among that number. Both held that it was evidence of God's great mercy to a sinful land that the plot had been discovered in time. Preaching at the end of 1681, when Oates had already been in prison for four months, Owen expressed this view:

> The large and wonderful discovery of the horrible plot, of the horrible popish plot, laid for the ruin, destruction and desolation of this nation, is evidence that England is not yet, I say, utterly forsaken of the Lord its God. It was not discovered by our rulers, from whom it was hid ... yet through the conduct of the holy providence of God, it hath broke forth [been disclosed].

So, concluded Owen, 'there is ground of encouragement yet remaining to apply ourselves to God'.[1] But even he could not foresee the ferocity of the trouble that was about to overtake the Dissenting churches.

Angry at the attempt to oust James from the succession, the Royalist supporters (increasingly known as the Tory Party), looked round for a scapegoat on whom to vent their wrath. The Dissenters were a natural target. Informers found fresh opportunities for their dastardly work of betraying and ruining innocent neighbours and fellow citizens for their own personal gain. Some informers ran a lucrative business, employing a team of 'sub-informers' to scour the country, tracking down any known Dissenter to his home or meeting place. Magistrates, tipped off as to where a gathering for worship was in progress, would send constables to storm the meeting, driving the worshippers into the street, often beating them with swords, or even pikestaffs. Pulpits and pews were smashed and the wood grabbed by the poor for firewood; buildings were demolished before the very eyes of the dismayed congregation.

Fines, more ruinous than anything imposed before, were levied against those caught in the act of worship. Goods were confiscated, leaving families with no means of support. Once more the prisons were packed with Dissenters who were either unable or unwilling to pay these exorbitant fines. As before, towns differed markedly in their attitudes to Dissenters, with some being more lenient than others, but punitive measures were common in many towns and cities. Not all Dissenters stood quietly by while their property and livelihoods were destroyed; the records of the Broadmead Baptist Church in Bristol give a number of instances of intense resistance to such interference and downright robbery conducted in the name of the law.

Understandably, churches once more went 'underground', meeting in woods at dead of night, in dells, barns, or any secret place hidden from the prying eyes of the informers. After December 1681 we have only a few intermittent records of the Bedford Meeting, and virtually none at all between 1683 and 1688. Clearly Bunyan's church too went into hiding and certainly feared to record any of its activities. Caring for the spiritual life of the church under such conditions cannot have been easy for John Bunyan. Troubles seemed to press in on every hand. Quite apart from his own personal danger, he could say, with the apostle Paul, that he had been 'in perils by mine own countrymen ... in perils in the city ... in perils among false brethren ... besides ... that which cometh upon me daily, the care of all the churches'.[2]

Among other 'perils' which he endured at this time were the cruel accusations made by one church member, John Wildman, who had been reprimanded for an ugly display of anger, described as 'a kind of raillery and very great passion'. And what better way for Wildman to wreak his vengeance on the church for the discipline imposed than to lay a counter-accusation against Bunyan himself — one of dishonourable financial dealings? Incensed at such a suggestion, the church minutes labelled Wildman 'an abominable lyer and slanderer of our beloved brother Bunyan',[3] and at a church meeting on 2 November 1680 threatened Wildman with excommunication if he did not show evidence of repentance before the next meeting. This was not forthcoming and the matter rumbled on for almost three years. Even as late as April 1683, when Wildman wanted to be received back into membership, his attitudes were far from satisfactory.

Adding to the burdens weighing down on Bunyan, and on Elizabeth too, was the behaviour of Thomas, second son of John's first marriage. Now a young man of twenty-two, Thomas had grown up while his father was in prison and his wild, even criminal, behaviour brought deep shame on his parents. Clearly Thomas had mixed in bad company and now, in 1680, one of his friends, William Robinson, was serving a prison sentence for being accessory to a crime involving counterfeit coinage. To gain the release of both his friend and another criminal also in the jail, young Thomas Bunyan and an accomplice (the son of another church member), planned to rob travellers at night and with the proceeds bribe the jailer to release the two men. It seems that the plan was discovered before Thomas was able to execute it, but he was indicted to appear at the next assizes. No more is known of the case, but it is probable that his older brother John stood surety for Thomas, perhaps paying his fine, so that Thomas was not imprisoned for his offence.

If times were hard for the Dissenters of England, conditions were even worse for the Covenanters in Scotland. Although some resorted to arms to defend their cause, most wanted nothing more than to worship their God peaceably according to the dictates of conscience, refusing to compromise with the strictures of the state church. But the 1680s, known as the Killing Times, were days when men, women and young people were hounded, hunted and slaughtered without mercy. Stories like that of the two Margarets, Margaret Wilson and Margaret MacLachlan — the former a girl of eighteen and the latter aged sixty-three — tied to posts and drowned by the incoming tide in the Solway Firth for refusing to 'conform', are familiar. So too is the gruelling account of John Brown of Priesthill, whose pregnant widow sat weeping over the mutilated and murdered body of her godly husband. 'How will you answer for this morning's work?' she asked the cruel John Graham of Claverhouse, who had just shot Brown as he knelt in prayer. 'To man I can be answerable,' replied the pitiless dragoon, 'and as for God, I will take him into my own hand.'

Whether John Bunyan knew of these fearsome acts of wickedness, we do not know, but one loss that he would have felt keenly was one from natural causes — that of his fellow elder, Samuel Fenne, a friend who had shared Bunyan's sufferings, both in hefty fines and imprisonment; his death in November 1681 added to John's heavy burden of responsibility. It seemed that God was removing some of the most resolute and godly men in the land at this time, taking them from the scenes of their strenuous labours and perhaps sparing them the grief of witnessing the renewed sufferings of Christian people. Only the previous year the eminent Puritan preachers Walter Marshall, Thomas Brooks, Stephen Charnock and Thomas Goodwin had all died.

During these years John Bunyan was tireless in his toils, both in preaching and writing. Exposed to all weather conditions, he could be found wherever he might secretly and safely gather a congregation. It is not hard to imagine the difficulties of such a ministry. The state of the roads was appalling; some of them were merely rutted tracks with deep potholes that turned to muddy ponds in winter, or wet weather. Gingerly picking its way along, Bunyan's horse carried its owner often at dead of night to many isolated places where eager congregations were expecting him. The nickname 'Bishop Bunyan', playfully given to one whose dislike of episcopacy was a byword, relates to these days, as such a ministry took him not only to the villages of Bedfordshire, but to all the surrounding counties, and further afield.

Before the intense persecution made it impossible, Bunyan could also be found preaching in London from time to time. In 1682, now aged fifty-four, he preached a sermon on Mark 8:37 on 'The Greatness of the Soul' with the subtitle 'and [the] unspeakableness of the loss thereof'. The venue was one of the best-known Nonconformist pulpits, the Pinners' Hall. Built by the Pinmakers' Company in 1636, the hall had been leased by the guild to the Dissenters for their weekly lectures and as a place of worship. Together with other guildhalls, such as Haberdashers' Hall, Salters' Hall and Girdlers' Hall, Pinners' Hall had become a significant pulpit by the 1680s and was therefore being targeted for closure by the Tory and High Church party in their crackdown against all Dissenting worship.

However, it was still open in 1682, and Bunyan's invitation to preach there demonstrates his increasing popularity as a preacher and a writer. By this date eight editions of *The Pilgrim's Progress* had come off Nathaniel Ponder's presses, though scarcely four years had passed since its first publication — a fact that added enormously to Ponder's personal success as a printer. As the tall, serious, yet kindly-looking preacher rose to address the men and women gathered there in the Pinners' Hall at some risk to themselves, they would receive an unforgettable challenge.

Basing his words on Mark 8:37, Bunyan did not spare his hearers as he developed his theme of the fearful peril of losing one's soul. The days were dangerous and his opportunities to preach uncertain; he himself could be thrown back into prison at any time. Nothing mattered more than the soul. 'House and land, trades and honours, places and preferments, what are they to salvation? To the salvation of the soul?' he demanded. Throughout this sermon the fearful flames of hell are ever present in the preacher's mind, as he warns his hearers again and again of the importance of the soul and the results of its neglect. The days were urgent with the looming possibility of the total destruction of Dissenting churches, and even of all Protestant churches, when the avowed Roman Catholic, James, Duke of York, became king.

> The soul that is lost is never to be found again, never to be recovered again, never to be redeemed again. Its banishment from God is everlasting; the fire in which it burns and by which it must be tormented, is a fire that is [for]ever, everlasting fire, everlasting burnings...[4]

If such words make uncomfortable reading in cold print, it is not hard to imagine the overpowering effect they would have had on Bunyan's first hearers, riveted by the terrifying descriptions of the fate of those who pay little heed to the soul. Degrees of punishment in hell formed a key emphasis in Bunyan's sermon. As he pointed out, a log daubed with a little oil will not burn as fiercely as one soaked in oil for many years. The more grievous the sins committed, therefore, the worse the punishment. 'The lowest hell is for the biggest sinners, and theirs will be the greater damnation,'[5] he maintained; the justice of God demands that it should be so.

There is little relief anywhere in this sermon, no hiding place from Bunyan's soul-piercing oratory. Some rejected such a message. We know of one hearer listening to another of Bunyan's sermons at this time who could hardly condescend to acknowledge his excellence as a preacher — none other than the young Samuel Wesley, later to be the father of John and Charles Wesley. He was attending an academy for Nonconformist students in Stoke Newington, the same one that Isaac Watts would attend eight years later. With characteristic pride, Samuel Wesley described hearing 'Friend Bunnian', but dismissed him for his lack of formal education. Before long Samuel Wesley had returned to the fold of the state church.

John Owen

Far different was Bunyan's friend John Owen. Renowned for his great learning and his contribution as the leading Puritan thinker and theologian, he was not too proud to acknowledge the gifts of other men, particularly one like John Bunyan, who had spent the best years of his manhood in a degrading and filthy jail for his convictions. During his own lifetime of preaching and writing Owen had published over eighty different theological works and many individual sermons, but now, in 1682, he was far from well. With his health undermined by repeated attacks of asthma, and his body wracked with pains for which there were no relief-giving analgesics, Owen was unable to preach as often as before. At such times he would listen to his Bedford friend, who had come to London both to preach and perhaps to bring some new work for his publisher. Occasionally Owen would ask Bunyan to fill his own pulpit.

'Why do you listen to a tinker prate?' Charles II had disdainfully asked Owen.

'Had I the tinker's abilities [to preach], please your Majesty,' replied Owen, 'I would most gladly relinquish my learning.'[6]

In fact Owen had little more than a year left to live, and a hard year it proved. Plots and counter-plots were in the air, as many with Whig sympathies did all in their power to promote the claim to the throne of James, Duke of Monmouth, Charles II's dashing thirty-three-year-old son by his mistress Lucy Walters. Some unwise Dissenters may well have been accessories to the plotting, so anxious were they that the Catholic James should not become king on his brother's death. And, on the thinnest of pretexts, the Court Party laid the blame for any unrest on the Dissenters and their conventicles. As long as conventicles, those 'nurseries of rebellion', went on meeting, wrote one statesman, conspiracies and plots against the throne would continue.[7]

Betrayed by informers, more than fifteen London Dissenting ministers were charged with officiating at conventicles, and huge fines were levied against them. Included in this number were some of Bunyan's closest friends and associates, men such as John Owen, George Cokayne, Matthew Meade, John Howe and others. Even William Kiffin, the Particular Baptist leader, a man who had given the king a gift of £10,000 on an earlier occasion, had his house searched and was fined a hefty £300.

Yet more trouble lay in store for John Owen when an absurd accusation linking him to the Rye House Plot was mooted. In a measure of desperation, certain men had planned an ultimate and indefensible way of securing the throne for the Duke of Monmouth. They would murder both the king and his brother James. In this conspiracy, named after Rye House, a manor in Hoddesdon, Hertfordshire, the plotters schemed to conceal a hundred armed men in the garden of the house. When the king and his brother came past in their coach, as they always did on the way back from the Newmarket races, the men in ambush would spring out and murder both of them. The Duke of Monmouth would then be the next and obvious claimant to the throne.

But, like many plots, it grievously miscarried. All was in readiness for it to be put into operation on 1 April 1683, but a devastating fire at Newmarket, which destroyed a greater part of the town, cut short the duration of the races and the royal brothers came home early, on 22 March. A few days later someone divulged the plot. Vengeance was swift and terrible. Judge George Jeffreys — a man with a heinous reputation for cruelty — rounded up any who could be remotely connected with a desire to see Monmouth on the throne, John Owen among them. It may well be that Owen, like many others, had some knowledge of this plot, or of an earlier one designed to force Charles to guarantee a Protestant succession. But knowledge does not denote approval. Sick and in pain, Owen was later released, but others, including Lord William Russell, the well-respected member of Parliament for Bedford, were executed on flimsy evidence. The Duke of Monmouth himself decided that he would be safer out of the country and escaped to the Low Countries to bide his time before making a further attempt to claim a throne he considered to be rightfully his.

Only a few months later John Owen died, his life no doubt cut short by the circumstances of recent months. Beyond the reach of malicious and vindictive men, he was buried in Bunhill Fields in London, a graveyard where many Dissenters lie awaiting the general resurrection. And, among many others, John Bunyan would have mourned his passing and doubtless thought wistfully of that land he had glimpsed in his 'dream', where all the bells of the city rang for joy when faithful pilgrims passed in through the gates.

42

The battle is the Lord's

Although the Whigs had been ousted from power, many still plotted ceaselessly, hoping to prevent the throne from passing to the Catholic James Stuart. The fear of renewed civil war was real, with memories of Charles I and the events of 1642 too recent and too painful to be easily forgotten. 'No Popery, No Slavery,' was a mantra on the lips of many Whig politicians and echoed by some Nonconformists and Dissenters. To tighten his control on the country, Charles II began to reinforce the terms of the Corporation Act of 1661, legislating against anyone holding position on the corporations of towns or cities who had not taken communion in the Church of England within the last year. This placed William Fenne, mayor of Bedford in 1678 and father of Bunyan's friends, Samuel and John Fenne, under considerable pressure. Before long there was a move afoot to remove all members of town corporations who might be sympathetic to Dissenting churches.

Renewed repression of conventicles and the cruel treatment of innocent men and women brought anxiety and indignation to men like John Bunyan. Nonconformists, in common with many others, had viewed the country's troubles since the Restoration as God's reply to a government which mercilessly oppressed its own people. War, plague, fire, and even the fear of the Popish Plot, had not checked the godlessness of the court and nation. Writing in 1681, Bunyan had exclaimed:

> Wickedness like a flood is like to drown our English world. It begins already to be above the tops of the mountains; it has almost swallowed up all; our youth, middle age, old age and all are almost carried away of this flood. O debauchery, debauchery, what hast thou done in England! Thou hast corrupted our young men and hast made our old men beasts...[1]

Against this background of unrest, fear and the unrestrained progress of evil, John Bunyan wrote his second great allegory, *The Holy War*.[2] A marathon work, it consisted of some 102,000 words. Bunyan must have written this in about ten months, between concluding *Israel's Hope Encouraged* in the spring of 1681 and the licensing of *The Holy War* ready for publication in February 1682. To accomplish this he would have needed to work at an astonishing speed.[3]

As with *The Pilgrim's Progress*, scholarly writers have been at pains to discover the sources from which Bunyan culled ideas for his epic description of the vicious and endless battle raging over the town of Mansoul between Emmanuel, representing Christ, and Diabolus, portraying the devil. Bunyan's thoughts can be primarily traced once again to the Scriptures, where warfare, both literal and metaphorical, is a frequent theme. Before the Israelites surrounded the walls of Jericho, Joshua was strengthened by an encounter with 'the captain of the host of the LORD'.[4] In the New Testament Christ refers to Satan as 'the strong man armed', while the apostles urge Christians to 'resist the devil', 'put on the whole armour of God' and 'fight the good fight of faith.'[5]

Completed early in 1682, *The Holy War* was printed by Dorman Newman and Benjamin Alsop,[6] instead of Nathaniel Ponder. It may be that the popularity of *The Pilgrim's Progress* gave Ponder little time for work on anything else. Demand for the first allegory was still as great as ever. Some even refused to believe that an unlettered tinker who had spent more than twelve

years in a degrading prison could possibly be the author of such a
work of genius. In a versified 'advertisement' attached to *The
Holy War*, Bunyan was ready with his reply, delivered with a
measure of indignation. He coupled it with a further claim — one
of originality for his new work.

> Some say The Pilgrim's Progress is not mine,
> insinuating as if I would shine
> in name and fame by the worth of another,
> like some made rich by robbing of their brother...
> I scorn it: John such dirt-heap never was
> since God converted him.

Continuing in the same piqued vein, Bunyan insists:

> Also for this thine eye is now upon,
> the matter in this manner came from none
> but the same heart, and head, fingers and pen,
> as did the other. Witness all good men;
> for none in all the world without a lie,
> can say that this is mine, excepting I.

However, few writers, if any, are totally original, and it is hard
to imagine that Bunyan had not heard of, or read, Richard
Bernard's classic work, *Isle of Man, or the Legal Proceedings in
Manshire against Sin.* A Puritan pastor, Bernard was born in
Epworth, Lincolnshire, in 1568. He had strong sympathies for the
Separatists and his most popular work, *Isle of Man,* was written in
1627 and reprinted many times during Bunyan's lifetime. In it
Bernard portrays the struggle between good and evil raging in
Manshire, where an inn, representing the heart of man, is the
grand epicentre of battle. Five doors lead into the inn, each being
one of the senses: sight, hearing, taste, touch and smell. All of
these elements have their counterparts in Bunyan's work, *The
Holy War,* as have some of Bernard's characters, such as Sir
Worldly Wise and Wilful-Will.

Probably the significance of Bunyan's claim that the work was
entirely his own lies in the phrase 'in this manner'; for, whatever
seed thoughts he may or may not have gleaned from Richard

Bernard, he improves and develops them beyond anything which Bernard attempted. Mr Outside, Sir Lukewarm and Sir Plausible Civil in *Isle of Man* have little personality beyond what is conveyed by their names alone. But in many cases Bunyan gives flesh and blood, colour and life, to his characters.

Another man whose writings are cited as a model for *The Holy War* is Bunyan's contemporary, Benjamin Keach, whose works, *War with the Devil* (1673) and *The Glorious Lover* (1679), would probably have been familiar to Bunyan. But despite these possible sources, John Bunyan, like a mighty eagle, soars above all lesser authors. Each of his books bears the characteristics of his own unmistakable genius.

So highly acclaimed was Bunyan's allegory that other writers were already producing works of inferior quality and claiming that they were by Bunyan, sometimes even using the initials 'JB' to gain rapid sales. So we can well understand the Bedford pastor's natural indignation as he continues:

> I write not this of any ostentation,
> nor 'cause I seek of men their commendation...
> Witness my name, if anagram'd to thee,
> the letters make — ' Nu hony in a B.'[7]

As in the opening words of *The Pilgrim's Progress*, when he 'walked through the wilderness of this world' and lighted on a den where he dreamed his dream, so in *The Holy War*, Bunyan introduces his readers to his subject with a personal allusion regarding its origins. The words are simple and memorable:

> In my travels, as I walked through many regions and countries, it was my chance to happen into that famous continent of Universe; a very large and spacious country it is.

And among the diverse towns and areas 'in this gallant country of Universe', Bunyan comes across 'a fair and delicate town, a corporation, called Mansoul'. So beautiful was this town in its original state that he reports that 'There is not its equal under the whole heaven.' This personal involvement with his

The frontispiece of the first edition of *The Holy War*, incorporating the only known full-length portrait of Bunyan

own narrative is deliberate, for like many of Bunyan's works, *The Holy War* contains a strong autobiographical content.

The stately town of Mansoul was the possession of King Shaddai,[8] and in it he had built for himself a pleasing palace. Peace and contentment reigned in Mansoul: 'There was not a rascal, rogue or traitorous person then within the walls.' Depicting the soul as first created by God, a fit companion for himself, upright and pure, Bunyan presents a splendid word-picture of the life of man before the Fall. Then onto the scene comes Diabolus, 'a great and mighty prince, and yet both poor and beggarly', who, with his fallen angels, seeks to conquer and possess the town of Mansoul as vengeance upon King Shaddai for casting him out of heaven.

In his introductory poem Bunyan aligns himself personally with Mansoul, both in its original glory and in its subsequent shame:

> For my part, I (myself) was in the town,
> both when 'twas set up, and when pulling down.
> I saw Diabolus in his possession,
> and Mansoul also under his oppression.
> Yea, I was there when she own'd him for lord,
> and to him did submit with one accord.

He knew only too well from his godless youth what it meant for a man to be 'pulled down' as he served Diabolus, or the devil. When Apollyon had fought Christian he had roared:

> Thou art one of my subjects, for all that country is mine, and I am the prince and god of it. How is it that thou hast run away from thy king?[9]

Mansoul had five gates, each representing one of the senses, but it is through Ear gate and Eye gate that Diabolus and his host of fallen angels seek to make their most subtle attack. Because the town cannot be taken without the consent of its people, Diabolus seeks by smooth words to persuade them to open the gates, suggesting, as he did to Eve in the Garden of Eden, that King Shaddai was depriving the town of its rightful benefits. Captain

Resistance, who guarded Ear gate, is shot dead; Captain Inno-
cency also dies, and Diabolus, with his evil troops, enters the
town and proceeds to take up residence in Heart Castle. The
town is remodelled; Shaddai's laws are revoked and his image,
which stood in the marketplace, defaced.

Throughout *The Holy War* Bunyan places marginal notes
which supply the key to his allegory. As he warns his readers:

> Nor do thou go to work without my key...
> it lies there in the window [margin]; fare thee well...[10]

By its very nature, allegory takes the reader one step back
from a factual representation of the truth, and it is found more
frequently under the old covenant than under the new. Christ
sometimes used a form of allegory in the parables, but it was not
to simplify truth so much as to hide it from the sceptical and
unbelieving. Even his disciples were forced to ask, 'What might
this parable mean?', after Jesus had spoken of the sower and his
seed. 'The seed is the Word of God,' Christ explains; the birds
that snatch away the seed represent the devil. If allegory hides,
rather than reveals, truth some have queried Bunyan's wisdom in
using such a method. But he himself defends it in his long, versified 'Apology' for *The Pilgrim's Progress:*

> Art thou offended, and dost thou wish I had
> put forth my matter in another dress
> or that I had in things been more express?

No, he maintains, he has written in allegorical form so that he
may stir up the minds of his readers. And certainly in *The Holy
War* this unusual presentation of truth stimulates thought and
clothes familiar concepts in fresh and arresting attire.

So when King Shaddai learns of the tragic fall of Mansoul into
the grip of Diabolus, he sends four brave captains, accompanied
by an army of 40,000 men, to lead an assault to regain the town.
These captains, Boanerges, Conviction, Judgment and Execution,
represent the initial blasts of conviction made against the soul
because of the broken law of God — an experience which
Bunyan himself knew all too well.

I saw the captains, heard the trumpets sound,
and how his forces covered all the ground.
Yea, how they set themselves in battle-ray,
I shall remember to my dying day.

We discover that Lord Understanding, the former mayor of the town, has been deposed by Diabolus and is safely locked up in his house, with a wall built around it so that no light may enter the darkened windows; My Lord Will-be-will has become the servant of Diabolus, and Mr Conscience, the recorder of Mansoul, is replaced by Mr Forget-good. The people of Mansoul are in a sorry state. They co-operate helplessly and willingly with all Diabolus' malevolent plans and purposes of evil, sincerely believing that Shaddai's laws were designed to rob them of their delights.

When the captains fail to retake the town, King Shaddai's own son, Emmanuel, offers to come himself to Mansoul. With five more captains, Credence, Goodhope, Charity, Innocent and Patience, he leads a further assault. Cringing and afraid, Diabolus sues for terms of peace, but is only ready for a partial surrender. Sending his ambassador Mr Loath-to-Stoop, he suggests that they share the town. Six times, as the devil tries to negotiate terms with Emmanuel which will leave him a foothold in Mansoul, Bunyan writes in the margin, 'Mark this'. Clearly he had a message for his readers about the dangers of trying to compromise with sin.

As Mansoul is resistant to all his offers of mercy and grace, Emmanuel at length calls upon his army to bring up the battering rams against Ear gate and Eye gate. Finally they crumble, allowing the triumphant captains to enter. They bombard Heart Castle, demanding that Diabolus comes out. News of his capture is conveyed to Emmanuel, who at last enters the town, chaining the whingeing Diabolus to his chariot wheels and parading him through the streets, in much the same way as the Romans treated their conquered generals.

Intricate and complex, Bunyan's allegory attempts to deal in detail with God's entire plan to rescue fallen man. He endeavours to pack an entire systematic theology into his story, crowding, or even overcrowding, his narrative with names and characteristics

typical of fallen man. We meet Mr Fury, Mr Stand-to-Lies and Mr
Drunkenness, aldermen of Mansoul. These die in combat. We also
learn of the evil machinations of Satan's infamous agents Lord
Beelzebub and others, as well as Emmanuel's undaunted captains,
among them Captain Conviction and Good-hope.

Throughout, a distinction is made between the original citizens
of Mansoul, who are powerless, sinful and misguided, and the
evil Diabolonians who have corrupted the town. Bunyan gives us
a moving glimpse into the eternal counsels between the Father
and the Son in which the Son agrees:

> That at a certain time prefixed by both, [Emmanuel]
> should take a journey into the country of Universe, and there
> in a way of justice and equity, by making amends for the follies
> of Mansoul, he should lay a foundation of her perfect deliver-
> ance from Diabolus and his tyranny.[11]

Perhaps the weakest point, and the point at which allegory
itself fails as a medium for expressing a full-orbed gospel, is in the
treatment of redemption by the cross of Christ. Not until the end
of the book do we discover, in perhaps one of the finest passages
of all, Emmanuel proclaiming his redeeming work on behalf of
Mansoul:

> O my Mansoul, I have lived, I have died, I live and will die no
> more for thee. I live that thou mayest not die. Because I live
> thou shalt live also. I reconciled thee to my Father by the
> blood of my cross, and being reconciled thou shalt live through
> me.[12]

Prince Emmanuel sets up his rule in Mansoul once more,
having proclaimed his undeserved forgiveness for such rebellion.
He clothes the citizens in pure white garments, so that they may
be known as his. Certain of the most vicious Diabolonians are
tried and crucified, in line with the apostle's words that believers
'have crucified the flesh with the affections and lusts'.[13] These
include Mr False-peace, Mr Atheism and Mr Lustings. The former
Lord Mayor under Diabolus, Mr Incredulity, manages to escape

shortly before his execution and returns to Diabolus on Hell-gate-hill.

With Emmanuel making his home in the town, and setting up God's Peace as the new governor, all seems well with the town of Mansoul. Forgiven for his cowardice, Mr Conscience is once again installed as the 'subordinate preacher', and the Lord Chief Secretary — the Holy Spirit — resides in Heart Castle. Each day Emmanuel visits the homes of his people, expresses his love and assures them of his purposes of mercy towards them. 'Was there ever a town so favoured, so blessed?' Bunyan enquires.

A town redeemed from the hand and from the power of Diabolus — a town that the King Shaddai loved, and that he sent Emmanuel to regain from the prince of the infernal den — yea a town that Emmanuel loved to dwell in?[14]

But, sadly, there were Diabolonians still left in the town, skulking in corners or hidden in the homes of some who had intermarried with them and whose children were of mixed race.

Can such peace and tranquillity last while Diabolus still has a foothold in Mansoul? Never one to minimize the conflicts of the Christian life, Bunyan's further description of that lifelong battle that rages between nature and grace is gripping and relevant.

43

The wiles of the devil

When Rudyard Kipling's only son, John, was killed during World War I at the Battle of Loos in April 1915, the intense grief of his father was such that even the passing of time seemed unable to bring healing. When he read John Bunyan's *The Holy War*, Kipling interpreted the life-and-death struggle depicted in the allegory in terms of the Great War. He felt Bunyan's graphic descriptions carried a prophetic note in view of the appalling conflict in which his son had died — a conflict he could only describe as 'Armageddon':

> A tinker out of Bedford,
> a vagrant oft in quod [prison]
> a private under Fairfax,
> a minister of God —
> Two hundred years and thirty
> ere Armageddon came,
> his single hand portrayed it,
> and Bunyan was his name.

He mapped for those who follow
the world in which we are —
'This famous town of Mansoul'
that takes the Holy War.
Her true and traitor people,
the gates along her wall,
from Eye Gate unto Feel Gate,
John Bunyan showed them all.

The outbreak of the First World War had occurred approximately 'two hundred years and thirty' after the publication date of *The Holy War*. But Kipling knew well that Bunyan portrayed no earthly warfare, however terrible. He was describing a fight that was more relentless, more unending and, as Kipling ends his fascinating poem, his words indicate this:

The craft that we call modern
The crimes that we call new,
John Bunyan had 'em typed and filed
In Sixteen Eighty-two....

One watchword through our armies
One answer through our lands —
'No dealings with Diabolus
As long as Mansoul stands...'

Eight blinded generations
ere Armageddon came,
he showed us how to meet it,
and Bunyan was his name.[1]

'No dealings with Diabolus' might well sum up Bunyan's entire allegory of *The Holy War*, but the reader may be forgiven for wondering why he is only halfway through the book when Diabolus has been cast out of Mansoul and finally all is peace and joy in the streets and homes of the town. Yet, as Bunyan well knew from his own experience, the Christian is involved in a lifelong conflict with the powers of darkness, and the story of Mansoul is one of an unfinished battle.

Although many Diabolonians were still left behind in Mansoul, all was well while the town remained sensitive to the directions of the Lord High Secretary (the Holy Spirit) and valued the visits of Emmanuel. But when a certain Mr Carnal Security, a former activist for Diabolus who pretended to be serving Emmanuel, gained influence in the town, the picture changed. Bunyan lists the subtle evidences of backsliding in the Christian's heart:

> They [the townspeople] left off their former way of visiting Emmanuel; they came not to his royal palace as afore. They did not regard, nor yet take notice that he came, or came not to visit them. The love-feasts that had wont to be between their Prince and them, though he made them still ... yet they neglected to come at them or be delighted in them. They waited not for his counsels, but began to be headstrong and confident in themselves.[2]

Predictably, the Lord High Secretary was grieved at such conduct and left the town, while Emmanuel returned to his Father's court to await a change in Mansoul's disposition. Mr God's Peace resigned his commission.

When Mr Carnal Security held a great feast for some of the people of Mansoul, he invited Mr Godly-fear to come. But the old gentleman was silent and depressed. Asked the reason for his unhappiness, he alerted the town to its predicament, pointing out that 'Emmanuel has been offended and now he is arisen and gone.' Hearing his grievous words, Mr Conscience, who was also at the feast, turned pale and looked as though he was going to pass out. The people, aroused from their state of spiritual stupor, realized too late the situation into which their negligence had brought them. Taking Mr Carnal Security, they bustled him back to his own house and set it on fire with him inside.

But the way back for Mansoul is hard. Diabolonians who had been in hiding come out into the open. Bunyan tells us some of their names: Lord Fornication, Lord Adultery, Lord Murder, Lord Anger, Lord Evil-eye, Lord Blasphemy, and many others. While such enemies are running riot in the town, Mr Profane takes a message to Diabolus that it is an excellent opportunity for him to attack and retake the town. Diabolus has three suggestions as to the best method to gain access: either make Mansoul careless and conceited, or drive the people to despair, or blow up the town with the gunpowder of pride. Deciding that despair is the best tactic, Diabolus sends three henchmen in disguise whose activities in Mansoul will keep their Prince from heeding the repeated cries of the people for him to return and help them. Lord Covetousness changes his name to Prudent-thrifty, Lord Lasciviousness calls himself Harmless-mirth, and Lord Anger says his name is Good-zeal. These three, mingling with the inhabitants of Mansoul, deceive the people, and before long it is hard to distinguish between the townsfolk and the Diabolonians. Some in the town still cry repeatedly to Emmanuel to come to their aid:

> ... but he answered all with silence [for] they did neglect reformation, and that was as Diabolus would have it... Yea, there seemed now to be a mixture in Mansoul, the Diabolonians and the Mansoulians would walk the streets together.[3]

The next tactic employed by Diabolus is to send an army of Doubters against Mansoul. Here we are reminded most forcibly of Bunyan himself as he struggled against the onslaughts of Satan described in *Grace Abounding*. Aided by Emmanuel's captains who are still in the town, Mansoul manages to keep the Doubters — including Election-doubter, Salvation–doubter, Grace-doubter and others — at bay, but the noise of their drums terrifies the people. However, Bunyan is not merely retelling his own story in another form. Thirty years of spiritual experience have passed since those early days of his long-running battles with Satan's wiles. As a wise and experienced pastor, he incorporates into his allegory much that he has observed and learnt, since those days, of God's ways and the devil's strategies to undermine and destroy the church.

Camping outside the town, Diabolus keeps up the fearsome noise of drums to undermine the resistance of the people. Then Mansoul makes a fatal mistake. It chooses to send out its captains on a night foray led by Captain Credence (a symbol of faith) and others. But darkness proves a poor time to attack, and Credence is wounded, with Mansoul suffering a number of casualties. Diabolus determines to attack again at night, and chooses Feel gate as the weakest point. As his troops storm through, yelling, 'Hell-fire! Hell-fire!', they accost, injure, and even murder, many of the citizens. Taking up residence in every cottage, they turn the rightful owners out onto the street. Doubters are stationed all around Heart Castle, but they cannot enter, for Mansoul's captains have barricaded themselves within. By this Bunyan is demonstrating that, although a believer may seriously backslide, never again can Satan take entire possession of him.

Ah, poor Mansoul [comments Bunyan], now thou feelest the fruits of sin, and what venom was in the flattering words of Mr Carnal Security![4]

Bunyan then makes a curious reference to his own experience, for he tells his readers that this state of siege in Mansoul lasted for two and a half years.[5] Throughout this time, 'the people of the town were driven into holes and the glory of Mansoul was laid in the dust'. In *Grace Abounding*, not long before his own final deliverance from his doubts and fears, he records, 'I could not be delivered nor brought to peace again, until well-nigh two years and an half were completely finished.'[6]

But, as in Bunyan's case, this period was also a turning point for Mansoul. With renewed desperation the people cry out to Emmanuel to help them. At last Mr Godly-fear tells the chiefs of Mansoul that their prayers have been rejected by Emmanuel because they were not written in conjunction with the Lord High Secretary and endorsed by him. Once again, Bunyan is pointing out that all acceptable prayer must be offered through the agency of the Holy Spirit, a point he had made in his earliest book on prayer, written from prison in 1663. Mansoul now seeks the help of the Lord High Secretary, and Emmanuel hears the cries of his people, coming into the field to help the beleaguered town. The Diabolonians are routed, caught between the armies of Emmanuel in the field and those of Mansoul itself under the leadership of Captain Credence, supported by a wounded Captain Experience leaning on his crutches.

Welcomed home by the trumpeters of Mansoul, playing 'the best music that heart could invent', Prince Emmanuel returns to his town. Many Diabolonians flee and others are caught, judged and slaughtered by the now courageous citizens of Mansoul.

But the battles of Mansoul are far from over. An enraged Diabolus raises a fresh army consisting of 10,000 more Doubters, who hail from the Land of Doubting that lies between the Land of Darkness and the Valley of the Shadow of Death. Bunyan intends his readers to search out the hidden meaning behind each point in his allegory, and is showing that doubts can often continue to threaten the believer, particularly in times of depression and of illness or death.

Yet more significantly, this army of Doubters is augmented by 15,000 Bloodmen from the Province of Loath-good. Here Bunyan is taking advantage of his allegorical style to make a political and topical illusion. The Bloodmen undoubtedly stand for those responsible for the cruel and merciless persecution of the Dissenters, which was growing ever more intense at the time Bunyan was writing. These Bloodmen, as Bunyan explains, serve under the banners of such captains as Captain Cain (a murderer), Captain Ishmael (one who mocked and scorned Isaac in the biblical narrative), Captain Saul (who tried to murder an innocent David), Captain Judas (who, like the dastardly informers, was willing to betray a man for money) and Captain Pope (standing for the threat of persecution and even annihilation under a Catholic James Stuart). The standard-bearer for this last-named captain carried a banner depicting the image of someone perishing in the flames at one of Mary Tudor's stakes.

Of considerable interest in terms of Bunyan's own views on the sufferings of Christian people is the fact that in the allegory Emmanuel instructs his men to destroy the captured Doubters, but the Bloodmen must not be killed. They are to be rounded up and brought before Emmanuel. 'All Bloodmen are chicken-hearted men,' comments Bunyan, 'when they once come to see themselves matched and equalled.' These Bloodmen came from the towns of Blindmanshire, Blindzealshire and Malice, and, though they are unrepentant, Emmanuel binds them over to appear before King Shaddai on that last great day of judgement, to receive their due. In this way Bunyan is emphasizing that it is wrong for a Christian to take up arms against his persecutors, as some of the Covenanters in Scotland had done, and as many

Dissenters were tempted to do at that time. Later he would develop this theme in his work *Advice to Sufferers*, urging his readers to suffer patiently in days of persecution, knowing that their God would eventually vindicate them.

Many have read 'sub-texts' into John Bunyan's *The Holy War*, and in the case of the treatment of Bloodmen this is undoubtedly correct. Some, however, have tried to maintain that this allegory is a protracted comment on Charles II and his Restoration government, told in this form to avoid censorship. This is far from the truth. Although Richard Greaves suggests that there are 'multiple levels of meaning', he is categorical that 'the most fundamental and consistent'[7] is the whole panorama of salvation from the fall of man, the salvation of the sinner, the unending battle against the 'wiles of the devil' and the final destiny of the believer where sin and temptation can never assail him again.

A many-sided and intricate allegory, *The Holy War* has never achieved the popular appeal of *The Pilgrim's Progress*. One writer describes it as 'the most complex and, arguably, the least engaging of Bunyan's fictions'.[8] Perhaps one cause of the problem is that Bunyan is trying to combine within his allegory both Satan's attack on the whole church and also his stratagems against the individual believer. Under the image of a town, made up of many different citizens, he is describing the composite body of Christ — the church. But he is also relating the experiences of one believer, with his personal failures, struggles and conquests. It is a dual war: against the church of Christ, but also against the Christian as he progresses from a state of rebellion against God, through a lifetime of spiritual experiences, until at last the battle is over and he is taken to glory. This adds to its complexity.

Another problem is that *The Holy War* lacks the spontaneity of *The Pilgrim's Progress*. Whereas Bunyan tells us of his first allegory that 'still as I pull'd it came, and so I penned it down', we sense that with this second one he sat down and structured his book in a far more orderly fashion, sometimes piling on double, or even treble, significance into the names of his people and places. The compass of the two books is the same, one developing the Christian life as a pilgrimage, the other as a battle. But a significant difference lies in the fact that in *The Pilgrim's Progress* we can identify with Christian, Faithful and Hopeful, whereas in the crowded canvas in which we meet Mr Hatebad, Mr Affection, Mr Godly-fear, Mr Diligence and Mr Trueheart, among a host of others, it is not easy to do so.

There is one exception: depicted in lines both simple and splendid, the character of Prince Emmanuel dominates the whole, both when he is present, visiting and cherishing his people, and when absent, grieving at their backsliding. Among some of the most striking and evocative words which Bunyan ever wrote are found in Emmanuel's last charge to Mansoul. Gathering the whole town into the marketplace, he addresses them in unforgettable language:

> You, my Mansoul, and the beloved of my heart, many and great are the privileges I have bestowed upon you. I have singled you out from others and have chosen you to myself, not for your worthiness, but for my own sake.

He speaks of their redemption, bought with 'a price of blood, mine own blood, which I have freely spilt upon the ground to make thee mine'. As he turns to their backsliding, he is tender and forgiving:

> Thou seest, moreover, my Mansoul, how I have passed by thy backsliding, and have healed thee. Indeed I was angry with thee, but I have turned my anger from thee, because I loved thee still.

It was he who took the necessary measures to restore them from their careless state:

> It was I who made thy sweet bitter, thy day night, thy smooth ways thorny ... it was I that put life into thee, O Mansoul, to seek me, that thou mightest find me, and in thy finding, find thine own health, happiness and salvation.

But the battle must go on — there can be no truce for Mansoul, for Diabolonians are still lurking within the town. Emmanuel urges the people:

> Show me then thy love, my Mansoul, and let not those that are within thy walls take thy affection off from him that hath redeemed thy soul...

And the future for Mansoul will be glorious:

> For yet a little while, O my Mansoul, even after a few more times are gone over thy head, I will ... take down this famous town of Mansoul, stick and stone to the ground. And will carry the stones thereof and the timber thereof, and the walls thereof, and the dust thereof, and the inhabitants thereof, into mine own country, even into the kingdom of my Father, and will there set it up with such strength and glory as it never did see in the kingdom where it is now.

Bunyan describes in words of outstanding beauty, too many to be quoted here, the glories that await the believer in that kingdom yet to come where Emmanuel will set up his town of Mansoul once more. Only one warning remains:

> Nothing can hurt thee but sin; nothing can grieve me but sin; nothing can make thee base before thy foes but sin; Take heed of sin, my Mansoul.

And then, in words of final exhortation which reveal all the poetry of Bunyan's prose:

> Remember, therefore, O my Mansoul, that thou art beloved of me; as I have therefore taught thee to watch, to fight, to pray and to make war against my foes, so now I command thee to believe that my love is constant to thee. O my Mansoul, how have I set my heart, my love upon thee, watch... Hold fast till I come.[9]

The Holy War may be more difficult to read than *The Pilgrim's Progress*, but it more than repays the effort. George Offor, who edited Bunyan's works, had read it through forty times in as many years, and described it as 'the most beautiful and extraordinary that mere human genius ever composed in any language'.[10]

44

Travels of a pilgrim church

John Bunyan was holding a book in his hands, turning it over and over and examining it with a degree of curiosity mingled with a measure of indignation. Written by a certain 'T S',[1] the book bore the bold title, *The Second Part of Pilgrim's Progress from this present world of Wickedness and Misery, to an Eternity of Holiness and Felicity, exactly described under the similitude of a dream.* Such appalling plagiarism was a deliberate attempt on the part of the writer to correct various emphases in Bunyan's work which he considered to be wrong. Too much humour marred the book in the opinion of 'T S', and so his account excluded any elements of the cheerful interchange that had made *The Pilgrim's Progress* so human and well loved. In addition, this upstart writer felt that at certain points John Bunyan was theologically incorrect. Why, he wondered, was there no account of mankind's fall into sin? Even Bunyan's description of conversion was inadequate according to this writer, and he could find no mention of baptism. Little wonder that Bunyan commented with a mixture of amazement and irritation:

'Tis true, some have of late, to counterfeit
my pilgrim, to their own title set,
Yea others, half my name and title too
have stitched to their books to make them do;
yet they, by their features, do declare
themselves not mine to be, whose e'er they are.

It seemed to Bunyan that only one alternative remained. He must write his own sequel to *The Pilgrim's Progress*, and in 1684 that is exactly what he did. He had attempted this before in *The Life and Death of Mr Badman*, published three years earlier, but the public had not been satisfied with the book.

Part II of *The Pilgrim's Progress* was never meant to stand alone, and Bunyan assumed that anyone reading it would already be familiar with Part I. As he 'sent out' his book into the world, he had a message for it:

Go now, my little book, to every place
where my first Pilgrim has but shown his face,
call at their door. If any say, 'Who's there?'
then answer thou, CHRISTIANA is here.
If they bid thee come in, then enter thou
with all thy boys.

Bunyan had received some early criticism of his first book from those who thought that it was unmanly of Christian to set off on pilgrimage, leaving his wife and children to fend for themselves in the City of Destruction. Such a criticism only underlines the amazing success of *The Pilgrim's Progress*, for in no sense was Bunyan advocating a *literal* journey, forsaking wife and family. So vivid had been the narrative that these readers had almost forgotten that this was only an allegory, a pictorial representation of the spiritual life. So into the second edition of *The Pilgrim's Progress*, printed within months of the first, Bunyan had inserted two passages to correct this misunderstanding. One demonstrated his wife's early opposition to his spiritual anxiety and the other explained to Charity in the Palace Beautiful how hard he had tried to persuade her to join him.

Like Part I of *The Pilgrim's Progress*, Bunyan begins this second part with a further dream, but this time he is in a wood rather than a den, a hint that he was now at liberty. Bunyan then gives his dream a strange twist. An old man named Mr Sagacity comes past and in his dream Bunyan joins him on his travels. Before long they speak of the family that Christian had left behind, and Mr Sagacity shares the news that the entire family has gone on pilgrimage. As she grieved over the death of her husband, Christiana had recalled with pangs of regret her neglect of all his urgent exhortations to leave the City of Destruction. 'Sons, we are all undone. I have sinned away your father, and he is gone,' she confesses to her four boys, adding, 'I have also hindered you of life.'

A vivid dream further alerts Christiana to her spiritual danger, and she and her boys decide to set out on pilgrimage. Unhelpful neighbours try to dissuade the family with dire predictions of the folly of such an enterprise, but one of them, a young woman called Mercy, decides to accompany them for a short distance. Old Mr Sagacity continues with the narrative until after the family has managed to cross the Slough of Despond safely, having avoided the struggle that Christian experienced because they saw the stepping stones[2] leading through the mire. At this point John Bunyan realized that the structure of his book, telling his story at second hand through Mr Sagacity, was not going to work, so with little ceremony he dismisses the old man, merely informing his readers, 'And now Mr Sagacity left me to dream out my dream by myself.'

Part II of *The Pilgrim's Progress* follows in almost all respects the same pattern as Part I. Christiana and Mercy, together with the four 'sweet babes', Christiana's sons, come first to the Wicket Gate, a scene that Bunyan describes with particular tenderness. Mercy, who now longs with all her heart to be a pilgrim herself, knocks with vehement desire at the gate, dropping down in a dead faint before the Keeper can open to her. Bunyan's treatment of this incident may have reminded his readers of his sermons on John 6:37 published in *Come and Welcome to Jesus Christ*. In them he constantly urges the despairing sinner who desires to come to Christ to take courage: 'Be sure, therefore, if the Father hath given thee an heart to come to Jesus Christ, the gate of

mercy yet stands open to thee,' he tells those that tremble for fear
of being rejected, and adds, 'Coming sinner, Christ inviteth thee
to dine with him ... his banner over thee shall be love.'[3]

The fact that Bunyan chooses to make two women his central
characters is of particular interest because only a few months
earlier he had published a pamphlet entitled *A Case of Conscience
Resolved*. In it he had dealt with a question that had been put to
him by two of his friends. Addressing their query to 'Brother
Bunyan', they wished to know whether certain 'godly women
whose custom for a long time hath been to meet together to
pray' were right to do so in the light of Scripture. These women
had been encouraged in their endeavour by a certain 'Mr K', who
had cited a number of passages from the Bible supporting the
practice of women praying on their own together, notably Acts
16:13, where the women of Philippi were meeting by a river
when Paul spoke to them.

Surprisingly, in terms of our modern thinking, Bunyan was
much against the practice, and in a somewhat ill-tempered
pamphlet expressed his opinion of 'Mr K', who had encouraged
these women. He reasoned that the fact that God had heard the
prayers of women praying like that in the past did not make it
right. Using Eve's transgression in the Garden of Eden as a strong
reason why women should be silent in the church, he extends the
principle to any gathering together, even when only women are
present. To understand Bunyan, we must appreciate that he was a
seventeenth-century man and had lived through days of acute
religious disorder. He was certainly not as extreme as Richard
Baxter in this matter,[4] but his anxiety to maintain scriptural
principles of worship and fear of any disorder in the church led
him to frown on such practices. His attitude seems all the more
strange to us when we remember how he himself had been
powerfully affected before his conversion when he had overheard
the women of Bedford talking together of the things of God.

In case his views on this matter should lead his readers to think
that he had a low view of womanhood, Bunyan would wish his
Part II of *The Pilgrim's Progress* to act as a corrective. The characters
of Christiana and Mercy are both drawn with a delicate pen and
present a beautiful picture of feminine graces and qualities. Quite
different from each other, Christiana is determined, sensible,

motherly and wise, whereas Mercy is a lovely-looking girl, tender, hesitant, and yet courageous. Some have even wondered whether the character of Elizabeth, Bunyan's second wife, was the role model for Christiana. Perhaps he was also recalling the characteristics of his first wife, Mary, young, diffident, yet patient, in his description of Mercy.

Although many compare Part II of *The Pilgrim's Progress* adversely with Part I, and agree with George Cheever that 'the First Part is so superior to the second that it loses in comparison',[5] this is an imperfect assessment. Bunyan was setting out with a far different perspective as he wrote Part II, and did not mean it to stand alone. It was intended to complement Part I, adding a dimension that the former lacked. Brave, rugged and lonely, Christian had fought his way through to the Celestial City from first to last, even struggling in the waters of the last river. That book was the product of a man who was enduring severe deprivation resulting from long years of imprisonment, cut off from wife and family, a man who had been helpless to prevent the sufferings of his blind child. But Part II was different. Calmer, happier and more mature, Bunyan was now writing as a family man and the pastor of a church. The story was not of one solitary pilgrim accompanied first by Faithful and then by Hopeful, but of a company of women and children, later joined by others, all journeying together to the Celestial City, guarded and guided by a pastor figure, Mr Great-heart. It is the story of the gathered church of Jesus Christ travelling through this world in company — a mixed band, but all with a common goal.

The two women, together with Christiana's four boys, follow the same journey as Christian travelled, and wherever they go they are warmly welcomed for Christian's sake. At the House of the Interpreter the lessons and word-pictures given by the Interpreter are quite different from those that Christian learnt. Perhaps the most memorable, and what has come to be one of the best-known of Bunyan's symbols, is 'the man with the muck-rake' — a man who 'could look no way but downwards, with a muck-rake in his hand'. Yet all the time there was another standing by, offering to exchange his muck-rake for a celestial crown. 'But the man did neither look up nor regard, but raked to himself the straws, the small sticks and the dust of the floor.' Interpreter then points out that many, oblivious of heaven and glory, spend all their time preoccupied with the 'straws, sticks and dust'[6] of this life.

Here, at the House of the Interpreter, the pilgrims are given robes of white to wear, marking them out as belonging to the King of the Celestial City. And here too a guide is appointed who will protect them on their journey. Armed with sword, helmet and shield, Mr Great-heart will lead them on, fight their battles, care for the children and instruct the pilgrims. Throughout Part II Mr Great-heart figures as the courageous leader who has gone that way before and knows all the pitfalls. It could well be interpreted as a picture of Bunyan himself, carefully guarding and directing those committed to his care.

A strange inattention to the passage of time characterizes Part II of *The Pilgrim's Progress*. When Christiana's boys set out on pilgrimage they are described as 'sweet babes'. We discover Mercy coaxing Matthew, the eldest boy, to take his medicine, prescribed because he had eaten some poisoned fruit. Yet not many pages later, we find her marrying him. By the end of the book it appears that most of the boys have been married.[7]

The dominant note throughout is one of cheerfulness and confidence. Many songs punctuate the text. As the pilgrims rest at Palace Beautiful, Christiana thinks she can hear heavenly music. 'Wonderful!' declares Mercy, 'Music in the house, music in the heart and music also in heaven for joy that we are here.'[8] Even the Valley of Humiliation, where Christian had fought Apollyon, is carpeted with lilies, and here Mercy, in particular, finds herself happier and healthier than she has ever been before. Here too they meet a shepherd boy, poorly clad, but singing to himself:

He that is down needs fear no fall,
he that is low, no pride;
he that is humble ever shall
have God to be his guide.

Bunyan's emphasis on joy and well-being may be deliberate in view of the sufferings which the Dissenters were experiencing at that very time. The Tory reaction to the discovery of the Rye House Plot in 1683 had been relentless and cruel. Perhaps this note of cheerfulness was introduced to raise many downcast spirits. Even the Valley of the Shadow of Death, though danger-ous, is less fearsome now than it was for Christian. The pilgrims go through it in daylight without those frightening incidents that he experienced. Bunyan may wish to emphasize that pilgrims all face different trials; most are not called upon to pass through the hardships that he had endured.

As the party journeys onwards, Mr Great-heart fights their battles, and even destroys the giants that seek to capture them unawares. Giant Grim, who tries to stop pilgrims reaching Palace Beautiful, is the first to be destroyed; the next is Giant Maul, who sits outside the cave where Christian had met Giant Pope. These giants probably symbolize the persecuting state church, which determined by legal measures to prevent men, women and children from entering the Dissenting churches. The state, like the giants, harassed with the utmost severity any who entered. Even Mr Great-heart scarcely escapes with his life as he fights Maul, but finally he deals him a fatal blow and puts his head on a pillar as a message to future pilgrims. In the same way the heads of some Dissenters, allegedly involved in the Rye House Plot, had been displayed as a warning to other would-be plotters.

Because this pilgrimage is more leisurely than in Part I, Bunyan is able to pack into his book much instruction by means of conversations along the way or at the inns and homes where they are entertained. At the home of Gaius, where the travellers rest for some time, Bunyan draws a highly attractive picture of communal church life among the Independent churches. And if any should still think he has a low view of womanhood, the words he gives to Gaius dispel such a thought:

> When the Saviour was come ... I read not that any man did give unto Christ so much as one groat; but the women fol-lowed him and did minister unto him of their substance. It was a woman that washed his feet with tears and a woman that anointed his body to the burial... They were women that wept when he was going to the cross... Women, therefore, are highly favoured, and show by these things that they are sharers with us of the grace of life.[9]

Unlike *The Holy War*, where a multiplicity of characters crowd the scene, in Part II of *The Pilgrim's Progress* Bunyan draws far fewer, but these are depicted with consummate skill.

Old Father Honest is one. Shortly after the defeat of Giant Maul, the travellers find him asleep under an oak tree. In a few deft lines Bunyan sketches his character and we feel that we know this kindly, honourable and wise old gentleman. Because the church is made up of all ages, Bunyan includes this elderly fellow traveller among Mr Great-heart's pilgrims. On occasions during prolonged conversations as they rest at wayside inns, he nods off to sleep and has to be jogged awake. Despite his age, Mr Honest helps Mr Great-heart fight and destroy Giant Despair — an episode that must have given Bunyan much satisfaction to write, considering his own long battles with despair. The last river, a picture of death in Bunyan's allegory, was in full spate, overflowing all its banks when the time came for old Father Honest to cross, but his long-standing friend Good-conscience 'lent him a hand and so helped him over'.

The account of Mr Fearing, one who had 'the root of the matter in him', is also ably and warmly drawn. Mr Honest had known this pilgrim well, and tells his story. Bunyan's understanding of the timidity and trials of such people is apparent and compassionate; we may well suppose that he was describing members of his own congregation. This man 'was always kept very low', his constant fears making him 'so burdensome to himself, and so troublesome to others'. He was sensitive to sin and so afraid of hurting others that he preferred to deny himself things that might be quite lawful. All through his journey he battled against fears, and when he came to the last river, a river without a bridge, he was yet more afraid. He thought 'he should be drowned for ever and so never see that face with comfort that he had come so many miles to behold'. But when Mr Fearing arrived at the bank, the narrator observes:

> ... the water of that river was lower at this time than ever I saw it in all my life. So he went over at last, not much above wet-shod.[10]

Mr Feeble-mind, Mr Ready-to-Halt, Mr Despondency and his daughter Much-afraid all join the pilgrims as they travel along under the guidance of Mr Great-heart. Rescued just in time from the grip of Giant Slay-good, Mr Feeble-mind was 'a man of no strength at all of body, nor yet of mind', yet of resolute spirit. Determined to continue his pilgrimage, he undertook 'to run when I can, to go when I cannot run, and to creep when I cannot go'. Some of Bunyan's early austerity, even impatience at the failures of others, has clearly melted away as he has learnt from his pastoral experience that many in a church may suffer from marked weaknesses, needing constant care and understanding — yet they are true pilgrims none the less. Each of Mr Great-heart's company crosses that last river satisfactorily. Mr Despondency was heard declaring, 'Farewell night! Welcome day!' as he crossed over, while his daughter sang as she went, though none could catch the words of her song. Mr Ready-to-Halt no longer needed his crutches, for he saw horses and chariots awaiting him on the other side, and, as Mr Feeble-mind ventured through, he called out, 'Hold out, faith and patience.'

Perhaps the noblest and most memorable of all the pilgrims who join the company as they journey along are Mr Valiant-for-Truth and Mr Standfast. When Great-heart and the pilgrims met the former, he had just fought for three hours against some vagabonds who had accosted him. Wounded and weary, his face covered with blood, he had not yielded to their uncouth demands and had at last put them to flight. 'When the blood ran through my fingers, then I fought with most courage,' he declares. Great-heart examines Mr Valiant's sword and discovers it to be 'a right Jerusalem blade'. Mr Valiant adds that 'Its edges will never blunt. It will cut flesh and bones, and sword and spirit and all' — an apt description, as Bunyan doubtless intended, of the 'sword of the Spirit'.[11]

Bunyan's poems in Part II reach a higher standard than anywhere else, with 'The Song of the Shepherd Boy' and Mr Valiant-for-Truth's grand hymn gaining a place in most national collections of English verse. Describing his fierce conflict with his three opponents, Mr Valiant-for-Truth breaks into song, challenging others to a life of Christian courage:

Who would true valour see,
let him come hither;
one here will constant be,
come wind, come weather.

Words from this popular hymn have entered English phraseology,
with a number of its expressions still in current use: 'Come wind,
come weather,' is perhaps the best example. A tradition exists that
Bunyan himself wrote the original tune, a supposition which is
certainly feasible, considering his musical ability.[12]

When the company of pilgrims led by Mr Great-heart have
almost crossed over the Enchanted Ground they discover a man
kneeling in prayer, his arms lifted to heaven in earnest supplication. Rising from his knees, this man begins to run as if fleeing
some dreadful threat. Catching up with him, Mr Great-heart
discovers that his name is Mr Standfast, and learns that he is
fleeing the attractions of a seductive woman who offered him 'her
body, her purse and her bed'. Despite his repeated rejections,
Madam Bubble (whom Bunyan tells us in his marginal notes is a
picture of 'this vain world'), persists in her offers and the only
way of deliverance lies in earnest prayer and in running from her.
As Mr Standfast joins the pilgrim company, they discuss the
alluring pull of the world and its deceptive nature. Mr Great-heart
points out that many would-be pilgrims have been entangled in
Madam Bubble's snares — men such as Judas, who betrayed his
Lord, and Absalom, who attempted to use his charms to dethrone
his father, David.

Most significant of all is Bunyan's account of Mr Standfast's last
days. Even those who have downgraded Part II of *The Pilgrim's
Progress* grant that this prayerful pilgrim's final words as he crosses
the cold river of death are among the most magnificent and
moving that Bunyan ever wrote. Many believers since Bunyan's
day have found consolation and courage through them in the face
of death:

Now there was a great calm at that time in the river; wherefore Mr Standfast, when he was about halfway in, stood a
while and talked to his companions that had waited upon him
thither; and he said, This river has been a terror to many; yea

the thoughts of it have often frightened me. But now, methinks, I stand easy... The waters indeed are to the palate
bitter, and to the stomach cold, yet the thoughts of what I am
going to and the conduct that waits for me on the other side,
doth lie as a glowing coal at my heart. I see myself now at the
end of my journey, my toilsome days are ended. I am going now
to see that head that was crowned with thorns, and that face
that was spit upon for me.

I have formerly lived by hearsay and faith; but now I go where
I shall live by sight, and shall be with him in whose company I
delight myself. I have loved to hear my Lord spoken of; and
wherever I have seen the print of his shoe in the earth, there I
have coveted to set my foot too... His voice to me has been
most sweet; and his countenance I have more desired than they
that have most desired the light of the sun. His word I did
gather for my food, and for antidotes against my faintings...

Now while he was thus in discourse, his countenance
changed, his strong man bowed under him; and after he had
said, 'Take me, for I come unto thee,' he ceased to be seen of
them.[13]

It is impossible to read such words without thinking of John
Bunyan himself, one to whom the name Standfast most aptly
applies.

45

Troubled times

Charles II was dying. Although only fifty-four years of age, his lifestyle of immorality and abandon may well have undermined his health. Marked by a sudden collapse, his last illness — now thought to have been kidney failure — began on 1 February 1685. The royal physicians hurried to the king's bedchamber and began to administer a flurry of unwelcome though well-intended medical treatments. They blistered and bled their dying king, applying red-hot irons to his shaved head and bare feet. Added to this they tried all manner of purges and emetics to restore him. We cannot be surprised that Charles apologized to the nobles and physicians standing around his far-from-private deathbed because it was taking him so long to die.

More significant than the attempts to revive the king was the arrival of a strange-looking figure into his bedchamber. Disguised in wig and cassock, it was none other than Father Huddleston, a Roman Catholic priest well known to Charles. He had come with a vial of oil to anoint the king, and welcome him into the Catholic Church. When all the confessions, prayers and administration of the last rites were finally complete, Father Huddleston pressed a crucifix into the dying monarch's hand to aid his last thoughts, then disappeared as suddenly as he had come through a secret door. Charles II died the following day, 6 February, a fully-accepted member of the Roman Catholic Church.

The transition of the crown from Charles to his brother James went smoothly, but James was a man with a desire for retribution in his heart. And the chief subjects for his vengeance were the defenceless Nonconformists and Dissenters, for some had supported the Whigs in their attempt to exclude him from the throne. Persecution, more intense than anything previously experienced, broke out against them. Writing of this period, G. R. Cragg says:

> Fines of staggering magnitude were levied on the more prosperous nonconformists. Their homes were pillaged, their goods seized. Even the humblest members found no immunity. Those who owned little lost it all. Tradesmen were ruined. In some districts the dislocation of business was serious, and the cry was raised that the economic prosperity of the country was threatened. In the streets the nonconformists were exposed to such violent abuse that their leaders hesitated to venture abroad.[1]

At the beginning of the new reign one man in particular faced delayed justice for his actions. Titus Oates, responsible for the allegations of the Popish Plot which had sent a number of innocent men to the executioner's block, had been in prison since 1681. Apparently his deceptions did not carry the death penalty, but James still planned that he should die.

First put in the stocks, Oates was then taken out and whipped all the way through the London streets from one side of the city to the other, not once but twice over. Some three thousand lashes struck his back and legs as he ran. Somehow he managed to survive the ordeal and spent the next few years in prison once more.

Scarcely three weeks after James had replaced his brother as king, a blow was struck at a prominent Puritan leader, none other than Richard Baxter himself. Elderly, frail, and bereaved of his well-loved wife Margaret, Baxter was thrown into prison to await

Titus Oates in the pillory

trial — a dark and contemptible blot on the new reign, and an even darker reproach on the coarse character of Judge George Jeffreys, whom James had made his new Lord Chancellor. The flimsy pretext for Baxter's arrest was that his newly published book, *The Paraphrase of the New Testament*, was said to contain veiled references to the corrupt lifestyle of various bishops and statesmen.

On 18 May 1685, while Titus Oates was standing in the stocks at the mercy of the jibes and missiles of passers-by, Baxter's trial opened and the emaciated old man, a pitiful sight, stood at the mercy of Jeffreys' verbal jibes and missiles. 'If Baxter did but stand on the other side of the pillory with him [Oates], I would say that two of the greatest rogues and rascals in the kingdom stood there,' roared the merciless judge. The full trial — a travesty of justice — took place at the London Guildhall on 30 May with a striking contrast between the calm dignity of Baxter and the flaming fury of Judge Jeffreys. Attempting to mock the worship of Nonconformists, Jeffreys clasped his hands together in fake prayer and sang out his petitions in nasal tones. 'This old rogue has poisoned the world with his Kidderminster doctrine,' snarled the judge, now scarlet with rage. Baxter's defence was silenced, and only the intervention of Jeffreys' more merciful colleagues prevented him from sentencing the old Puritan to be flogged through the streets of London as Oates had been. Describing Baxter's bearing under such circumstances, Archbishop Tillotson[2] was to say of him, 'Nothing more honourable than when Baxter stood at bay, berogued, abused, despised: never more great than then.'

If so prominent a Puritan could be treated in such a way, John Bunyan must have wondered whether he would be King James' next victim. Had he not recently written scorching words against 'professors' of religion whose lives fell far short of their claims?

> There are a great many professors now in England that have nothing to distinguish them from the worst of men... What greater contempt can be cast upon Christ than by such wordy professors?[3]

To add to this, he had made some stinging indictments on the pretended righteousness of many religious men of his day in his sermons on the parable of *The Pharisee and the Publican*, a work published shortly after James had come to the throne. Perhaps it was the popularity of *The Pilgrim's Progress*, now in its tenth edition, which acted as a saving factor for Bunyan, causing the hierarchy to hesitate before arresting him once more.

Alternatively, he may have been spared by an event that took place only a few weeks after the conclusion of Baxter's trial — the Monmouth Rebellion. As we have seen, James, Duke of Monmouth, illegitimate son of Charles II, had always believed that the throne of England was rightfully his. As a Protestant, he had the backing of the Whigs and the almost mindless loyalty of many Dissenters, who saw in his accession to the throne an end to their trials. Foiled in his previous efforts to secure the crown by means of the Rye House Plot, Monmouth had conspired together with Archibald Campbell, 9th Duke of Argyll, and some of the Scottish Covenanters, to remove James from the throne, so taking it for himself. He landed at Lyme Regis in Dorset on 11 June 1685, hoping for a large following of West Countrymen who would join forces with Argyll's men, and together they would march on London. But with an ill-equipped army, and disappointed by the lack of such support, his attempted coup suffered a serious setback when Argyll was captured not far from Glasgow and subsequently executed.

Only a few months earlier John Bunyan had published a series of sermons which he called *Seasonable Counsel or Advice to Sufferers*. It had been written soon after the discovery of the Rye House Plot, with its attempted murder of the royal brothers. The sufferings of men like John Owen and other Dissenters, most of them wrongly accused of complicity in the plot, had convinced Bunyan even more strongly of the Christian duty of submission to the state and the sin of attempting to undermine or fight against those appointed to rule. If the Dissenters who flocked in considerable numbers to join Monmouth had read and heeded Bunyan's strongly urged words in *Advice to Sufferers*, they might well have avoided a fearful and untimely death.

Addressing himself specifically to the 'many at this day exposed to sufferings', Bunyan took words from 1 Peter, an epistle directed to Christians about to undergo torture and violent death at the hands of the Roman emperor Nero: 'Wherefore let them that suffer according to the will of God, commit the keeping of their souls to him in well doing, as unto a faithful Creator' (1 Peter 4:19). Few had a greater right to speak on such a subject than John Bunyan. Almost thirteen years of humiliating imprisonment in Bedford jails lay behind him. From his own experience he could say:

> He [God] can make those things that in themselves are most fearful and terrible to behold, the most pleasant, delightful and desirable things. He can make a gaol more beautiful than a palace; restraint more sweet by far than liberty; and the reproach of Christ greater riches than the treasures of Egypt.[4]

The thrust of Bunyan's *Advice to Sufferers* is that the only way to suffer rightly is to commit your cause and your soul to God the Creator — for he who brought a world into being out of nothing can surely protect, sustain and recreate, bringing good out of an evil situation. Bunyan remembered the lesson he had learnt as he faced his first imprisonment, one that had carried him through fear, bereavement and despair:

> I was made to see that if ever I would suffer rightly, I must first pass a sentence of death upon everything that can properly be called a thing of this life, even to reckon myself, my wife, my children, my health, my enjoyments and all as dead to me, and myself as dead to them.[5]

Now he reiterates that vital principle:

> A cat at play with the mouse is sometimes a fit symbol of the way of the wicked with the children of God. Wherefore, as I said, be always dying; die daily; he that is not only ready to be bound, but to die is fit to encounter any amazement.[6]

But, a reader might ask, should a Christian attempt to escape in the face of impending suffering? In certain cases Bunyan suggests that he may do so, though he himself had not. Certainly it was wrong actively to seek persecution, as some had done in the past. Nor must the Christian place limits on how much he is prepared to endure for Christ's sake:

> Say not to thy afflicters, Hitherto and no further... I say take heed of doing thus, for fear God should let them go beyond thee ... and find thee unprovided. Christ sets their bounds at the loss of life, and no nearer.[7]

Again this was a lesson hammered out of bitter experience in Bunyan's early prison days.

Although *Advice to Sufferers* was written primarily with the situation facing the Dissenters in the early 1680s in mind, since its publication it has proved to be a book for all Christians as they face grief, persecution or other trials. As Bunyan points out time and again, suffering is the lot of the Christian while here on earth, but it is not a token of God's anger:

> ... it is rather, a token of his love ... it is indeed a dignity put upon us... Count it therefore a favour that God has bestowed upon thee his truth and graces to enable thee to profess it, though thou be made to suffer for it.[8]

Writing before the fearful fiasco at the Battle of Sedgemoor, when the Duke of Monmouth and his untrained army were routed by the king's far superior troops, Bunyan could not have known what cruel reprisals would be exacted against all who took part in that rebellion. Many Dissenters had joined Monmouth's West Country recruits, believing such action to be right.

At least eight hundred of Monmouth's supporters were exiled to far-off Barbados — a severe punishment, for they would never again see their homes or families. But an even worse fate awaited three hundred or more other men and women; some were executed for merely giving food and shelter to desperate fugitives of the battle. The name of Judge George Jeffreys and the Bloody Assize have gone down in English history as synonymous with injustice, even judicial murder.

Corpses and mutilated body parts could be seen at every street corner in the West Country where military executions had taken place, but it was those condemned to death on trumped-up charges and at prejudiced trials that made the Bloody Assize notorious. Judge Jeffreys jeered, swore and laughed at the calamity of these men and women, as he pronounced a guilty verdict upon them. In contrast, many of his victims died with a courageous testimony of their love for Jesus Christ on their lips. Among the most notable were the two grandsons of William Kiffin, the Particular Baptist leader who had been Bunyan's protagonist in the controversy over baptism in the 1670s. Benjamin and William Hewling were fine and godly young men and were as close to Kiffin as if they were his own sons.

Nineteen-year-old William was being educated in Holland at the time and knew Monmouth personally. He accompanied him on his voyage to Lyme Regis. Meanwhile Benjamin enthusiastically joined the rabble army, believing that this invasion was God's reply to the sufferings of Dissenters. Despite the efforts of William Kiffin to save his grandsons, both were condemned to be hung, William in Lyme Regis and Benjamin in Taunton. And both died with Christian fortitude. On the evening before he endured the hangman's rope, William said:

> O how great were the sufferings of Christ for me; beyond all I can undergo! How great is the glory to which I am going. It will soon swallow up all our sufferings here.

Benjamin showed an equal composure even at the prospect of a violent death. 'We have no cause to fear death if the presence of God be with us,' he said. 'There is no evil in it, the sting being taken away.'[9] He was twenty-two when he died.

Persecution of the Dissenters, already intense, became even more severe following Monmouth's abortive uprising and his execution. The Tory Party, now back in the political ascendancy, laid the blame for the rebellion squarely onto the Dissenting churches. W. T. Whitely, a Baptist historian, has stated that many embryonic Baptist and Independent fellowships were completely wiped out at this time, and even a number of stronger societies almost eliminated, their places of worship reduced to rubble and their early records destroyed.[10]

As vengeance for Argyll's part in Monmouth's rebellion, Scottish Covenanters suffered even more. When the prisons of Edinburgh were crowded beyond capacity, more than 150 men and women were driven like cattle to Dunottar Cattle on the east coast, and there thrust into a foul underground vault, full of sludge, with only one small window. Here they remained, crammed together, during the summer months. Not surprisingly many died from jail fever, and others as a result of the torture administered to both men and women indiscriminately. These days were rightly called the Killing Times.

News from across the Channel was equally alarming. Louis XIV, with whom Charles II had schemed to impose Catholicism on England, determined to enforce it throughout his own country. In October of that grievous year of 1685, he revoked the Edict of Nantes, which had been in force for almost ninety years, and had given legal protection to French Protestants, known as Huguenots. Huguenot churches were to be destroyed and their schools closed down, and they were all ordered to convert to Catholicism or be subjected to dire persecution. Although forbidden to emigrate, with roads and ports carefully watched for any who might be attempting to escape, an estimated 400,000 Huguenots fled the country. Many sought refuge in England;[11] others in Holland, Denmark and some as far afield as America and South Africa. The result was a grievous loss to France of thousands of her most skilled and industrious people. According to Louis' own boast, fewer than 1,500 Huguenots remained in France — a loss of expertise, and more importantly of true Christian faith, that has affected France ever since.

Understandably, Bunyan's church at Bedford had gone into hiding once more. Only a few stray, undated notes exist recording the church's activities at this time. Bunyan was still preaching whenever he was able. Charles Doe had heard him preach on 'The Desire of the Righteous Granted' at a secret location in the Southwark area of London during 1685 — a sermon he could never forget. This is clear evidence that John Bunyan was pre-pared to risk imprisonment, torture, or worse, to bring the consolations of God's Word to the people. One desire in the hearts of many of his hearers at this time was for that heavenly land where suffering and sorrow were gone for ever.

> This desire [of the righteous] is a desire that hath a long neck; for it can look over the brazen wall of this, quite into an-other world... This desire makes a man willing rather to be ab-sent from all enjoyments that he may be present with the Lord — this is a famous desire; none hath this desire but a righteous man.[12]

Much of Bunyan's time during 1685 and 1686 was spent on his writing, for in this way he could reach more people than by preaching. He began a commentary on the book of Genesis, but was only able to complete chapters 1-10 and part of chapter 11, the blank sheets at the end giving a clear sign that he had hoped to continue. Some evidence also exists that, for a while at least, Bunyan returned to his work as a brazier. With his youngest child, Joseph, still only thirteen, his family may well have needed such support.

Perhaps too, this was why he chose 1686 as the best time to publish *A Book for Boys and Girls or Country Rhimes for Chil-dren.* In all probability Bunyan had been writing these forty-nine 'Country Rhimes' over a number of years, particularly for Joseph, whose childhood he had been able to share, unlike that of his older children. Here we see John Bunyan relaxing from the stresses of his pastoral duties and the constant tension of possible renewed persecution as he stoops with intense delight to the level of his child, pointing out the wonders of nature. We are given a unique insight into Bunyan as a father and a man of warm and homely personality.

Like Aesop, the seventh-century storyteller, John Bunyan describes natural and everyday things which he notices all around him, and then points the child to the moral, or hidden meaning, which may be learnt from them. But in Bunyan's case these 'morals' are spiritual lessons and, not surprisingly, bear a striking resemblance to those which Christian and Christiana learnt at the House of the Interpreter as they set out on pilgrimage. So John can write in 'Meditations on an Egg':

An egg's no chick by falling from a hen,
nor man a Christian till he's born again.
The egg's at first contained in the shell;
Man, afore grace, in sins and darkness dwell.
The egg, when laid, by warmth is made a chicken,
And Christ, by grace, those dead in sin doth quicken.

Many of Bunyan's verses comprise two parts: first a description of some aspect of nature, followed by 'a comparison' — the lesson he wishes children to learn from what they see. Perhaps as he looked out of his study window he noticed an apple tree laden with blossom:

A comely sight indeed it is to see
A world of blossoms on an apple tree:
Yet far more comely would this tree appear
If all its dainty blooms young apples were.

Pressing home the moral, he continues:

This tree a perfect emblem is of those
which God doth plant, which in his garden grows...
Behold then how abortive some fruits are
Which at the first most promising appear.
The frost, the wind, the worm, with time doth show,
there flows, from much appearance, works but few.

Or he may describe the activities of a bee. So we read, 'The bee goes out, and honey home doth bring,' but, perhaps drawing on personal experience, he adds, '... and some who seek that honey find a sting.' This may be why he writes in his 'comparison':

This bee an emblem truly is of sin
whose sweet unto a many death hath been.

Many objects from nature are included in these verses, showing
that Bunyan was ever a keen observer of the world around him.
Seeing a lovely rose on a thorny bush, he notes that any who
approach too near will have their hands torn. So Christ resembles
the rose, but was born into Adam's sinful race — a race which,
like the angry thorns, tries to prevent those who approach from
benefiting from the beauties of the rose.

Bunyan draws parables from such unexpected situations as a
boy whose watch has broken, a woman who looks into a mirror
but does not notice her own defects, inflation (as the cost of a
penny loaf rises to twenty pence), a skilled musician playing to an
unmusical and unappreciative audience, and even the different
styles of riding a horse:

Now every horse has his especial guider
Then by his going you may know the rider...

So, by the way a person lives, an observer can tell who is his
'guider'. Some keep to 'a right way' and go in correct paths, while
others, hell-bent, ride recklessly, regardless of right or wrong.

Perhaps the most fascinating of Bunyan's 'rhimes', and the
longest, is called 'The Sinner and the Spider' and stretches to some
two hundred lines. Doubtless he had many opportunities to
observe the ways of spiders in his dingy and dirty prison; maybe
too they found their way into the Bunyans' cottage in St
Cuthbert's Street. This poem takes the form of a dialogue between
the sinner and the spider in much the same style as that of Bunyan's first prison work, *Profitable Meditations,* a long dialogue
between Christ and the sinner.[13] This present poem opens with the
sinner's antipathy to the spider. 'What black, what ugly crawling
thing art thou?' he asks, as he proudly declares his own superiority:

I am a man, and in God's image made,
I have a soul shall neither die nor fade,
God has possessed me with human reason,
speak not against me lest thou speakest treason.

The spider, however, has an unanswerable reply:

But though thy God hath made thee such a creature,
thou hast against him often played the traitor.
Thy sin has fetched thee down: leave off to boast;
nature thou hast defiled, God's image lost.

The sinner remains impenitent, and heaps additional abuse upon the spider:

Ill-shaped creature, there's antipathy
'Twixt man and spiders, 'tis in vain to lie;
I hate thee, stand off, if thou dost come nigh me,
I'll crush thee with my foot; I do defy thee.

The spider has a further answer:

They are ill-shaped who warpèd are by sin
Antipathy in thee hath long time been
To God...
Come, I will teach thee wisdom, do but hear me,
I was made for thy profit, do not fear me.

Gradually, as the argument progresses, the sinner has less and less to say for himself as the spider demonstrates that he fulfils God's creation purposes for spiders, whereas man has defiled and degraded God's design for *his* creation. The spider begins to instruct the sinner:

I spin, I weave, and all to let thee see
Thy best performances but cobwebs be.
Thy glory now is brought to such an ebb
it doth not much excel the spider's web.

His web, the spider claims, demonstrates the different ways in which a sinner, like the fly, may be trapped and destroyed. Not only is it hung in unexpected places, but:

I hide myself when I for flies do wait,
So doth the devil when he lays his bait.
If I do fear the losing of my prey
I stir me, and more snares upon her lay...

At last the sinner, listening to the spider, is humbled and subdued and admits:

Well, my good spider, I my errors see,
I was a fool for railing upon thee...
Thy way and works do also darkly tell
How some men go to heaven, and some to hell.
Thou art my monitor, I am a fool;
They learn may, that to spiders go to school.

A quaint and intriguing poem, 'The Sinner and the Spider' shows John Bunyan's poetic gift at its best. Whether written in prison or at home, it demonstrates his ingenious turn of mind, and writing such verse would have been a relaxation from the intensity of his circumstances. In early editions two of the poems[14] are accompanied by a tune possibly set for a flute or a violin. With his love of music, Bunyan may well have composed the tunes himself, to be accompanied by his flute made from the leg of the prison stool or his home-made violin.

As John Bunyan prepared his *Country Rhimes* for Nathaniel Ponder to publish, he knew well that at any moment a loud knock on his door could signal that the magistrates had come to arrest him and cast him into prison once more. If this should happen all his goods would be confiscated and Elizabeth left destitute — an all-too-likely possibility. John therefore decided to make a Deed of Gift to Elizabeth. Sometimes called his will, it was in fact a transfer of all his possessions to her. If he were then incarcerated once more, their goods could not be touched, for she would be the legal owner of the house, his money and all their household chattels. This left Elizabeth in a more secure position. With four church members as witnesses, Bunyan drew up the Deed of Gift, describing his occupation as that of 'a brazier'. Duly signed and dated on 23 December 1685, the document was

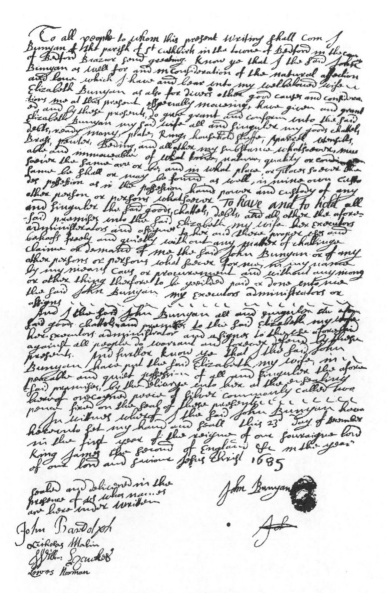

John Bunyan's 'Deed of Gift'
Reproduced by kind permission of Bunyan Meeting Free Church, Bedford, England

hidden at the back of the chimney — a commentary in itself on how apprehensive he was for his own and his family's future.[15]

Having done all he could, Bunyan was ready to 'commit the keeping of his soul to God 'in well doing, as unto a faithful Creator',[15] as he had urged in his *Advice to Sufferers:*

> Let us wait upon God, walk with God, believe in God, and commit our souls, our body to God to be kept. Yea, let us be content to be at the disposal of God, and rejoice to see him act according to all his wondrous works.[17]

46

A passionate preacher

Although John Bunyan is remembered today pre-eminently as a writer, it was also as a preacher that he made a profound impression on his own generation. As we have seen, apart from his allegorical work, his writings were usually little more than an expanded form of his sermons. And in the last years of his life he had many opportunities to preach to large congregations — something that was previously denied to him because of the onslaught of persecution against the Dissenters. Despite being a free man between 1672 and 1676 and again after 1677, Bunyan had still been forced to conduct much of his ministry in secret for fear of informers and the threat of further imprisonment. How then, we may wonder, could a situation so dire and hostile that Nonconformists hardly dared to walk the streets change in such a remarkable way as to make it possible for Bunyan to preach freely and publicly to packed congregations and in the open air? The answer must be twofold: the overruling power of God and the incredible follies of an earthly monarch, James II.

The Monmouth Rebellion may have been crushed with ease, but its repercussions were not so easily eliminated. The cruelty

Bunyan in later life (based on a portrait painted in 1685)

with which adherents and supporters had been removed or liquidated appalled and disgusted many Englishmen. The early popularity that James had enjoyed began to drain away. Added to this, James increased his regular standing army from a mere 6,000 to almost 30,000 men, many of them encamped permanently on Hounslow Heath as if protecting the capital. Memories of the horrors of the Civil War were rekindled in the minds of the people, together with the absolutist powers of a Stuart monarch, Charles I, father of James II. Soldiers were encouraged to attend mass at a specially erected chapel and priests enlisted to urge the troops to espouse Catholicism.

Englishmen also looked with fear across the Channel at what was happening to the Huguenots, listening with dismay to the stories from those who had escaped as they described the torture and death meted out to many peace-loving French citizens. Was James also about to stamp out English Protestantism in a similar way? Fears of the Popish Plot were still fresh and vividly remembered. Rumour had it that the influential Bishop of Valence was urging Louis XIV to unite with the King of England for the very purpose of imposing Catholicism on the English people. James had begun dismissing powerful Tory officials, replacing them with prominent Catholics. Clearly he had little understanding of his people and of the nation's long-standing fears dating back to the reign of the last Catholic monarch, Mary Tudor. As he played fast and loose with laws designed to prevent Catholics from occupying influential positions, James lost yet more support. The High Church Tory Party watched with dismay as their influence was steadily eroded.

Two years of serious misrule followed. The king dismissed his Parliament, allowing him a free hand with the laws of the land. Magistrates who supported his policies were appointed to administer justice, and the new king's influence on the universities was soon felt. The fellows at Magdalen College, one of the oldest and proudest of the Oxford colleges, were turned out and replaced by their Catholic counterparts. At last, early in 1687, little more than two years into his reign, James discovered to his dismay that he had few friends left.

Then an amazing thing happened. Instead of crushing Dissenters still further, the king suddenly turned to them for support. A Declaration of Indulgence, issued on 4 April 1687, based on his royal prerogative, granted freedom of worship to all Dissenters and Catholics alike. Few could fail to see the underlying strategy that James was pursuing in this policy, and many Dissenters were deeply uneasy at accepting toleration on such terms. In fact, rather than uniting these persecuted churches, the declaration had the opposite effect. Some Dissenters were implacably opposed to it, knowing full well that this was only a ruse both to gain their support and to facilitate the advance of Catholicism. Others preferred a cautious acceptance of the indulgence with the proviso that they would keep their position under review. Yet others endorsed the king's action wholeheartedly, taking advantage of their new liberty. Some eighty Dissenting churches sent messages of congratulation and thanks to the king.

The Bedford church experienced some division of opinion over the new situation, but, judging by the freedom Bunyan now enjoyed to preach in London, and elsewhere, it appears that he was prepared to make the most of any opportunity without constant fear and the constraint of reprisals. The anonymous writer of *A Continuation of Mr Bunyan's Life*, attached to *Grace Abounding*, suggests that Bunyan was fully aware of the king's schemes:

> His piercing wit [maintains this writer] penetrated the veil and found that it was not for the Dissenters' sake that they were so suddenly freed from prosecutions that had long laid heavy upon them.[1]

From this same writer we learn that Bunyan was also unhappy at the reorganization that was taking place in the town corporation of Bedford, and those of other towns. These changes were stipulated by the king in order to recruit representatives for a new parliament favourable to his policies. Bunyan himself was offered an official position, but he was unwilling even to attend an interview with the one who had been commissioned to bring the offer to him.

For John Bunyan was a man with a single purpose. Nothing could divert him from that one steady aim: to preach the gospel of Christ. Free from intimidation, the people now flocked to hear him. Charles Doe records that, with only a single day's notice that Bunyan was due to preach in London, crowds would pack a meeting house to capacity, with as many again turned away for lack of room. One such place where he preached was at his friend George Cokayne's church in the City of London, or sometimes it would be at the newly-built Zoar Street Chapel in Southwark, where Doe lived. By seven o'clock in the morning on a weekday in winter, regardless of the dark and cold, more than 1,200 would gather to hear the well-loved preacher. Doe recalled one occasion when some 3,000 men and women were clamouring to hear him. Bunyan had a struggle to reach his pulpit even by a back door and had to be 'pulled almost over people to get upstairs to his pulpit'. This was probably at a Dissenting meeting house in Stepney, the only one large enough to accommodate such numbers.

What was it about his preaching that attracted the people in such numbers? Bunyan himself probably provides us with the best answer: 'I preached what I felt, what I smartingly did feel, even that under which my poor soul did groan and tremble to astonishment.' Drawing on his deep study of the Scriptures, Bunyan covered a wide range of subjects in his sermons, but the sufferings and temptations that he had endured formed the raw material for many of his applications and illustrations. It has been rightly said that in assailing John Bunyan as he did, Satan overreached himself, providing the church of Jesus Christ with a guide heavenwards through many subsequent generations. Much of Bunyan's most effective preaching, therefore, had a strong biographical content; as he looked back on his personal experience he was like his own pilgrim, fleeing from the City of Destruction and urging others to flee also.

We discover a description of Bunyan's earnest pulpit manner from an unlikely source — the poet, Robert Browning, writing two centuries later. In a fascinating piece Browning depicts the trial of a fraudulent rogue named Ned Bratts, a publican, who, with his wife Tab, was appearing before the judges at Bedford Assizes. The poet packs into his lines many references to the persecuted Dissenters, and especially to a certain tinker presently serving a prison sentence 'for gospelling'. At the trial Tab tells how angry she became when that tinker would no longer allow his blind daughter to sell them any of the tagged laces he had been making in prison. Bent on revenge, she had gone to the jail to confront the prisoner, but was rooted to the spot by the way he spoke:

> ... a fiery tear he put in every tone ...
> 'tis my belief God spoke: no tinker has such powers.[2]

Bunyan preaching in the open air

Browning had clearly read and sincerely admired Bunyan's writings — writings which mirrored his preaching style.

The testimony of his contemporaries is unanimous. As we have noted, John Owen said he would gladly relinquish his learning to be able to preach like the tinker. His friends John Wilson and Ebenezer Chandler could add

> In his latter years few if any were more successful in their work, we mean with respect to conversion. God was with him from first to last.

These two spoke of Bunyan's outstanding ability with words and commented on his mental agility. 'His wit was sharp and quick, his memory tenacious,' was their assessment, but they pointed out that Bunyan never relied on mere natural gifts unaccompanied by hard work. He was 'laborious in preaching and diligent in his preparation for it, not doing the work of God negligently', they said. But, yet more importantly, it was Bunyan's own devotion to Christ and his personal communion with him that lent passion and power to his preaching. They testified that:

> His business was to converse much with the Word of God and to pray over it; his labours therein were indefatigable, and God blessed him in so doing with a more than ordinary degree of knowledge...

As we have noted, another contemporary description of Bunyan's preaching comes from Charles Doe, after he had first heard Bunyan preach in 1685. 'Mr Bunyan,' he declared, 'preached so New Testament-like that he made me admire and weep for joy.' As he thought back on the preaching he had heard, Doe could add that those present felt 'as if an angel had touched their souls with a coal of holy fire from the altar'.[3] Bunyan had become like the picture of the preacher which he had first seen at Interpreter's House — 'one of a thousand' — a man who had eyes lifted up to heaven, the best of books in his hand, the law of truth written upon his lips, who stood as if he pleaded with men.[4]

Agnes Beaumont had also discovered this. Describing his preaching, she could write:

> Oh how we did feel our hearts stirred by the wonderful preaching of that godly Mr Bunyan... We heard him with profit to our souls. I was so full of joy that it was as if I had been in heaven.

Nor was this a mere riot of emotion. It produced in Agnes an ardent love for Jesus Christ and a desire for communion with him in prayer. In her earnest and simple account of those days, she tells us that:

> There was scarce a corner, in the house or barns, cowhouses or stable, under the hedges or in the wood where I did not pour out my soul to God. This often made me cry so that some would say, 'Agnes, why do you grieve or go crying thus?' while all the time my tears were for joy and love of Jesus Christ.

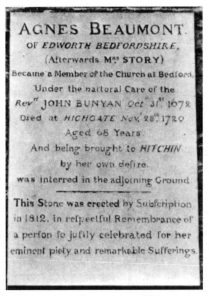

Memorial tablet to Agnes Beaumont

Despite all her subsequent sufferings, Agnes remained a faithful believing woman, dying in London at the age of sixty-nine.[5]

One of the last series of sermons preached by John Bunyan was based on three words only from Luke 24:47: 'Beginning at Jerusalem...' This sermon, *The Jerusalem Sinner Saved or Good News for the Vilest of Men*, is one that affords many illustrations of John Bunyan's most mature, moving and effective style in the pulpit. From it we may identify some of the elements in his preaching that made it so powerful, not only on the occasion itself, but also in the printed records.

First, Bunyan always gives his sermons a doctrinal basis, placing the passage chosen into its correct scriptural context. In the case of this sermon, Christ had said to his disciples before his ascension that the gospel must first be preached at Jerusalem, the very city over which he had wept because of its hardness and unbelief. Its worship had become corrupt, and at the crucifixion only a few weeks earlier 'Jerusalem sinners' had cried out, 'His blood be upon us and upon our children.' For the gospel to be preached 'beginning at Jerusalem' was evidence of the astounding mercy of God. As Bunyan observes, 'Jesus Christ would have mercy offered, in the first place, to the biggest sinners' — therefore to the least deserving.

To drive his message home to the hearts of his hearers, Bunyan engages in constant interaction with his congregation. He did not preach *at* the people; he preached *to* them, seeking to lay hold of their minds and hearts at every point. Again and again he addresses them personally, often by means of question and answer. He imagines the objections of some of the first 'Jerusalem sinners' of Peter's day:

Objector: But I was one of them that bare false witness against him. Is there grace for me?
Peter: For every one of you.
Objector: But I railed on him, I reviled him, I hated him, I rejoiced to see him mocked at by others. Can there be hopes for me?
Peter: There is, for every one of you.

Or he may widen the application to any who feel the weight of sin:

Objection: But I have a heart as hard as a rock.
Answer: Well, but this doth prove thee a biggest sinner.
Objection: But my heart continually frets against the Lord.
Answer: Well, but this doth prove thee a biggest sinner.
Objection: But my grey head is found in the way of wickedness.
Answer: Well, thou art in the rank of the biggest sinners...
Objection: But I am a reprobate.

Answer: Now thou talkest like a fool, and meddlest with
                what thou understandest not.

Bunyan can scarcely forebear crying out: 'Oh the greatness of
the grace of Christ that he should thus be in love with the souls of
Jerusalem sinners!'[6] If the biggest sinners are 'first served', he urges
anyone who is convicted of his sin to 'Put thy name, man, among
the biggest, lest thou be made to wait until they are served'.[7]
Another noticeable means that Bunyan often employs in his
sermons, and therefore in his written works, is what has been
called 'the argument of faith'. By this the believer uses revealed
scriptural truth and, arguing from it, presents to God the grounds
on which he is now basing his plea for mercy; he argues from
certainty to those things of which he is less sure.[8] It is a form of
debating with God. Because 'Christ is able to save to the utter-
most,' Bunyan reasons:

> What ground is now here for despair? If thou sayest, the
> number and burden of my sins; I answer, Nay: that is rather a
> ground for faith; because such an one, above all others, is
> invited by Christ to come unto him, yea, promised rest and
> forgiveness if they come... What! despair of bread in a land
> that is full of corn! Despair of mercy when our God is full of
> mercy![9]

He even anticipates arguing with the devil, and turning his
accusations into grounds for encouragement and hope for mercy:

> What, my true servant, quoth he [i.e. said Satan], wilt thou
> forsake me now? Having so often sold thyself to me to work
> wickedness, wilt thou forsake me now? Thou horrible wretch,
> dost not know that thou hast sinned thyself beyond the reach
> of grace, and dost thou think to find mercy now? ... Dost thou
> think that Christ will foul his fingers with thee? It is enough to
> make angels blush.
> And what did you reply? saith the tempted. Why, I granted
> the whole charge to be true, says the other. And what, did you
> despair, or how? No, saith he, I said, 'I am Magdalene, I am the
> thief, I am the publican, I am the prodigal, and one of Christ's

murderers, yea, worse than any of these, and yet God was so
far off from rejecting of me, as I found afterwards that there
was music and dancing in his house for me, and for joy that I
was come home unto him.[10]

Throughout his sermons, Bunyan draws on his own experience
to add weight to his arguments. For the most part these references
are implicit, and would only be recognized by hearers who knew
his personal background, but occasionally they are explicit, as in
this sermon. He too had been a 'Jerusalem sinner', he tells the
people, and when John Bunyan found forgiveness, many other
'Jerusalem sinners' in Elstow sought mercy as well:

> I speak by experience. I was one of these lousy ones, one
> of the great sin breeders ... wherefore Christ Jesus took me
> first; and taking me first, the contagion was much allayed all the
> town over. When God made me sigh, they would hearken, and
> inquiringly say, What's the matter with John? ... When I went
> out to seek the bread of life some of them would follow and
> the rest be put into a muse [made to wonder].[11]

Bunyan's use of graphic imagery adds sparkle and life to his
sermons. The mind that composed *The Pilgrim's Progress* and *The
Holy War* was clearly adept at introducing vivid imagery into his
preaching. Illustrating the fact that those whose sins may seem
outwardly less heinous than others can also find grace, he points
out:

> Now, I say, if there is room for those [sinners] of the big-
> gest size, certainly there is room for the lesser size. If there be
> a door wide enough for a giant to go in at, there is certainly
> room for a dwarf.[12]

Changing the metaphor, Bunyan demonstrates the breadth of
Christ's love for sinners of all sorts:

> Christ Jesus has bags of mercy that were never yet bro-
> ken up or unsealed. Hence it is said, He has goodness laid
> up, things reserved in heaven for his. And if he breaks up one

of these bags, who can tell what he can do? Hence his love is said to be such as passeth knowledge.[13]

Throughout this sermon Bunyan is full of tenderness, full of pleading and arguments to draw burdened sinners to Christ. This aspect was not always foremost in his preaching for, as we have seen, some of his sermons can be terrifying in their intensity and description of the fearful end of the unbeliever. But whether Bunyan woos or threatens, he has a great and passionate concern for the souls of men and women. His desires for the lost to be reconciled to God filled him with an unquenchable zeal to preach, and when forbidden to do so he was prepared to languish in a prison, or even suffer a violent death, rather than consent to stop preaching. His earnestness is caught in such words as these:

> O that they who have heard me speak this day did but see as I do what sin, death, hell and the curse of God is; and also what the grace and love and mercy of God is through Christ to men... And, indeed, I did often say in my heart before the Lord, That if to be hanged up presently before their eyes would be a means to awaken them ... I gladly should be contented.[14]

Above everything else, above eloquence, illustration, pleadings or threatenings, John Bunyan looked for the assistance and power of the Holy Spirit in his preaching to make it effectual in the lives of his hearers. He expresses it quaintly but vividly. At times, he tells us, he became suddenly aware that 'an Angel of God had stood by at my back to encourage me'. And when that happened, everything changed:

> Oh, it hath been with such power and heavenly evidence upon my own soul, while I have been labouring to unfold it, to demonstrate it, and to fasten it upon the consciences of others, that I could not be content with saying, I believe, and am sure; methought I was more than sure.[15]

On such occasions his contemporaries tell us that he preached with 'no small degree of liveliness and vigour'.

And, as we glance through Bunyan's sermons, we may detect many occasions when the Angel of the Covenant stood at his back, assisting, and empowering him to preach effectively. And here, in *The Jerusalem Sinner Saved*, nothing that the troubled, awakened sinner can plead will revoke the extraordinary offer of mercy that God holds out in first calling those most conscious of their sins — the 'Jerusalem sinners':

> Stand away, devil, Christ calls me; stand away unbelief, Christ calls me; stand away, all ye my discouraging apprehensions, for my Saviour calls me to receive of his mercy... Is this not an encouragement to the biggest sinners to make their application to Christ for mercy? 'Come unto me all ye that labour and are heavy laden', doth also confirm this thing; that is, that the biggest sinner, and he that has the biggest burden is he who is first invited.[16]

Little wonder that the people flocked to hear John Bunyan preach!

47

Sharpening his quill

Ever since his conversion, Bunyan had lived with eternity in view.
The Celestial City was as real to him as if he had seen it with his
own eyes. Like his pilgrims waiting in the Land of Beulah for the
summons to cross the river, he could say, 'I have a desire to
venture the tugs and pains and the harsh handling of the king of
terrors [death] so I may be with Jesus Christ.'[1]

As 1687 drew to its close and 1688 dawned, it may well be
that John Bunyan anticipated that the day might be near when
this desire would be fulfilled. Perhaps soon he too would hear the
summons to come, and be able to say, like Mr Valiant-for-Truth:

> I am going to my Father's, and though with great difficulty I
> am got hither, yet now I do not repent me of all the trouble I
> have been at to arrive where I am.

If John Bunyan did have any premonition that the end might
be close, he certainly did not slacken in his endeavours to 'serve
his generation' while the opportunity remained. If possible, he did
even more. Ten new titles came from his ready pen during 1687–

1688. Five of these were published during 1688; others were added to the pile on his desk still remaining in manuscript form. Some of these unpublished manuscripts were either not quite complete, or else consisted of matter that was still judged unwise to circulate, given the strictures of the times and the witch-hunt for books deemed to promote the Dissenting cause. Quite

Pocket-knife thought to have been used by Bunyan

apart from the mental agility required to produce all this new material, such an accomplishment was an even more remarkable achievement in days when everything had to be written by hand. Patiently Bunyan must have had to keep sharpening the ends of his quills with his pen-knife, dipping them again and again in his inkpot. In a computer age, it is scarcely imaginable how he could have done all this in such a short space of time. Nor were these mere booklets; some were of considerable length.

The Jerusalem Sinner Saved was one such labour during 1688; another was *The Water of Life*, a series of sermons based on the words in Revelation 22:17: 'Whosoever will, let him take the water of life freely.' We can well imagine that this subject was one that brought the preacher much joy. In this flowing river of life, streaming out from under the throne of God, he saw an emblem of divine grace — a life-theme for Bunyan — for here, in such a river, was 'grace abounding even to the chief of sinners'. Whether preaching or writing about such a subject, Bunyan delighted to portray 'the richness and glory of the grace and spirit of the gospel', as the subtitle declares. The theme was one that was well suited to Bunyan's imaginative turn of mind. This unbounded river of grace was deep and broad.

[And] if thou canst swim, here thou mayest roll up and down as do fishes in the sea. Nor needest thou fear drowning in this river, it will bear thee up, and carry thee over the highest hills, as Noah's water did carry the ark.[2]

The Water of Life included a message for Christians, as Bunyan urged his hearers to avail themselves freely of the plentiful grace of Christ for every situation. But, like *The Jerusalem Sinner Saved*, it was particularly addressed to troubled 'seekers'. He refers several times to the custom, growing in popularity amongst the well-to-do, of trekking down to Bath, Epsom or Tunbridge Wells to bathe in the spa waters, which were thought to contain medicinal qualities. Some people even bought property nearby. Better far, Bunyan assures his hearers, to live near this River of Life and to bathe in its waters, for it brings healing for the soul's diseases. Firmly believing as he did in the electing love of God, he nevertheless emphasizes in these words the 'whosoever will' of the gospel:

> Sinner, here is laid a necessity upon thee; one of two must be thy lot; either thou must accept of God's grace ... notwithstanding all thy undeservings and unworthiness, or else thou must be damned for thy rebellion.[3]

Bunyan concludes this warm, experimental book with words that apply equally to believer and non-believer alike:

> Wherefore, despairing soul, for it is to thee I speak, forbear thy mistrusts, cast off thy slavish fears, hang thy misgivings as to this upon the hedge, and believe ... a river is before thy face. And as for thy want of goodness and works, let that by no means daunt thee; this is a river of water of life, streams of grace and mercy.[4]

Of a far different character, and probably not preached as a series of sermons, is a further book which Bunyan published during the early part of 1688. Called *Solomon's Temple Spiritualized*, this was a subject which gave him full scope for his flair for symbolism. As he developed an intricate interpretation of the details given in the Old Testament of the temple King Solomon built in Jerusalem, he saw many spiritual parallels for the Christian life. The subtitle, *Gospel Light fetched out of the Temple at Jerusalem*, sums up Bunyan's theme. In seventy numbered sections he roams in imagination around Solomon's temple, pointing out the hidden gospel implications of all that he sees. We might well wonder whether some of the typology is too far-fetched, but by the time Bunyan has provided Scripture references for all his allusions, we have to admit that he may well be right in his interpretation.

Each numbered section follows the same sequence. First, he describes the particular item upon which he has alighted: the windows, the doors, the walls, the stairs, the carvings, and even the golden nails of the inner temple. He also includes paragraphs on the functions of the priests, the significance of the veil of the temple, and other details. Having depicted the primary purpose for the chosen item, Bunyan then shows its spiritual meaning for the New Testament Christian.

As he reads of the chains engraved in gold on the outer pillars of the temple, for example, Bunyan finds in them a type of 'gospel obligations' — those spiritual duties that the believer is bound to perform out of love for Christ. But, he adds:

> ... this strength to bind lieth not in outward force but in sweet constraint by virtue of the displays of undeserved love. 'The love of Christ constraineth us.'[5]

Even Bunyan was not always sure that he was correct in his suggestions. Like a miner digging for precious jewels, he recognizes that he may sometimes misjudge his discovery. 'I dare not presume to say that I know I have hit it right in everything,' he confesses, 'but this I can say, I have endeavoured so to do.' He pleads for the charity of the reader:

> Wherefore, courteous reader, if thou findest anything either in word or matter that thou shalt judge doth vary from God's truth, let it be counted no man's else but mine. Pray God also to pardon my fault.[6]

Certainly, Bunyan is at his strongest as he deals with those representations in the temple that touch on the heart of the gospel — one being the mercy seat. The mercy seat rested upon the ark containing the tablets on which the Ten Commandments were written. Here was a subject highly significant in Bunyan's own experience:

> [Because] the mercy seat was set above upon the ark, it teacheth us to know that mercy can look down from heaven, though the law stand by... The law out of Christ is terrible as a lion; the law in him is meek as a lamb... Wherefore, sinner, come thou for mercy that way; for there, if thou meetest with the law, it can do thee no harm. Come therefore, come boldly to this throne of grace, this mercy seat, thus borne up by the ark.[7]

Although Bunyan was absorbed in his subject, he would have been well aware that the political situation in the nation was steadily deteriorating. Muttered conspiracies were the order of the day, as worried politicians and church leaders alike plotted and planned some means of ridding the country of another Stuart king, especially one determined to re-establish Roman Catholicism as the state religion. Naturally, minds turned across the North Sea to where the heir to the throne, the Princess Mary, eldest daughter of the king by his first wife, Anne Hyde, was living. Married to the Protestant William of Orange, who already had an eye on the throne of England, Mary seemed the only possible solution to the problem.

Alarm intensified when James not only reissued the Declaration of Indulgence on 27 April 1688, but insisted that in every parish church in the land it should be read out, first in London during May, and then everywhere else in June. Seven of the most prominent bishops of the Anglican Church refused, not so much from animosity to Dissent as from fear of the steadily growing influence of Catholicism. Furious at having his will countermanded in such a way, James had the seven clerics, one of whom was Archbishop William Sancroft, arrested on charges of seditious libel and confined in the Tower of London. Public outrage rose to new heights, as this was seen as an outright assault on the Church of England. After seven days in the Tower, the bishops were released on bail pending their trial in Westminster Hall at the end of June. The members of the jury, initially unable to agree, were locked up without food, light or heat until they could reach a verdict. After a night spent in such deliberation, they at last proclaimed a 'Not Guilty' verdict on the seven bishops — a further humiliating failure for James, as shouts of celebration rang out across London.

And the final factor in the demise of the last Stuart king occurred the very next week. The king's second wife, Mary of Modena, gave birth to a son. All Mary's previous infants had died apart from one girl, and after fifteen years of marriage it seemed strange indeed to a sceptical people that Mary should produce a son at such a critical stage of events.[8] A prince would naturally take precedence for the succession over his half-sisters, Mary and Anne, daughters of James' first marriage. With this birth a Catholic heir to the throne of England was ensured. Without any further delay, a secret invitation was sent to Holland by representatives of both political parties inviting William of Orange and his wife Mary to come to England to 'rescue English religion and liberty'.

While these transactions and conspiracies were taking place, John Bunyan became seriously ill. Accounts suggest that his condition was due to 'a sweating distemper'. This was not the sweating sickness which had last swept the country in 1552, taking many thousands to the grave; nor was it a further outbreak of the plague. Less serious than these, it was probably what we would call influenza, but even so, this was a disease well able to kill in its more virulent forms. And John Bunyan's robust constitution had already suffered severe strain after almost thirteen years of insanitary prison conditions. Added to this, the Bedford preacher was exhausted. Constantly bending over his manuscripts as he wrote for hour after hour, he had provided eight or nine theological treaties in the last two years. When he was not writing, he was preaching wherever he had opportunity, riding long distances, sometimes as far afield as London.

We can well imagine the anxiety with which Elizabeth must have watched over him. Their youngest son, Joseph, was still only sixteen and at an age when he needed a father's guidance. Of the thirty years in which they had been married, only seventeen had been spent together. Great was her relief as John gradually rallied and began to regain his strength once more. No sooner was he well enough to leave his bed than he was bowed over his books again. 'I have a manuscript that I must finish,' he would have told his troubled wife, 'for I wish to take it to my printer when I go to London in a few weeks' time. I have an engagement to fulfil to preach for John Gammon in Whitechapel Meeting House.' Unable to dissuade her determined husband from his labours, Elizabeth would have had no option except to acquiesce.

The manuscript on which John was working was one which he called *The Excellency of a Broken Heart*. More generally known as *The Acceptable Sacrifice*, it is drawn from King David's great psalm of penitence, Psalm 51, after his double sin of adultery and murder. Grieving over his fall, David presents to God the only sacrifice which he will accept: 'a broken spirit ... and a contrite heart'. As Bunyan develops his thoughts on this theme, it is immediately evident that his words spring from intense personal experience. He sees himself as that broken-hearted man, standing in the presence of a God of infinite majesty. Humbled by his sins, he declares, 'Verily, this consideration is enough to make the broken-hearted man creep into a mouse-hole to hide himself from such majesty.'⁹ Possibly he was thinking of some discreet mouse-hole in his own small home.

In our own day, when a depth of conviction of sin is rarely to be found, Bunyan's description of the fears that a broken sinner may experience is of great pastoral value. Such a person often doubts whether there can be mercy for him:

> They are afraid that this is but the beginning of death, and a token that they shall never see the face of God with comfort, either in this world or in that which is to come.

Of the broken-hearted, he says:

> He stands, as he sees, not only in need of mercy, but of the tenderest mercies. God has several sorts of mercies, some more rough, some more tender. God can save a man, and yet have him a dreadful way to heaven! This the broken-hearted sees, and this the broken-hearted dreads, and therefore pleads for the tenderest sorts of mercies.[10]

And Christ has a particular concern for such people:

> Behold, therefore, the care of God which he has for the broken in heart; he has given a charge to Christ his Son to look well to them, and to bind up and heal their wounds.[11]

In developing his theme, Bunyan illustrates the value God places on this condition, for:

> [A] broken heart prizes Christ and has a high esteem for him... As bread to the hungry, as water to the thirsty, as light to the blind, and liberty to the imprisoned, so, and a thousand times more, is Jesus Christ to the wounded, and to them that are broken-hearted.[12]

Such a disposition is like an unlocked cabinet 'where God lays up the jewels of the gospel'.

The Excellency of a Broken Heart is among the most moving of all Bunyan's lesser-known writings and is both pastoral and personal. Bunyan is anxious that Christians should remain sensitive to the Spirit of God, whose work it is to convict of sin. 'Take heed that you choke not those convictions that at present do break your hearts,' he warns, for these are the most evident signs of God's favour.

A confirmation that John Bunyan was including much personal experience in this treatise, the last he would ever write, comes from the pen of his long-standing friend George Cokayne, who wrote a lengthy 'Preface' to the work. Also a Bedford man, Cokayne may well have known Bunyan from their early days.[13] In his preface Cokayne states, 'What is here written is but a transcript out of his own heart.' He then suggests (whether rightly or wrongly, it is impossible to judge) that Bunyan had a lifelong problem with the sin of pride, and therefore the many trials he met with were God's chastening hand on his servant that his usefulness might not be impaired. He writes:

> God was still hewing and hammering him by his Word, and sometimes by more than ordinary temptations and desertions ... humbling of him and keeping him low in his own eyes. The truth is, as himself sometimes acknowledged, he always needed the thorn in the flesh, and God in mercy sent it to him, lest,

under his extraordinary circumstances he should be exalted above measure, which perhaps was the evil that did beset him more than any other.[14]

Meanwhile, as he was preoccupied with his writing, the country was teetering on the verge of revolution, and maybe even of another civil war as bloody as the one in which John himself had fought. Bunyan makes no allusion to the situation. As he slowly recovered from his illness, his concerns were increasingly wrapped up with those of a better world soon to come. Perhaps he realized that his opportunities to speak to his present generation were fast slipping away. Drawing his current work to a close, he had one final warning to both believer and unbeliever alike — the last words he was known to write:

> Come broken, come contrite, come sensible of and sorry for thy sins, or thy coming will be counted no coming to God aright; and if so, consequently thou wilt get no benefit thereby.[15]

It was now the middle of August 1688. With a final glance through the manuscript he had just completed, Bunyan began to prepare for his sixty-mile ride to London. His friends at Whitechapel Meeting had heard of his serious illness and were eagerly hoping that John might be sufficiently recovered to come. But it was a long ride for a man only just regaining his strength, and we can well imagine that Elizabeth was anxious. Then, doubtless, to her dismay, a young neighbour who had fallen out with his father, and was therefore fearful of losing his inheritance, begged Bunyan to call at his family home in Reading on his way to Whitechapel and plead with his father for him. Ever a Mr Greatheart, John kindly agreed, even though it involved him in a long detour, almost trebling the distance he had to travel. Such a journey would have been wearisome enough for a man in good health, but was unwise for someone of almost sixty who was just recovering from serious illness. Undeterred, John Bunyan said a last goodbye to his wife, and set off for Reading.

48

Crossing the river

Bound for Reading in mid-August 1688, John Bunyan rode steadily west, over roads that were often little more than rough tracks, a journey that would have taken him two days in his weakened condition. He had visited the town in the past and possibly knew his young neighbour's irate father. Tradition has it that when persecution against Dissenters was at its height Bunyan had once come to Reading disguised as a carter, complete with whip in hand. Word of his true identity quickly spread, with men and women gathering secretly to benefit from his words, before 'the carter' cracked his whip and disappeared again into the distance.

This present visit was far different. Irenic and warm-hearted by nature, Bunyan was on a mission. He hoped he might be able to pacify the young man's father and bring about a reconciliation between them. Never at a loss for words, Bunyan plied the offended father with 'such pressing arguments and reasons against anger and passion, as also for love and reconciliation,' that the man was completely melted down. Nor was his forgiveness a mere grudging concession to an erring boy, but a wholehearted change of heart towards his son. Instead of wishing to disinherit him, he now longed to see him again and to repair the damaged relationship.

On the following day, Bunyan saddled up his horse, cheerful at the success of his endeavours. He had a long ride to accomplish before nightfall, but at least he had been able to do good and — who could tell? — maybe the young man in question would be disposed to consider the message he preached of an even greater reconciliation — one between man and God.

As he turned his horse's head towards London he no doubt glanced anxiously at the darkening sky and hoped that the threatened storm would not break before he reached his destination. But

John Strudwick's house on Snow Hill

as he rode along the atmosphere grew even more sultry and humid. Clearly a storm was now imminent. Anxiously spurring his horse onwards, Bunyan knew he must reach Snow Hill in Holborn by nightfall. John Strudwick, a member and deacon of George Cokayne's church, had invited the Bedford pastor to stay with him during his visit to London and was expecting him that night. Strudwick, who ran a grocery business from his home, known as The Sign of the Star, had become a valued friend in recent years.

Before long John caught the sound of the first ominous rumblings of thunder: then flashes of lightning tore through the sky and finally torrential rain began to sheet down. With little protection against the elements, both horse and rider were soon drenched. The roads, never much better than rubble-filled ditches, turned to mud tracks and then to running streams. Had Bunyan sought shelter along the way, perhaps in Maidenhead or Slough, all might have been well, but he struggled on, blinding rain driving into his eyes. At last he reached the outskirts of London. Heading north, he finally arrived, shivering and exhausted, in Snow Hill and was knocking thankfully at the door of John Strudwick's tall four-storeyed home.

Alarmed at his state, Strudwick quickly drew the bedraggled traveller inside; his saturated clothing was removed and before long John Bunyan was able to rest in a warm bed. But the damage was done. Not fully recovered from his earlier illness, he once again manifested symptoms of fever, as the chill and fatigue of his journey brought on a relapse. For several days his condition was far from good, but by Sunday, 19 August, the fever had abated. Bunyan rose thankfully from his bed, drained but feeling better. And only one thing was on his mind — his promise to preach for John Gammon, the pastor of the church that met in Petticoat Lane,[1] Whitechapel. He may have been unwise in his determination to carry on despite his health, but concern over disappointing the expectant people weighed heavily with him. Accompanied by John Strudwick and other friends, Bunyan set out on the mile-long walk to his preaching appointment.

Usually reticent and thoughtful in company, Bunyan seemed unnaturally bright that day as they walked along. He had many things to say to his companions, and later they recalled some of his words and noted them down. Above all, they remembered the comments he had made on the trials of a Christian — and who better qualified to speak on such a subject than John Bunyan? 'Why do we find affliction so hard to bear?' someone had asked. 'Out of dark affliction comes a spiritual light,' John had replied, and added unforgettable words drawn directly from those hard early days of imprisonment:

> In times of affliction we commonly meet with the sweetest experiences of the love of God. Did we heartily renounce the pleasures of this world, we should be very little troubled for our afflictions.[2]

The walk seemed short to Bunyan's friends, and soon they had reached the chapel in Petticoat Lane. Relieved and thankful to see the well-loved preacher again, the congregation listened attentively as he addressed them on John 1:13: '... born, not of blood, nor of the will of the flesh, nor of the will of the man, but of God.' Although it was a short sermon, for the preacher was still far from well, it has been preserved because one of his hearers made extensive notes and later wrote up all he had heard. The burden of Bunyan's message was one that had concerned him through the years: the importance of holiness in the lives of those who professed faith. As he concluded he urged:

> Consider that the holy God is your Father, and let this oblige you to live like the children of God, that you may look your Father in the face with comfort another day.[3]

And that 'other day' was close at hand for John Bunyan himself. On the Monday he probably had opportunity to see the first part of his new manuscript, *The Excellency of a Broken Heart*, through the press, but when he returned to the Sign of the Star he was struck down once more with fever. It would appear that Strudwick and other close friends who had gathered to spend time with him did not realize the serious nature of his condition. Apparently an outbreak of epidemic proportions of 'distemper', or influenza, was rife in the community, but it was rarely proving fatal, so it does not seem that anyone thought of sending for Elizabeth or other members of his family.

At intervals John was still able to talk to those who gathered around his bed, and many of his sayings were carefully noted down by those who came in and out of the room where he lay.[4] But, as his condition deteriorated, his thoughts were gradually turning ever more often to the joys of a better world. He knew, even if his friends did not, that he had come to the brink of that bridgeless river which each must cross alone. Like Mr Valiant-for-Truth, John Bunyan had indeed been a fearless and noble pilgrim, constant to the end, and now he too could say:

> My sword I give to him that shall succeed me in my pilgrimage, and my courage and skill to him that can get it. My marks

and scars | carry with me, to be a witness for me that | have fought his battles, who will now be my rewarder.[5]

Those 'marks and scars' that John Bunyan would carry with him were created by unremitting government persecution, a weakened constitution after almost thirteen years spent in jail and the personal jibes and wicked innuendoes so often levelled against him by his enemies. These, together with his tireless endeavours in preaching and writing, had taken an exacting toll on his remaining strength. Not quite sixty years of age, he might well have expected to serve Christ's church for some years yet. Now he knew he must leave his family, his church and his friends behind. Would they be able to stand firm if persecution grew more intense once more? He did not know. Soon, however, all the trials of earth would be over for ever, not just for him but for them as well, for even the longest life is short at best. As he exclaimed in anticipation of that day:

O! what acclamations of joy will there be when all the children of God shall meet together without fear of being disturbed by the antichristian and Cainish brood![6]

Despite the best attentions and concern that his friends could give, Bunyan's condition only worsened. Then all hope of recovery vanished. Now they could see he was dying. His friend George Cokayne stayed by him, and to him Bunyan committed the remainder of his manuscript on *The Excellency of a Broken Heart* to complete its progress through the press. But John Bunyan was well prepared for this day. Long years ago he had struggled against the fear of death; he had come to terms with the reality of it when he realized that his imprisonment might easily end in a verdict of public execution. In that crisis he had found that the only way to endure was to 'pass a sentence of death upon everything that can properly be called a thing of this life'. He had learnt 'to count the grave my home, to make my bed in darkness ... that is to familiarise these things to me'. John Bunyan also knew, as the Shining Ones had told the trembling pilgrims before they entered the dark River of Death, that the waters would prove 'deeper or shallower as you believe in the King of the place'.

During ten feverish days of illness John thought much about that city he had once glimpsed and those 'streets paved with gold'. Now he could declare with confidence to those who stood around, 'O! who is able to conceive the inexpressible, inconceivable joys that are there? None but they who have tasted of them!' Perhaps he even recalled some words he had once written about his pilgrims as they looked across the river to the Celestial City beyond:

> You must there receive the comforts of all your toil, and have joy for all your sorrow; you must reap what you have sown, even the fruit of all your prayers and sufferings for the King by the way.

But those who watched by him could think of little else except the enormity of their loss. Tears streamed down their faces, for John Bunyan was dearly loved. Noticing their obvious distress, the dying man could only whisper, 'Weep not for me but for yourselves.' Then, as in the case of many other Christians brought face to face with death, that last and bitterest enemy, Bunyan's thoughts were clearly turning away from anything he might have been, had achieved, or even had suffered in his life. Only that solid foundation of his faith laid in the atoning sacrifice of Christ could give him confidence in the face of death:

> I go to the Father of our Lord Jesus Christ, who will, no doubt through the mediation of his blessed Son, receive me, though a sinner; where I hope we ere long shall meet and sing the new song and remain everlastingly happy, world without end.

These words, spoken with much difficulty but in assurance and hope, were his last. Far from his wife Elizabeth, far from his family and home, John Bunyan had crossed the river of death. It was Friday, 31 August 1688. Once, as he had followed his pilgrims to the gates of the Celestial City, he had heard all the bells ringing out for joy and listened to the jubilant praises of those already

Bunyan's tomb in Bunhill Fields

there. Then he had 'wished myself among them'. Now God had granted his faithful servant his heart's desire.

A messenger was quickly dispatched to Bedford to carry the grievous news to Elizabeth and to the church. Meanwhile the funeral must go ahead, and on the following Monday, 2 September, the great preacher and writer was buried in a corner of the Bunhill Fields graveyard known as 'Baptist Corner'. Situated off City Road in London, this graveyard was not attached to any parish church, and was one where thousands of plague victims had been hastily interred twenty-three years earlier in 1665. After the Act of Uniformity in 1662, when two thousand principled pastors and teachers had been ejected from their livings, many were refused the privileges of a burial in the parish church graveyard. A number of these Nonconformists were buried in Bunhill Fields, as also were the London Dissenters. Certainly John Bunyan's internment, not far from where his friend John Owen and also Thomas Goodwin lay, was highly appropriate.

No details of Bunyan's funeral have survived — one which neither Elizabeth nor any family member could have attended. His friend George Cokayne is thought to have conducted it, and in his foreword to *The Excellency of a Broken Heart*, he hints at the depth of sorrow felt on that day, and long after, as he describes 'the great loss and inexpressible grief of many precious souls'.[7] John Strudwick, in whose home Bunyan had died, intended that when his own impressive family vault was next opened, John Bunyan's coffin should be removed from its resting place in Baptist Corner and placed within it, as a suitable tribute to his friend. And this, it is generally supposed, took place ten years later when Strudwick himself died in 1698.

The imposing vault, standing not far from the entrance to Bunhill Fields, was restored in 1861. Complete with a new inscription to Bunyan and a life-sized figure of the preacher resting on it, it is a remarkable sight. In the hand of the figure is a book, and two emblems are carved on the sides of the grave: one of a man bowed beneath his burden; and the other of the same man as he loses his burden.[8] This vault, shared with a number of members of John Strudwick's family, stands as a silent reminder to all who visit Bunhill Fields graveyard of the pilgrimage of life — one which John Bunyan trod both nobly and well — and always in hope of a glorious resurrection.

49

Through the centuries

Stunned grief marked every face as news of their pastor's death was brought to his church in Bedford, possibly gathered for worship at the time. A brief note recorded the event in the church minute book:

> Wednesday the 4th of September was kept in prayer and huemilyation for this heavy stroak upon us, the death of deare brother Bunyan.[1]

The two following Wednesdays were also set aside by the church for the same purpose.

Distressed by her loss, Elizabeth herself had not long to live. Not yet fifty, her whole adult life had been spent in caring for John and his children. Now only three difficult years remained for her. Despite John's care in making all his possessions over to Elizabeth in 1685, it appears that she had either never known of the Deed of Gift or had forgotten where he had hidden it.[2] In fact she was obliged to file that he had died intestate. And when all his affairs were finally sorted out it was discovered that his total estate amounted to only forty-two pounds and nineteen shillings.[3] His forty-four books, poems and treatises already published, some of which had gone through multiple editions, can have brought little income for their author.

To preserve the memory of the man so suddenly and unexpectedly taken from them, two of his friends recorded their recollections of Bunyan — an account to be used later as a preface to an edition of his collected works. Ebenezer Chandler and John Wilson had known Bunyan well; Chandler would succeed him as pastor of the church, while Wilson, who had previously been a church member, was at the time pastor of the nearby church in Hitchin. They described him as 'grave and sedate', and remembered the unusual air of seriousness that had characterized this man; his whole manner was 'affable and meek towards others, yet bold and courageous for Christ'.

This did not mean that Bunyan was dour or lacking in warmth. Far from it. He had a lively sparkle in his eyes and a cheerful sense of humour — in fact he was sometimes criticized for being too light-hearted. 'He has sweetness and enterprise in his air,'[4] commented his publisher, Nathaniel Ponder, who had had plenty of opportunity to observe him as they worked together on the many editions of *The Pilgrim's Progress.* Some might even try to suppress a smile as they recollected a certain 'earthiness' in the way John spoke and wrote; occasionally his expressions, particularly in books such as *The Life and Death of Mr Badman,* could be described as coarse and might upset the more fastidious. But the ordinary people loved them. His homely metaphors drawn from familiar circumstances enlivened his preaching, making it yet more memorable and persuasive.

Quick-witted and with a tenacious memory, Bunyan had thrown all his natural gifts — gifts which amounted to little less than genius — into the service of his God and his fellow men. His knowledge of the Scriptures was comprehensive, coupled with an amazing gift of recall. Yet he was not overbearing in company. Often silent, he listened carefully to the opinion of others, not contributing himself until asked for his opinion. Even then, if he was unsure about the matter under discussion, he would say that where the Scripture was silent he dared not express an opinion.

Although George Cokayne had implied in his introduction to *The Excellency of a Broken Heart* that Bunyan had a lifelong struggle with the sin of pride, he must have overcome this to a considerable extent, for Chandler and Wilson could also say:

> This great saint was always in his own eyes the chiefest of sinners and the least of saints, esteeming any, where he did perceive the truth of grace, better than himself.[5]

Tentative and apprehensive when he had first submitted *The Pilgrim's Progress* into the hands of Nathaniel Ponder to be printed, he must have been delighted at its immediate success, especially in the light of the frequent scorn cast on him for his lack of formal education and his humble occupation. Reprinted within months of publication and then a further nine times before his death, *The Pilgrim's Progress* was acclaimed on every side. Little wonder that when he sent Part II to the printer he could write:

> My Pilgrim's book has travelled sea and land...
> In France and Flanders where men kill each other
> my Pilgrim is esteemed a friend, a brother.
> In Holland too, 'tis said, as I am told,
> my Pilgrim is with some worth more than gold.
> Highlanders and wild Irish can agree
> my Pilgrim should familiar with them be.
> 'Tis in New England under such advance...

Twenty-two editions of *The Pilgrim's Progress* would come off the presses by the turn of the century, with Dutch and French editions in 1682 and 1685 respectively. A further forty-eight editions were published by the year 1800. As the great missionary movement began to accelerate during the nineteenth century, many missionaries left their home countries with a copy of *The Pilgrim's Progress* packed in their trunks together with their Bibles. This resulted in a further explosion of popularity as the book was translated into many diverse languages. By the end of the 1800s the allegory could be found in Mandarin, Cantonese, Japanese, Hindi, Greek, Portuguese, Russian, Hungarian, Swedish and a host of other languages. By the beginning of the twenty-first century, one writer estimated that it had been translated into eighty different African languages.[6]

Elizabeth Bunyan little realized what recognition would be accorded to her husband's book in the future. For her the days were hard. She had sold what she could of John's possessions, but this yielded little financial support. His study had been left virtually untouched since that August day in 1688 when he had set off to Reading with the manuscript of *The Excellency of a Broken Heart* in his saddlebag. As the months passed, Elizabeth found she had little money left and wondered how she could afford her few modest expenses. We can imagine her going into John's study one day, where a layer of dust now covered his desk and papers. She would look wistfully around until her gaze rested on a pile of manuscripts. Ten separate treatises were stacked there, all in John's scrawling handwriting, prepared and awaiting publication. If only she could get them published, she might be able to gain a modest income to help her through this difficult time.

At length a bold plan struck Elizabeth. She would compose an advertisement notifying the public at large that these works existed, but adding that she was not in a position to publish them. Perhaps someone would see it and help her. And, in the overruling purposes of God, Charles Doe, the Southwark comb-maker, responded to Elizabeth's advertisement. Doe had found spiritual assurance through Bunyan's ministry; the Bedford pastor stood supreme in his estimation.

The sequel is told in Doe's own quaint style. When he woke up one morning, perhaps not long after seeing Elizabeth's advertisement, he felt unusually full of 'the sense of the peculiar love of God'. If only, he thought to himself, there was something he could do for the kingdom of God to express the love he felt welling up within. He stood at the top of his staircase musing. Then, as he slowly descended, he records that at '... about the middle of the stairs I reckoned that to sell books was the best I could do.' And by the time he had reached the bottom he had come to another conclusion: he would publish and sell John Bunyan's manuscripts that Elizabeth had advertised. And so, he later wrote, 'I began to sell books, and have sold about 3000 of Mr Bunyan's.'[7]

Doe lost no time in calling at 17, St Cuthbert's Street, in Bedford. He had probably met Elizabeth before because of his personal friendship with Bunyan during the last two years of the preacher's life. Among the manuscripts lying there on Bunyan's desk was the very sermon that had brought him spiritual life in 1685, *The Desire of the Righteous Granted* — undoubtedly a confirmation to this warm-hearted comb-maker of the guiding hand of God. Bunyan's unfinished commentary on Genesis was also there, together with eight other titles.

Offering Elizabeth the very best terms he could obtain for them, Doe went off carrying with him some of Bunyan's best work — writings that have enriched the Christian church ever since. His initiative would make the final months of life for John Bunyan's noble widow a little easier. Early in 1692 Elizabeth followed her pilgrim husband over the river. Like Christiana, having committed all her concerns to God, Elizabeth too could say, 'Come wet, come dry, I long to be gone.'

Doe, however, faced considerable problems in publishing Bunyan's works. His original plan was to collect all his previous publications and bind them together in one reasonably priced folio edition. Advertising for subscribers to finance the venture, he gained some four hundred names, but his greatest problem arose from some of Bunyan's former publishers,[8] who were unwilling to forgo the financial gain received from the books they had published. In a preface to his edition of Bunyan's work which he called *The Struggler,* Doe complained of 'the many discouragements I have met with in my struggles in this so great work'. Among these 'struggles' he added that 'an interested bookseller [had] opposed it'. By 1692 Doe had accomplished his objective as far as he was able, and had included twenty of Bunyan's titles in a folio edition, ten of them in print for the first time. He had planned to produce a second volume, but it seems that he met with too many obstacles, and this was only accomplished in 1736–37 under other editors.

Doe was, however, responsible for one other title — one that has been among the best known of Bunyan's shorter works, *The Heavenly Footman.* As we have seen, this was the very book that Bunyan was writing when he 'fell suddenly into an allegory' and ideas for *The Pilgrim's Progress* crowded into his mind. Bunyan's

eldest son, also called John, had kept this single title in his possession, but sold it to Doe, who promptly had it printed in 1698. In
his preface Doe described the book as 'the experience and
knowledge of a great convert — a monument to the mighty
power of grace'. He expressed his motivation in printing Bunyan's
works: 'I also do love them and would have you do the same.'

The only other title still held by the family was not printed
until 1767, more than a hundred years after its composition, and
that was Bunyan's *Relation of my Imprisonment*. Hannah Bunyan, great-granddaughter of the preacher, parted with it shortly
before her death, thus preserving for posterity the valuable
accounts of Bunyan's trials and of Elizabeth's heroic interventions
on his behalf.

John Bunyan's life had spanned one of the most tumultuous
periods of English history. As we saw in the opening chapter, he
was born in 1628, the same year that the Petition of Rights was
issued as the result of Parliament's demand for basic rights for the
people of England from the Crown. He died sixty years later, just
a few months before the 'Glorious Revolution' in December 1688
after James II had finally fled the country. William and Mary were
jointly proclaimed as king and queen on 13 February 1689.
Amongst the first benefits of the new regime was the 1689 Act of
Toleration, which granted religious liberty at last to all apart from
Roman Catholics and any who denied the doctrine of the Trinity.
Although still banned from civil or military office, Dissenters were
at last set free from the burden of constant harassment and
persecution and allowed to worship without fear of informer or
magistrate.

But the coming era was to prove 'enchanted ground' for some
Dissenters. Like Heedless and Too-bold, whom Mr Great-heart
and his company found asleep as they crossed this dangerous
plain, a number of churches relaxed their guard with the easing of
their circumstances. As a result a widespread loss of faith and zeal
gradually began to characterize many Independent churches
particularly after the death of Queen Anne in 1714. This, together
with the growth of rationalism and deism inspired by such
philosophers as John Locke and David Hume, resulted in a loss of
sympathy for works such as Bunyan's — indeed for Puritan works
in general.

However, Bunyan's writings never lost their appeal for the 'common people' — unlike the literary elite. In the words of N. H. Keeble:

> Amongst the literati of the early eighteenth century Bunyan's popularity was taken not as proof of his excellence but as confirmation of his vulgarity, and so of his inconsequentiality.

One critic arrogantly suggested that:

> ... no one could suppose that Bunyan, however popular with the rabble of the nation, could please and gratify the minds of men of quality and education.

His was 'the work of a Grub Street hack,' opined John Arbuthnot, 'fit only for maids and apprentices'; while David Hume himself saw an appreciation of Bunyan as evidence of bad taste.[9]

Even some who admired *The Pilgrim's Progress* were intimidated by the prevailing ethos. William Cowper, poet and hymn-writer, refers to Bunyan in one of his major works, but does not name him for fear of derision:

> Ingenious dreamer, in whose well-told tale
> Sweet fiction and sweet truth alike prevail;
> Whose humorous vein, strong sense, and simple style
> May teach the gayest, make the gravest smile;
> Witty, and well-employed, and, like thy Lord,
> Speaking in parables his slighted word;
> I name thee not lest so despised a name
> Should move a sneer at thy deserved fame...
> Revere the man whose PILGRIM marks the road,
> And guides the PROGRESS of the soul to God.[10]

The attitude of the leaders of the eighteenth-century Evangelical Revival was far different. Here were men who appreciated the spiritual value of Bunyan's writings. George Whitefield, renowned preacher, did not share Cowper's qualms. In 1767 he contributed a preface to the third edition of Charles Doe's 1692 edition of Bunyan's writings. In it he spoke of 'the success of his [Bunyan's] works in pulling down Satan's strongholds in sinners' hearts,' and added:

> [They] smell of the prison [for] ministers never write or preach so well as when under the cross: the Spirit of Christ and of glory then rests upon them.

John Wesley too was prepared to disregard literary opinion when he abridged *The Holy War*, including it in his *Christian Library*. John Newton of Olney added notes to a further edition of *The Pilgrim's Progress* Part I, and in 1775 another edition of the book was dedicated to Selina, Countess of Huntingdon.

It seems strange, however, that no authoritative biography of Bunyan was attempted during the whole of the eighteenth century. In 1809 Joseph Ivimey, a prolific Baptist historian, was the first to investigate Bunyan's life, but he did little more than reprint *Grace Abounding* with explanatory notes.[11] The first to devote an entire book to Bunyan's work was George Cheever, writing up his *Lectures on The Pilgrim's Progress*, which was first published in about 1828. With the tide of literary opinion beginning to turn, Robert Southey, poet laureate, wrote a hundred-page biographical sketch in 1830 as a preface to a further edition of *The Pilgrim's Progress*. Although unsympathetic in some respects, trying to whitewash the persecution of Dissenters, it at least reinstated John Bunyan as a trustworthy writer.

The following year, another literary heavyweight endorsed Bunyan — none other than the historian Thomas Babington Macaulay. Writing a review of Southey's book in December 1830, he described *The Pilgrim's Progress* as 'that wonderful book [which] has been read by many thousands with tears,' adding, '... by it every reader knows the straight and narrow path.' Bunyan's work, he suggested, was also invaluable for any who wished to gain a command of the English language. Indeed, he concluded, John Bunyan and John Milton were, in his view, the only two minds in the seventeenth century 'which possessed the imaginative faculty in a very eminent degree'.[12]

Throughout the nineteenth century Bunyan's allegory was prized ever more highly. Some of the well-known literary figures of the day added their warm endorsements, among them Sir

Walter Scott, Charles Lamb, John Keats, William Blake and even George Bernard Shaw.[13] The poet Samuel Coleridge was another who appreciated the literary and theological worth of *The Pilgrim's Progress*. He was unhappy about the reservations expressed by Southey and described the book as the best summary of evangelical theology 'ever produced by a writer not miraculously inspired'.[14]

But towering above the appreciation of these men of letters was the esteem of pulpit giants like C. H. Spurgeon. His printed sermons are full of references to Bunyan's writings. He gave it as his opinion that:

> Next to the Bible, the book that I value most is John Bunyan's *Pilgrim's Progress*, and I imagine I have read that through perhaps a hundred times; it is a book of which I can never seem to tire.

In it he recognized 'the Bible in another shape'[15] and once said of Bunyan's writings:

> Read anything of his, and you will see that it is almost like reading the Bible itself... He had read it until his whole being was saturated with Scripture, and though his writings are charmingly full of poetry, yet he cannot give us his *Pilgrim's Progress* — that sweetest of all prose poems — without continually making us feel and say, 'Why, this man is a living Bible!' Prick him anywhere; and you will find that his blood is bibline ... for his whole soul is full of the Word of God.[16]

Probably these years of the Victorian era were the high point of appreciation of John Bunyan's writings. Few homes were without a copy of *The Pilgrim's Progress*. Richard L. Greaves states that by 1938 as many as 1,300 editions of the book had been produced since it was first published in 1678.[17] Testimonies to its value and spiritual usefulness are legion, as also are the modifications based on it: versions for children, musical settings, stories and plays borrowing a similar theme, and even, more recently, a television production.

John Bunyan's statue, Bedford

The first full, though little recognized, biography of Bunyan was written by Robert Philip in 1839. In a hefty volume of almost 600 pages, Philip attempted to cover as many aspects of Bunyan's life and theology as possible, writing what he imagined to be the definitive life of the great Puritan.[18] Comprehensive as it certainly was, Philip's work would be eclipsed by that of the pastor of the Bunyan Meeting in Bedford, John Brown. The 1885 ornate and fully illustrated volume, *John Bunyan, his Life, Times and Work* remained the most authoritative account of Bunyan's life for many years, even though Brown himself had to revise it as new information came to light. George Offor, who had given unstinting years of his life to the study of Bunyan's writings, also wrote an informative memoir as a preface to his masterly three-volume edition of Bunyan's works. First published in 1854, Offor's volumes have been the standard resource until the late 1970s.[19]

But, with the growing influence of liberalism during the opening decades of the twentieth century, Bunyan's works became less sought after once more and, like other Puritan works of theology, were generally disregarded. Lone voices of appreciation could still be heard, however, particularly that of Alexander Whyte, popular Free Church of Scotland preacher, who wrote three titles based on the characters in *The Pilgrim's Progress.* Another voice was that of Gresham Machen, an American theologian who described it as 'that tenderest and most theological of books ... pulsating with life in every word'. [20]

A brief revival of interest was sparked by the tercentenary of Bunyan's birth in 1928, and a plethora of new biographies poured off the presses, some twenty in number. Among these was Frank Mott Harrison's revision of John Brown's biography,[21] although embroidered with a significant amount of imaginative fiction. Vera Brittain's well-researched 1950 biography, *In the Steps of John Bunyan* (marred also by over-much use of fictional extras), kindled further awareness of both the man and his background.

Since that date there has been a surprising revival of interest in John Bunyan, but its main preoccupation has been literary and social rather than biographical. Countless theses on every aspect of Bunyan's contribution can be found in the British Library. While a number of such writers are prepared to admire and study Bunyan's unique style and contribution, many find themselves in profound disagreement with his theology. It is refreshing therefore to read sympathetic scholastic works like those of Professor Richard Greaves[22] and of Michael Davies.[23] 'To read Bunyan aright,' Davies points out, 'it is vital to approach [him] with a spiritual mind.' Bunyan would have been horrified had he thought that his earnest gospel exhortations had become the subject of mere academic discussion.

So let John Bunyan himself have the last word. In a sermon entitled, 'The Saints' Knowledge of Christ's Love', based on Ephesians 3:18-19, one that Charles Doe included in his 1692 folio edition, Bunyan reveals the compelling motivation behind all his sufferings and his lifelong endeavour in the service of Christ and his church:

> Why should any thing have my heart but God, but Christ? He loves me, he loves me with love that passeth knowledge. He loves me and he shall have me: he loves me and I will love him: his love stripped him of all for my sake; Lord, let my love strip me of all for thy sake. I am a son of love, an object of love, a monument of love, of *free* love, of *distinguishing* love, of *peculiar* love, and of love that passeth knowledge: and why should I not walk in love?[24]

And this John Bunyan did to a remarkable extent. Down the long centuries his life and example have pointed out the path to Christians of every generation — and will continue to do so until, like Mr Standfast, we can say:

> I have formerly lived by hearsay and faith, but now I go where I shall live by sight, and shall be with him in whose company I delight myself.[25]

Appendices

Appendix I

A brief account of the build-up to the Civil War

If the long-term causes of the Civil War are debatable, the immediate steps leading to such conflict may be traced with relative ease. Charles I, whose tactless and obdurate confrontations with his people led him to dismiss his last Parliament in March 1629, had ruled alone for eleven years. Because of his desperate shortage of revenue, especially in view of the cost of his foreign wars, he had turned to the expedient of raising money through the sale of honours.

As this source of revenue dried up, he made himself even more unpopular by extending the levy of 'ship money' — initially a tax on coastal towns to support naval defences in time of war. He now demanded this tax from inland areas as well, causing widespread opposition. Although only nine years old at the time, John Bunyan must have caught something of the fury and frustration of locals required to contribute to this tax. Bedfordshire was ordered to raise £3,000, the cost of a 300 tonne ship — with many estates of local gentry being heavily charged to fund this levy.[1]

John Hampden, who had served as an MP before Charles dissolved his last Parliament in 1629, refused to pay the full amount of ship money demanded against his Buckinghamshire estates, declaring it to be an illegal tax. Although Hampden was ably defended by a Bedford lawyer in a famous test case in 1637, the ruling still went against him. But the case raised a furore amongst the public, for the people were already suffering from widespread inflation and food shortages.

Even more important than unjust taxation as a cause for the outbreak of Civil War was the religious policy fostered by the king and his High Church archbishop, William Laud. Soon after becoming archbishop in 1633, Laud had not only established unwelcome changes to church services, reintroducing Catholic procedures, but had banned the publication of certain popular books. Most notable of these was John Foxe's *Book of Martyrs*, second only to the Bible as standard reading. Some of Martin Luther's works also fell under the same axe. All publishers now had to obtain a licence from Laud, and any who offended could find themselves pilloried and publicly whipped.

Archbishop Laud's overriding aim was to bring about religious uniformity and to crush any form of Dissent. But his policy went one step too far when he tried to coerce the Scottish Kirk into submission. In 1637, with the aid of the Scottish bishops, he introduced certain amendments to the English *Book of Common Prayer*, and ordered it to be brought into use in the Scottish churches instead of John Knox's *Book of Common Order.* His strategy was thwarted at the very first reading from the new prayer book in St Giles Cathedral when, in an incident that has become proverbial, Jenny Geddes threw her stool at the Dean of Edinburgh, James Hannay, crying out, 'Villain, dost thou say Mass at my lug [ear]?'

Feelings ran high, and early the following year a 'National Covenant' was signed in Greyfriars Churchyard setting out the rights of the Scottish people. It commanded widespread support throughout the country. Still too obtuse to see that he was on a collision course with his northern subjects, Charles would not back down, declaring that he would force the Scots into unconditional submission. War quickly followed in 1639, but the English had little heart to help Charles in his fight against the Scots, who had their national pride and religious freedom at stake. Defeat was inevitable for Charles. Still determined to crush the recalcitrant Scots, the king was now desperate for more funds and had no alternative but to recall Parliament in order to raise the necessary revenue.

The new Parliament, summoned on 13 April 1640, was in no mood meekly to grant the king money for wars of which they seriously disapproved. They had other grievances to settle first, among them the policy of ship-money taxation, which Parliament insisted must be abandoned. Although the king agreed to this, Parliament still refused to grant him the massive subsidies he demanded to fight the Scots. After only three weeks Charles dismissed his Parliament yet again.

But the king had a staunch supporter in the person of Thomas Wentworth, Earl of Strafford. Wentworth, as Lord Deputy of Ireland, had ruthlessly subdued the Irish to the English Crown. Now, so it was alleged, he planned to raise an Irish army to aid the king's war effort against the Scots. Suspicion increased when Charles appointed Wentworth as commander-in-chief of his armed forces as he prepared once again to attack his northern kingdom. Reneging on his earlier promises of religious liberty, Charles initiated what became known as the Second Bishops' War. But a yet more humiliating defeat awaited Charles as the northerners crossed the Tyne, advancing into England itself.

Nothing now remained for the king but to swallow his pride and recall Parliament once again, for he was still unwilling to concede a final defeat in Scotland and was in dire need of money. In November 1640 Parliament reassembled, but this time the mood was even more belligerent. A list of reforms was presented to the king before any consideration of funding could be undertaken.

A proud nation, England had been humiliated by her own king and his main henchmen, Archbishop Laud and Thomas Wentworth. Now Parliament took its revenge against these allegedly 'evil councillors'. One of its first actions was to start impeachment proceedings against them. Archbishop Laud was accused of subverting the cause of true religion, and of high treason for his part in provoking the Bishops' Wars against Scotland. The Tower of London would be his prison for the next five years. Although it could not be proved that Thomas Wentworth had been plotting to bring over an Irish army to fight the king's cause, he became a scapegoat for the real culprit, Charles I. Despite his brilliant defence, the case went against him. The king reluctantly signed his death warrant and he was executed on 12 May 1641.

London was becoming chaotic and ungovernable with rioting mobs demanding further concessions from the king. Above all, no one knew how far the king could be trusted. Perhaps, it was suggested, he was just playing for time, making gestures which he planned to take back at the first opportune moment.

By the summer of 1641 a wary stand-off existed between the king and his Parliament, but in October a situation developed which became the immediate catalyst for outright civil war. The Irish, freed from the dominance of Wentworth's iron rule, rose up in rebellion against the English. Wild rumours flew around of 200,000 Protestants tortured or murdered, with the leaders of the uprising claiming that they had the support of Charles himself. Panic broke out in Parliament, and the king's slow return to London from a visit to Scotland only confirmed the rumours in many minds. English Catholics were joining their Irish counter-parts, or so it was alleged, in order to fight for the king against his Parliament.

Parliament's immediate reaction was to present the king with a document known as the Grand Remonstrance, listing over two hundred matters which the members wished to see reformed. Many clauses were aimed at curtailing the king's power: his advisers were to be approved by Parliament, the Court of the Star Chamber abolished, the powers of bishops reduced, with an 'Assembly of Divines' appointed to reform abuses that had crept into church life. The remonstrance went too far for many Members of Parliament. They began to fear the increasing power of Parliament as much as, or even more than, they feared the autocratic rule of the king.

Loud arguments broke out in Parliament amid scenes of wild disorder when the king's supporters tried to enter a protest against the proceedings. At midnight on 22 November 1641 the Grand Remonstrance was at last put to the vote. It only scraped through by eleven votes, with 159 in favour and 148 against. The opposing sides in the forthcoming Civil War were effectively formed that night as 'King versus Parliament'.

When further rumours reached Charles that Parliament purposed to impeach Queen Henrietta Maria herself for planning to secure French arms against England, the king's patience snapped. On 4 January 1642 he arrived in person at the House of

Commons to arrest and impeach five members whom he regarded as ringleaders in all these manoeuvres — but discovered that 'the birds have flown'. The members in question, having received prior warning, had fled the House, taking refuge in the City of London.

Both sides now began to prepare actively for war. The queen was dispatched to France, both for her own safety and to seek assistance from the French. Drums rolled and messengers travelled the length of the land, beating up support for their differing causes, while the king set up his court in York. Broadly speaking, the north, Wales and the west supported the king, while recruits for the parliamentary army were largely drawn from the south and east. Then, on 22 August 1642, Charles I, King of England, raised his standard in Nottingham, declaring war on his own people.

Appendix II
John Gifford's letter to his church
written shortly before his death in 1655

To the Church over which God made me an overseer when I was in the world:

I beseech you brethren beloved, let these following words (wrote in my love to you and care over you, when our heavenly Father was remooving me to the kingdome of his deare Son) be read in your Church gatherings together.

I shall not now, dearely beloved, write unto you about that which is the first, and without which all other things are as nothing in the sight of God, viz. The keeping the mystery of the faith in a pure conscience. I shall not, I say, write of these things (though the greatest) having spent my labours among you to root you and build you up in Christ (through the grace you have received) and to presse you to all manner of holynes in your conversations, that you may be found of the Lord without spot, and blameles at his coming.

But the things that I shall speake to you of, are about your Church affaires, which I feare have bene little considered by most of you; which things, if not minded aright and submitted unto according to the will of God, will by degrees bring you under divisions, distractions; and at last to confusion of that Gospell order and fellowship which now through grace you enjoy.

Therefore my brethren, in the first place I would not have any of you ignorant of this, that every one of you are as much bound now, to walke with the Church in all love, and in the ordinances of Jesus Christ our Lord, as when I was present among you; neither have any of you liberty to joyne your selves to any other society, because your pastor is removed from you, for you were not joyned to the ministery, but to Christ and the Church. And this is, and was, the will of God in Christ to all [the] churches of the saintes. Read Acts. 2.41 and compare it with Acts. 1.14, 15. And I charge you before the Lord, as you will answer it at the coming of our Lord Jesus, that none of you be found guilty herein.

Secondly. Be constant in your Church assemblyes. Let all the worke which concernes the Church be done faithfully amongst you; as admission of members, exercising of gifts, election of officers, as need requires, and all other things as if named, which the Scriptures being searched will lead you into through the Spirit. Which things if you doe, the Lord will be with you, and you will convince others that Christ is your head, and your dependency is not upon man. But if you do the worke of the Lord negligently, if you minde your owne things and not the things of Christ, if you grow of indifferent spirits, whether you minde the worke of the Lord in his Church or no, I feare the Lord by degrees will suffer the comfort of your communion to be dryed up, and the candlesticke which is yet standing, to be broken in pieces, which God forbid.

Now concerning your admission of members, I shall leave you to the Lord for counsaile, who hath hitherto bene with you. Onely thus much I thinke expedient, to stirre up your remembrance in, that after you are satisfyed in the worke of grace in the party you are to joyne with, the saide party do solemnly declare (before some of the Church at least), that union with Christ is the foundation of all saintes' communion, and not any ordinances of Christ, or any judgement or opinion about externalls. And the saide party ought to declare, whether a brother or sister, that through grace they will walke in love with the Church, though there should happen any difference in judgement about other things.

Concerning separation from the Church about baptisme, laying on of hands, anointing with oyle, psalmes, or any externalls, I charge every one of you respectively, as you will give an account for it to our Lord Jesus Christ, who shall judge both quick and dead at his coming, that none of you be found guilty of this great evill, which whiles some have committed and that through a zeale for God, yet not according to knowledge, they have erred from the lawe of the love of Christ, and have made a rent from the true Church which is but one.

I exhort you. brethren, in your comings together, let all things be done decently and in order according to the Scriptures. Let all things be done among you without strife and envy, without self-seeking and vaine glory. Be clothed with humility and submit to one another in love. Let the gifts of the Church be exercised according to order. Let no gift be concealed which is for edification: yet let those gifts be chiefely exercised which are most for the perfecting of the saintes. Let your discourses be to build up one another in your most holy faith and to provoke one another to love and good works. If this be not well minded much time may be spent and the Church reape little or no advantage. Let there be strong meate for the strong, and milke for babes. In your assemblies avoide all disputes which gender to strifes, as questions about externalls, and all doubt-full disputations. If any come among you who will be contentious in these things, let it be declared that you have no such order, nor any of the Churches of God. If any come among you with any doctrine contrary to the doctrine of Christ, you must not treat with such an one as with a brother or enter into dispute of the things of faith with reasonings (for this is contrary to the Scriptures) but let such of the brethren who are fullest of the Spirit and Word of Christ, oppose such an one stedfastly, face to face, and lay open his folly to the Church from the Scriptures.

If a brother (through weakenes) speake any thing contrary to any knowne truth of God (though not intended by him), some other brother of the Church must in love cleare up the truth, [lest] many of the Church lie laid under temptation. Let no respect of persons be in your comings together. When you are met as a Church, there's neither rich nor poor, bond nor free, in Christ Jesus. Tis not a good practise to be offering places or seates, when those who are rich come in. Especially 'tis a great evill to take notice of such in time of prayer or the Word: then are bowings and civill observances at such times not of God. Private wrongs are not presently to be brought unto the Church. If any of the brethren be troubled about externalls, let some of the Church (let it not be a Church busines) pray for and with such parties.

None ought to withdraw from the Church if any brother should walke disorderly, but he that walketh disorderly must beare his owne burthen according to the Scriptures. If any brother should walke disorderly, he cannot be shut out from any ordinance before Church censure. Study among yourselves what is the nature of fellowship, as the Word, prayer and breaking of bread, which whilest few, I judge, seriously consider, there is much falling short of duty in the Churches of Christ. You that are most eminent in profession, set a patterne to all the rest of the Church. Let your faith, love and zeale be very eminent: if any of you cast a dimme light, you will do much hurt to the Church.

Let there be kept up among you solemne dayes of prayer and thanksgiving, and let some time be set apart to seek God for your needs, which thing hath hitherto bene omitted. Let your deacons have a constant stock by them to supply the necessities of those who are in want. Truly, brethren, there is utterly a fault among you that are rich especially in this thing. Tis not that little which comes from you on the first day of the week that will excuse you. I beseech you be not found guilty of this sin any longer. He that sowes sparingly will reap sparingly. Be not backward in your gatherings together. Let none of you willingly stay till part of the meeting be come, especially such who should be examples to the flock.

One or two things are omitted about your comings together, which I shall here adde. I beseech you forbeare sitting in prayer, except parties be any way disabled. Tis not a posture that suites with the majesty of such an ordinance. Would you serve your prince so? In prayer let all self-affected expressions be avoyded and all vain repetitions. God hath not gifted, I judge, every brother to be a mouth to the Church. Let such as have most of the demonstration of the Spirit, and of power, shut up all your comings together, that ye may go away with your heartes comforted, and quickened. Come together in time, and leave off orderly, for God is a God of order amongst his saints. Let none of you give offence to his brother in indifferent things, but be subject to one another in love.

Be very carefull what gifts you approve of by consent for publick service. Spend much time before the Lord about choosing a pastor, for though I suppose he is before you whom the Lord hath appointed, yet it will be no disadvantage to you I hope if you walke a yeare or two as you arc before election. And then (if you be all agreed) let him be set apart according to the Scriptures.

Salute the brethren who walke not in fellowship with you, with the same love and name of brother or sister as those who do. Let the promises made to be accomplished in the latter dayes, be often urged before the Lord in your comings together, and forget not your brethren in bonds.

Love him much for the worke's sake who labours over you in the word and doctrine: let no man despise his youth. Muzzle not the mouth of the ox that treads out the corn to you. Search the Scriptures. Let some of them be read to you about this thing. If your teacher at any time be laide aside, you ought to meet together as a Church, and build up one another. If the members at such a time will go to a publick ministery, it must first be approoved of by the Church.

Farewell. Exhort, counsaile, support, reproove one another in love. Finally, brethren, be all of one minde. Walke in love one to another, even as Christ Jesus hath loved you and given himself for you. Search the Scriptures for a supply of those things wherein I am wanting.

Now the God of peace, who raised up our Lord Jesus Christ from the dead, multiply his peace upon you, and preserve you to his everlasting kingdome by Jesus Christ. Stand fast. The Lord is at hand. That this was written by me I have set my name to it, in the presence of two of the brethren of the Church.

John Gifford

Appendix III
John Bunyan's Deed of Gift
1685

To all people to whom this present writing shall com J Bunyan of the parish of St. Cuthbirts in the towne of Bedford in the county of Bedford Brazier send greeting. Know ye that I the said John Bunyan as well for and in consideration of the natural affection and love which I have and bear unto my welbeloved wife Elizabeth Bunyan as also for divers other good causes and considerations me at this present esspecially mouving, have given and granted, and by these presents do give, grant and conform unto the said Elizabeth Bunyan my said wife all and singular my goods, chattel, debts, ready mony, plate, Rings, household stuffe, Aparrel, utensills, Brass, pewter, Beding, and all other my substance whatsoever, moueable and immoueable of what kinde, nature, quality, or condition soever the same are or be, and in what place, or places soever the same be, shall or may be found, as well in mine own custody possession as in the possession, having power and custody of any other person or persons whatsoever, To have and to hold all and singular the said goods, chattels, debts, and all other the aforesaid premises unto the said Elizabeth, my wife her executors administrators and assigns to her and their proper uses and behoofs freely and quietly without any matter of challinge, claime or demand of me the said John Bunyan or of any other person or persons what soever for me, in my name by my means, caus or procurement and without any mony or other thing therefore to be yielded paid or done unto me, the said John Bunyan, my executors, administrators or assigns.

And I, the said John Bunyan, all and singular the aforesaid goods, chattels and premises to the said Elizabeth my wife her executors administrators and asignes to the use aforesaid against all people do warrant and for ever defend by these presents. And further know ye that I the said John Bunyan have put the said Elizabeth my wife, in a peaceable and quiet possession of all and singular the aforesaid premises, by the delivrye unto her at the ensealing hereof one coyned peece of silver commonly called two pence fixed on the seal of these presents...

In Wittnes whereof I the said John Bunyan have hereunto set my hand and seall this 23^{d} day of December, in the first year of the reigne of our souvraigne lord King James the Second of England &c, in the year of our lord and saviour Jesus Christ 1685.

John Bunyan

Sealed and delivered in the
presence of us whos names
are here under written

John Bardolph
Nicholas Malin
William Hawkes
Lewes Norman

Appendix IV

Bunyan's works

in order of writing, with dates of publication

1	Some Gospel Truths Opened	1656
2	Vindication of Some Gospel Truths Opened	1657
3	A Few sighs from Hell	1658
4	The Doctrine of Law and Grace Unfolded	1659
5	Profitable Meditations	1661
6	A Discourse Touching Prayer	1663
7	Christian Behaviour	1663
8	A map showing the order of salvation	1664
9	The Holy City	1665
10	One thing is Needful (poem)	1665
11	The Resurrection of the Dead	1665
12	Ebal and Gerizim (poem)	1665
13	Prison Meditations (poem)	1665
14	**Grace Abounding to the Chief of Sinners**	**1666**
15	The Heavenly Footman	1698*
16	**The Pilgrim's Progress**	**1678**
17	A Confession of my Faith	1672
18	A Defence of the Doctrine of Justification by Faith	1672
19	Differences in Judgment ... no bar to Communion	1673
20	The Barren Fig-tree	1673
21	Peaceable Principles and True	1674
22	Light for them that sit in Darkness	1673
23	Instruction for the Ignorant	1675
24	The Strait Gate	1676
25	Of Justification by Imputed Righteousness	1692*

*Titles published by Charles Doe

Bunyan did not write *An Exhortation to Peace and Unity*.
And there is considerable doubt over whether he wrote *Reprobation Asserted*.

Glossary

Apocrypha: Biblical writings appended to the Old Testament in the Vulgate and Septuagint versions but not considered (by Protestants) to be part of the canon of Scripture.

Assizes: Historical term for a court that sat at intervals in each county of England and Wales to administer civil and criminal law.

Brazier: Literally, a worker in brass, but the term was used in a wider sense to cover other kinds of metalwork.

Conventicles: Private gatherings for worship, frowned upon and often made illegal by the state church.

Court of the Star Chamber: A court of appeal in Tudor times, but under the Stuarts one that was increasingly used to suppress opposition to both royal and church dictates. Abolished in 1641.

Dissenters: Term used throughout this work to describe non-episcopal congregations, such as General Baptists, Particular Baptists, Congregationalists and Presbyterians.

Footman: A pedestrian; a (good, fast, etc.) walker or runner.

Independents: Sometimes a collective work for all Dissenters, but more accurately used as another name for Congregationalists.

Justice of the Peace: A lay magistrate appointed to preserve the peace in a county, town, etc., and discharge other local magisterial functions, as hearing minor cases and granting licences.

Levellers: Political radicals whose agenda included an extended franchise, religious toleration, reform of the law and free trade.

Nonconformists: Term used to describe those unwilling to consent unconditionally to everything contained in the 1662 *Book of Common Prayer* and therefore to subscribe to the Act of Uniformity.

Tinker: A person who made a living by travelling from place to place, mending pans and other utensils.

Notes

Works cited for which no author is given are by John Bunyan.

Foreword
1. *Grace Abounding to the Chief of Sinners* (Evangelical Press, 1978), p.122.

Preface and acknowledgements
1. Republished by the Banner of Truth Trust, 1991.

Prologue — 'Coals of holy fire'
1. The exact location of Stephen Moore's house is unknown. Roger Sharrock suggests Winchester Yard, Southwark, as the probable locality.
2. Quotations taken from *The Desire of the Righteous Granted, The Works of John Bunyan,* ed. George Offor (The Banner of Truth Trust, 1991), vol. 1. p.759. (Offor's edition is hereafter referred to as *Works.*)
3. Charles Doe, *A Collection of Experience,* 1700, British Library.

Chapter 2 — 'A hint of my pedigree'
1. John Brown, *John Bunyan, his Life, Times and Work,* London, 1885, p.33. In this first edition John Brown states that a further eighteen cottages had two hearths, eight had three, and the remaining ten homes had between four and seventeen hearths apiece.
2. Items such as tables, a bed, brass kettle, flaxen sheet and pillow, her best bolster and blanket, as well as listed items of clothing, were bequeathed to her five other children.
3. Also born in this same year of 1628 were three other prominent Puritans: Stephen Charnock, John Flavel and Walter Marshall. Richard Baxter was thirteen at the time.

Chapter 3 — Childhood days

1. *A Book for Boys and Girls*, *Works*, vol. 3, p.758.
2. *Grace Abounding to the Chief of Sinners*, *Works*, vol. 1, para. 3.
3. Bunyan refers in a poem to 'what I gained in a grammar school in my minority', *Works*, vol. 2, p.390.
4. *Grace Abounding*, para. 5.
5. *The Life and Death of Mr Badman*, *Works*, vol. 3, pp.596-7.
6. *Grace Abounding*, para. 5.
7. George Offor's *Memoir*, *Works*, vol. 1, p.v.
8. *Grace Abounding*, para. 6.
9. *Ibid.*, paras. 4-7.
10. *Ibid.*, para. 8.
11. *The Jerusalem Sinner Saved*, *Works*, vol. 1, p.79.
12. *Grace Abounding*, para. 11.
13. *Ibid.*, para. 12.
14. *Ibid.*, para. 10.
15. *Ibid.*

Chapter 4 — A soldier's lot

1. Paul Johnson, *A History of the English People* (London: Weidenfeld and Nicolson, 1985), p.187. For a brief account of the immediate causes of the Civil War, see Appendix I.
2. Out of the country's approximate population of five million, a figure of 250,000 men, made up of both Parliamentarians and Royalists, has been given as an estimate of those who died as a result of the Civil War.
3. Robert Devereux, 3rd Earl of Essex, son of Queen Elizabeth's one-time favourite who lost her goodwill — as well as his head — in 1601.
4. Earlier biographies of Bunyan suggest that he may have fought in the Royalist army, but the question was settled in 1896 when Bunyan's name was discovered in the muster rolls for Newport Pagnell garrison among the 'centinells'. Some have suggested that it may have been a different 'John Bunnion', but our subject's later close friendship with his first publisher, a Newport Pagnell man, and also with the minister of the Newport Pagnell church, John Gibbs, cannot be coincidental.
5. His name is also found on the muster rolls for each week in December 1644, January 1645, the first two weeks of February and of March, after which he served in a different company.
6. *Grace Abounding*, para.14.
7. Sir Samuel Luke, *The Letter Books, 1644-45*, ed. H. G. Tibbutt (HMSO, 1963), Letters 119, 121-2.
8. A committee set up in 1643 made up of twenty-one Scots and English Parliamentarians to oversee the conduct of the war.

9. Luke, *The Letter Books*, Letters 223-7.
10. *Ibid.*, Letter 187.

Chapter 5 — A babble of voices
1. *Grace Abounding*, para. 13.
2. Richard L. Greaves, *Glimpses of Glory, John Bunyan and English Dissent* (Stanford University Press, 2002).
3. *The Life and Actions of Mr John Bunyan from his Cradle to his Grave, 1692*, pp 17-18. (This was bound with a spurious Part 3 of *The Pilgrim's Progress*.)
4. Cited by Christopher Hill, *A Tinker and a Poor Man, John Bunyan and his Church, 1628-1688* (New York: Alfred A. Knopf, 1989), p.54.
5. *Grace Abounding*, para. 12.

Chapter 6 — The young brazier
1. Hill, *A Tinker and a Poor Man*, p.63.
2. Diggers, described as communist pacifists, wanted total equality for all. See Paul Johnson, *A History of the English People*, London, 1972, p.200.
3. Ranters were a fanatical sect who were both antinomian and pantheistic, substituted inward experience for the authority of Scripture and debunked traditional moral standards. The term 'Ranter' was inappropriately used in the nineteenth century to refer to the Primitive Methodists and other Nonconformist preachers.
4. *The Doctrine of Law and Grace Unfolded, Works*, vol. 1, p.548.
5. See Richard L. Greaves, *Glimpses of Glory*, chapter 2, 'Spiritual and Psychological Crisis'.
6. *Grace Abounding*, para. 15.
7. This anvil is now displayed in the Bunyan Museum in Bedford.
8. *Grace Abounding*, para. 15.
9. Arthur Dent, *The Plaine Man's Path-way to Heaven, a sermon on repentance*, 1601, p.158.
10. Republished 1974.
11. Recently reprinted by Soli Deo Gloria Publications.
12. *Grace Abounding*, para. 16.
13. *Ibid.*, paras. 16, 17.
14. *Ibid.*, para. 20.
15. *Ibid.*, para. 21.

Chapter 7 — A 'kind of despair'
1. *Grace Abounding*, para. 22.
2. Bunyan uses words of Hopeful in *The Pilgrim's Progress* to describe a similar experience. Hopeful says, 'I did not see him with my bodily eyes, but with the eyes of my understanding. [But] ... suddenly, as I thought, I

saw the Lord Jesus Christ look down from heaven upon me...' *Pilgrim's Progress, Works,* vol. 3, p.155.
3. *Grace Abounding,* para. 23.
4. *Ibid.*
5. *Ibid.,* para. 24.
6. *The Jerusalem Sinner Saved, Works,* vol. 1, p.79.
7. *The Doctrine of Law and Grace Unfolded, Works,* vol. 1, p.549.
8. *Grace Abounding,* para. 26.
9. *Ibid.*
10. *Ibid.,* para. 27.
11. *Ibid.,* para. 28.
12. *Ibid.,* para. 30.
13. *Ibid.,* para. 32.
14. *Ibid.*
15. This violin can be seen in the Bunyan Museum in Bedford.
16. *Ibid.,* para. 33.
17. *Ibid.,* para. 34.
18. From the preface to *Grace Abounding.*
19. Michael Davies, *Graceful Reading,* OUP, 2002.

Chapter 8 — What the tinker overheard
1. The exact title is unknown, but it was probably Robert Bolton's *The Four Last Things: Death, Judgment, Hell and Heaven,* 1635.
2. *Minutes of the First Independent Church at Bedford, 1656–1766,* ed. H. G. Tibbutt, 1976, p.17.
3. The probable time of these events was in the summer of 1651.
4. *Grace Abounding,* para. 37.
5. Quotations from *Grace Abounding,* paras. 37-39.
6. *Ibid.,* para. 40.
7. *Ibid.,* para. 41.
8. *Ibid.,* para 45.
9. Romans 8:6-7.
10. *Grace Abounding,* para 44.
11. *Ibid.,* para. 45.
12. *Ibid.,* para 46.
13. *The Doctrine of Law and Grace Unfolded, Works,* vol. 1, p.549.
14. *Ibid.*

Chapter 9 — The roaring lion
1. *Grace Abounding,* para. 48.
2. *Ibid.,* para. 51.
3. *Ibid.,* paras. 53, 54.
4. *Ibid.,* para. 57.

5. *Ibid.*, paras. 61, 62.
6. Ecclesiasticus 2:10.
7. *Grace Abounding*, para. 68.
8. *Ibid.*, para. 73.
9. *Ibid.*, paras. 77, 78.
10. John Walford, *The Life and Labours of Hugh Bourne*, reprinted Berith Publications, 1999, vol. 1, p.43.
11. John Cennick (1718–1755), Autobiographical Preface to *Cennick's Hymns*, 1741, ed. J. R. Broome, Gospel Standard Trust, 1988, p.xxxiv.
12. *Grace Abounding*, para. 79.
13. *Ibid.*, para 82.
14. *Ibid.*, para. 83.
15. *Ibid.*, para. 92.

Chapter 10 — 'Satan has desired to have you'

1. A play on the name of one of the members for London, a leather merchant called Praise-God Barbon.
2. The eleven years from 1649 to the Restoration of the Monarchy in 1660 are often referred to as the Commonwealth period, but this is in fact a misnomer.
3. *The Law and Grace Unfolded, Works*, vol. 1, p.549.
4. Charles Doe, *The Struggler*, Bunyan's *Works*, vol. 3, p.765.
5. *Grace Abounding*, para. 97. The Koran was first translated into English in 1649.
6. *Ibid.*, para. 106.
7. C. H. Spurgeon's *Autobiography, compiled … by his wife*, Passmore and Alabaster, 1897, vol. 1, p.86.
8. *Grace Abounding*, para. 115.
9. *Ibid.*, para. 116.
10. *Ibid.*, para. 117.
11. The clue to this being the case lies in his references to the Quakers, how he studied the errors of their teaching (paras. 119-23) and how he gained spiritual assurance soon afterwards (paras. 126-9). He refers to these same events in his *Doctrine of Law and Grace Unfolded* (*Works*, vol.1, p.549), which we are able to date because we know that the Quakers became active in Bedford in 1656. I will therefore leave paragraphs 119-28 until what appears to be their appropriate place in his life story.
12. Paragraphs 129-30 were in any case added six years after the original publication in 1666, while paragraphs 124 and 125, detailing the teaching of the Quakers, were not added until 1677.

Chapter 11 — 'Sell him, sell him!'

1. Preface to *Grace Abounding*, vol. 1. p.5.
2. Davies, *Graceful Reading*, p.89. Davies continues: 'One self-evident way of denouncing, depopularizing and demonising those who held a non-rationalist, providentialist and separatist view of faith is, therefore, to refer to them as insane fanatics who intend to tear the fabric of social order apart' (*Ibid.*, p.90).
3. Edward Fowler, *Dirt wip'd off, or a manifest discovery of the gross ignorance, erroneousness, and most unchristian and wicked spirit of one Bunyan ...*, London, Royston, 1672.
4. *Ibid.*, pp 2,3,70.
5. J. A. Froude, *Bunyan*, Macmillan & Co., 1902, p.47.
6. Josiah Conder, preface to an edition of *The Life and Writings of John Bunyan*, New York, 1850.
7. Gaius Davies, *Genius and Grace*, Hodder and Stoughton, 1992, p.62.
8. *Ibid.*, p.64.
9. The Keswick Movement, inaugurated in 1875, with its emphasis on victorious Christian living, frowned on any admission of weakness, depression or failure among those claiming to be Christians.
10. See Thomas Goodwin, *A child of light walking in darkness*, Edinburgh, James Nichol, 1861, vol. 3, p.235; William Bridge, *A lifting up for the downcast*, Banner of Truth Trust, 1961; Richard Sibbes, *The bruised reed and smoking flax*, Edinburgh, James Nichol, 1862, vol. 1, p.42. See also D. Martyn Lloyd-Jones, *Spiritual Depression, its Causes and its Cure*, Pickering and Inglis, 1964.
11. *Grace Abounding*, para. 132.
12. *Ibid.*, para. 133.
13. *Ibid.*, para. 135.
14. *Ibid.*, paras. 139-40.
15. *Ibid.*, para. 142.
16. *Ibid.*, paras. 143-4.
17. Mark 3:29.
18. *Grace Abounding*, para. 149.
19. Nathaniel Bacon, *A Relation of the fearful estate of Francis Spira in the year 1548*, London, 1672, p.62.
20. *Grace Abounding*, para. 163.
21. He only added it in the third edition, probably published after 1672. The first edition was 1666, and the second, of which no copy remains, probably 1667.
22. *Grace Abounding*, para. 175.
23. *Ibid.*, para. 226.
24. *Ibid.*, para. 224.
25. *Ibid.*, paras. 229-30.

26. *Ibid.*, para. 231.
27. Alexander Whyte, *Bunyan Characters, Bunyan himself as seen in his Grace Abounding.* London, 1908, p.257.

Chapter 12 — 'Gold in my trunk'
1. *Grace Abounding,* para. 232.
2. See 1 Corinthians 1:30.
3. *Grace Abounding,* para. 246.
4. *Ibid.*, para. 250.
5. *Ibid.*, para. 252.
6. *Ibid.*, paras. 252-3.
7. The building was demolished in 1838. The site is now marked with a plaque.
8. For John Gifford's dying instructions to his church see Appendix II, pp.468-72.
9. See chapter 10, notes 11 and 12 (p.483). The following passage regarding Luther fits in naturally at this point, although Bunyan did not insert it into his narrative until 1672, six years after the original publication.
10. *Grace Abounding,* para. 129.
11. *Ibid.*
12. *Ibid.*
13. Martin Luther, *Commentary on the Epistle to the Galatians,* first published 1535, James Clarke edition, 1953, p.24.
14. *Grace Abounding,* para. 229.
15. Cf. Romans 7:13.
16. *Grace Abounding,* para. 130.
17. *Ibid.*, para. 257.
18. *Ibid.*, para. 259.
19. *Minutes of the First Independent Church at Bedford,* p.21.
20. *Grace Abounding,* para. 124.
21. *The Doctrine of Law and Grace Unfolded, Works,* vol. 1, p.549.
22. *Ibid.*
23. Probably Anne Blaykling, one of the early Quaker missionaries.
24. Grimshaw's experiences bear remarkable similarities to those of Bunyan. He writes, 'Young Christians are by and by, like their Master led into the wilderness... At this time we think that we are not God's child, that we are not justified nor pardoned, that we are mistaken with ourselves... After the devil has tried us thus for a season, he then assaults us with evil imaginations and blasphemous thoughts, doubts about the authority of the holy Scriptures, scruples about the divinity of our Saviour... At these times we are apt to reason with ourselves, saying, Surely we are not born again; surely we are not sons of God, for if we

were, why are we thus?' (See Faith Cook, *William Grimshaw of Haworth*, Banner of Truth Trust, 1997, pp.72-3).
25. *Grace Abounding*, para. 128.

Chapter 13 — Called to preach
1. *The Doctrine of Law and Grace Unfolded*, p.549.
2. *Ibid.*
3. *Grace Abounding*, para. 265.
4. *Ibid.*, para. 266.
5. *Works of John Owen*, ed. William Orme, 1826, vol. 2, p.88.
6. *Grace Abounding*, para. 268.
7. *Ibid.*, para. 269.
8. *Ibid.*
9. *Ibid.*, para 274.
10. *Ibid.*, para. 276.
11. *Ibid.*, paras. 276-7.
12. John Newton, *Memoirs of the Life of the Late Rev. William Grimshaw, A. B, in Six Letters.* Hamilton, 1814, pp.44, 46.
13. *Grace Abounding*, para. 275; cf. I Corinthians 9:2.
14. *Ibid.*, para. 278.
15. *Ibid.*, para. 282.

Chapter 14 — Defending the faith
1. *Some Gospel Truths Opened, Works*, vol. 2, pp.141, 147, 149-50, etc.
2. *Ibid.*, p.152.
3. Galen K. Johnson elaborates further: 'For Bunyan, conscience was not autonomous, for only when it learns from the preached scriptures to feel the terrible burden of personal sin does it begin its progression towards Christ' (*Prisoner of Conscience*, Milton Keynes: Paternoster, 2003, p.12).
4. *Some Gospel Truths Opened*, p.162.
5. *Ibid.*, p.175.
6. *Ibid.*, from 'the Author to the Reader', pp.132-8.
7. *Ibid.*, p.141.
8. *Ibid.*
9. *Grace Abounding*, para. 260.
10. *Ibid.*, para. 263.

Chapter 15 — Repercussions
1. The absence of a capital letter for 'son' was significant to the Quakers.
2. Edward Burrough, *The True Faith of the Gospel of Peace*, London: 1657, p.137.
3. *A Vindication of Gospel Truths, Works*, vol. 2, p.181.
4. *Ibid.*, p.183.

5. *Ibid.*, p.201.
6. *Ibid.*, p.193.
7. *Ibid.*, p.210.
8. John Brown, *John Bunyan, his Life, Times and Work,* London, 1918, vol. 1, p.110.

Chapter 16 — Reproaches for Christ's sake

1. This concept was based on Daniel's vision in Daniel 2 of the four kingdoms that crumbled and of Christ's everlasting kingdom which was to be the fifth and final kingdom.
2. George Cokayne, also a Bedfordshire man and a friend of Bunyan's, was another.
3. In a later treatise entitled *The Work of Jesus Christ as an Advocate,* Bunyan refers to this: 'I did use to be much taken with one sect of Christians; for that it was usually their way when they made mention of the name of Jesus, to call him "The blessed King of Glory".' (*Works,* vol.1 p.193). A discussion of this is found in Richard L. Greaves, *John Bunyan and English Nonconformity,* The Hambleton Press, 1992, ch. 8.
4. *Grace Abounding,* para. 289.
5. *Ibid.*, para. 283.
6. *Minutes of First Independent Church at Bedford,* p.29 (entry for 25 December 1657).
7. 'It was concluded ... that the members of the Church of Christ in and around Steventon may breake bread with us and we with them' (*Minutes of First Independent Church at Bedford,* p.23).
8. *Grace Abounding,* paras. 311-12.
9. Henry Denne, 1605–66, a fearless controversialist and defender of Baptist principles, but a tolerant and just man with broad sympathies.
10. *Works,* vol. 1, p.xliii. The scholar's name has not been preserved.
11. *Grace Abounding,* para. 288.
12. *Ibid.*, para. 296.
13. *Ibid.*, paras. 300-301.
14. *Ibid.*, paras. 306-8.
15. Bunyan spells her name like this, but she was probably Anne Blaykling, one of the early Quakers.
16. *A Vindication of Gospel Truths, Works,* vol. 2, p.201.
17. Preface to *Works of John Bunyan,* 1692, written by Ebenezer Chandler and John Wilson.
18. *A Few Sighs from Hell, Works,* vol. 3. p.682.
19. *Ibid.*, p.694.
20. Quotations from the introduction to *A Few Sighs from Hell, Works,* vol. 3. p.677. George Offor wrongly ascribes this introduction to John

Gifford (whose initials were the same). However, Gifford had been dead three years by this time.

21. Although the term 'Dissenter' did not come into general use until after 1688, it is used throughout this work to describe non-episcopal congregations, such as Baptists (General and Particular), Congregationalists and Presbyterians. The term 'Independent' is strictly speaking another word for Congregationalists, but references to Independent churches can refer to the entire grouping. Those ejected from the Church of England after 1662 are sometimes called Dissenters but it is more common to use the term 'Nonconformists' in reference to them.

Chapter 17 — The gathering storm

1. Many who write on Bunyan confine their comments to his better-known works, omitting the biographical content in his other writings, so presenting a less than accurate picture of the man.
2. Martin Luther, *The Epistle to the Galatians*, James Clarke, 1953, p.160.
3. *The Doctrine of Law and Grace Unfolded, Works*, vol. 1, p.523.
4. *Ibid.*, p.563.
5. *Ibid.*, p.550.
6. *Ibid.*, pp.572-3.
7. *Ibid*, p.496.
8. *Ibid.*, p.495.
9. *Minutes of First Independent Church at Bedford*, p.34.
10. Eric C. Walker, *William Dell, Master Puritan*, Cambridge, 1970, p.35.
11. *Ibid.*, p.2.

Chapter 18 — 'One here will constant be'

1. *Minutes of First Independent Church at Bedford*, p.36.
2. *Ibid.*
3. *Grace Abounding, Works*, vol. 1, p.50.
4. *Ibid.*
5. Nehemiah 6:11.
6. *Grace Abounding*, p.51.
7. *The Saints Knowledge of Christ's Love, Works*, vol. 2, p.13.
8. *Grace Abounding*, p.51.
9. *Ibid.*, pp.51-2.

Chapter 19 — By the light of a candle

1. *Grace Abounding*, p.52.
2. *Ibid.*, para. 283.
3. The full text reads: 'As every man hath received the gift, even so minister the same one to another, as good stewards of the manifold

grace of God. If any man speak, let him speak as the oracles of God; if any man minister, let him do it as of the ability which God giveth.'

4. Although Bunyan did not mention the name of the one whom his friends had consulted, except to call him 'a pretended friend,' it was almost certainly William Foster, a Doctor of Law in Bedford, who, as we shall see, appeared on the scene in Harlington at that moment.

5. *Grace Abounding*, p.52.

6. This is a reference to Psalm 55:21.

7. Foster was actually Francis Wingate's brother-in-law, husband of his sister Amy, who had recently died.

8. *Grace abounding*, para. 326.

9. *Ibid.*, p.54.

10. *Grace Abounding*, paras. 324-5.

11. Then called Gaol Lane.

Chapter 20 — A prisoner of conscience

1. One of these can now be seen in the Bunyan Museum, next door to the Bunyan Meeting Free Church. Another is in the Moot Hall museum, Elstow.

2. Description taken from John Howard, *The State of the Prisons in England and Wales*, London, 1785, p.283.

3. Francis Smith, one of Bunyan's early publishers, was imprisoned in 1661. At one point he was charged £5 for the privilege of sleeping for three nights without chains. Sometimes prisons were so overcrowded that there was no space to lie, and men had to sleep standing against a wall (See G. R. Cragg, *Puritanism, The Great Persecution*, Cambridge, 1957, pp.95-101).

4. *The Resurrection of the Dead, Works*, vol. 2, p.111.

5. *Grace Abounding, Works*, vol. 1, p.54.

6. *Ibid.*

7. *Ibid.*, paras. 328-9.

8. Froude, *Bunyan*, p.72. Another biographer, Dr Robert Southey, also suggests that Bunyan was both unreasonable and intolerant before the magistrates in *Cromwell and Bunyan* (1830), John Murray — Select Biographies 1846. Alfred Noyes, who set out to discredit Bunyan in *The Bookman* in 1928, can also be added to the list, together with W. H. Hutton, also writing in 1928.

9. *The Baptist Confession of Faith*, originally compiled in 1677 but published in 1689, states the doctrine succinctly: 'The way appointed by Christ for the calling of any person, fitted and gifted by the Holy Spirit unto the office of bishop or elder in a church, is that he be chosen thereunto by the common suffrage of the church itself, and solemnly set

apart by fasting and prayer, with imposition of the hands of the eldership of the church' (Section entitled 'Of the Church', para. 9).

10. *Prison Meditations, Works,* vol. 1, p.64.

11. Cragg, *Puritanism, The Great Persecution,* p.94.

12. *Grace Abounding,* para. 329.

Chapter 21 — The trial

1. *Grace Abounding,* p.57.

2. Thomas McCrie, *The Story of the Scottish Church,* reprinted 1988, p.258.

3. *Grace Abounding,* p.54.

4. *Ibid.,* para 332-3.

5. *Ibid.,* para. 336.

6. *Ibid.,* para. 337.

7. *Ibid.,* paras. 338-9.

Chapter 22 — Seeking a royal pardon

1. *Grace Abounding,* p.58.

2. These included pronouncing baptized infants regenerate; granting communion to unbelievers; using the sign of the cross; using words at a funeral that suggested that all die as believers — as well as the compulsory imposition of everything else in the Prayer Book, which included about six hundred changes to wording.

3. John Brown, *John Bunyan,* vol. 1, p.149.

4. Highway robbers operating on foot.

5. This confusion could well be due to a misreading of Bunyan's manuscript.

6. *Profitable Meditations,* printed by Francis Smith, 1661, p.18. Smith himself was imprisoned in August 1661, so he must have received this manuscript earlier that year. The work was not republished until it came to the attention of George Offor in 1860, and was therefore not included in his 1854 edition of *The Works of John Bunyan,* published by W. G. Blackie, from which the Banner of Truth Trust reprint was taken.

7. *Grace Abounding,* para. 323.

Chapter 24 — Living on the invisible God

1. Brown, *John Bunyan,* vol. 1, p.162, cited from State Papers of Charles II.

2. *Minutes of First Independent Church at Bedford,* p.37.

3. *Grace Abounding,* p.62.

4. *Ibid.*

5. This was a high fee; when John Howard, the prison reformer, was writing in 1775, over a hundred years later, it amounted to seventeen shillings and fourpence with an extra two shillings for the turnkey.

6. *Grace Abounding*, para. 326.
7. *Ibid.*, para. 321.
8. *Ibid.*, para. 323.
9. *Ibid.*
10. *Prison Meditations, Works*, vol. 1, p.64.
11. *Letters of Samuel Rutherford*, Banner of Truth Trust, 1984, p.354.
12. G. R. Cragg, *Puritanism in the Period of the Great Persecution*, CUP, 1957, p.7.
13. Among the better known of those who were thrown out of their livings in addition to Baxter were Oliver Heywood, John Howe, Edmund Calamy, Matthew Poole, whose *Commentary* is still used today, Thomas Manton, Joseph Alleine, John Owen, Thomas Goodwin, Stephen Charnock, Samuel Annesley, John Wesley's grandfather, and John Flavel, to name but a few.
14. Cragg, *Puritanism in the Period of the Great Persecution*, p.8.
15. Cited by L. F. Lupton in *Free Grace Record*, 1962, p.30.
16. *Works*, vol. 1, p.630. Also *Prayer*, Banner of Truth Trust reprint, 1965, pp.59-60.

Chapter 25 — A prisoner of hope
1. For example, the anonymous songs, 'There is a lady sweet and kind' and 'Barbara Allen', both of which date from the seventeenth century.
2. See B. A. Ramsbottom, *Stranger than Fiction, The Life of William Kiffin*, Gospel Standard Trust Publications, 1989, pp.47-50.
3. Quotes from *Prison Meditations, Works*, vol. 1, pp.64-6.
4. Reprinted, Banner of Truth Trust, 1965.
5. *A Discourse Touching Prayer, Works*, vol. 1, p.623.
6. *Ibid.*, p.631. Also Banner of Truth edition, p.32.
7. *Minutes of First Independent Church at Bedford*, p.38.
8. *Christian Behaviour, Works*, vol. 2, p.569.
9. *Ibid.*, p.574.

Chapter 26 — The city of gold
1. The flute, together with the violin, can still be seen displayed in the Bunyan Museum, Bedford.
2. As George Wither found to his cost, when he produced *Hymns and Songs of the Church* in 1623 and suffered persecution for his pains.
3. Named after its chief architect, Edward Hyde, 1st Earl of Clarendon, Charles II's Lord Chancellor.
4. Newhouse Baptist Church, Smeatharpe, in Devon, once bordered Devon, Somerset and Dorset. The first meeting house on that plot dates from this time, with the original 1652 pulpit still in use today in the present building.

5. The attitude displayed towards Dissenters may be illustrated by lines quoted by W. Y. Tindall in *John Bunyan, Mechanic Preacher*, 1934, p.70.

This kind of vermin swarm like caterpillars
and hold conventicles in barnes and sellars
some preach (or prate) in woods, in fields, in stables,
in hollow trees, on tubs or tops of tables.

6. Brown, *John Bunyan*, vol. 1, p.167.
7. *The Holy City, Works*, vol. 3, pp.397-8.
8. *Ibid.*, p.429.
9. *Ibid.*, p.401.
10. Revelation 13:18.
11. By 'Antichrist' Bunyan understood not so much one individual as a whole world system opposed to Christ, headed up and ruled over by Satan (See *Antichrist and his Ruin, Works*, vol. 2, p.46).
12. Bunyan would later express regret over 'the forwardness of some ... who have predicted concerning the time of the downfall of Antichrist, to the shame of them and their brethren' (*Works*, vol. 2, p.59).
13. E.g. in *Prison Meditations*, 1661, stanza 50, he had written:

Just thus it is we suffer here
for him a little pain
who, when he doth again appear
will with him let us reign.

14. *The Holy City*, p.412.
15. *Ibid.*, p.426.
16. *Ibid.*, p.413.
17. *Ibid.*, p.409.
18. *Ibid.*, p.431.
19. *Ibid.*, p.440. Although there is no proof, it is likely that Bunyan had been influenced by the work of Joseph Mede, *The Key of the Revelation*, trans. Richard More, 1650. A summary on page 123 of *The Key* relates well to Bunyan's interpretation. Also John Henry Alsted states that '... the overthrow of the antichrist shall immediately go before, not the last judgment, but the happiness of the church which shall happen in this life' (*The Beloved City*, 1643, p.37).
20. *The Holy City*, p.459.

Chapter 27 — 'A drop of honey from the carcase of a lion'
1. *The Autobiography of Richard Baxter*, Everyman Classics, 1985, p.196.
2. In all probability, and particularly with the devastation of the plague in mind, it was at this time that Bunyan wrote a treatise called *The Resurrection of the Dead and Eternal Judgment* (*Works*, vol. 2, p.41), and also two long poems, *One Thing is Needful* and *Ebal and Gerizim*, which deal with similar subjects — death, judgement, heaven and hell.
3. *Grace Abounding*, *Works*, vol. 1, preface, p.4.
4. *Ibid.*, p.5.
5. George B. Cheever, *Lectures on The Pilgrim's Progress and the Life and Times of John Bunyan*, 1872, p.25.
6. From *Scriptures Self-evidence, to prove its existence, authority, certainty it itself...*, London, 1667, pp.191-2.
7. See chapter 11, pp. 114-15.
8. Andrew Fuller (1754–1815), *The Complete Works of Andrew Fuller*, Sprinkle Publications, 1988, vol. 1, p.3.

Chapter 28 — A masterpiece in the making
1. *Autobiography of Richard Baxter*, p.198.
2. *Scriptures Self-evidence...*, pp 191-2.
3. *The Struggler*, *Works*, vol. 3, p.765.
4. *The Heavenly Footman*, *Works*, vol. 3, p.382.
5. *Ibid.*, p.386.
6. *Ibid.*, p.391.
7. *Ibid.*, p.383, where he speaks of 'that little time that I have been a professor...'
8. See Chapter 11, pp.112-16.
9. *The Pilgrim's Progress*, 'Author's Apology', *Works*, vol. 3, p.85.
10. *The Heavenly Footman*, p.382.
11. *Pilgrim's Progress*, p.85.
12. A plaque on the bridge announces this as the certain place where the book was composed.
13. For further details see Joyce Godber, *The Imprisonments of John Bunyan, Transactions of the Congregational Historical Society*, 1949.
14. Other suggestions, such as *The Strait Gate* (1676) and even *A Confession of my Faith* (1672), have been made for the book Bunyan had been writing, but these bear only marginal resemblance to the theme of *Pilgrim's Progress*.
15. Bunyan rarely gives exact indications of dating, but one reference in *Pilgrim's Progress* tells of a character whom he calls Temporary. He had been 'forward in religion', but had turned back '*about ten years ago*'. This suggests that Bunyan was writing this part of *Pilgrim's Progress* in 1669–70, and is referring to the year 1660, ten years earlier, when

persecution of Dissenters had begun. This corroborates our dating for the book. *Pilgrim's Progress*, p.160.

16. *The Heavenly Footman*, p.384.

Chapter 29 — From a den in the wilderness

1. Historian G. M. Trevelyan writes, 'Of all the words of high imagination that have enthralled mankind, none opens with a passage that more instantly places the reader in the heart of all the action' (Commemorative address delivered in Cambridge on 19 January 1928 to mark the tercentenary of Bunyan's birth).

2. No modern scholar apart from Beth Lynch (in *John Bunyan and the Language of Conviction*, Cambridge, 2004, p.88) appears to have noticed this biblical source.

3. In the Old Testament 'the wilderness' is used both literally and metaphorically as a representation of the terrain through which God's people pass on their way to Canaan, a type of heaven. The prophet Jeremiah records God's description of the way he had led his people 'through the wilderness, through a land of deserts and of pits, through a land of drought and the shadow of death' (Jeremiah 2:6).

4. Lord Macaulay, *Critical and Historical Essays*, London, 1879, vol. 1, p.140.

5. Hebrews 11:8-10.

6. 1 Peter 2:11.

7. Benjamin Keach, *War with the Devil*, 1673, pp.152, 207.

8. Psalms 69:2,14; 40:2; cf. Psalm 38:4.

9. This passage regarding Mr Worldly Wiseman, and also an early passage where Christian's wife and family cannot understand his burdened state of mind, was not inserted until the second edition of the book.

10. See chapter 12, pp.122-4.

11. *The Doctrine of Law and Grace Unfolded*, p.563.

12. Matthew 7:13, AV.

13. John 10:9; 14:6.

14. Dr Barry Horner, whose excellent work *Pilgrim's Progress — Themes and Issues* (EP, 2003) deals extensively with this matter, has calculated that in 3,561 published sermons, Spurgeon refers to Bunyan no less than 779 times, in addition to references in many other works. Spurgeon's small book *Around the Wicket Gate* is especially designed for those seeking after the truth.

15. I Corinthians 2:2. C. H. Spurgeon, *Metropolitan Tabernacle Pulpit*, 1900, p.212.

16. Bunyan himself later expounds his view of the order of salvation in *The Pharisee and the Publican*, *Works*, vol. 2, pp.248ff. He places the

imputation of Christ's justifying righteousness before faith or repentance, arguing that without it nothing that the sinner does can be acceptable to God.

17. From one of Grimshaw's unpublished MSS. See Cook, *William Grimshaw of Haworth*, p.79.

18. Matthew 16:16, 22.

Chapter 30 — Beyond the Wicket Gate

1. Formerly called the *Naseby*.

2. Rudyard Kipling, 'The Dutch in the Medway,' *Collected Poems*, Wordsworth Editions Ltd, 1994, p.752.

3. Clifford, Arlington, Buckingham, Ashley and Lauderdale.

4. *Pilgrim's Progress*, p.98.

5. A picture of Christ's imputed righteousness

Chapter 31 — Palace Beautiful

1. *A Confession of my Faith and a Reason of my Practice, Works*, vol. 2, p.594.

2. Houghton House was built around 1620 for Lady Pembroke, sister of Sir Philip Sidney. The Bruce family lived in it during Bunyan's lifetime.

3. See Horner, *Pilgrim's Progress — Themes and Issues*, pp.261-8.

4. *Minutes of First Independent Church at Bedford*, p.19.

5. *A Confession of my Faith*, pp.606-7.

6. *Ibid.*, p.605.

7. *Pilgrim's Progress*, pp.107-8.

8. *Ibid.*, p.108.

9. *Minutes of First Independent Church at Bedford*, p.25.

10. Introduction to *The Works of John Bunyan*, 1692.

11. John Kelman, *The Road*, vol. 1, p.110.

12. *Pilgrim's Progress*, p.110.

13. *Christian Behaviour, Works*, vol. 2, p.550.

14. *The Desire of the Righteous Granted, Works*, vol. 2, pp.757-8.

15. *Christian Behaviour*, p.550.

Chapter 32 — The pilgrim path

1. George Cheever, *Lectures on Pilgrim's Progress*, 1872, p.16.

2. C. S. Lewis, *Selected Literary Essays*, ed. Walter Hooper, CUP, 1969, p.147.

3. Richard Johnson, *The Seven Champions of Christendom*, 1596, ed. J. Fellows, 2003.

4. Lewis, *Selected Literary Essays*, p.147.

5. *Pilgrim's Progress*, p.112.

6. Compare *Grace Abounding,* paras. 106-7, with the following words: 'One of the Wicked Ones got behind him [Christian] and stept up softly to him, and whisperingly suggested many grievous blasphemies to him which he verily thought proceeded from his own mind.'

7. Pagan is dead, so Christian learns later.

8. See chapter 17, pp.165-6.

9. *Pilgrim's Progress,* p.131.

10. *Advice to Sufferers, Works,* vol. 2, p.720.

11. *Pilgrim's Progress,* pp.131-2.

Chapter 33 — The suffering church

1. '30th day of the 8th moneth', according to the Julian calendar.

2. *Minutes of the First Independent Church at Bedford,* p.39.

3. *The Jerusalem Sinner Saved, Works,* vol. 1, p.92.

4. *Minutes of the First Independent Church at Bedford,* p.40.

5. According to figures provided by Richard L. Greaves, the Bishop of London calculated that there were at least 12,000 worshippers gathering in conventicles on a single Sunday in London in May 1670 (Greaves, *Glimpses of Glory,* p.268).

6. Brown, *John Bunyan,* vol. 1, pp.201-2.

7. *The Life and Death of Mr Badman, Works,* vol. 3, p.625.

8. *Advice to Sufferers,* p.723.

Chapter 34 — A strange conclusion

1. *Pilgrim's Progress,* p.161.

2. Isaiah 62:4.

3. The nineteenth-century American preacher Edward Payson used this imagery when he was dying. To his sister he wrote, 'Were I to adopt the figurative language of Bunyan, I might date this letter "From the Land of Beulah" of which I have been for some weeks a happy inhabitant. The celestial city is full in my view, its glories beam upon me, its breezes fan me... Nothing separates me from it but the river of death' (See *Singing in the Fire,* Banner of Truth Trust, 1995, p.120).

4. *Pilgrim's Progress,* p.166.

5. Emeth had worshipped Tash, a personification of the devil, but Aslan accepts his devotion because he was sincere (C. S. Lewis, *The Last Battle,* HarperCollins, 1997, p.154).

6. Lewis, *Selected Literary Essays,* p.152. J. A. Froude, another biographer, also hopes that Bunyan was 'a mistaken interpreter' and claims that 'the fierce inferences of Puritan theology are no longer credible to us' (*Bunyan,* p.171).

7. *Grace Abounding,* para. 229.

8. *Pilgrim's Progress,* pp.157-9.

9. From 'The Vicar of Bray', an anonymous eighteenth-century song:

In good King Charles' golden days,
When loyalty had no harm in't,
A zealous High Churchman I was,
And so I gained preferment.
To teach my flock I never missed:
Kings were by God appointed;
And they are damned who dare resist
Or touch the Lord's anointed.

When Royal James obtained the Throne
And Popery grew in fashion,
The Penal Law I hooted down,
And read the Declaration [i.e. of Indulgence to Dissenters — 1687];
The Church of Rome I found would fit
Full well my constitution
And I had been a Jesuit
But for the Revolution [of 1688].

And this is law, I will maintain
Until my dying day, sir,
That whatsoever King shall reign,
I'll still be Vicar of Bray, sir.

10. *A Defence of the Doctrine of Justification, Works*, vol. 2, p.322.
11. Edward Fowler, *The Design of Christianity*, London, 1671, p.6.
12. *A Defence of the Doctrine of Justification*, p.322.
13. Edward Fowler, *Dirt Wip'd Off*, 1672, p.67.

Chapter 35 — Freedom at last
1. *A Confession of my Faith and a Reason of my Practice, Works*, vol. 2, p.593.
2. Some have wondered whether Bunyan believed in 'eternal justification' from the fact that here he places 'justification' in order before the other doctrines. Pieter de Vries, in his doctoral thesis *John Bunyan on the Order of Salvation*, 1994, rules this out, and suggests that, like other Puritans, Bunyan was convinced that 'we can only have a sound perception of election in the light of our justification by faith' (p.90).
3. *Minutes of the First Independent Church at Bedford*, p.70.

Chapter 36 — A painful controversy

1. Henry Jessey, *A Storehouse of Provision*, 1650, pp.84ff.
2. *A Reason of my Practice in Worship*, *Works*, vol. 2, p.604.
3. *Ibid.*, p.606.
4. *Ibid.*, p.613.
5. *Ibid.*, p.606.
6. *Differences about water baptism no bar to communion*, *Works*, vol. 2, p.617.
7. *Ibid.*, p.631.
8. *Peaceable Principles and True*, *Works*, vol. 2, p.649.
9. See chapter 16, p.151.
10. *Peaceable Principles and True*, pp.648-9.
11. A short treatise entitled *An Exhortation to Peace and Unity* is included in George Offor's *Works of John Bunyan*. However, even Offor doubts that this is Bunyan's work, and a careful reading makes it obvious that in style and content it is not, for it is propounding the opposite position on baptism. It is thought to be the work of one of Bunyan's antagonists, Henry D'Anvers.
12. Bunyan's son John was received into church membership in 1693; Thomas appears to have had only formal links with St Cuthbert's parish church, while Joseph would link up with St Paul's parish church in Bedford.

Chapter 37 — The Bedford pastor

1. Cited by Greaves, *Glimpses of Glory*, p.289, from the Tanner MSS 43.
2. *Minutes of the First Independent Church at Bedford*, p.75.
3. This was not published in 1682 as suggested by Offor, but on 24 November 1673 by a Jonathan Robinson at *The Golden Lion, St Paul's Churchyard*. Only two copies of the first edition exist — one of which was sold to the University of Alabama and the other, at one time the possession of Ralph E. Ford, is now in the British Library.
4. *The Barren Fig-tree*, *Works*, vol. 3, p.566.
5. *Ibid.*, p.572.
6. *Ibid.*, p.579.
7. *The Strait Gate*, *Works*, vol. 1, p.390.
8. *Grace Abounding*, paras. 307-8.
9. *Ibid.*, paras. 314, 315, 317.
10. *Ibid.*, para. 312.

Chapter 38 — Tenuous liberty

1. According to the Gregorian, or New Style, calendar. Under the Julian calendar, which was in operation at the time, the new year did not start until 25 March and the warrant therefore bears the date '1674'.

2. A letter signed by John Bunyan in the church minute book is dated as the 12th month 1676, which in the Gregorian calendar was February 1677.
3. *Instruction for the Ignorant, Works,* vol. 2, p.676.
4. *Saved by Grace, Works,* vol. 1, pp.341-2.
5. Cokayne published one of Bunyan's last books, *The Acceptable Sacrifice,* and wrote a warm description of him in the preface.
6. Doe, *A Collection of Experience,* p.57.
7. *Saved by Grace,* p.346.

Chapter 39 — A publishing venture
1. This view was proposed by Joyce Godber in her book *The Imprisonments of John Bunyan* and promoted by such writers as Vera Brittain (*In the steps of John Bunyan,* Rich and Cowan, 1950, pp.19-22).
2. Although no copy of this fourth edition has survived, it is most likely that paragraphs 306-317 were added to this edition, rather than to the fifth, which was not published until 1680, six years after the events concerned.
3. *Come and Welcome to Jesus Christ, Works,* vol. 1, p.297.
4. Called *A Continuation of Mr Bunyan's Life* and added to *Grace Abounding* in 1692.
5. Thomas Barlow (1607-91) became Bishop of Lincoln in 1675, just prior to Bunyan's second imprisonment (See 'The Vicar of Bray', quoted above, ch. 34, note 9, p.497).
6. This bond was discovered in Aylesbury Museum in 1887.
7. Information taken from John Asty's *Life of Owen,* written in 1721 by one who knew Owen personally. It is cited by William Orme in a *Memoir of Owen,* appended to his *Works,* 1826, p.304.
8. *Grace Abounding, Continuation,* p.63.

Chapter 40 — A time of fear
1. *Israel's Hope Encouraged, Works,* vol. 1, p.585.
2. *Grace Abounding,* paras. 247, 350.
3. *Come and Welcome to Jesus Christ,* pp.279-80.
4. *A Treatise on the Fear of God, Works,* vol. 1, p.448.
5. *Ibid.,* p.485.
6. Cited by G. M. Trevelyan, *England under the Stuarts,* p.389, from George Treby's *Collection,* 1681.
7. *The Pilgrim's Progress,* p. 133.
8. See chapter 6, pp.65-6.
9. *The Life and Death of Mr Badman, Works,* vol. 3, p.625.
10. *Ibid.,* p.652.

Chapter 41 — 'Come wind, come weather'
1. *Works of John Owen*, vol. 16, pp.116-17. For the Baptists, Edward Terrill (1635–86) of Broadmead Baptist Church in Bristol wrote in the church records:

> As papists still do seek to kill
> the governors of our land,
> the Lord of might doth bring to light
> the plots they take in hand.

2. See 2 Corinthians 11:26-28.
3. *Minutes of the First Independent Church at Bedford*, pp.85,88.
4. *The Greatness of the Soul, Works*, vol. 1, p.124.
5. *Ibid.*, p.149.
6. Cited from Joseph Ivimey, *History of the English Baptists*, vol. 2, p.41, from Owen's early biographer, John Asty, *Works of John Owen*.
7. Cited by Greaves, *Glimpses of Glory*, p.459.

Chapter 42 — The battle is the Lord's
1. *Life and Death of Mr Badman, Works*, vol. 3, p.593.
2. The full title was: *The Holy War, made by Shaddai upon Diabolus for the regaining of the Metropolis of the World, or The Losing and Taking again of the town of Mansoul*.
3. According to the calculations of Richard Greaves, he would need to have written 475 words a day, working five days a week. Because of his extensive travels and preaching at this time, it is likely that he wrote even more intensively, perhaps devoting fewer days each week to the work. Bunyan's ability to write quickly is demonstrated by the fact that he produced a treatise of 46,000 words in reply to Edward Fowler in a six-week period (see chapter 34, p.309).
4. Joshua 5:14.
5. See, for example, Ephesians 6:11-17; 1 Timothy 6:12; 2 Timothy 2:4.
6. Both were men of Nonconformist and radical principles.
7. *The Holy War*, p.374. In the anagrammed name for John Bunyan read 'j' for 'i'.
8. From the Hebrew meaning 'God Almighty', 'the Self-Existent One'.
9. *Pilgrim's Progress*, p.111.
10. *Holy War*, 'Advertisement to Reader', p.374.
11. *Holy War*, p.266.
12. *Ibid.*, p.372.
13. Galatians 5:24.
14. *Holy War*, p.325.

Chapter 43 — The wiles of the devil

1. 'The Holy War', *Collected Poems of Rudyard Kipling*, Wordsworth Poetry Library, 1994, p.301.
2. *Holy War*, p.326.
3. *Ibid.*, p.339.
4. *Ibid.*, p.350.
5. *Ibid.*, p.351.
6. *Grace Abounding*, para. 198.
7. Greaves, *Glimpses of Glory*, p.419.
8. Arlette Zinck, cited by Galen Johnson, *Prisoner of Conscience*, p.178.
9. From Emmanuel's last charge, *The Holy War*, pp.367-73.
10. *Works*, vol. 3, p.252.

Chapter 44 — Travels of a pilgrim church

1. This author was later discovered to be Thomas Sherman.
2. The promises of God.
3. *Come and Welcome to Jesus Christ*, pp.253, 281.
4. 'Except it be very few,' thought Baxter, 'women are betwixt a man and a child, some few have more of the man, and many have more of the child' (*The Christian Directory*, p.399).
5. Cheever, *Lectures on Bunyan*, p.307.
6. *Pilgrim's Progress*, p.184.
7. Cf. reference to Christiana, her sons and her sons' wives, *ibid.*, p.230.
8. *Ibid.*, p.198.
9. *Ibid.*, p.219.
10. *Ibid.*, pp.213-14.
11. *Ibid.*, p.233. See Hebrews 4:12.
12. The usual tune, 'Monk's Gate', was arranged by Ralph Vaughan Williams (1872–1958) and is said to be based on 'a traditional English melody'.
13. *Pilgrim's Progress*, pp.243-4.

Chapter 45 — Troubled times

1. Cragg, *Puritanism, the Great Persecution*, p.26.
2. John Tillotson was Archbishop of Canterbury from 1691.
3. *A Holy Life, the Beauty of Christianity*, *Works*, vol. 2, pp.508-9.
4. *Advice to Sufferers*, p.700.
5. *Grace Abounding*, para. 325.
6. *Advice to Sufferers*, p.738.
7. *Ibid.*, p.737.
8. *Ibid.*, p.737.
9. Quoted from B. A. Ramsbottom, *Stranger than Fiction, The Life of William Kiffin*, Gospel Standard Publications, 1989, pp.58-9.

10. W. T. Whitely, *A History of British Baptists*, 1923, p.149.
11. Many street names in London bear evidence of this influx, for example Petty France in Westminster.
12. *The Desire of the Righteous Granted*, *Works*, vol. 1, p.758.
13. See chapter 22, pp.208-9
14. 'The child with a bird at the bush' and 'Of the rose bush', *Works*, vol. 3, pp.756-7.
15. The full text of the Deed of Gift, with original spelling, is in Appendix III.
16. 1 Peter 4:19.
17. *Advice to Sufferers*, p.732.

Chapter 46 — A passionate preacher
1. *Works*, vol. 1, p.63.
2. 'Ned Bratts', from *The Poetical Works of Robert Browning*, OUP, 1957, p.599.
3. Doe, *A Collection of Experience.*
4. *Pilgrim's Progress*, p.98.
5. Agnes Beaumont, retold in *Behind Mr Bunyan.* London: The Fauconberg Press, 1963, p.6.
6. *The Jerusalem Sinner Saved*, *Works*, vol. 1, p.72.
7. *Ibid.*, pp.88-9.
8. Perhaps the clearest example in Scripture is Romans 8:31-36.
9. *The Jerusalem Sinner Saved*, p.91.
10. *Ibid.*, p.80.
11. *Ibid.*, p.79.
12. *Ibid.*, p.94.
13. *Ibid.*, p.98.
14. *Grace Abounding*, para. 281.
15. *Ibid.*, para. 282.
16. *The Jerusalem Sinner Saved*, p.90. (The Banner of Truth Trust has recently republished this as a separate book.)

Chapter 47 — Sharpening his quill
1. *The Desire of the Righteous Granted*, p.759.
2. *The Water of Life*, *Works*, vol. 3, p.543.
3. *Ibid.*, p.547.
4. *Ibid.*, p.559.
5. *Solomon's Temple Spiritualized*, *Works*, vol. 3, p.472.
6. *Ibid.*, 'Preface,' p.464.
7. *Ibid.*, 503-4.

8. This infant is often referred to as the 'warming-pan' baby, because of rumours that he had been smuggled into the royal apartments, and was not in fact the child of James and Mary.
9. *The Excellency of a Broken Heart, Works,* vol. 1, p.690.
10. *Ibid.,* p.699.
11. *Ibid.,* p.692.
12. *Ibid.,* p.711.
13. Some suggest that the anonymous author of *A Continuation of Mr Bunyan's Life,* added to *Grace Abounding,* was in fact Cokayne, who was then pastor of a Congregational church in St Giles, Cripplegate. However, the inaccuracies included in it suggest that it was the work of someone less well acquainted with Bunyan.
14. *Ibid.,* 'Preface', p.686.
15. *Ibid.,* p.720.

Chapter 48 — Crossing the river
1. Now renamed Middlesex Street.
2. *Bunyan's Dying Sayings, Works,* vol. 1, p.65.
3. *Mr Bunyan's Last Sermon, Works,* vol. 2, p.758.
4. Richard Greaves expresses doubt as to the authenticity of the document recording Bunyan's 'Dying Sayings'. Certainly some scarcely sound like the words of a dying man. Perhaps they had been culled over several years from Bunyan's occasional remarks. They were first published only weeks later, in September 1688, and were then added to the *Continuation of Mr Bunyan's Life.*
5. *Pilgrim's Progress,* Part II, p.243.
6. *Dying Sayings,* p.66.
7. *Excellency of a Broken Heart, Works,* vol. 1, p.688.
8. No details of Bunyan's original burial can be found in the cemetery register, and even the first inscription was not discovered until 1864 — a commentary perhaps on the despised status of Dissenters in the 1680s.

Chapter 49 — Through the centuries
1. *Minutes of the First Independent Church at Bedford,* p.89.
2. It only came to light in 1838 when the house in St Cuthbert's Street was being demolished.
3. John Owen's estate in contrast was nearer £2,000.
4. John Dunton, *The Life and Errors of J D,* London, 1705, p.437.
5. Wilson and Chandler, Preface to *Bunyan's Works,* 1692.
6. Isabel Hofmeyr, *The Portable Bunyan,* Princeton University Press, 2004.
7. Doe, *A Collection of Experience,* p.57.
8. Bunyan had used thirteen different publishers.

9. Quotations cited by N. H. Keeble (*John Bunyan: Conventicle and Parnassus, Tercentenary Essays*, ed. N. H. Keeble, Clarendon Press, Oxford, 1988, pp.246ff.), to whom I am indebted for parts of this chapter.
10. *Poetical Works of William Cowper, Tirocinium, or a Review of Schools*, OUP, 1892, p.336.
11. Joseph Ivimey, *The Life of Mr John Bunyan*, 1821.
12. Thomas Macaulay, *Critical and Historical Essays* (first published in *The Edinburgh Review*, 1831), 1874, p.140.
13. For more detail see H. G. Tibbutt, *What they said about John Bunyan*, Bedfordshire County Council, 1981.
14. Samuel Coleridge (1772–1834) *Literary Remains*, London, 1836–39, vol. 3, p.392.
15. C. H. Spurgeon, *Metropolitan Tabernacle Pulpit*, vol. 47, pp 259-60.
16. C. H. Spurgeon, *Autobiography*, London, Passmore and Alabaster, 1897, vol. 4, p.268.
17. See Greaves, *Glimpses of Glory*, pp.610-15.
18. Robert Philip, *The Life and Times and Characteristics of John Bunyan*, London, 1839.
19. Superseded only by Roger Sharrock's, *The Miscellaneous Works of John Bunyan*, OUP, 1979.
20. J. Gresham Machen (1881–1937), cited by Barry E. Horner. For an excellent account of Bunyan's work and theology see Dr Horner's work, *Pilgrim's Progress — Themes and Issues*.
21. Reprinted by the Banner of Truth Trust, 1964.
22. Greaves, *Glimpses of Glory*.
23. Davies, *Graceful Reading*.
24. *The Saints' Knowledge of Christ's Love*, *Works*, vol. 2, p.39.
25. *Pilgrim's Progress*, p. 243.

Appendix I — The build-up to the Civil War
1. Wilstead (then known as Wilshamstead), a village only a mile or two from Elstow, has records dating from 1637 of ship money tax amounting to £25. 10s. 11d to be raised from individual households. Bedfordshire was among the five counties that defaulted on the tax.

Bibliography

Primary sources

The Works of John Bunyan, ed. George Offor. Reprinted, Banner of Truth Trust, 1991

The Works of John Bunyan, edited by Roger Sharrock and others

Profitable Meditations, in a conference between Christ and the sinner. London: Francis Smith, at Sign of the Elephant and Castle, 1661

A true and impartial account of some illegal and arbitrary proceedings by certain Justices of the Peace... 1670, British Library

Bacon, Nathaniel. *A Relation of the fearful estate of Francis Spira in the year 1548.* London: at Adam and Eve, Little Britain, 1672

Bailey, Louis. *The Practice of Piety.* Reprinted, Soli Deo Gloria, from 1842 edition

Baxter, Richard. *The Autobiography of,* ed, N. H. Keeble. Everyman, 1985

Bernard, Richard. *The Isle of Man or the Legall proceeding in Man-shire against sinne.* London: Blackmore, 1628

Besse, Joseph. *A Collection of the Sufferings of the people called Quakers, 1650–1698.* London, 1753

Burrough, Edward. *The Memorable Works of a Son of Thunder and Consolation,* including *The True Faith of the Gospel of Peace* (1657). London, 1672

Chandler, Ebenezer and Wilson, John. 'Preface' to *The Works of that eminent Servant of Christ, Mr John Bunyan...* London:

printed and sold by William Marshall at the Bible in New-
gate Street, 1692

Dent, Arthur. *The Plaine Man's Path-way to Heaven, a sermon on
repentance.* 1601, Robert Dexter, to be sold at the Signe of
the Brazen serpent in Powles Church-yard

Doe, Charles. *A Collection of Experience or the work of grace.*
London: printed for Cha. Doe, a Comb-maker in the
Burrough, between the Hospital and London Bridge, 1700

Doe, Charles. *Some account of Mr Bunyan and his Ministry.*
London: printed by John Marshall at The Bible in Grace
Church Street, 1692

Fowler, Edward. *Dirt wip'd off, or a manifest discovery of the
gross ignorance, erroneousness, and most unchristian and
wicked spirit of one Bunyan...* London, Royston, 1672

Jesse, Joseph. *A Collection of the Sufferings of the People called
Quakers, for the testimony of a good conscience, 1650–
1689.* London, 1753

Jessey, Henry. *A Storehouse of Provision*, 1650

Keach, Benjamin. *Antichrist Stormed or Mystery Bablyon ...
proved to be the present Church of Rome.* London: Nathaniel Crouch at the Bell in the Poultrey near Cheapside,
1689

Keach, Benjamin. *War with the Devil.* London, 1673

Luke, Sir Samuel. *The Letter Books of, 1644–1645*, ed. H. G.
Tibbutt. HMSO, 1963

Mede, Joseph. *The Key of the Revelation*, trans. Richard More,
1650

Minutes of the First Independent Church at Bedford, 1656–1766,
ed. H. G. Tibbutt. Bedfordshire Historical Record Society,
1976

Souldiers Pocket Bible, 1643

Books on John Bunyan

Bacon, Ernest. *Pilgrim and Dreamer.* Exeter: The Paternoster Press,
1983

Brittain, Vera. *In the steps of John Bunyan.* London: Rich and
Cowan, 1950

Brown, John. *John Bunyan, His Life, Times and Work.* London, 1885

Calhoun, David L. *Grace Abounding, Life, Books and Influence of John Bunyan.* Christian Focus, 2005

Cheever, George B. *Lectures on* The Pilgrim's Progress *and the Life and Times of John Bunyan.* London, 1872

Davies, Michael. *Graceful Reading.* Oxford University Press, 2002

Evans, Vivienne. *John Bunyan, his Life and Times.* Dunstable: Book Castle, 1995

Froude, J. A. *Bunyan.* Macmillan & Co, 1902

Fullerton, W. Y. *The Legacy of John Bunyan.* London, 1928

Furlong, Monica. *Puritan's Progress.* New York: Coward, McCann & Geoghenan, 1975

Greaves, Richard L. *Glimpses of Glory, John Bunyan and English Dissent.* Stanford University Press, 2002

Greaves, Richard L, *John Bunyan.* The Sutton Courtenay Press, Abingdon, 1969

Greaves, Richard L, *John Bunyan and English Nonconformity.* The Hambleton Press, 1992

Griffith, G. O. *John Bunyan.* Hodder and Stoughton, 1928

Harper, Charles. *The Bunyan Country.* London, 1928

Harrison, F. Mott. *John Bunyan, a story of his life.* 1928, reprinted, Banner of Truth Trust, 1964

Harrison, G. B. *John Bunyan, A Study in Personality.* J. M. Dent, 1928

Hill, Christopher. *A Tinker and a Poor Man, John Bunyan and his Church.* Oxford University Press, 1988

Hofmeyr, Isabel. *The Portable Bunyan,* Princeton University Press, 2004

Ivimey, Joseph. *The Life of Mr John Bunyan.* London, 1825

Johnson, Galen K. *Prisoner of Conscience, John Bunyan on Self, Community and Christian Faith.* Carlisle: Paternoster Press, 2003

Keeble, N. H., ed. *John Bunyan: Conventicle and Parnassus, Tercentenary Essays.* Oxford: Clarendon Press, 1988

Lynch, Beth. *John Bunyan and the Language of Conviction.* Cambridge, 2004

Pestell, John. *Travel with John Bunyan.* Day One, 2000

Philip, Robert. *The Life, Times and Characteristics of John Bunyan.* London, 1839

Sargent, G. E. *The Bedfordshire Tinker.* London: Benjamin Green, 1848

Sharrock, Roger. *John Bunyan.* London: Macmillan, 1968

Southey, Robert. *Cromwell and Bunyan* (1830). John Murray – Select Biographies, 1846

Speight, Harold. *The Life and Writings of John Bunyan.* Harper Brothers, 1928

Talon, Henri. *John Bunyan.* Rockcliff, 1950

Tindall, William York. *John Bunyan, Mechanic Preacher.* New York: Columbia University Press, 1934

Vries, Pieter de. *John Bunyan and the Order of Salvation.* 1994

Wakefield, Gordon. *John Bunyan, The Christian.* HarperCollins, 1994

Willcocks, M. P. *Bunyan Calling.* London, 1943

Social background

Adair, John. *By the Sword Divided.* London: Century Publishing, 1983

Anderson, Angela. *An Introduction to Stuart Britain.* Hodder and Stoughton, 1999

Ashley, Maurice. *The English Civil War.* Guild Publishing, 1990

Ashley, Maurice. *The Glorious Revolution of 1688.* Hodder and Stoughton, 1966

Bate, Frank. *The Declaration of Indulgence, 1672, A Study in the Rise of Organised Dissent.* London and Liverpool, 1908

Briggs, Asa. *A Social History of England.* Penguin, 1983

Calamy Edmund. *The Nonconformist Memorial, being an account of the ministers who were ejected or silenced after the Restoration ...* abridged and corrected by Samuel Palmer, London, 1775.

Cragg, G. R. *Puritanism in the Period of the Great Persecution 1660–88,* Cambridge University Press, 1957

Firth, Katharine. *The Apocalyptic Times in English Dissent, 1530–1645,* Oxford University Press, 1979

Fox, George. *George Fox's Journal,* vol. II. Everyman, 1924

Fraser, Antonia. *King Charles II.* Weildenfeld and Nicolson, 1979

Greaves, Richard L. *Saints and Rebels: Seven Nonconformists in Stuart England.* Mercer University Press, 1985

Greaves and Zaller. *Bibliographical Dictionary of British Radicals*

Howard, John. *The State of Prisons in England and Wales,* London, 1792

Hutchinson, Lucy. *Memoirs of the Life of Colonel Hutchinson,* ed. N. H. Keeble. Everyman, 1995

John Bunyan and his England, eds. Anne Laurence, W. R. Owens, and Stuart Sim. The Hambleton Press, 1990

Keeble, N. H. *The Literary Culture of Nonconformity in later Seventeenth Century England.* Leicester University Press, 1987

Noble, Vernon. *The Man in Leather Breeches.* London: Elek Books, 1953

Trevelyan, G. M. *English Social History.* Longmans, Green and Co., 1942

Trevelyan, G. M. *England under the Stuarts.* Methuen, 1904

Vipont, Elfrida. *George Fox and the Valiant Sixty.* London: Hamish Hamilton, 1975

Wedgewood, C. V. *The Trial of Charles I.* Reprint Society, 1964

Wedgewood, C. V. *Oliver Cromwell.* Duckworth, 1972

On John Bunyan's works

Calhoun, David B. *Grace Abounding.* Christian Focus, 2005

Horner, Barry. *Pilgrim's Progress — Themes and Issues.* Evangelical Press, 2003

Kelman, John. *The Road, A Study of John Bunyan's Pilgrim's Progress.* Edinburgh, 1911

Whyte, Alexander. *Bunyan Characters,* vols. 1-3. Oliphant, Anderson and Ferrier, 1895

Pamphlets, single chapters and articles

Beaumont, Agnes. *Behind Mr Bunyan,* ed. L. F. Lupton, 1964

Bunyan Studies: *John Bunyan and his Times,* vol. 1, 1988

Conder, Josiah. Introductory Memoir to *The Life and Works of John Bunyan*, 1850

Davies, Gaius. *Genius and Grace*. Hodder and Stoughton, 1992

Dix, Kenneth. *John Bunyan, Puritan Pastor*. Fauconberg Press, 1978

Ford, R. E, *The lesser known works of John Bunyan*, 1957

Godber, Joyce. *John Bunyan of Bedfordshire*. Bedfordshire County Council, 1972

Howard, Kenneth W. H. His detailed notes for a prospective biography of Bunyan were made available to me by Dr Robert Oliver

Kapic and Gleason, eds. *The Devoted Life. 'Pilgrim's Progress'*, by J. I. Packer, IVP, 2004

Knott, J. R. 'Bunyan and the Language of Martyrdom', *Discourses of Martyrdom in English Literature*. Cambridge University Press, 1993

Lewis, C. S. *Selected Literary Essays*, ed. Walter Hooper. Cambridge University Press, 1969

Loane, Marcus. *Makers of Puritan History*. Baker Book House, 1961

Macaulay, T. B. *Critical and Historical Essays*, vol. 1. London, 1879

Oliver, Robert W., ed. *John Owen, The Man and his Theology, his Life and Times*. Evangelical Press, 2002

Talon, Henri. *John Bunyan, Writers and their Work*. Longmans, 1956

Watkins, Owen C. *John Bunyan and his Experience*. Puritan Papers, vol. 1, P&R Publishing, 2000

Westminster Conference Report, London, 1978. *Light from John Bunyan* (3 papers)

Westminster Conference Report, London, 1988. *Not by Might, nor by Power* (1 paper)

Other related topics

Nuttall, Geoffrey F. *The Puritan Spirit*. Epworth Press, 1967

Ramsbottom, B. L. *Stranger than Fiction, Life of William Kiffin*. Gospel Standard Publications, 1989

Underwood, A. C. *A History of the British Baptists.* London: Carey Kingsgate, 1947

Walker, Austin. *The Excellent Benjamin Keach.* Joshua Press, 2005

Walker, Eric C. *William Dell, Master Puritan.* Cambridge: Heffer & Sons Ltd, 1970

Watts, Michael. *The Dissenters*, vol. 1. Oxford: Clarendon Press, 1978

Whitely, W. T. *A History of British Baptists*, 1923

Index